OXFORD WORLD'S CLASSICS

JOHN MILTON

Paradise Lost

Edited with an Introduction and Notes by
STEPHEN ORGEL and JONATHAN GOLDBERG

OXFORD
UNIVERSITY PRESS

OXFORD
UNIVERSITY PRESS

Great Clarendon Street, Oxford OX2 6DP

Oxford University Press is a department of the University of Oxford.
It furthers the University's objective of excellence in research, scholarship,
and education by publishing worldwide in

Oxford New York

Auckland Bangkok Buenos Aires Cape Town Chennai
Dar es Salaam Delhi Hong Kong Istanbul Karachi Kolkata
Kuala Lumpur Madrid Melbourne Mexico City Mumbai Nairobi
São Paulo Shanghai Taipei Tokyo Toronto

Oxford is a registered trade mark of Oxford University Press
in the UK and in certain other countries

Published in the United States
by Oxford University Press Inc., New York

Introduction and Select Bibliography © Stephen Orgel and Jonathan Goldberg 2004
Notes © Stephen Orgel and Jonathan Goldberg 1991, 2004

The moral rights of the author have been asserted

Database right Oxford University Press (maker)

First published as an Oxford World's Classics paperback 2004

British Library Cataloguing in Publication Data

Data available

Library of Congress Cataloging in Publication Data

Data available

ISBN 0–19–283319–7

5

Typeset in Ehrhardt
by RefineCatch Limited, Bungay, Suffolk
Printed in Great Britain by
Clays Ltd, St Ives plc

CONTENTS

INTRODUCTION

FROM almost the moment of its publication in 1667, *Paradise Lost* was considered a classic. It has, moreover, become so central a monument in British literary history that it is difficult, from where we stand, to see both how audacious an undertaking it represents, and how astonishing its immediate and continued success was. In 1667, Milton was about as far from the centre of English cultural, political, and even poetic life as it was possible to be. The Commonwealth he had served was gone; he had been imprisoned and narrowly escaped execution; he was blind, and lived in a straitened retirement with his daughters, a relic of a past that few thought of as heroic. And yet Milton's life constitutes, in the history of poetry, an amazing success story. He was the first English poet to succeed in making poetry what it had been for Virgil or Horace: both a vocation and a career, an honourable and honoured profession. *Paradise Lost*, indeed, insists on this. The blind bard of the epic may recall Homer, but he undoubtedly is Milton.

Biography

John Milton was a native Londoner, born in 1608. His father, also named John, was a scrivener, a profession that combined the functions of legal adviser, notary, banker, accountant, and moneylender: he prospered, and the family was well off. Milton was the eldest son, and therefore stood to inherit the bulk of his father's estate. By avocation, the father was a musician and scholar; he published songs, and had a wide acquaintance in the musical world of the time. Milton's parents were Protestant, with Puritan leanings, though this had caused serious problems because Milton's grandfather was Roman Catholic, and his son's conversion occasioned a break with the family, upon which the senior John Milton had been disinherited. The situation was not an uncommon one in the period; Donne went through a similar family crisis. Milton was destined for the Church, a good career for a poet and scholar, though the increasing regulation and ceremonialism of the Anglican Church under Archbishop Laud finally alienated him so that he never took holy orders. And though his own politics and religion were ultimately to be more radical than those of the rest of his family, the relations remained close. His younger brother Christopher was a Royalist and conservative, even during the Commonwealth, and was appointed a judge under Charles II, at a time when his brother John was in danger of indictment for treason.

Milton had a superb education, in both classic and modern subjects. Initially he was tutored at home; among his tutors was a Scots Presbyterian churchman, Thomas Young: the choice indicates the family's religious sympathies. From the age of 11 he attended St Paul's School in London. He learned Latin, Greek, and Hebrew, pursuing on his own the study of French and Italian, and reading recent English poets, such as Spenser and Sidney. As a schoolboy he was already writing poetry in both Latin and English, and declared his ambition to write a poem on the creation. It was at St Paul's, too, that he met his dearest friend, Charles Diodati.

At the age of 16 he went to Cambridge, probably because it was more hospitable to Puritan ideas than Oxford. Here, however, education was another matter entirely. Teaching was done by the traditional method of disputation, a system based on rhetoric and debate and deeply involved with scholastic philosophy. Students were set to arguing abstract and often pointless theses—a typical topic would be whether day is better than night. In his first year he was rusticated for several months, apparently for being insubordinate to his tutor. He spent the time happily at his family's country house, and returned to Cambridge the following term, where the very civilized solution was simply to change his tutor. During this period he wrote a good deal of verse, mostly in Latin; it was not until the early 1630s that he began writing primarily in English. *On the Morning of Christ's Nativity*, dated 1629, can be taken as the poem in which Milton announces his own poetic coming of age. He stayed at Cambridge for seven years, taking both the BA and MA degrees (his Puritan principles did not yet preclude his signing the necessary Articles declaring himself a member of the Anglican communion). Clearly there was no hurry: he was taking a long time to prepare himself.

For another seven years after leaving Cambridge he lived with his family, studying on his own: he read classics, mathematics, and music. His first published verse was the unsigned dedicatory poem 'On Shakespeare' in the second Shakespeare folio (1632). By the end of his stay with his family, in 1638, he had written an impressive body of poetry in both Latin and English, including *L'Allegro*, *Il Penseroso*, Comus, and *Lycidas*.

Lycidas is the last English poem of this period, and it can be read as a determination to move on—it concludes, 'tomorrow to fresh woods, and pastures new'—beyond both pastoral and the phase of his life concluded by the untimely death of his Cambridge classmate Edward King, the young poet and divinity student whom the elegy commemorates, and whose ambitions paralleled Milton's own. But the untimeliness is not only in King's death; *Lycidas* also implies that the poet's own career has been interrupted by the necessity of writing before he feels ready. And it must be relevant to the sense of both disruption and the necessity of moving on that his mother also died in 1637, a few months before King. We know little about his mother beyond the fact that she was very devout, which suggests that the theological vocation, to which Milton obviously had a very complicated relationship, was significantly involved with his feelings about her.

In 1638 he travelled to Italy, and remained there for fifteen months. This was more than a grand tour or a search for the sources of his passion for the classical world: he sought out most of the important Italian intellectuals, who were of course Roman Catholics, but with whom he formed intense and mutually admiring friendships that continued by correspondence after his return. When he was in Florence he managed to visit Galileo, who was under house arrest—a good index to his intellectual range, curiosity, and independence. The visit is recorded in *Paradise Lost*, where Galileo is called 'the Tuscan artist' (i. 288; this is the only use of the word *artist* in Milton's poetry, and Galileo is the only contemporary of Milton's mentioned in the poem), and the view Milton had of the moon through his telescope in Fiesole provides a striking analogy for the appearance of Satan's gigantic shield after the fall from heaven (i. 287–90). It is surely significant that the audacious science that so fascinated Milton is associated with Satan, not God. There is a second, more neutral, allusion to Galileo in Book V, line 263; but both the intensity and the complexity of his interest in the new science are evident when, in Book VIII, Adam is rebuked by Raphael for his questions about astronomy. Whatever Milton's interest in Galileo in 1638, the allusion in *Paradise Lost* gains a particular poignancy from the fact that Galileo was blind and was persecuted for his beliefs, as Milton was to be when writing his epic.

During his Italian travels he learned that his closest friend Charles Diodati had died, prompting his greatest Latin poem, the elegy *Epitaphium Damonis* (*Damon's Epitaph*). This loss motivated him much more profoundly than the death recorded in *Lycidas*. He says in *Damon's Epitaph* that he has chosen a subject for an epic he intends to write on the Arthurian legends (modelling himself, that is, on Spenser) and resolves to write thenceforth in English—this Latin poem signals a real choice of a career. He returned to England, slowly, in response to news of the impending Civil War.

He then lived in London, and supported himself by teaching his nephews and a few other boys. In 1640 his notebook records that he is meditating on subjects for a 'great work'. The list of possibilities reveals that the Arthurian epic has been abandoned; most of the subjects are from the Old Testament, with some also from the Gospels and from British history. These are described, however, as subjects for a tragedy rather than an epic—the model now is not Spenser but the ancient Greek dramatists and Shakespeare; and the remnants of the original dramatic impulse are clearly evident in Satan's great monologues in *Paradise Lost*. There are, moreover, four drafts of a tragedy on the loss of Eden, among them a cast list under the title *Paradise Lost* and a more extensive draft for a drama to be called 'Adam unparadiz'd'.

Milton's move into the political world came initially through his involvement in the debate over episcopacy, the increasingly rigid government of the Church by the hierarchy of bishops and archbishops under Archbishop Laud. Much of the country favoured the more democratic presbyterian system, in which a group of elders of equal rank governed the Church; and when in 1639 Charles I attempted to impose the Anglican Prayer Book on the Presbyterian Church of Scotland—in effect replacing the Scottish Presbyterian Church with the Church of England—he precipitated an open rebellion. We need to remind ourselves of how overwhelming a presence religion was in every aspect of seventeenth-century British life, whether private or public, social or political. The four nations that comprised the British Isles under Charles I, England, Scotland, Wales, and Ireland, were culturally, politically, religiously, even linguistically, extremely diverse, and sectarian hostilities especially abounded. Nevertheless, the transformation of all parts of the kingdom into a single Anglican community, with the King as its spiritual and temporal head, was one of the most actively pursued aims of Charles's government. But the royal army that marched north to enforce religious conformity on the Scots was decisively defeated, and the King, faced with an uncontainable religious crisis, was forced to summon Parliament for the first time in ten years. The nominal issue was the reform of Church government, but with the King at the head of the Church, any changes mandated by Parliament necessarily impinged on the royal prerogatives. And there were, in addition, a multitude of perceived abuses that the new Parliament insisted on debating: monopolies, judicial corruption, the imposition of taxes by royal fiat, and indeed the whole structure by which the King had succeeded in ruling for a decade without a Parliament to vote subsidies or support onerous policies.

In 1641 a group of Presbyterian ministers, including Milton's old tutor Thomas Young, published a pamphlet attacking episcopacy, a reply to an earlier pamphlet in defence of the bishops. In the same year Milton lent his support to the Presbyterian cause with his first published tract, *Of Reformation Touching Church Discipline*, and continued with energetic defences of Young and his colleagues, and with virulent attacks on their critics. Milton's personal life changed significantly at this period too: in the following year he married Mary Powell, the daughter of an old family friend and client of his father's. The marriage has traditionally been declared unhappy, since Mary returned to her family after only a few months, and Milton published his notorious divorce tracts in 1643 and 1644. Although the inference is probably correct, it is possible that once Civil War broke out in 1642, and the Powells strongly favoured the Royalist cause, Mary's family may have wanted her in the country with them. Milton at this time was a staunch supporter of the Presbyterian and Parliamentary side (although he would soon break with them over what he saw as their reinstatement of the Church hierarchy and their intolerance of any diverging religious viewpoints, and would join with other Independents). Nevertheless, after the King's defeat in 1645 Mary returned to her husband's house, and over the next seven years bore him three daughters and a son. She died in childbirth in 1652, and the son died shortly after. Milton subsequently married twice more, but had no other surviving children.

He published two more pamphlets in 1644, *Of Education*, and his most famous prose work, *Areopagitica*, but he wrote no more prose until 1649, when the King's trial for treason elicited Milton's most important work of political philosophy, *The Tenure of Kings and Magistrates*. This argued against the divine right of kings, and maintained the right of the people to remove a tyrannical monarch. His poetic career, however, was still very much on his mind during these years. He wrote sonnets, on both personal and political subjects, some of which are among the greatest in English, and in 1646 he published his collected poems (dated, in the old style, 1645), a very small volume that was eventually to be recognized as a major literary achievement. *Poems of Mr John Milton, both English and Latin* (it also includes several poems in Italian) appeared with a striking display of testimonials. The title page notes that 'The songs were set in music by Mr. Henry Lawes, Gentleman of the King's Chapel, and one of His Majesty's private music'; the publisher's preface assures the reader that 'these are not without the highest commendations and applause of the learnedest academics, both domestic and foreign' including 'that renowned Provost of Eton, Sir Henry Wotton', and compares Milton with Spenser and Waller; and the Latin poems (which for educated readers throughout the Western world would have been the more impressive achievement) are prefaced with a series of adulatory poems contributed by the Italian Catholic intellectuals Milton had met in 1638. The book, in short, positively flaunted its author's Royalist and Catholic connections. If this seems surprising, given Milton's political sympathies, it probably only reveals the permeability of the divisions between the factions in the Civil War. Even the most militant Parliamentarians maintained at this period that what they sought was reform and reconciliation, not regicide.

The Royalist forces were decisively defeated by Cromwell's army in 1645; the King took refuge with the Scots, but thereafter was in fact a prisoner. The trial of Charles I was difficult to defend. The Parliament that voted to indict him was blatantly rigged, all its Royalist members having been forcibly ejected before the debate. Charles considered the court that tried him to be illegally constituted, and refused to defend himself, holding that it had no jurisdiction over him. The King's execution in 1649 was a profound shock, to the country and the world at large, and it was disastrous for England's foreign relations. Cromwell's government required an erudite and articulate spokesman to justify its position and argue for its legitimacy. The author of *The Tenure of Kings and Magistrates* was an obvious choice, especially given Milton's fluency in Latin, the international language of diplomacy and learning. Milton was offered the post of Secretary for Foreign Tongues to the Council of State.

His first and most urgent task was the refutation of the *Eikon Basilike* (*The Royal Image*), a hagiographic work published under the King's name shortly after his execution. This gave a version of the conflict with Parliament from the royal perspective, and represented Charles as a saint and martyr. The book was immediately and immensely popular, going through sixty editions in 1649–50 alone. Milton's *Eikonoklastes* (*The Image Breaker*) attempted a point-by-point rebuttal. The effort could hardly have succeeded, and *Eikon Basilike*

continued to circulate not only in England but in Continental trans-
lations. He then dealt with a major critique of the regicide by the
influential French legal scholar Claude Saumaise (Salmasius).
Milton's reply, in Latin, *Defensio pro Populo Anglicano* (*Defence of the
English People*), in this case was entirely effective, and gave him an
international reputation for learned polemic. But within a short time
he was forced to turn his attention from responding to Continental
critics of the new Commonwealth to defending himself against
personal attacks by Royalists on the one hand, and by Puritans
more doctrinaire than he on the other. Moreover, his eyesight had
begun to fail in the mid-1640s, and he was by 1652 completely blind.
Responses to such attacks and an account of his blindness are
memorably included in his second reply, *Defensio Secunda* (1654).
Nevertheless, he served his employers well, and after he retired in
1655 continued to hold the nominal title of Secretary to the Council,
and his salary continued to be paid. His replacement was the other
great poet of the period, Andrew Marvell, who remained a close and
supportive friend.

After Cromwell's death in 1658, the Commonwealth essentially
fell apart. Richard Cromwell, who briefly succeeded his father, had
little support, and Parliament was too factionalized to form a
government. The army, and much of the nation, favoured a return to
the monarchy, and in 1660 Charles II, who had been in exile in France,
was invited to return and assume his father's throne. Milton held
out, courageously (or quixotically), for a republican solution, and his
final political pamphlet, issued shortly before the new king's return,
was *The Ready and Easy Way to Establish a Free Commonwealth*.

After the Restoration, Milton was in great danger. He had been an
influential spokesman for the regicides, and could have been charged
with treason and executed. He was in fact briefly placed under
arrest and heavily fined, and *Eikonoklastes* and *Defensio pro Populo
Anglicano* were called in and publicly burnt; but whether because his
blindness seemed to render him now harmless, or because he had
enough friends and admirers in the new government (Marvell, for
example, was a Member of Parliament, and Milton's brother
Christopher was an influential jurist) to mitigate his situation, he was
allowed to live the rest of his life in quiet retirement. He had written
some poetry during the Commonwealth: great sonnets, probably
Samson Agonistes, and some of *Paradise Lost*—his nephew Edward
Phillips reported that Milton had shown him Satan's monologue at
the beginning of Book IV in the 1640s, as part of a projected tragedy.

But the main work on the poem probably took place from 1658 to 1665, at a time of the greatest pessimism and danger for the poet. It was was published in 1667. In the last two years of his life he published *Paradise Regained* and *Samson Agonistes* and revised versions of the 1645 *Poems* and of *Paradise Lost*. He died in 1674.

Paradise Lost

Owing to Milton's blindness, *Paradise Lost* was written by dictation, to whatever willing amanuensis was at hand. It appeared in two distinct versions. The 1667 version was in ten books, perhaps recalling its dramatic beginnings, a two-part tragedy in ten acts, or more likely taking Lucan's ten-book republican epic *Pharsalia* as its model. In the year of his death, however, a revised version in twelve books appeared: the change was apparently instigated by the publisher, and transferred the epic model to the *Aeneid*. The revision required very few alterations—two long books were split, and some transitional lines were added—but the conceptual change from tragedy and Lucan to Virgilian epic is significant.

The 1667 *Paradise Lost* was a handsomely printed but distinctly austere volume. It included none of the eulogistic prefatory verse usual for volumes of poetry in the period, nor did Milton supply a dedication or an introduction of any sort. The title page reads simply *Paradise Lost. A Poem Written in Ten Books By John Milton*, and notes that the book has been duly licensed for publication; on the next page the poem begins. The publisher, however, soon sensed that something more was required, so he asked Milton to supply an Argument. Prose summaries of each of the books were therefore inserted before the poem, along with an explanation of the poet's decision to write in blank verse, rather than rhyme. Almost at once, that is, explanations and justifications seemed to be required; the poem was puzzling and challenging. The 1674 version (which has become the standard one for us) looks much more normal: it is supplied with two dedicatory poems, in Latin and English, the latter by Andrew Marvell; the note on the verse has become the author's preface, and the plot summaries have been placed where they would be expected, before each book. *Paradise Lost* had become, in those seven years, the normative English epic.

Milton's defence of his use of blank verse is worth pausing over. It could have been simply a conservative argument: blank verse had first been used in English, after all, over a century earlier, in the Earl of

Surrey's translation of the *Aeneid*. It was devised as a vernacular equivalent to Virgil's Latin hexameters, and Milton might have argued that he was returning, as far as it was possible to do in English, to his poetic sources. But he makes a different, and more provocative claim, 'rhyme being', he says, 'no necessary adjunct or true ornament of poem or good verse . . . but the invention of a barbarous age, to set off wretched matter and lame metre'. The enemy here is partly the Middle Ages, when Latin poetry first started to be rhymed, and partly the fantastic subject matter of romances; but the enemy is also firmly in the present, for example in recent epics such as Sir William Davenant's very popular *Gondibert*, a chivalric tale in rhymed quatrains, published in 1651. Most of all, Milton rejects the simple pleasure rhyme gives us, viewing it as a distraction from, or a substitute for, genuine poetic accomplishments apt for a civilized and culturally sophisticated society. The pressure of justification extends to questions of taste; and making the wrong choice, following false gods, is as much an aesthetic issue as a moral and theological one.

For a seventeenth-century English poet, however, the real problem with rejecting rhyme and the matter of romances was how to deal with the great example of 'our sage and serious poet Spenser' (as he is called in *Areopagitica*), for whom Milton had an enormous, though equivocal, admiration. Despite his decision to abandon his projected epic on the Arthurian legends, Spenser's *Faerie Queene* was an unavoidable poetic precedent—Dryden reported, indeed, that Milton told him that 'Spenser was his original', his model. So Milton acknowledges that there are some great modern poems in rhyme, but asserts that they would have been even better poems without it; and he concludes that he has given to the nation an example, 'the first in English, of ancient liberty recovered to heroic poem from the troublesome and modern bondage of rhyming'. The language is still that of the Puritan revolutionary; even in his prosody Milton is preserving ancient liberty from modern bondage. In his recovery of 'ancient liberty', Milton proposes an alternative modernity. The move away from chivalric legend (and from rhymed stanzas) is represented as an affirmation of truth and freedom, but these are *ancient*. The modern, the present, is the danger, what keeps us in bondage.

As a recent model for a Protestant biblical epic, Milton had Guillaume Salluste, Sieur du Bartas's enormously influential poem on the creation *Les Semaines et les Jours* (1578), which appeared in English in Joshua Sylvester's translation as *Divine Weeks and Days* in 1605. Milton admired the poem, and declares his indebtedness to it by many allusions. But *Paradise Lost* is as little like du Bartas as it is like the traditional epic descending from Homer and Virgil, with its martial context and idealistic nationalism. Milton's project was far more audacious and original, not least in its avowed intention to 'justify the ways of God to men': the underlying assumption was that God's ways need justification and that Milton was authorized to be God's spokesman. In fact, Milton was theologically quite unorthodox: his treatise *Christian Doctrine*, which remained unpublished until the nineteenth century, is in many respects heretical, for example rejecting the Trinity and the immortality of the soul. Both doctrinally and politically, *Paradise Lost* is to all appearances uncontroversial—as it would have had to be in order to be published—but dramatically it confronts the fallen Christian nation with its failures, and offers only a distant and doubtful hope of an eventual return to grace.

'Of man's first disobedience . . . Sing heavenly muse': the poem establishes its claims to poetic authority at once, as Milton identifies himself first with Virgil and Homer and then with Moses, and even more profoundly in the announced intention to soar above the mount of the muses, beyond the world of classical poetry, and approach God's knowledge. The justification of God's ways requires more than an exhortation to belief; it requires a complex drama whose source is both historical and deeply personal. This undertaking is Milton's heroic Christian mission; but the conception—with its assertion of the dangerous flight, the intention to venture beyond the mean, to do what nobody else has ever dared to do—allies the poetic enterprise with Satan's pride, and his attempt to regain the paradise that he too has lost. The poem acknowledges from the outset that God's ways are not self-evident, any more than the good is.

The opening books focus on Satan, a figure of magnificent will and passionate intensity. The essential evil he represents is a given, but the tone is nevertheless profoundly and movingly elegiac, dramatically established with Satan's first words, as he recognizes his comrade Beelzebub: 'If thou beest he; but O how fallen! how changed . . .' (i. 84). Readers since Blake and Shelley have observed that Milton seems to be on Satan's side without realizing it. Certainly, in the first half of the poem, it is Satan whose motivation and psychology are comprehensible to us, who is, ironically, the most human character we encounter. Even the account of the primal sin, the revolt in heaven, resonates with human experience throughout history: the decision to rebel against authority, the ambition to be free, not to be subservient, would have had a particular force for readers who had lived through the Civil War and the changing fortunes of the King and the Commonwealth. Even in acknowledging defeat, Satan denies that the rebellion was wrong—it might have succeeded; it was worth a try: 'till then who knew | The force of those dire arms?' (i. 93–4).

Who knew—how could one know? It is a question that resonates dangerously, subversively, throughout the poem. How do you know anything except by trial, by experience? What would *we* know if Adam and Eve had not eaten the forbidden fruit? In fact, the central experience throughout all Milton's moral work is the experience of temptation, of trial, and the point is made over and over that innocence is no protection against its dangers. In *Areopagitica*, Milton argues against Parliament's order to censor manuscripts before publication, and his point is that people's innocence must not be preserved; they must be free to choose if choice is to have any moral meaning at all—and that means they must be free to make the wrong choice, to learn by their mistakes.

Satan's decision to rebel against God was clearly the wrong one. Nevertheless, as Milton sets it up, the issues are essentially the same as they are to be with Adam and Eve: they choose wrongly, but they do not really understand what they are choosing. God's omnipotence is a given, but it is not a reality until it is tested, and to test it is to fall. In the same way, in Spenser's *Faerie Queene*, throughout the first two books the heroes fall, over and over: yield to temptation, are deceived or seduced from their duty, neglect their quest. This is the nature of moral experience as Spenser introduces it into his epic—we fall, and then we pick ourselves up; that is how we learn, and that is why Milton told Dryden that 'Spenser was his original'. In dramatic terms, moreover, God's omnipotence never becomes a reality, simply because Satan never fully acknowledges it. He will not 'sue for grace | With suppliant knee, and deify his power', he declares (i. 111–12), and thereby makes the point: God's divinity depends on his worshippers— if there were nobody to worship him, he would not be God. This is theologically quite incorrect—it would have to be, for God to be omnipotent. Theologically, God does not *need* anybody; God is self-sufficient. The creation was not necessary; it did not prove that he needed worshippers, or anything else; it was simply an emanation of his goodness, his omnipotence in action. But even after the defeat and explusion from heaven, Satan does not see it that way; neither does Beelzebub (who wonders why God won, whether 'by strength, or chance, or fate': i. 132); neither, in their inexperience and gullibility, do Eve and Adam; and finally, as the whole poem acknowledges, neither do we. That is why we are still capable of making tragic choices, and why God's ways have to be—keep having to be—justified to us: because his goodness is still not self-evident, because our lives are, as they have always been, full of conflicting goods.

The realities Milton dramatizes are not primarily theological ones, they are the realities of the human spirit as understood by a radical Christian thinker; and it is extraordinarily courageous of him to acknowledge that our ties are more profoundly with Satan than with God, that we understand the world through the model of Satan's experience, not through the model provided by God's law. This is why Satan is not presented as simply hideous and perverse. He appears, in fact, far more recognizably human than God or Christ. For a Renaissance reader, imbued with the epic tradition, he would have been a familiar type, but not simply a type of evil, a villain. He is a figure of genuinely heroic stature who cannot bear not being first—pride is the tragic flaw, the original sin. The classic model is Achilles, the flawed hero, but the greatest of heroes none-theless. Satan's choice, not Eve's and Adam's, really constitutes the great moral exemplum in the poem. To say that the angels have free will but can only choose to obey is saying nothing at all: freedom implies, at a minimum, more than one choice. It is the rebel angels who make obedience meaningful—there is no notion of good with-out a notion of evil: we know things by their contraries. Even to make a rational choice to obey, we have to be able to imagine what the alternative is. Satan's rebellion legitimates the angels who refuse his call, as Milton attempts to dramatize, in the confrontation between Satan and Abdiel, the only angel who is represented as first seduced and then repelled by Satan's revolt.

We get our sense of Satan initially through long, powerful, beauti-fully realized dramatic speeches, and, even when he makes assertions that we know to be mistaken or blasphemous, there is a magnificence to the figure that derives precisely from Milton's sense of him as an epic hero, or a figure out of Shakespearean or Marlovian tragedy: Faustus, Macbeth, Richard III. The double sense of such figures, and of the way it complicates the moral quality of the poem's whole action, is something Milton manages to keep continually in sight, and is one of the poem's greatest triumphs. Consider the description of Mammon in Book I, lines 678 ff. He is 'the least erected spirit that fell'; even before the fall, his gaze was always downward, toward the golden pavement of heaven. In hell, he is the architect of the palace of

Pandaemonium ('all the devils'; the name appears to be Milton's coinage), a prototype of the lavish works of Israel's godless enemies. But after forty lines of this, Milton gives us another view of Mammon:

> Nor was his name unheard or unadored
> In ancient Greece; and in Ausonian land
> Men called him Mulciber; and how he fell
> From heaven, they fabled, thrown by angry Jove
> Sheer o'er the crystal battlements; from morn
> To noon he fell, from noon to dewy eve,
> A summer's day; and with the setting sun
> Dropped from the zenith like a falling star,
> On Lemnos the Aegaean isle: thus they relate,
> Erring . . .

> (i. 738–47)

The account moves from condemnation and contempt to an astonishing reversal, in which Mammon can be legitimately admired—'adored' is Milton's word, or more precisely (and cautiously), 'nor . . . unadored'. Mammon is a biblical analogue to the Greek Hephaestos, the Roman Vulcan; we are offered a classical version of the fall of the rebel angels, in which it is no longer sinful or painful but beautiful, and Milton's eloquent account is full of compassion for the loss of a particularly ephemeral beauty. It is, moreover, specifically the *fall* that is beautiful. 'From morn | To noon, he fell, from noon to dewy eve, | A summer's day . . . Dropped from the zenith like a falling star': there are no negative overtones now; the verse has become rich, sensuous, and full of pity—so much so that Milton pulls himself back from it, with that final 'Erring'.

This sort of double vision occurs throughout the poem, and Milton's sense of classical literature makes it possible. To the Renaissance humanist, the classical world is a version of the biblical one, but its stories are fables, the result of an imperfect understanding of the truth of scripture, an incomplete revelation. At such moments, Milton finds in classical myth a version of his story that does not involve the pressures of judgment, allowing him to acknowledge that much of what we treasure most in our history is also most problematic morally, the subjects of tragedy and epic. These moments also acknowledge that we would be justified in condemning those subjects only if we were God.

The willingness to accept, to admire, not to condemn, makes such passages most human, most touching and evocative; but also, ironically, makes us, and Milton, least godlike. There is certainly a tone of heavy moralizing in the poem, but it is largely reserved for God. Even the angels make mistakes, and both good and rebel angels have their ties with us. As a dramatic figure in the poem, God is, not surprisingly, a major problem. There are a number of critical moments when Milton makes it clear that God's perspective, even on the action of the poem, is not, and cannot be, ours. One way to understand this is to say that it means we cannot play God; but another is to say that God is the element in the poem that Milton has most trouble with. In Book III God, addressing Christ, predicts Satan's success in bringing about the fall of man:

> man will hearken to his glozing lies,
> And easily transgress the sole command,
> Sole pledge of his obedience: so will fall
> He and his faithless progeny: whose fault?
> Whose but his own? ingrate, he had of me
> All he could have; I made him just and right,
> Sufficient to have stood, though free to fall.
>
> (iii. 93–9)

This is the first appearance of God in the poem, and, dramatically, it is what establishes him as a character. He asserts in the course of this speech that the failure of absolute obedience to one's father is a sufficient cause for a sentence of death, not only on Adam but on all his descendants—notice those 'faithless progeny': Adam's children are not even born yet; how are they implicated? Doubtless a strongly patriarchal culture, or one in which Augustine's notion of original sin had become a matter of unquestioned belief, would have had less trouble than we do in accepting the validity of the claim that the sins of the fathers are properly visited on the children. But Milton does nothing to mitigate the tone, to make God compassionate and regretful rather than angry and vindictive. The charge that Adam is an 'ingrate' is particularly unattractive, because it is particularly inhuman; it refuses to acknowledge that there are any reasons why one might do the wrong thing, or any mitigating circumstances: and from God's point of view, there are indeed none.

If this were the poem's point of view, the question of justification would not be an issue—God's ways would not have to be justified. Adam and Eve are disobedient and wicked, Satan is the devil, and that's the end of it: there's no problem, and if there's no problem, there's no poem. But this is not the poem's point of view. The fall, the decision to eat the forbidden fruit, as it is presented dramatically, is anything but an easy transgression. It is an intricately linked series of small actions no one of which is clearly understood by any of the participants; and the final outcome is far more the result of ignorance and inexperience than of intentional disobedience. God's sense of the ease of the sin will be dramatically countered by the human sense of the real difficulties of dealing with temptation.

As for God's accusation of ingratitude, the charge ignores the realities of anybody's life except God's. In eating the forbidden fruit, Adam is caught between conflicting loyalties; he chooses the wrong side—his wife—but he really understands too little about the implications of the choice to choose the right one. What he has to decide is where his loyalty lies; and his decision—to be loyal to his wife rather than to his father (or his patron)—is one that could not have seemed alien to any but the most doctrinaire of Milton's readers, even in the seventeenth century. The very terms of the marriage ceremony, indeed, for doctrinaire readers, would have dictated Adam's choice: we promise to be faithful to our wives and husbands for better or worse, till death. What Adam has to do is not to choose good over evil, loyalty over disloyalty, but to decide between conflicting goods, conflicting loyalties; and Adam and Eve really are not in possession of enough information or experience to enable them to make a free choice. What they know is that the penalty for eating the fruit is death—'Whatever thing death be', Satan says to Eve (ix. 695), and thereby reveals the extent of their ignorance and inexperience, and the problems with this as a valid test of their will. What does the threat of death mean in a world where no one has ever died? Death is a concept no one in the poem has any experience of: not Satan, not the angels, not even God— Death exists in the poem only as an allegorical figure on the outskirts of hell. The threat, therefore, can have meaning only for us, readers millennia later in a fallen world. There is, moreover, a significant slippage in the way the sin is described: God says he forbade Adam and Eve to eat the fruit, but in fact that is not what he did. He imposed on the act a penalty which they were at liberty to incur. They chose to incur it, but they had no way of understanding what they were choosing. The will, in such conditions, cannot be said to be free. What is remarkable, even unique, about Milton's vision of the fall is that he acknowledges all this, and presents the fall as sinful but also comprehensible, human, inescapable, and ultimately even a good thing.

The issue of responsibility for the fall is a complex one. Satan, who has already produced in Eve a dangerous dream of aspiration, finds the innocent serpent and takes possession of it. This is a significant departure from the narrative in Genesis, in which Satan is not involved. The serpent is described as the most 'cunning' of the beasts, both the most knowledgeable and naturally mischievous, a sort of Edenic trickster; this is his character, the way he is created, and he acts on his own. The original story is a folk tale about the pointless perversity of nature, about how you can trust some animals and not others, and about how naturally gullible humans are. Such a story does not lend itself to a strong moral line—it is a comedy, not a tragedy—and over the centuries biblical commentators introduced Satan into the equation to make it workable in the moral scheme, to introduce a concept of evil and responsibility. Milton's version elaborates the biblical narrative in a perfectly orthodox way, but it depends deeply on a history of interpretation.

What delivers Eve into Satan's hands is precisely the central issue of the poem, the exercise of free will. Eve has decided to separate herself from Adam and work in the garden by herself. Adam protests; but if the will is free Eve must be free to choose as well as Adam. In Eve's insistence, however, we become aware of a new tone in the poem, and a change in their relationship:

> That such an enemy we have, who seeks
> Our ruin, both by thee informed I learn,
> And from the parting angel overheard . . .
> But that thou shouldst my firmness therefore doubt
> To God or thee, because we have a foe
> May tempt it, I expected not to hear.
>
> (ix. 274–81)

The tone is full of subtlety, pride, and manipulativeness, and a wheedling quality that looks forward to Restoration comedy—she is, suddenly, being presented as an utterly conventional figure, a conniving woman who knows how to get what she wants, and she wants to feel free, not to feel subservient.

But what is wrong with that? She wants a freedom, the implied argument would go, that she cannot handle. Nevertheless, the subtlety, pride, and disingenuousness are clearly not learned behaviour. Milton's idea must be that they are qualities natural to women; and it is true that seventeenth-century medical opinion held that women were naturally less perfect than men. But the case is clearly being loaded; Eve is being set up. In a sense, Milton has to load the case: suppose Eve asserted forthrightly that she was entitled to her free choice and independence just as Adam is. It would then be much more difficult to justify God's judgment: she exercised her power of choice, and because she was lied to by a charming con-man, she made the wrong choice—in the fallen world, it happens all the time. Eve must be represented as incapable of rational choice, as ripe for seduction; her sin is not in wanting to be free, but in presuming that she is, in not knowing her place in the natural hierarchy, in presuming that she does not require Adam's constant advice and protection—whereas, ironically, Adam's sin is in presuming that he *does* require hers. Adam is aware that her trial has begun, and urges that they endure it together. But her reply, again, indicates that it is already too late, that the fall has already taken place:

> If this be our condition, thus to dwell
> In narrow circuit straitened by a foe . . .
>
> (ix. 322–3)

The garden has already started to look different, insular and restrictive, a narrow circuit. It is surrounded by a wall, its inhabitants sequestered from the rest of creation; it could be looked at in the way Eve has suddenly started to do—it could always have been seen that way—but paradise has not seemed like a prison until just now. The sin has been committed as soon as it is acknowledged that there is another way of looking at things. The fall is a matter of perspective. But even in the poem's terms, if, as God said, he made humankind sufficient to have stood though free to fall, what is there to fear? The answer can only come from experience, from hindsight, after it is too late.

What is there to fear? The answer to this question provides the largest ironic dimension of the poem. The fearful thing is precisely choice, the freedom of the will—just what we want most. In Book VIII, Adam recounts how God appeared to him in a dream and warned him not to eat the fruit of the tree of knowledge. 'The rigid interdiction', Adam tells Eve, 'resounds | Yet dreadful in mine ear, though in my choice | Not to incur' (viii. 334–6). What is it that is dreadful? Precisely the rigid interdiction, the fear that the will in fact will turn out not to be free; and the only way to know its freedom is to test it and to choose the forbidden alternative. Milton's greatest difficulty throughout the poem is in conceiving of choice in the way Adam fears, as something negative or passive—'though in my choice | Not to incur'. Choosing not to act, choosing to stay as we are, contradicts the whole attitude toward knowledge in the poem. We only know what we are, what our good is, when we know what the alternatives are. Experience is the chief form of knowledge in the poem (as it is throughout Milton), and the principal mode of experience is 'try it and see'. This also means that we know what we have only through losing it; this is the essential means to knowledge, but the whole pressure of the poem is also to regain what we have lost, to repair the loss, just as in the creation of man God was repairing the loss of the rebel angels.

But even before the fall, in creation itself, Milton finds a sense of loss, or of something missing. Before the creation of Eve, Adam finds his solitude intolerable, and asks God for a companion. We are naturally incomplete, unsatisfied; God created us this way. Even the solitary creation, life closest to God, life at its most perfect and innocent, constitutes a trial for man. And God, creating Eve out of Adam, taking something out of Adam to create Eve, replicates and perpetuates that sense of incompleteness in both of them. Independence, free will, means always searching for the missing element in ourselves, even in paradise before the fall.

This complex vision contradicts any simplistic judgment about man's first disobedience. It also means, however, that what ought to be the strongest and most comforting voice in the poem—God's—turns out to be the most problematic. Throughout, we find our ties are not with God but first with Satan, and then (as Satan grows less and less heroic as the action proceeds) with Adam and Eve. Milton also provides a number of mediating figures in the poem, to mitigate the abstractness of God's justice, which in dramatic terms expresses itself as so inhuman and cold. There are the angels, who make mistakes, and chat affably with Adam, and offer information about life and love above the moon, and blush when Adam is inquisitive about angelic sex (viii. 615 ff.); but who also warn Adam against asking too many questions, especially about astronomy, the knowledge that, in cosmological terms, would bring us closest to God. Such moments undeniably provide a humanizing dimension to the celestial elements of the poem, but that is not really why the angels are there. They have been sent specifically to warn Adam to be on guard against the coming temptation, and not so that Adam and Eve can avoid it, but, as God explicitly puts it, so that Adam cannot say he was not warned. Milton spells it out explicitly, in the prose Argument to Book V: 'God to render man inexcusable sends Raphael to admonish him of his obedience.' To render man inexcusable: the angels look as if they are on our side, but in another sense—God's sense—they are only there to make things worse for us.

Most of all, and first of all, in Book III Milton provides the mediating figure of Christ, who agrees to become a man himself, and, though utterly innocent, agrees not only to die but to suffer an excruciating death. This is the greatest act of generosity in the poem—perhaps the only pure act of generosity Milton can imagine, one done entirely for someone else's benefit, from which the giver gains nothing at all— but in a way Christ's sacrifice, too, only makes things worse, only sets us farther off from God. What it means is that at the centre of Milton's Christianity is a father whose justice can only be satisfied by the torture and death of his son, who, in a biblical passage Milton does not—perhaps cannot—deal with, cries to God from the cross: 'Why hast thou forsaken me?' Even Christ, becoming a man, feels forsaken by God. This is the version of Christianity Milton must justify, the reason God's ways have to be justified: it is very difficult for us to understand both how universal and how uncompromising Christianity was in the period.

There is, however, one genuinely mediating voice in *Paradise Lost*, and it is Milton's own, entering at critical moments that do a good deal to control our response to the action. The famous opening of Book III, the apostrophe to light, moves from abstract and theoretical to mythological, and then, startlingly, to autobiographical:

> thee I revisit safe,
> And feel thy sovereign lamp; but thou
> Revisit'st not these eyes, that roll in vain
> To find thy piercing ray, and find no dawn . . .
> . . . Thus with the year
> Seasons return, but not to me returns
> Day, or the sweet approach of even or morn,
> Or sight of vernal bloom, or summer's rose,
> Or flocks, or herds, or human face divine;
> But cloud instead, and ever-during dark
> Surrounds me . . .
>
> (iii. 21–4, 40–6)

In passages like these, Milton becomes the central figure in the poem. The autobiographical voice is especially striking at the opening of Book VII, the midpoint of the epic. The war in heaven has been described, and the poem returns to earth, and to the crucial experience that must be accounted for, man's first disobedience, and the entrance into the world of death and all our woe. The muse invoked at the beginning of Book I is only now finally named: 'Descend from heaven, Urania'—Urania is the muse of both epic poetry and of astronomy, muse of the highest and most dangerous knowledge. The implications of Milton's audacity become clear—astronomy is what Adam was warned against asking questions about; and we recall Milton's fascination with Galileo. The danger, moreover, is not generalized or metaphorical, but real and autobiographical:

> Standing on earth, not rapt above the pole,
> More safe I sing with mortal voice, unchanged
> To hoarse or mute, though fallen on evil days,
> On evil days though fallen, and evil tongues;
> In darkness, and with dangers compassed round,
> And solitude . . .
>
> (vii. 23–8)

This is life, and poetry, after the fall, and its muse is Urania. The one tree in Eden forbidden to humankind was the tree of knowledge; in the unfallen world, knowledge, the desire for learning and understanding, are evil. The knowledge is, explicitly, the knowledge of good and evil— and therefore also the ability to distinguish between them and thereby to choose between them: the knowledge that makes our free will free, gives our choices meaning. It is not only Satan, but Milton himself, who now exemplifies the dangers of aspiring too high. It grows harder and harder to distinguish virtues from vices; and the poem's virtues, more and more, exist only in a lapsed world.

> Return me to my native element:
> Lest from this flying steed unreined, (as once
> Bellerophon, though from a lower clime)
> Dismounted, on the Aleian field I fall
> Erroneous there to wander and forlorn.
>   . . . still govern thou my song,
> Urania, and fit audience find, though few.
> But drive far off the barbarous dissonance
> Of Bacchus and his revellers, the race
> Of that wild rout that tore the Thracian bard
> In Rhodope, where woods and rocks had ears
> To rapture, till the savage clamour drowned
> Both harp and voice; nor could the muse defend
> Her son. So fail not thou, who thee implores:
> For thou art heavenly, she an empty dream.
>
> (vii. 16–20, 30–9)

These magnificent passages establish the terms and the tone of the second half of the poem. In the flight of Bellerophon (the hero who attempted to ascend to heaven on the muses' winged horse Pegasus and was thrown down by Jove, to live out his life in blindness and solitude), in the death of the archpoet Orpheus at the hands of the outraged followers of Bacchus, Milton saw an allegory of his own audacity in defending the Commonwealth to the bitter end, in writing *Paradise Lost*, in presuming to justify God's ways to man. He saw the same complex and ambiguous analogy in Satan's pride, in Eve's aspiration, in Adam's hunger for knowledge: the poem creates a context where aspiration and heroic knowledge are the sources not only of sin and woe but also of poetic strength, the substance of epic and tragedy. Satan's temptation of Eve is, after all, a temptation to imagine another kind of life, not a life of pastoral contentment but one of epic and tragic aspiration—to imagine herself, in short, in another kind of poem. All the metaphoric play on the idea of 'the fall' gets brilliantly, tragically localized as Milton sees in it his own situation. As the poem moves toward Adam's sin, the poet asserts, from a depth of experience that will always be denied to most of us, and is certainly denied to Adam and Eve, that we fall with the best of intentions.

The Critical History of the Classic Text

In so far as *Paradise Lost* invites identification with the fallen condition and thereby distances itself from any easy Christian consolation, its status as a canonical text cannot simply coincide with the delivery of normative values. Rather, from the very start, treating the poem as a classic has involved the attempt to foist such values upon it. John Dryden's responses to the poem are, in this respect, illuminating. In 1674, the very year that *Paradise Lost* appeared in its final twelve-book incarnation, Dryden rewrote it as an opera, *The State of Innocence*, recasting it into rhymed couplets in an attempt to refashion the epic to meet contemporary literary formal and generic demands in much the same way that Elizabethan plays were being rewritten for the Restoration stage. Dryden's attempt to modernize the poem made Milton's epic a classic—and instantly old-fashioned. Where Milton had ascribed a revolutionary value to his verse form, one that connected it to an ancient liberty, Dryden sought to fetter it. Safely circumscribed, Dryden could then hail it, as he does in a poem accompanying the 1688 edition of the epic, as equal in stature to Homer or Virgil. The elevation of the text to classic status is coincident with the distancing of the text, the denial to it of contemporaneity, and hence of any religious or political implications that might question the Restoration.

This can be seen in the terms of Dryden's critical estimation of *Paradise Lost* in the preface to *The State of Innocence*, as 'one of the greatest, most noble, and most sublime poems which either this age or nation has produced'. The coupling of such terms as 'noble' and 'sublime' ascribes to the poem quasi-aristocratic value; the coupling of generic and class markers 'elevates' the poem in ways that safeguard it against revolutionary or republican readings. This is perhaps even more the case in the series of essays on the poem that Addison contributed to *The Spectator* in 1712. Treating the poem as a supreme instance of 'the highest kind' of poetry, an epic that deserved to be called 'divine', Addison sought at the same time to make it normative, the realization of its genre, and, beyond that, the embodiment of a comfortable and conforming Christianity. For Addison, the poem is 'universal' in its scope—and 'useful' too, for it teaches the great moral of obedience. Addison's *Paradise Lost* brings its readers up to a level of critical judgment and of belief that is no different from their social refinement. Hence, in his twelve essays on the 'beauties' of each book of *Paradise Lost*, Addison was at pains to show the meanings that 'ordinary' readers might miss, and to guide them to what is 'capable of pleasing the most delicate reader' and to raise his readers to that 'delicate' capacity. Thus, for instance, Addison's readers learn that Eve is 'soft and womanish', while Adam is 'more masculine and elevated'; what Addison terms the 'universal' is never far from a very restricted and hierarchized vision of a gendered social decorum. 'His subject', Addison sums up, 'is the noblest that could have entered into the thoughts of man.' What this means, among other things, is that Milton's imagination is 'conformable to ... Scripture', 'finely imagined, and grounded upon what is delivered in sacred story'. Hence 'the more the reader examines the justness and delicacy of its sentiments, the more he will find himself pleased with it'. The poem, then, is educative, at once teaching what is best in poetry, best to believe, best if one is to reform oneself into that which makes one most noble and elevated, in a word, socially decorous and refined in taste and sensibility. Milton, Addison assured his readers, 'took the greatest care to avoid anything that might be offensive to religion or good manners'.

Through complicated byways, views like Addison's have continued to prevail in Milton criticism and scholarship, if not quite in the same terms, none the less in the sense that Milton's poem represents enduring values, saving beliefs, comfort and consolation. For much of the twentieth century Milton was extolled as a Christian humanist poet, and in such generalized terms that even his Protestantism faded into ecumenism, while a more recent emphasis on Milton as a Protestant poet always hastens to insist on the poet's rationality, in effect delivering, once again, a Christian humanism, albeit of a more sectarian slant. Much Milton criticism supports a view of canonical literature which assumes that such texts instil time-transcending universal values, that what the Bible or the classics teach are dehistoricized truths, or truths reached once the Reformation succeeded.

In Addison and Dryden one can see the origins of such critical beliefs as part of the post-revolutionary settlement, and, in one respect at least, such responses to Milton's poem are not entirely misguided. For one end of the revolution was, in a fashion, realized in the Glorious Revolution of 1688 which for ever subordinated the monarch to Parliament. This change in politics was not, however, matched by any such change in private hierarchies, and, arguably, was accompanied by a further sequestration of women to a private domain. In countless ways, *Paradise Lost* represents the first couple as a proto-modern bourgeois couple; labour is divided between them; she prepares the meals, he talks to angels. Even the decision to represent the fall as a choice of domestic happiness against more strenuous obligations to God, pits individual happiness against socio-political demands in a way that forecasts much in later understandings of the relationship between individual and society.

None the less, there is another legacy of the poem, and a recognition almost as early as Dryden's or Addison's of elements in the poem that disturb the post-revolutionary settlement. It can be seen, for instance, in Richard Bentley's 1732 edition of *Paradise Lost*, which regards the poem as hardly perfect in execution or exemplary in its meanings. Bentley desired to save the poem's faults from Milton, and thus ascribed its supposed errors to an editor or to the printer. On the one hand, this saving gesture raised Milton above the vagaries of the production of the text. But on the other hand—since the 'errors' that Bentley found were in fact features of Milton's poem—Bentley's reading confronted much that was unassimilable to the conforming response of Addison and his followers. So William Empson argued in *Some Versions of Pastoral* (1935), in an essay that reclaimed the errors of Bentley for a contemporary reading project—in Empson's case, one directed as much against prevailing orthodox readings of Milton (which became the standard academic critical tradition) as against a new orthodoxy, the rejection of the poet advanced by modernist critics. These followed the lead of T. S. Eliot, who, in his 1921 essay on 'The Metaphysical Poets' had condemned Milton as the writer who had introduced a 'dissociation of sensibility' that Eliot saw as his task to repair. Modernist rejections of Milton that followed (including, famously, F. R. Leavis's attempt to rewrite the canon of English literature without Milton in it) depended precisely on a reading of Milton as a deadly upholder of calcified poetic form and language. That is, modernist readings depended on the Milton that the tradition of Addison espoused. Yet just below the surface of the assaults of Eliot or Leavis can be seen something else: a defence against Milton, a dislike of his wresting of language away from the ordinary, of his stretching of literary form to the breaking point, and, hence, of the revolutionary politics that arguably underlies the formal features of the poem. And ironically, as is more than suggested by Eliot's final recantation in a 1947 essay that somewhat grudgingly acknowledges Milton as a great poet, what modernist criticism wanted from Milton was precisely what it also claimed he did not offer: the consolations of order and art against the depredations of ordinary life. When Eliot found himself at home in the Established Church, he was willing to admit Milton into the literary pantheon after all. Both the rejection and the admission of Milton were couched in the terms laid out much earlier by Dryden and Addison. Or, as Empson astutely noted, both those academic critics who rally around Milton as the embodiment of eternal values, and those modernist critics who followed in the wake of Eliot, were united in their neo-Christianity and social conservatism.

The terms for modern literary criticism were invented in the eighteenth century, and it was around Milton (and Shakespeare and Spenser) that its programme developed. Empson, arguably the greatest critic of Milton in the twentieth century, looked back not only to the extravagant example of Milton's early editors. Implicitly, his arguments about the poem have everything to do with Dr Johnson, the most brilliant eighteenth-century critic of Milton. In some respects, Johnson shared the normative views of his predecessors, and there are passages in his life of Milton (in his *Lives of the Poets*, 1779) that could be put beside Addison, as, for instance, his claim that *Paradise Lost* is a 'useful' text that shows 'the reasonableness of religion, and the necessity of obedience to the Divine Law'. Johnson's resistance to Milton's republican politics is strongly registered and worth noticing because it suggests how hard-won his admiration for *Paradise Lost* was. His reading of the poem testifies to its overwhelming force— the reader of the poem is described, for instance, as 'harassed and overburdened'—its imposition on him the weight not merely of its learning, but its vast abilities to displace the forms it inhabits. Also, and perhaps most important to Empson, Johnson measures the material force of Milton's language, its refusals of the protocols of sense, its joining of abstract and concrete, 'the confusion of spirit and matter' that Johnson saw as the consequence of one dilemma that Milton faced, 'the description of what cannot be described, the agency of spirits'. Although Johnson assumed that Milton shared his view of the separation of matter and spirit, what Johnson responds to is the materiality of a language that refuses to mark spirit as different in kind from matter; this is the representational equivalent of the poet's heretical materialism that led him to question the immortality of the soul.

Johnson's response to the materialism of the poem spurred twentieth-century criticism. William Kerrigan's 1975 account of Milton's beliefs and their impact on *Paradise Lost* details the effects of his heresies on the poem. More recently, this materialism has been explored by Stephen Fallon (1991), while John Rogers (1996) assimilates it to a 'vitalist' science of the mid-seventeenth century, a materialism that Rogers credits as well with the more liberal political aspects of Milton's political thought. One can make a connection from these aspects of Milton's imagination to the arguments of Empson's *Milton's God* (1961), which suggested nothing less than the ways in which the poem's beliefs are anything but normative, that Milton puts God on trial and he comes off wanting; but it can almost be heard even in the course of Johnson's account of the poem, for what he described as the most 'useful' aim of the poem, its instilling of reasonable belief and obedience to divine law, he also recognized as 'most arduous: "to vindicate the ways of God to man" '.

Empson's reading could be assimilated to the Romantics' Milton, to Blake's proclamation in *The Marriage of Heaven and Hell* that Milton 'was of the Devil's party without knowing it', for instance. Such a belief is not unprecedented, however; Dryden had much earlier opined that *Paradise Lost* failed precisely in so far as it had made Satan its hero. Empson was close enough to eighteenth-century rationalism to want what he saw as the truth about Milton's God to have been what Milton intended, to assault the values of Christianity; that is, Empson read the poem as an attack on Christianity written from within its beliefs. The poem is assumed to express Milton's conflicts, and, beyond that, the inherent conflicts within Christianity. 'As a rule,' Empson wrote in his essay on Milton and Bentley, 'if Milton's sympathies were divided, he understood the conflict he was dramatising, and if the result is hard to explain, it is easy to feel.' There is much in Milton's theology that supports Empson's views, as has recently been suggested by Victoria Silver (2000), rare among contemporary Milton critics in acknowledging the force of Empson's intervention, although Silver's main aim is to explore complications within Christian belief and to ally them to issues in twentieth-century philosophical thought.

One can also trace a path from the Romantics back to Dr Johnson. For Johnson's response to the poem suggests the ways in which it compels in him beliefs that run counter to his own, counter to the normalizing tendencies that marked earlier eighteenth-century critics. Thus, for instance, Johnson echoes Addison in describing the poem as sublime; but for him, unlike Addison, this does not mean that the poem elevates one to a higher plane of civilized and polite consciousness. Rather, Johnson sees that the poem is profoundly inhuman, not merely because its task is to represent spirits, but also because until their fall even Adam and Eve are not human beings we can ever hope to approximate, not the basis for characters that one might find in a novel; hence, the poem gives 'little assistance to human conduct'. There is, Johnson claims, a 'want of human interest' throughout the poem, and its sublimity lies in the ways in which it stretches the reader to breaking point. Johnson can be wickedly nasty about this, as when he reports that '*Paradise Lost* is one of the books which the reader admires and lays down, and forgets to take up again', and concludes: 'none ever wished it longer than it is.' This all too human response to the poem also serves to register its demands. And indeed the sublimity of the poem is captured in descriptions that seem proto-Romantic, as the poem becomes a virtually ungraspable landscape of highs and lows, light and darkness, too vast to fill any mind except, as Johnson repeats over and again, the capacious imagination of a poet at home in 'the power of displaying the vast, illuminating the splendid, enforcing the awful, darkening the gloomy, and aggravating the dreadful'. Given these qualities, Johnson continues, Milton 'chose a subject on which too much could not be said, on which he might tire his fancy without the censure of extravagance'. Indeed, despite Johnson's attempts to find fault with the poem, he continued to register the fact that what he calls its weaknesses are at the same time signs of its inhuman strength.

Johnson recalls Addison's estimation that 'our language sunk under him', and recasts this as he describes the reader of the poem 'in captivity to a higher and nobler mind'; 'criticism', he concludes, 'sinks in admiration'. Whereas in Addison, the poem's elevation of the reader served a profoundly social function, Johnson's reader/critic is the site of a displacement by a poem that 'crowds the imagination', a dislocation that makes the scene of the reception of the poem a struggle between the Miltonic mind and the reader's. If this serves further to elevate and distance Milton it also paves the way for the privatization of the reading experience, conferring on any literate, cultivated reader the additional burden of a privacy that affords one the luxury of the agonized measuring of one's own individual imaginative capacities. It is in this sense that Johnson leads the way towards Romantic criticism and provides another path to modern criticism—indeed, to the so-called New Criticism—with its dehistoricizing valuation of the ability of literature to increase the reader's stock in imaginative responsiveness. Johnson's insights also stand behind Harold Bloom's arguments in *The Anxiety of Influence* (1973) and *A Map of Misreading* (1975), in which the legacy of Milton for the Romantics and their successors is the sense of having been displaced and overburdened by the example of Milton. Keats memorably writes of Milton that 'life to him would be death to me', while Wordsworth opens *The Prelude* by echoing the closing lines of *Paradise Lost*. Johnson might even be behind the argument of Stanley Fish's *Surprised by Sin* (1967), in which the reader, according to Fish, succumbs again and again to the temptation to identify with the fallen condition only to be upbraided by an awareness of and subjection to the divine plan and meaning.

Johnson's criticism holds out these modern legacies, and the route from him to Empson, especially through the intervention represented by *Milton's God*, has led to a modern project of reading that continually engages the resistance which Milton's *Paradise Lost* offers to privatizing, normalizing, and simply adulatory responses to the poem. In criticism of the 1980s and 1990s, such enquiry was conducted by readers for whom the representation of gender or race were matters that necessarily complicated the achievements of the classic text. Feminist criticism in particular (as represented by the essays of Mary Nyquist, or Janet Halley's 'Female Autonomy in Milton's Sexual Poetics', 1988), has powerfully shown how the poem solicits female subordination even as its agenda is complicated by the fact that the male author also represents himself in a subordinate position, an argument that resonates in essays on the poem by John Guillory. Some of the impetus for such inquiry can even be found in Empson, who describes Eve as 'set up' by the scheme of the poem and its religion; indeed, even Johnson excoriates the poet's masculinism, his 'Turkish contempt of females, as subordinate and inferior beings', though it is of course noteworthy that Johnson would have such behaviour characterize Islamic rather than Western European cultures; moreover, as Kevin Pask demonstrates in his *The Emergence of the English*

Author (1996), Johnson takes Milton's support of domestic tyranny to give the lie to his republicanism, a suspect conflation.

Empson's desire to embed Milton's critique within his Christianity led the way to a further historicizing of the poem, not least because theological issues do not merely count as religious, but are sites for the most contested struggles in seventeenth-century England, at the centre of debates over social relations and institutions. Political criticism that followed this impulse is best represented by Christopher Kendrick's *Milton: A Study in Ideology and Form* (1986), work also indebted to the crucial arguments of Christopher Hill. Despite the invigorating enquiries of late-twentieth-century criticism, Milton criticism continues to be dominated by traditional Miltonists. The full effect of the poem as the product of a revolutionary conscious-ness—and its continuing possibilities for disruption—remain to be measured, and perhaps will remain so for quite a while. Hill's attempts to align Milton's prose with other radical writing of the period, as well as his claims that Milton was forced in *Paradise Lost* to disguise his revolutionary commitments, have been modified by more recent historicizing work that seeks to read Milton as a Restoration poet or that wishes to situate Milton as a republican (a representative example of the latter point would be David Norbrook's treatment of *Paradise Lost* in *Writing the English Republic*, 1999). The project of treating Milton as a republican has its own limits, both in denying him a more radical edge, but also in having to sidestep some of the unpleasant features of Milton's politics—his belief, for example, that a right-minded minority could dictate the people's best interest. Part of the pathos of self-presentation in *Paradise Lost* comes, after all, from Milton's self-representation as a solitary voice who alone knows what is best. In this way, Milton offers an image of a beleaguered and knowing individual. To focus there might be to lose sight of the extra-individual forces that animate *Paradise Lost* in its search for ancient liberty.

NOTE ON THE TEXT

MODERNIZATION of Milton's spelling has been carried out according to the principles established by Stanley Wells in *Modernizing Shakespeare's Spelling* (Oxford, 1979). This has meant a loss of quaintness—e.g. sovran, quire, and faery have become sovereign, choir, and fairy—but it is hoped that most readers will agree with us that Milton in his own time was not quaint. In the spelling of proper names, an uneasy compromise has been attempted. Where the modern spelling leaves pronunciation and rhythm unaffected, we have modernized; but Milton's biblical names are those of the Latin Bible, not the Authorized Version, and his geography cannot be brought up to date. Hence we retain Fesole, Rhene, Danaw, but we use Moloch (not Moloc), Moscow (not Mosco), Astrakhan (not Astracan). In general, the sound of English has changed so much since Milton's time that it has seemed pointless, if not positively misleading, to retain old spellings merely because they seem to preserve a particular Miltonic pronunciation. Punctuation is a more complex matter, and one to which Milton paid careful attention. His practice is not entirely consistent, but to modernize it is to lose not only a good deal of rhetorical force, but often his most individual syntax. Here again, the language has changed, and grammatical structures that were possible, and even commonplace, in the seventeenth century are now solecisms. For example, a question mark does not invariably indicate the end of a sentence for Milton; to capitalize the lower-case word following the question mark, as most modern editors routinely do, constitutes a grammatical change. In general, we have undertaken to alter the original punctuation only when it seemed patently incorrect or when not to modernize it would be confusing or misleading. We have not attempted to produce a Milton in modern syntax.

Line numbers in the margin indicate a gloss in a footnote below; line numbers set in italic font, however, are for the reader's convenience only (where text is unglossed for more than a few lines).

SELECT BIBLIOGRAPHY

Other Editions

There is no authoritative edition of Milton's poetry; frequently cited are Merritt Y. Hughes (ed.), *John Milton: Complete Poems and Major Prose* (New York, 1957) and John Carey and Alastair Fowler (eds.), *The Poems of John Milton* (New York and London, 1968, 1997; cited in notes as 'Fowler'). A more recent edition is Roy Flannagan (ed.), *The Riverside Milton* (Boston, 1998). All these offer annotations fully in tune with traditional Milton scholarship.

Biography

A full-scale modern biography is William Riley Parker, *Milton: A Biography* (Oxford, 1968); revised edn. Gordon Campbell (Oxford, 1997); another is Barbara K. Lewalski, *The Life of John Milton: A Critical Biography* (Oxford, 2000). These are worth supplementing with the seven volumes of David Masson, *The Life of John Milton* (Cambridge and London, 1859–94) and Helen Darbyshire (ed.), *The Early Lives of Milton* (London, 1932). A stimulating account of the construction of Milton's life is offered in Kevin Pask, *The Emergence of the English Author* (Cambridge, 1996).

Twentieth-Century Criticism of Paradise Lost

A strong collection of original essays indicative of trends in 1980s criticism is Mary Nyquist and Margaret W. Ferguson (eds.), *Re-membering Milton* (New York and London, 1987); a convenient collection of previously published work is Annabel Patterson (ed.), *John Milton* (London, 1992). Other recommended studies:

Sharon Achinstein, *Milton and the Revolutionary Reader* (Princeton, 1994).
Denise Albanese, *New Science, New World* (Durham, NC, 1996).
Catherine Belsey, *John Milton: Language, Gender, Power* (Oxford and New York, 1988).
Harold Bloom, *The Anxiety of Influence* (London and New York, 1973).
—— *A Map of Misreading* (London and New York, 1975).
William Empson, *Milton's God* (London, 1961, 1965; Cambridge, 1981).
—— *Some Versions of Pastoral* (London, 1935).
Stephen M. Fallon, *Milton Among the Philosophers: Poetry and Materialism in Seventeenth-Century England* (Ithaca, NY, 1991).
Stanley Fish, *Surprised by Sin: The Reader in Paradise Lost* (London and Berkeley, 1967).
—— *How Milton Works* (Cambridge, Mass., 2001).
Linda Gregerson, *The Reformation of the Subject: Spenser, Milton and the English Protestant Epic* (Cambridge, 1995).

John Guillory, 'From the Superfluous to the Supernumerary: Reading Gender into *Paradise Lost*', in Elizabeth D. Harvey and Katharine Eisman Maus (eds.), *Soliciting Interpretation: Literary Theory and Seventeenth-Century Poetry* (Chicago, 1990).

—— 'Milton, Narcissism, Gender: On the Genealogy of Male Self-Esteem', in Christopher Kendrick (ed.), *Critical Essays on John Milton* (New York, 1995)

—— *Poetic Authority: Spenser, Milton, and Literary History* (New York, 1983).

Janet E. Halley, 'Female Autonomy in Milton's Sexual Poetics', in Julia M. Walker (ed.), *Milton and the Idea of Woman* (Champaign, Ill., 1988).

Geoffrey Hartman, 'Adam on the Grass with Balsamum' and 'Milton's Counterplot', in *Beyond Formalism* (New Haven, 1970).

Christopher Hill, *Milton and the English Revolution* (London and New York, 1978).

Christopher Kendrick, *Milton: A Study in Ideology and Form* (New York and London, 1986).

William Kerrigan, 'The Heretical Milton: From Assumption to Mortalism', *English Literary Renaissance*, 5 (1975), 125–66.

—— *The Prophetic Milton* (Charlottesville, Va., 1974).

—— *The Sacred Complex: On the Psychogenesis of Paradise Lost* (Cambridge, Mass., 1983).

Edward Semple LeComte, *Milton's Unchanging Mind* (Port Washington, NY, 1973).

Mary Nyquist, 'Fallen Differences, Phallologocentric Discourses: Losing *Paradise Lost* to History', in Derek Attridge, Geoff Bennington, and Robert Young (eds.), *Post-Structuralism and the Question of History* (Cambridge, 1987); reprinted in Patterson (ed.), *John Milton*.

—— 'The Father's Word/Satan's Wrath', *PMLA* 100 (1985), 187–202.

—— 'The Genesis of Gendered Subjectivity in the Divorce Tracts and in *Paradise Lost*', in Nyquist and Ferguson (eds.), *Re-membering Milton*.

Patricia Parker, *Inescapable Romance* (Princeton, 1979).

Maureen Quilligan, 'Freedom, Service, and the Trade in Slaves: The Problem of Labor in *Paradise Lost*', in Margreta de Grazia, Maureen Quilligan, and Peter Stallybrass (eds.), *Subject and Object in Renaissance Culture* (Cambridge, 1996).

Balachandra Rajan and Elizabeth Sauer (eds.), *Milton and the Imperial Vision* (Pittsburgh, 1999).

John Rogers, *The Matter of Revolution: Science, Poetry, and Politics in the Age of Milton* (Ithaca, NY, 1996).

Victoria Silver, *Imperfect Sense: The Predicament of Milton's Irony* (Princeton, 2000).

Further Reading in Oxford World's Classics

The Bible: Authorized King James Version, ed. Robert Carroll and Stephen Prickett.

Homer, *The Iliad*, trans. Robert Fitzgerald, ed. G. S. Kirk.
—— *The Odyssey*, trans. Walter Shewring, ed. G. S. Kirk.
John Milton, *Selected Poetry*, ed. Stephen Orgel and Jonathan Goldberg.
—— *The Major Works*, ed. Stephen Orgel and Jonathan Goldberg.
Virgil, *The Aeneid*, trans. C. Day Lewis, ed. Jasper Griffin.

A CHRONOLOGY OF JOHN MILTON

1608	9 December: John Milton born in Cheapside, London, first son of John Milton, scrivener and musician, and his wife Sara.
c.1615/17–24	Attends St Paul's School, London.
1625	Enters Christ's College, Cambridge.
1626	Probably rusticated (suspended) from Cambridge for part of Lent term.
1629	BA.
1632	MA; Milton's first published poem, 'On Shakespeare', appears in the dedicatory verses to the second Shakespeare folio.
1632–4	Lives at the family home in Hammersmith.
1634	*A Masque Presented at Ludlow Castle* ('*Comus*') performed.
1635–8	Lives at the family's country house at Horton, Bucks.
1637	Death of Sara Milton. Milton's Cambridge contemporary Edward King drowned.
1638–9	Travels in Italy.
1638	Publication of *Lycidas* in a volume of elegies for Edward King. Milton's closest friend, Charles Diodati, dies in August and is memorialized in *Epitaphium Damonis*.
1639	Milton returns to England and lives and teaches in London.
1640	Long Parliament convened 3 November.
1641	Publication of Milton's first political tracts: *Of Reformation Touching Church Discipline*, *Of Prelatical Episcopacy*, *Animadversions upon the Remonstrant's Defence against Smectymnuus*.
1642	Civil War begins 22 August. Publication of *The Reason of Church Government*, *Apology for Smectymnuus*. Milton marries Mary Powell, who soon after returns to her family.
1643	Publication of *The Doctrine and Discipline of Divorce*.
1644	*Of Education*, *The Judgement of Martin Bucer Concerning Divorce*, *Areopagitica*, and a revised and enlarged edition of *Doctrine and Discipline* published.
1645	Publication of *Tetrachordon* and *Colasterion*. Mary Powell Milton returns to live with Milton.
1646	*Poems of Mr John Milton, both English and Latin* (dated 1645) published. Milton's daughter Anne born.
1647	Death of John Milton, Sen.

1648   Milton's daughter Mary born.

1649   King Charles executed. Publication of *The Tenure of Kings and Magistrates* and *Eikonoklastes*. Milton appointed Secretary for Foreign Tongues to the Council of State.

1651   Publication of *Defensio pro Populo Anglicano*. Milton's son John born.

1652   Milton becomes totally blind. His wife Mary dies after giving birth to their daughter Deborah. His son John dies.

1654   *Defensio Secunda* published. Cromwell becomes Protector.

1655   *Pro Se Defensio* published.

1656   Marries Katherine Woodcock.

1657   Birth of a daughter, who dies six months later.

1658   Death of Katherine Woodcock Milton. Death of Cromwell.

1659   Publication of *A Treatise of Civil Power* and *Considerations touching the Likeliest Means to Remove Hirelings out of the Church*.

1660   Publication of *The Ready and Easy Way to Establish a Free Commonwealth*. Charles II enters London. Milton arrested and imprisoned; released some months later.

1663   Marries Elizabeth Minshull.

1667   *Paradise Lost* published in a ten-book version.

1670   *The History of Britain* published.

1671   *Paradise Regained* and *Samson Agonistes* published.

1673   Revised and enlarged edition of *Poems* (1645) published. *Of True Religion* published.

1674   *Paradise Lost* published in a twelve-book version. Milton dies 8 November.

PARADISE LOST

THE VERSE

The measure is English heroic verse without rhyme, as that of Homer in Greek, and of Virgil in Latin; rhyme being no necessary adjunct or true ornament of poem or good verse, in longer works especially, but the invention of a barbarous age, to set off wretched 4 matter and lame metre; graced indeed since by the use of some famous modern poets, carried away by custom, but much to their own vexation, hindrance, and constraint to express many things otherwise, and for the most part worse than else they would have expressed them. Not without cause therefore some both Italian and Spanish poets of prime note have rejected rhyme both in longer and shorter works, as have also long since our best English tragedies, as a thing of itself, to all judicious ears, trivial and of no true musical delight; which consists only in apt numbers, fit quantity of syllables, 13 and the sense variously drawn out from one verse into another, not in the jingling sound of like endings, a fault avoided by the learned ancients both in poetry and all good oratory. This neglect then of rhyme so little is to be taken for a defect, though it may seem so perhaps to vulgar readers, that it rather is to be esteemed an example set, the first in English, of ancient liberty recovered to heroic poem from the troublesome and modern bondage of rhyming.

4 **invention of a barbarous age**] In Latin poetry, rhyme first began to be used regularly in Christian hymns of the fifth and sixth centuries. 13 **apt numbers**] Appropriate rhythm.

BOOK I

The Argument

This first book proposes, first in brief, the whole subject, man's disobedience, and the loss thereupon of Paradise wherein he was placed; then touches the prime cause of his fall, the serpent, or rather Satan in the serpent; who revolting from God, and drawing to his side many legions of angels, was by the command of God driven out of heaven with all his crew into the great deep. Which action passed over, the poem hastes into the midst of things, presenting Satan with his angels now fallen into hell, described here, not in the centre (for   8 heaven and earth may be supposed as yet not made, certainly not yet accursed) but in a place of utter darkness, fitliest called Chaos: here   10 Satan with his angels lying on the burning lake, thunderstruck and astonished, after a certain space recovers, as from confusion, calls up him who next in order and dignity lay by him; they confer of their miserable fall. Satan awakens all his legions, who lay till then in the same manner confounded; they rise, their numbers, array of battle, their chief leaders named, according to the idols known afterwards in Canaan and the countries adjoining. To these Satan directs his speech, comforts them with hope yet of regaining heaven, but tells them lastly of a new world and new kind of creature to be created, according to an ancient prophecy or report in heaven; for that angels were long before this visible creation, was the opinion of many ancient Fathers. To find out the truth of this prophecy, and what to determine thereon he refers to a full council. What his associates thence attempt. Pandaemonium the palace of Satan rises, suddenly   24 built out of the deep: the infernal peers there sit in council.   *coherence*

> OF MAN'S first disobedience, and the fruit
> Of that forbidden tree, whose mortal taste
> Brought death into the world, and all our woe,
> With loss of Eden, till one greater man   4
> Restore us, and regain the blissful seat,
> Sing heavenly muse, that on the secret top   6

---

8 **not in the centre**] Not at the centre of the earth (which had not yet been created). 10 **utter**] Both absolute and outer.   24 **Pandaemonium**] Lit. 'all the demons'; the name is Milton's coinage.

4 **one greater man**] Jesus, as the Messiah.   6 **heavenly muse**] Urania, the muse of astronomy, and therefore of heavenly matters generally, invoked by name in Book vii: as the inspiration of Moses, she is identified here with the divine word.   **secret top**] Summit hidden from public view, where God spoke alone with Moses.

Of Oreb, or of Sinai, didst inspire   7
That shepherd, who first taught the chosen seed,   8
In the beginning how the heavens and earth   9
Rose out of chaos: or if Sion hill   10
Delight thee more, and Siloa's brook that flowed   11
Fast by the oracle of God; I thence   12
Invoke thy aid to my adventurous song,
That with no middle flight intends to soar
Above the Aonian mount, while it pursues   15
Things unattempted yet in prose or rhyme.
And chiefly thou O Spirit, that dost prefer
Before all temples the upright heart and pure,
Instruct me, for thou know'st; thou from the first
Wast present, and with mighty wings outspread
Dove-like sat'st brooding on the vast abyss   21
And mad'st it pregnant: what in me is dark   22
Illumine, what is low raise and support;
That to the height of this great argument   24
I may assert eternal providence,
And justify the ways of God to men.
   Say first, for heaven hides nothing from thy view
Nor the deep tract of hell, say first what cause   28
Moved our grand parents in that happy state,
Favoured of heaven so highly, to fall off
From their creator, and transgress his will

7 **of Oreb, or of Sinai**] God delivered the Ten Commandments to Moses either on Mount Horeb (Deuteronomy 4: 10) or on nearby Mount Sinai (Exodus 19: 20). Here, as throughout, Milton uses the Vulgate form of biblical names.   8 **shepherd**] Moses is identified as the shepherd of Jethro's flock in Exodus 3, but the term is also used figuratively for him as leader of his people.   **seed**] Literally translating *semen*, God's offspring, the children of Israel.   9 **In the beginning**] The opening words of Genesis and John.   10 **out of chaos**] Technically a heretical position: orthodox doctrine held that God created the world not out of unformed matter (the *chaos* of Neoplatonic philosophy) but *ex nihilo*, out of nothing, the 'void' of Genesis 1: 2.   **Sion hill**] The sacred Mount Zion, on which Solomon's Temple stood.   11 **Siloa's brook**] The Pool of Siloam, which flows alongside the Temple mountain, and with whose waters Jesus cured a blind man (John 9: 7).   12 **Fast by**] Close.   15 **Aonian mount**] Helicon, in Aonia in Boeotia, sacred to the classical muses.   21 **Dove-like**] The Holy Spirit is a dove descending on Jesus in John 1: 32.   17–22 **And chiefly thou ... pregnant**] The Holy Spirit, that in Genesis 1: 2 'moved upon the waters' and was the agent of creation. Milton's 'brooding' (l. 21) gives a more precise translation of the Hebrew.   24 **height**] Milton's normal spelling, and standard usage in the seventeenth century, is 'highth'   **argument**] Subject.   28 **Nor**] Not even.

For one restraint, lords of the world besides?
Who first seduced them to that foul revolt?
The infernal serpent; he it was, whose guile
Stirred up with envy and revenge, deceived
The mother of mankind, what time his pride   36
Had cast him out from heaven, with all his host
Of rebel angels, by whose aid aspiring
To set himself in glory above his peers,
He trusted to have equalled the most high,   40
If he opposed; and with ambitious aim
Against the throne and monarchy of God
Raised impious war in heaven and battle proud
With vain attempt. Him the almighty power
Hurled headlong flaming from the ethereal sky
With hideous ruin and combustion down
To bottomless perdition, there to dwell
In adamantine chains and penal fire,   48
Who durst defy the omnipotent to arms.
Nine times the space that measures day and night   50
To mortal men, he with his horrid crew
Lay vanquished, rolling in the fiery gulf
Confounded though immortal: but his doom
Reserved him to more wrath; for now the thought
Both of lost happiness and lasting pain
Torments him; round he throws his baleful eyes   56
That witnessed huge affliction and dismay   57
Mixed with obdurate pride and steadfast hate:
At once as far as angels' ken he views
The dismal situation waste and wild,   60
A dungeon horrible, on all sides round
As one great furnace flamed, yet from those flames
No light, but rather darkness visible
Served only to discover sights of woe,
Regions of sorrow, doleful shades, where peace

---

36 **what time**] When; the diction is Latinate, but the expression was in common
English usage.   48 **adamantine**] Unbreakable: adamant was a mythical substance
of impenetrable hardness.   50 **Nine times . . . night**] The nine days of the rebel
angels' fall is based not on biblical authority but on Hesiod's account of the fall of
the Titans who rebelled against Zeus (*Theogony*, 664–735), which was considered
another version of the same event.   56 **baleful**] Both malign and full of pain.
57 **witnessed**] Both regarded and testified to.   60 **dismal**] Ominous, disastrous.

And rest can never dwell, hope never comes   66
That comes to all; but torture without end
Still urges, and a fiery deluge, fed   68
With ever-burning sulphur unconsumed:
Such place eternal justice had prepared
For those rebellious, here their prison ordained
In utter darkness, and their portion set   72
As far removed from God and light of heaven
As from the centre thrice to the utmost pole.   74
O how unlike the place from whence they fell!
There the companions of his fall, o'erwhelmed
With floods and whirlwinds of tempestuous fire,
He soon discerns, and weltering by his side   78
One next himself in power, and next in crime,
Long after known in Palestine, and named
Beelzebub. To whom the arch-enemy,   81
And thence in heaven called Satan, with bold words   82
Breaking the horrid silence thus began.

   If thou beest he; but O how fallen! how changed   84
From him, who in the happy realms of light
Clothed with transcendent brightness didst outshine
Myriads though bright: if he whom mutual league,   87
United thoughts and counsels, equal hope
And hazard in the glorious enterprise,
Joined with me once, now misery hath joined   90
In equal ruin: into what pit thou seest
From what height fallen, so much the stronger proved
He with his thunder: and till then who knew
The force of those dire arms? yet not for those,

---

66 **hope never comes**] Recalling Dante's inscription on the gate of hell, '*Lasciate ogni speranza, voi ch'entrate*' ('Abandon all hope, you who enter', *Inferno*, iii. 9). 68 **Still urges**] Continuously presses.   72 **utter**] Both total and outer.   74 **As from the centre . . . pole**] Milton imagines a Ptolemaic universe with the earth at the centre of nine concentric spheres. The distance from hell to heaven is three times as far as the centre of the earth is from a point on the outermost sphere.   78 **weltering**] Writhing.   81 **Beelzebub**] The name in Hebrew means 'god of flies'.   82 **And thence . . . called Satan**] The name means 'enemy'; his original name was Lucifer, 'bringer of light'.   84 **If . . . changed**] The words contain a double echo, of Aeneas seeing a vision of the dead Hector on the night Troy fell, '*quantum mutatus ab illo | Hectore*' ('how changed from that other Hector', *Aeneid*, ii. 274-5), and of Isaiah 14: 12, 'How art thou fallen from heaven, Lucifer, son of the morning.'   87 **if he**] 'Thou beest' is understood.

Nor what the potent victor in his rage
Can else inflict, do I repent or change,
Though changed in outward lustre; that fixed mind
And high disdain, from sense of injured merit,
That with the mightiest raised me to contend,
And to the fierce contention brought along   *100*
Innumerable force of spirits armed
That durst dislike his reign, and me preferring,
His utmost power with adverse power opposed
In dubious battle on the plains of heaven,   *104*
And shook his throne. What though the field be lost?
All is not lost; the unconquerable will,
And study of revenge, immortal hate,   *107*
And courage never to submit or yield:
And what is else not to be overcome?
That glory never shall his wrath or might   *110*
Extort from me. To bow and sue for grace
With suppliant knee, and deify his power,
Who from the terror of this arm so late
Doubted his empire, that were low indeed,   *114*
That were an ignominy and shame beneath
This downfall; since by fate the strength of gods
And this empyreal substance cannot fail,   *117*
Since through experience of this great event
In arms not worse, in foresight much advanced,
We may with more successful hope resolve   *120*
To wage by force or guile eternal war
Irreconcilable, to our grand foe,
Who now triumphs, and in the excess of joy
Sole reigning holds the tyranny of heaven.
     So spake the apostate angel, though in pain,
Vaunting aloud, but racked with deep despair:
And him thus answered soon his bold compeer.
     O prince, O chief of many thronèd powers,
That led the embattled seraphim to war
Under thy conduct, and in dreadful deeds   *130*

---

104 **dubious**] 'Of uncertain issue or result' (*OED*).   107 **study of**] Zeal for
(Lat. *studium*).   114 **Doubted**] Feared for.   117 **empyreal**] Heavenly (lit. made
of fire, the purest element).

Fearless, endangered heaven's perpetual king;
And put to proof his high supremacy,   132
Whether upheld by strength, or chance, or fate,
Too well I see and rue the dire event,
That with sad overthrow and foul defeat
Hath lost us heaven, and all this mighty host
In horrible destruction laid thus low,
As far as gods and heavenly essences
Can perish: for the mind and spirit remains
Invincible, and vigour soon returns,   140
Though all our glory extinct, and happy state
Here swallowed up in endless misery.
But what if he our conqueror (whom I now
Of force believe almighty, since no less   144
Than such could have o'erpowered such force as ours)
Have left us this our spirit and strength entire
Strongly to suffer and support our pains,
That we may so suffice his vengeful ire,   148
Or do him mightier service as his thralls
By right of war, whate'er his business be   150
Here in the heart of hell to work in fire,
Or do his errands in the gloomy deep;
What can it then avail though yet we feel
Strength undiminished, or eternal being
To undergo eternal punishment?
Whereto with speedy words the arch-fiend replied.

   Fallen cherub, to be weak is miserable
Doing or suffering: but of this be sure,   158
To do aught good never will be our task,
But ever to do ill our sole delight,
As being the contrary to his high will
Whom we resist. If then his providence
Out of our evil seek to bring forth good,
Our labour must be to pervert that end,
And out of good still to find means of evil;
Which oft-times may succeed, so as perhaps
Shall grieve him, if I fail not, and disturb   167

---

   132 **proof**] Test.   144 **Of   force**] Perforce.   148 **suffice**] Satisfy.
158 **Doing or suffering**] Whether active or passive.   167 **fail**] Mistake.

His inmost counsels from their destined aim.
But see the angry victor hath recalled
His ministers of vengeance and pursuit
Back to the gates of heaven: the sulphurous hail
Shot after us in storm, o'erblown hath laid   172
The fiery surge, that from the precipice
Of heaven received us falling, and the thunder,
Winged with red lightning and impetuous rage,
Perhaps hath spent his shafts, and ceases now
To bellow through the vast and boundless deep.
Let us not slip the occasion, whether scorn,   178
Or satiate fury yield it from our foe.
Seest thou yon dreary plain, forlorn and wild,
The seat of desolation, void of light,
Save what the glimmering of these livid flames
Casts pale and dreadful? Thither let us tend
From off the tossing of these fiery waves,
There rest, if any rest can harbour there,
And reassembling our afflicted powers,   186
Consult how we may henceforth most offend   187
Our enemy, our own loss how repair,
How overcome this dire calamity,
What reinforcement we may gain from hope,
If not what resolution from despair.
     Thus Satan talking to his nearest mate
With head uplift above the wave, and eyes
That sparkling blazed, his other parts besides
Prone on the flood, extended long and large
Lay floating many a rood, in bulk as huge   196
As whom the fables name of monstrous size,
Titanian, or Earth-born, that warred on Jove,
Briareos or Typhon, whom the den   199

172 **laid**] Put down.   178 **slip**] Neglect.   186 **afflicted**] Lit. 'cast down'.
187 **offend**] Injure.   196 **rood**] Or rod, a variable measure, from six to eight
yards.   198–9 **Titanian ... Typhon**] The hundred-armed Briareos was a Titan,
the monster Typhon (or Typhoeus) a giant with a hundred serpent-heads. Both Titans
and giants made war on the Olympian gods and were thrown back to earth and crushed
or cast into the classical hell, Tartarus. See Hesiod, *Theogony*, 713–16 and 819–85, and
Ovid, *Metamorphoses*, v. 325–31 and 346–58. The Typhon story was moralized by
Renaissance mythographers as an allegory of the destructive potential of ambition (see
the standard Renaissance compendium, Natale Conti, *Mythologiae* (first published at
Venice 1551; innumerable editions thereafter), vi. 22).

By ancient Tarsus held, or that sea-beast   200
Leviathan, which God of all his works   201
Created hugest that swim the ocean stream:
Him haply slumbering on the Norway foam
The pilot of some small night-foundered skiff,
Deeming some island, oft, as seamen tell,
With fixèd anchor in his scaly rind   206
Moors by his side under the lee, while night   207
Invests the sea, and wishèd morn delays: 208
So stretched out huge in length the arch-fiend lay
Chained on the burning lake, nor ever thence   210
Had risen or heaved his head, but that the will
And high permission of all-ruling heaven
Left him at large to his own dark designs,
That with reiterated crimes he might
Heap on himself damnation, while he sought
Evil to others, and enraged might see
How all his malice served but to bring forth
Infinite goodness, grace and mercy shown
On man by him seduced, but on himself
Treble confusion, wrath and vengeance poured.   220
Forthwith upright he rears from off the pool
His mighty stature; on each hand the flames
Driven backward slope their pointing spires, and rolled
In billows, leave i' the midst a horrid vale.
Then with expanded wings he steers his flight
Aloft, incumbent on the dusky air   226
That felt unusual weight, till on dry land
He lights, if it were land that ever burned   228
With solid, as the lake with liquid fire;
And such appeared in hue, as when the force

---

200 **Tarsus**] According to Pindar, Typhon dwelt in a cave in Cilicia, of which Tarsus was the principal city (*Pythian Odes*, i. 17).   201 **Leviathan**] A mysterious sea-monster in Job 41, a 'piercing' and 'crooked serpent' in Isaiah 27: 1, hence associated with Satan; also frequently identified as a whale. The story of the whale appearing a safe haven to unwary sailors was often cited as a parallel to the dangerous deceptiveness of Satan.   206 **rind**] The skin of an animal.   207 **under the lee**] In its shelter. 208 **Invests**] Envelops.   210 **Chained on**] Confined to.   226 **incumbent**] Lying (lit. 'pressing upon'; see l. 227).   228 **lights**] Alights. **ever**] Always.

Of subterranean wind transports a hill   231
Torn from Pelorus, or the shattered side
Of thundering Aetna, whose combustible   233
And fuelled entrails thence conceiving fire,
Sublimed with mineral fury, aid the winds,   235
And leave a singèd bottom all involved
With stench and smoke: such resting found the sole
Of unblessed feet. Him followed his next mate,
Both glorying to have scaped the Stygian flood   239
As gods, and by their own recovered strength,
Not by the sufferance of supernal power.
    Is this the region, this the soil, the clime,
Said then the lost archangel, this the seat
That we must change for heaven, this mournful gloom
For that celestial light? Be it so, since he
Who now is sovereign can dispose and bid
What shall be right: furthest from him is best
Whom reason hath equalled, force hath made supreme
Above his equals. Farewell, happy fields
Where joy forever dwells: hail horrors, hail   250
Infernal world, and thou profoundest hell
Receive thy new possessor: one who brings
A mind not to be changed by place or time.
The mind is its own place, and in itself
Can make a heaven of hell, a hell of heaven.
What matter where, if I be still the same,   256
And what I should be, all but less than he
Whom thunder hath made greater? Here at least
We shall be free; the almighty hath not built
Here for his envy, will not drive us hence: 260
Here we may reign secure, and in my choice
To reign is worth ambition though in hell:
Better to reign in hell, than serve in heaven.

231 **subterranean wind**] Ovid describes underground winds creating a hill in
Metamorphoses, xv. 296–377; seventeenth-century meteorology held that the earth is
'full of wind . . . which, sometimes breaking out, causeth horrible earthquakes' (Robert
Burton, *Anatomy of Melancholy*, 1621, II. ii. 3).   232–3 **Pelorus . . . Aetna**] Cape
Faro, in north-east Sicily, and the volcano nearby.   235 **Sublimed with mineral
fury**] Vaporized by the volcano's violence.   239 **Stygian flood**] The Styx, one of
the four rivers of hell. *Stygian* implies impenetrable darkness.   256 **What matter
where**] 'I am' understood.

But wherefore let we then our faithful friends,
The associates and eopartners of our loss
Lie thus astonished on the oblivious pool,   266
And call them not to share with us their part
In this unhappy mansion, or once more   268
With rallied arms to try what may be yet
Regained in heaven, or what more lost in hell?
    So Satan spake, and him Beelzebub
Thus answered. Leader of those armies bright,
Which but the omnipotent none could have foiled,
If once they hear that voice, their liveliest pledge
Of hope in fears and dangers, heard so oft
In worst extremes, and on the perilous edge   276
Of battle when it raged, in all assaults
Their surest signal, they will soon resume
New courage and revive, though now they lie
Grovelling and prostrate on yon lake of fire,
As we erewhile, astounded and amazed,
No wonder, fallen such a pernicious height.   282
    He scarce had ceased when the superior fiend
Was moving toward the shore; his ponderous shield
Ethereal temper, massy, large, and round,   285
Behind him cast; the broad circumference
Hung on his shoulders like the moon, whose orb
Through optic glass the Tuscan artist views   288
At evening from the top of Fesole,   289
Or in Valdarno, to descry new lands,   290
Rivers or mountains in her spotty globe.
His spear, to equal which the tallest pine
Hewn on Norwegian hills, to be the mast
Of some great admiral, were but a wand,   294
He walked with to support uneasy steps
Over the burning marl, not like those steps   296

---

266 **astonished**] Stunned. **oblivious**] Producing forgetfulness.   268 **man-sion**] Dwelling-place (not necessarily a building).   276 **edge**] Front line (Latin *acies*).   282 **pernicious**] Ruinous, fatal.   285 **Ethereal temper**] Tempered in heavenly fire.   288 **optic glass**] Telescope. **Tuscan artist**] Galileo, who first devised a telescope sufficiently powerful to reveal the surface of the moon. Milton alludes to a visit to him in *Areopagitica*.   289 **Fesole**] Fiesole, a hill-town near Florence.   290 **Valdarno**] The Arno valley, in which Florence is located. 294 **admiral**] flagship.   296 **marl**] Soil.

On heaven's azure, and the torrid clime
Smote on him sore besides, vaulted with fire;
Natheless he so endured, till on the beach   299
Of that inflamèd sea, he stood and called
His legions, angel forms, who lay entranced
Thick as autumnal leaves that strew the brooks
In Vallombrosa, where the Etrurian shades   303
High overarched imbower; or scattered sedge   304
Afloat, when with fierce winds Orion armed   305
Hath vexed the Red Sea coast, whose waves o'erthrew
Busiris and his Memphian chivalry,   307
While with perfidious hatred they pursued
The sojourners of Goshen, who beheld   309
From the safe shore their floating carcasses
And broken chariot wheels, so thick bestrewn
Abject and lost lay these, covering the flood,
Under amazement of their hideous change.   313
He called so loud, that all the hollow deep
Of hell resounded. Princes, potentates,
Warriors, the flower of heaven, once yours, now lost,
If such astonishment as this can seize   317
Eternal spirits; or have ye chosen this place
After the toil of battle to repose
Your wearied virtue, for the ease you find   320
To slumber here, as in the vales of heaven?
Or in this abject posture have ye sworn
To adore the conqueror? who now beholds
Cherub and seraph rolling in the flood   324

299 Natheless] Nevertheless.   303 Vallombrosa] Lit. 'valley of shadows',
near Florence. Etrurian shades] Tuscan foliage.   304 sedge] Seaweed.
305 Orion] One of the giants, a great hunter slain by Diana and transformed
into a constellation. It was associated with storms because its evening rising during
autumn signals the approach of winter.   307 Busiris] Pharaoh, here given the
name of a legendary Egyptian tyrant. Memphian chivalry] Egyptian cavalry.
306–7 whose waves . . . chivalry] After Moses parted the Red Sea and the Israelites
passed safely to the opposite shore, the waters closed over the pursuing Egyptians,
destroying Pharaoh's army (Exodus 14: 21ff.).   309 Goshen] The area in Egypt
where Jacob and his descendants settled, and from which the Israelites were
fleeing.   313 amazement] Stupefaction.   317 astonishment] 'Loss of sense
. . . mental prostration, stupor' (*OED*; cf. l. 266).   320 virtue] Strength.
324 Cherub and seraph] The two highest orders of angels, first established by
Dionysius the Pseudo-Areopagite (fourth century AD) in *De Coelesti Hierarchia*, vi. 2

With scattered arms and ensigns, till anon
His swift pursuers from heaven gates discern
The advantage, and descending tread us down
Thus drooping, or with linkèd thunderbolts
Transfix us to the bottom of this gulf.
Awake, arise, or be forever fallen.   330
    They heard, and were abashed, and up they sprung
Upon the wing, as when men wont to watch
On duty, sleeping found by whom they dread,   333
Rouse and bestir themselves ere well awake.
Nor did they not perceive the evil plight
In which they were, or the fierce pains not feel;
Yet to their general's voice they soon obeyed
Innumerable. As when the potent rod
Of Amram's son in Egypt's evil day   ، 339
Waved round the coast, up called a pitchy cloud
Of locusts, warping on the eastern wind,   341
That o'er the realm of impious Pharaoh hung
Like night, and darkened all the land of Nile:
So numberless were those bad angels seen
Hovering on wing under the cope of hell   345
'Twixt upper, nether, and surrounding fires;
Till, as a signal given, the uplifted spear
Of their great sultan waving to direct
Their course, in even balance down they light
On the firm brimstone, and fill all the plain;
A multitude, like which the populous north
Poured never from her frozen loins, to pass
Rhene or the Danaw, when her barbarous sons   353
Came like a deluge on the south, and spread
Beneath Gibralter to the Lybian sands.
Forthwith from every squadron and each band
The heads and leaders thither haste where stood
Their great commander; godlike shapes and forms
Excelling human, princely dignities,
And powers that erst in heaven sat on thrones;   360

---

333 whom] The one whom.   339 Amram's son] Moses, whose 'potent rod'
invoked the plague of locusts on the Egyptians (Exodus 10: 12–15).   341 warping]
Whirling.   345 cope] Canopy.   353 Rhene . . . Danaw] Rhine, Danube.
360 erst] Formerly.

Though of their names in heavenly records now
Be no memorial, blotted out and razed
By their rebellion, from the books of life.   363
Nor had they yet among the sons of Eve
Got them new names, till wandering o'er the earth,   365
Through God's high sufferance for the trial of man,
By falsities and lies the greatest part
Of mankind they corrupted to forsake
God their creator, and the invisible
Glory of him that made them, to transform
Oft to the image of a brute, adorned
With gay religions full of pomp and gold,   372
And devils to adore for deities: 373
Then were they known to men by various names,
And various idols through the heathen world.
Say, muse, their names then known, who first, who last,   376
Roused from the slumber, on that fiery couch,
At their great emperor's call, as next in worth
Came singly where he stood on the bare strand,
While the promiscuous crowd stood yet aloof?   380
The chief were those who from the pit of hell
Roaming to seek their prey on earth, durst fix
Their seats long after next the seat of God,
Their altars by his altar, gods adored
Among the nations round, and durst abide
Jehovah thundering out of Sion, throned
Between the cherubim; yea, often placed
Within his sanctuary itself their shrines,
Abominations; and with cursèd things
His holy rites, and solemn feasts profaned,
And with their darkness durst affront his light.
First Moloch, horrid king besmeared with blood   392
Of human sacrifice, and parents' tears,

363 **books of life**] The term is used in the Old and New Testaments for the record of God's faithful, those destined for eternal life in heaven.   365 **Got them new names**] The transformation of the fallen angels into pagan deities is attested by many Church Fathers; see e.g. Tertullian, *Apologeticum*, xx. 22–4. 372 **religions**] Religious rites.   373 **devils ... deities**] 'They sacrificed unto devils, not to God' (Deuteronomy 32: 17).   376 **then**] i.e. subsequently, in the 'heathen world' of l. 375.   380 **promiscuous**] 'Massed together without order' (*OED*).   392 **Moloch**] The name means *king*.

Though for the noise of drums and timbrels loud
Their children's cries unheard, that passed through fire   395
To his grim idol. Him the Ammonite   396
Worshipped in Rabba and her watery plain,   397
In Argob and in Basan, to the stream
Of utmost Arnon. Nor content with such   399
Audacious neighbourhood, the wisest heart
Of Solomon he led by fraud to build
His temple right against the temple of God
On that opprobrious hill, and made his grove   403
The pleasant valley of Hinnom, Tophet thence
And black Gehenna called, the type of hell.   405
Next Chemos, the obscene dread of Moab's sons,   406
From Aroar to Nebo, and the wild   407
Of southmost Abarim; in Hesebon   408
And Horonaim, Seon's realm, beyond   409
The flowery dale of Sibma clad with vines,
And Eleale to the Asphaltic Pool.   411

394–5 **Though for the noise . . . unheard**] The cries of sacrificial children were drowned out by the sound of drums and timbrels.   396 **Ammonite**] The Ammonites were enemies of Israel, ultimately conquered by Jephtha.   397 **Rabba**] Rabbah, the Ammonite capital; modern Amman, in Jordan.   398–9 **Argob . . . Basan . . . Arnon**] The lands east of the Dead Sea, roughly the northern section of modern Jordan. Argob was the southern part of the region of Bashan, in the north, and the area in which Moloch was worshipped extended into Ammon, as far south as the Arnon river.   401–3 **Of Solomon . . . that hill**] 'Solomon loved many strange [i.e. foreign] women'; among his seven hundred wives were Ammonites and Moabites, who 'turned away his heart after other gods', and he built a temple 'for Moloch, the abomination of the children of Ammon' on the Mount of Olives, hence 'that opprobrious hill' (1 Kings 11: 1–7).   404–5 **Hinnom, Tophet . . . Gehenna**] The valley of Hinnom runs along the western and southern edges of Jerusalem. Tophet, in the valley's south, was the site of Moloch's shrine where the child sacrifices of ll. 394–5 were performed. The Hebrew name of the valley, Ge-hinnom, was transliterated into Greek as Geenna, in its English form *Gehenna*, and, because of the abominations practised there, this became the New Testament word for hell.   406 **Chemos**] 'Chemosh, the abomination of Moab', also worshipped at Solomon's shrine (1 Kings 11: 7).   407 **Aroar**] Aroer (modern Arair, in Jordan), an important northern Moabite city. **Nebo**] The name of both a southern Moabite town and the mountain in Moab from which Moses saw the promised land of Canaan.   408 **Abarim**] A range of hills, including Mount Nebo, at the western edge of Moab, overlooking the Jordan valley and the Dead Sea.   408–9 **Hesebon . . . Horonaim . . . Seon's realm**] Heshbon and Horonaim were Amorite cities; Sihon (*Seon*) was king of the Amorites.   410–11 **Sibma . . . Eleale**] Sibma, east of the Jordan in the Moabite hills, was famous for its wine; Elealeh was a nearby city. **the Asphaltic Pool**] The Dead Sea, which casts up bitumen, or asphalt.

Peor his other name, when he enticed   412
Israel in Sittim, on their march from Nile,
To do him wanton rites; which cost them woe.   414
Yet thence his lustful orgies he enlarged
Even to that hill of scandal, by the grove   416
Of Moloch homicide, lust hard by hate;   417
Till good Josiah drove them thence to hell.   418
With these came they, who from the bordering flood
Of old Euphrates to the brook that parts
Egypt from Syrian ground, had general names   421
Of Baalim and Ashtaroth, those male,   422
These feminine. For spirits when they please
Can either sex assume, or both; so soft
And uncompounded is their essence pure,
Not tied or manacled with joint or limb,
Nor founded on the brittle strength of bones,
Like cumbrous flesh; but in what shape they choose   428
Dilated or condensed, bright or obscure,
Can execute their airy purposes,
And works of love or enmity fulfil.
For those the race of Israel oft forsook
Their living strength, and unfrequented left   433
His righteous altar, bowing lowly down
To bestial gods; for which their heads as low   435
Bowed down in battle, sunk before the spear
Of despicable foes. With these in troop
Came Astoreth, whom the Phoenicians called

412 **Peor**] More fully Baal-Peor, the Moabite deity identified with Chemosh.
413–14 **Sittim . . . wanton rites**] Shittim, on the east bank of the Jordan opposite
Jericho, the last encampment of the Israelites before crossing into Canaan, where 'the
people began to commit whoredom with the daughters of Moab . . . and Israel joined
himself unto Baal-peor' (Numbers 25: 1–3).   415–16 **Yet thence . . . hill of
scandal**] The Mount of Olives, the 'opprobrious hill' of l. 403 (see note to ll. 404–5).
417 **hard by**] Adjacent to.   418 **good Josiah**] Extirpated idolatry from Israel and
destroyed the shrine of Topheth (2 Kings 23: 10).   420–1 **Euphrates . . . Syrian
ground**] From the northernmost to the southernmost border of Syria (the River Besor),
including modern Jordan.   422 **Baalim and Ashtaroth**] Baal (plural Baalim) was
the general name given to the chief god of the Canaanite pantheon, particularized in
various cults by the addition of a surname (e.g. Baal-peor; cf. l. 412); Ashtoreth (plural
Ashtaroth) is the biblical form of Ishtar or Astarte, analogous to Venus in the Roman
pantheon, goddess of sex and, in the Middle Eastern cults, of war.   428 **cumbrous**]
Cumbersome.   433 **their living strength**] i.e. the God of Israel.   435 **bestial**]
Because they were worshipped in the form of animals.

Astarte, queen of heaven, with crescent horns;   439
To whose bright image nightly by the moon
Sidonian virgins paid their vows and songs,   441
In Sion also not unsung, where stood
Her temple on the offensive mountain, built
By that uxorious king, whose heart though large,   444
Beguiled by fair idolatresses, fell
To idols foul. Thammuz came next behind,
Whose annual wound in Lebanon allured
The Syrian damsels to lament his fate
In amorous ditties all a summer's day,   449
While smooth Adonis from his native rock
Ran purple to the sea, supposed with blood   451
Of Thammuz yearly wounded: the love-tale
Infected Sion's daughters with like heat,
Whose wanton passions in the sacred porch
Ezekiel saw, when by the vision led   455
His eye surveyed the dark idolatries
Of alienated Judah. Next came one
Who mourned in earnest, when the captive ark
Maimed his brute image, heads and hands lopped off   459
In his own temple, on the groundsel edge,   460
Where he fell flat, and shamed his worshippers:
Dagon his name, sea monster, upward man
And downward fish: yet had his temple high
Reared in Azotus, dreaded through the coast   464
Of Palestine, in Gath and Ascalon
And Accaron and Gaza's frontier bounds.   466

438-9 **Astoreth ... Astarte**] Worshipped as the moon goddess, hence 'with crescent horns', l. 439.   441 **Sidonian**] Phoenician (from Sidon, the chief city of Phoenicia).   444 **uxorious king**] Solomon, who had seven hundred wives. 446-9 **Thammuz . . . summer's day**] Astarte's lover Tammuz, a god of fertility and vegetation, was identified with Adonis. His death was annually celebrated at the summer solstice.   450-1 **Adonis ... purple**] The River Adonis, in Lebanon, becomes discoloured with reddish mud each summer.   455 **Ezekiel ... led**] For Ezekiel's vision of the Israelite 'women weeping for Tammuz' see Ezekiel 8: 14.   457-9 **came one ... brute image**] The Philistines placed the captured ark of the Lord in the temple of their god Dagon; the next morning the idol of Dagon was found destroyed (1 Samuel 5: 4).   460 **groundsel**] Threshold.   464 **coast**] Philistia lay along the Mediterranean coast.   464-6 **Azotus ... Ascalon ... Accaron**] Vulgate names of the Authorized Version's Ashdod, Askelon, Ekron; these, with Gath and Gaza, were the five principal Philistine cities.   **frontier bounds**] Ekron was the northernmost of the five cities, Gaza the southernmost.

Him followed Rimmon, whose delightful seat   467
Was fair Damascus, on the fertile banks
Of Abbana and Pharphar, lucid streams.
He also against the house of God was bold:
A leper once he lost and gained a king,   471
Ahaz his sottish conqueror, whom he drew   472
God's altar to disparage and displace
For one of Syrian mode, whereon to burn
His odious offerings, and adore the gods
Whom he had vanquished. After these appeared   476
A crew who under names of old renown,
Osiris, Isis, Orus and their train   478
With monstrous shapes and sorceries abused
Fanatic Egypt and her priests, to seek
Their wandering gods disguised in brutish forms
Rather than human. Nor did Israel scape
The infection when their borrowed gold composed
The calf in Oreb: and the rebel king   484
Doubled that sin in Bethel and in Dan,   485
Likening his maker to the grazèd ox,
Jehovah, who in one night when he passed
From Egypt marching, equalled with one stroke   488
Both her first born and all her bleating gods.   489

  467 **Rimmon**] The chief Syrian deity.   471 **A leper once he lost**] When Elisha told the Syrian general Naaman that washing in the Jordan would cure his leprosy, Naaman scoffed, but when he subsequently followed the prophet's advice and was cured, he acknowledged the God of Israel (2 Kings 10ff.).   472 **sottish**] Foolish.   471–6 **a king ... vanquished**] King Ahaz in alliance with the king of Assyria conquered Damascus, but he then converted to the cult of Rimmon and placed a Syrian altar in the temple of Jerusalem (2 Kings 16: 9–17).   478 **Osiris, Isis, Orus**] Isis, Egyptian moon goddess, represented with the horns of a cow, was the mother of Orus (or Horus), a hawk-headed god, and wife and mother of the sun god Osiris. 483–4 **borrowed gold ... Oreb**] While Moses was on Mount Sinai receiving the ten commandments, his brother Aaron, the high priest, erected a golden idol of a calf, claiming it as the god who had delivered Israel from Egypt. The worship of the golden calf so enraged Moses when he returned that he broke the tablets of the law and destroyed the idol (Exodus 32: 1–20).   484–5 **rebel king ... Dan**] When Jereboam led the rebellion of the Ten Tribes of Israel against King Rehoboam, he set up two golden calves, in Bethel and Dan, as alternative centres of worship to the temple at Jerusalem (1 Kings 28–32).   488 **equalled**] i.e. made equal by destroying. 487–9 **Jehovah ... bleating gods**] For God's destruction of the Egyptian firstborn, see Exodus 12: 12.

Belial came last, than whom a spirit more lewd   490
Fell not from heaven, or more gross to love
Vice for itself: to him no temple stood
Or altar smoked; yet who more oft than he
In temples and at altars, when the priest
Turns atheist, as did Eli's sons, who filled
With lust and violence the house of God.   496
In courts and palaces he also reigns
And in luxurious cities, where the noise
Of riot ascends above their loftiest towers,
And injury and outrage: and when night
Darkens the streets, then wander forth the sons
Of Belial, flown with insolence and wine.   502
Witness the streets of Sodom, and that night
In Gibeah, when the hospitable door
Exposed a matron to avoid worse rape.   505
These were the prime in order and in might;
The rest were long to tell, though far renowned,
The Ionian gods, of Javan's issue held   508
Gods, yet confessed later than Heaven and Earth
Their boasted parents; Titan Heaven's first born   510
With his enormous brood, and birthright seized
By younger Saturn, he from mightier Jove
His own and Rhea's son like measure found;   513
So Jove usurping reigned: these first in Crete

490 **Belial**] Not a god in the Old Testament, but a personification: the Hebrew word means 'worthless', and the biblical 'sons of Belial' were not worshippers at a particular shrine but good-for-nothings. Milton is partly aware of this: see ll. 492–3. 495–6 **Eli's sons . . . God**] Eli was a priest at Shiloh, who took the young Samuel into his care. His two profligate sons 'lay with the women that assembled at the door of the tabernacle'; for this iniquity God pronounced the irremediable doom of Eli's house (1 Samuel 2–4). 502 **flown**] Swollen. 503–5 **Sodom . . . rape**] The story is in Judges 19: a Levite travelling with his concubine was given shelter by an old man in the city of Gibeah, and 'certain sons of Belial beset the house round about, and beat at the door' demanding to be allowed to rape the Levite. They were given the concubine instead (the 'matron' of l. 505) and raped her to death. Milton's notion that there are preferable kinds of rape is entirely consistent with the biblical account. 508 **Ionian**] Greek. **Javan**] son of Japhet and grandson of Noah, here identified with Ion, progenitor of the Ionian Greeks. 509–10 **Heaven and Earth . . . parents**] Uranus and Ge (in Latin, Coelus and Terra) were the parents of the Titans, and grandparents of Zeus (Jove) and the Olympian gods. 510–13 **Titan . . . found**] Titan, the oldest of Uranus' children, was overthrown by his younger brother Saturn, who in turn was overthrown by his son Jove. **Rhea**] Saturn's wife, Jove's mother.

And Ida known, thence on the snowy top   515
Of cold Olympus ruled the middle air
Their highest heaven; or on the Delphian cliff,
Or in Dodona, and through all the bounds   518
Of Doric land; or who with Saturn old   519
Fled over Adria to the Hesperian fields,   520
And o'er the Celtic roamed the utmost isles.   521
All these and more came flocking; but with looks
Downcast and damp, yet such wherein appeared   523
Obscure some glimpse of joy, to have found their chief
Not in despair, to have found themselves not lost
In loss itself; which on his countenance cast
Like doubtful hue: but he his wonted pride
Soon recollecting, with high words, that bore   528
Semblance of worth, not substance, gently raised
Their fainting courage, and dispelled their fears.
Then straight commands that at the warlike sound
Of trumpets loud and clarions be upreared   532
His mighty standard; that proud honour claimed
Azazel as his right, a cherub tall: 534
Who forthwith from the glittering staff unfurled
The imperial ensign, which full high advanced
Shone like a meteor streaming to the wind   537
With gems and golden lustre rich emblazed,   538
Seraphic arms and trophies: all the while
Sonorous metal blowing martial sounds:
At which the universal host upsent
A shout that tore hell's concave, and beyond   542
Frighted the reign of Chaos and old Night.   543

514–15 **Crete . . . Ida**] Jove was born on Mount Ida in Crete.   517–18 **Delphian cliff . . . Dodona**] The oracle of Apollo was at Delphi, that of Zeus at Dodona. 519 **Doric land**] Greece   **Saturn . . . fled**] Saturn was banished from heaven by Jove, and roamed the earth.   520 **Adria**] The Adriatic Sea.   **Hesperian fields**] Italy.   521 **Celtic**] French.   **utmost isles**] Britain and Ireland.   523 **damp**] Depressed, 'with dampened spirits'.   528 **recollecting**] Summoning up, rallying. 532 **clarions**] Shrill-sounding trumpets with a narrow tube, 'formerly much used as a signal in war' (*OED*).   534 **Azazel**] Not an angel in the Bible, but in cabbalistic writers one of four standard-bearers of Satan's army; the name means 'scapegoat' (see Leviticus 16: 8, 20).   537 **meteor**] In the seventeenth century both a shooting star and a comet.   538 **emblazed**] 'Adorned with heraldic devices' (*OED*). 542 **concave**] Vault.   543 **reign . . . Night**] In ii. 894 ff. Chaos and Night rule over a Kingdom of 'eternal anarchy', the formless void between hell and heaven.

All in a moment through the gloom were seen
Ten thousand banners rise into the air
With orient colours waving: with them rose   546
A forest huge of spears: and thronging helms   547
Appeared, and serried shields in thick array
Of depth immeasurable: anon they move
In perfect phalanx to the Dorian mode,   550
Of flutes and soft recorders; such as raised
To height of noblest temper heroes old
Arming to battle, and instead of rage
Deliberate valour breathed, firm and unmoved
With dread of death to flight or foul retreat,
Nor wanting power to mitigate and swage   556
With solemn touches, troubled thoughts, and chase
Anguish and doubt and fear and sorrow and pain
From mortal or immortal minds. Thus they
Breathing united force with fixèd thought
Moved on in silence to soft pipes that charmed
Their painful steps o'er the burnt soil; and now
Advanced in view, they stand, a horrid front   563
Of dreadful length and dazzling arms, in guise
Of warriors old with ordered spear and shield,
Awaiting what command their mighty chief
Had to impose: he through the armèd files
Darts his experienced eye, and soon traverse   568
The whole battalion views, their order due,
Their visages and stature as of gods,
Their number last he sums. And now his heart
Distends with pride, and hardening in his strength
Glories: for never since created man,   573
Met such embodied force, as named with these
Could merit more than that small infantry   575
Warred on by cranes: though all the Giant brood   576

---

546 **orient**] Bright.   547 **helms**] helmets.   550 **phalanx**] 'A body of heavy-armed infantry drawn up in close order, with shields joined and long spears overlapping' (*OED*). **Dorian mode**] The gravest of the Greek musical modes, considered especially suitable to men preparing for battle (Plato, *Republic*, x. 389).   556 **swage**] Assuage.   563 **horrid**] The word retains its etymological sense of 'bristling' (with the 'forest huge of spears' of l. 546).   568 **traverse**] All across.   573 **created man**] Man was created.   575 **infantry**] The word also meant a group of infants and puns on their size.   575–6 **small infantry . . . cranes**] Homer describes the pygmies slaughtered by cranes in *Iliad*, iii. 1–5.

Of Phlegra with the heroic race were joined   577
That fought at Thebes and Ilium, on each side   578
Mixed with auxiliar gods; and what resounds   579
In fable or romance of Uther's son   580
Begirt with British and Armoric knights;   581
And all who since, baptized or infidel
Jousted in Aspramont or Montalban,   583
Damasco, or Morocco, or Trebizond,   584
Or whom Bizerta sent from Afric shore   585
When Charlemagne with all his peerage fell
By Fontarabia. Thus far these beyond   587
Compare of mortal prowess, yet observed
Their dread commander: he above the rest
In shape and gesture proudly eminent
Stood like a tower; his form had yet not lost
All her original brightness, nor appeared
Less than archangel ruined, and the excess
Of glory obscured: as when the sun new risen
Looks through the horizontal misty air
Shorn of his beams, or from behind the moon
In dim eclipse disastrous twilight sheds
On half the nations, and with fear of change
Perplexes monarchs. Darkened so, yet shone   599
Above them all the archangel: but his face
Deep scars of thunder had intrenched, and care
Sat on his faded cheek, but under brows
Of dauntless courage, and considerate pride   603

576–7 **Giant . . . Phlegra**] The giants battled the gods on the plains of Phlegra in Macedonia (Ovid, *Metamorphoses*, x. 151).   577–8 **heroic race . . . Ilium**] The Seven Against Thebes, epic subject of Statius' *Thebaid* and of Aeschylus' play. Ilium = Troy.   579 **auxiliar**] Assisting.   580 **Uther's son**] King Arthur, son of Uther Pendragon.   581 **Armoric**] From Brittany.   583 **Aspramont or Montalban**] Castles in the chivalric romances.   584 **Damasco, or Morocco, or Trebizond**] Scenes of jousts between Christian and pagan knights in chivalric romances. Damasco = Damascus. Trebizond was a Byzantine city on the Black Sea taken by the Turks in 1461.   585 **whom Bizerta sent**] The Saracens who invaded Spain and defeated Charlemagne's army embarked from Bizerta, in Tunisia.   586–7 **Charlemagne . . . Fontarabia**] Charlemagne did not fall, but his troops led by Roland were destroyed at Roncesvalles near Fontarabia (the modern Fuenterrabia) in Spain.   598–9 **with fear . . . monarchs**] Solar eclipses were from earliest times taken to be premonitions of the death of kings, as the king was identified with the sun.   603 **considerate**] Deliberate.

Waiting revenge: cruel his eye, but cast
Signs of remorse and passion to behold
The fellows of his crime, the followers rather
(Far other once beheld in bliss) condemned
Forever now to have their lot in pain,
Millions of spirits for his fault amerced
Of heaven, and from eternal splendours flung   610
For his revolt, yet faithful how they stood,
Their glory withered. As when heaven's fire
Hath scathed the forest oaks, or mountain pines,   613
With singèd top their stately growth though bare
Stands on the blasted heath. He now prepared
To speak; whereat their doubled ranks they bend
From wing to wing, and half enclose him round   617
With all his peers: attention held them mute.
Thrice he essayed, and thrice in spite of scorn,
Tears such as angels weep burst forth: at last
Words interwove with sighs found out their way.
    O myriads of immortal spirits, O powers
Matchless, but with almighty, and that strife
Was not inglorious, though the event was dire,   624
As this place testifies, and this dire change
Hateful to utter: but what power of mind
Foreseeing or presaging, from the depth
Of knowledge past or present, could have feared,
How such united force of gods, how such
As stood like these, could ever know repulse?   630
For who can yet believe, though after loss,
That all these puissant legions, whose exile
Hath emptied heaven, shall fail to reascend
Self-raised, and repossess their native seat?
For me be witness all the host of heaven,
If counsels different, or danger shunned   636
By me, have lost our hopes. But he who reigns
Monarch in heaven, till then as one secure

609-10 **amerced / Of heaven**] Both 'deprived of heaven' and 'punished by heaven'.
613 **scathed**] Injured.   617 **From wing to wing**] From one end of the phalanx to
the other.   624 **event**] Outcome.   636 **different**] Disagreeing; *counsels* and *dan-
ger* are both objects of *shunned*: Satan denies that he either ignored alternative proposals
or avoided danger.

Sat on his throne, upheld by old repute,
Consent or custom, and his regal state
Put forth at full, but still his strength concealed,   641
Which tempted our attempt, and wrought our fall.
Henceforth his might we know, and know our own
So as not either to provoke, or dread
New war, provoked; our better part remains
To work in close design, by fraud or guile   646
What force effected not: that he no less
At length from us may find, who overcomes
By force, hath overcome but half his foe.
Space may produce new worlds; whereof so rife
There went a fame in heaven that he ere long   651
Intended to create, and therein plant
A generation, whom his choice regard
Should favour equal to the sons of heaven:
Thither, if but to pry, shall be perhaps
Our first eruption, thither or elsewhere: 656
For this infernal pit shall never hold
Celestial spirits in bondage, nor the abyss
Long under darkness cover. But these thoughts
Full counsel must mature: peace is despaired,   660
For who can think submission? War then, war
Open or understood must be resolved.

    He spake: and to confirm his words, outflew
Millions of flaming swords, drawn from the thighs
Of mighty cherubim; the sudden blaze
Far round illumined hell: highly they raged
Against the highest, and fierce with graspèd arms
Clashed on their sounding shields the din of war,
Hurling defiance toward the vault of heaven.

      There stood a hill not far whose grisly top
Belched fire and rolling smoke; the rest entire
Shone with a glossy scurf, undoubted sign   672
That in his womb was hid metallic ore,   673
The work of sulphur. Thither winged with speed   674
A numerous brigade hastened. As when bands

---

641 **still**] Always.   646 **close**] Secret.   651 **fame**] Rumour.   656 **eruption**]
Lit. 'breaking out'.   672 **scurf**] Crust.   673 **his**] Its.   674 **The work of
sulphur**] Sulphur was a basic ingredient in the refining of metals.

Of pioneers with spade and pickaxe armed   676
Forerun the royal camp, to trench a field,
Or cast a rampart. Mammon led them on,   678
Mammon, the least erected spirit that fell
From heaven, for even in heaven his looks and thoughts
Were always downward bent, admiring more
The riches of heaven's pavement, trodden gold,
Than aught divine or holy else enjoyed
In vision beatific: by him first
Men also, and by his suggestion taught,
Ransacked the centre, and with impious hands   686
Rifled the bowels of their mother earth
For treasures better hid. Soon had his crew
Opened into the hill a spacious wound
And digged out ribs of gold. Let none admire   690
That riches grow in hell; that soil may best
Deserve the precious bane. And here let those
Who boast in mortal things, and wondering tell
Of Babel, and the works of Memphian kings   694
Learn how their greatest monuments of fame,
And strength and art are easily outdone
By spirits reprobate, and in an hour   697
What in an age they with incessant toil
And hands innumerable scarce perform.
Nigh on the plain in many cells prepared,   700
That underneath had veins of liquid fire
Sluiced from the lake, a second multitude
With wondrous art founded the massy ore,   703
Severing each kind, and scummed the bullion dross:
A third as soon had formed within the ground

676 **pioneers**] Lit. 'diggers', originally the foot-soldiers who preceded the main body of the army to dig protective trenches.   678 **Mammon**] Not a biblical devil but Aramaic for 'wealth', and this is how the word appears in the New Testament. But as a personification, the figure was associated with the Greek god of wealth, Plutus, and in turn identified with Pluto, god of the underworld. Milton's account of him is heavily indebted to the Cave of Mammon episode in Spenser's *Faerie Queene*, ii. 7.   686 **Ransacked the centre**] Mined the earth for precious metals. 690 **ribs**] Veins. **admire**] Marvel.   694 **Of Babel ... kings**] The tower in Nimrod's capital (Genesis 11: 4, and see below, xii 38–62), and the Egptian pyramids, monuments to earthly vanity.   697 **reprobate**] 'Rejected by God' (*OED*). 700 **cells**] Individual containers.   703 **founded**] Melted down (as in a foundry).

A various mould, and from the boiling cells   706
By strange conveyance filled each hollow nook,   707
As in an organ from one blast of wind
To many a row of pipes the sound-board breathes.
Anon out of the earth a fabric huge   710
Rose like an exhalation, with the sound   711
Of dulcet symphonies and voices sweet,   712
Built like a temple, where pilasters round   713
Were set, and Doric pillars overlaid   714
With golden architrave; nor did there want   715
Cornice or frieze, with bossy sculptures graven,   716
The roof was fretted gold. Not Babylon,   717
Nor great Alcairo such magnificence   718
Equalled in all their glories, to enshrine
Belus or Serapis their gods, or seat   720
Their kings, when Egypt with Assyria strove
In wealth and luxury. The ascending pile
Soon fixed her stately height, and straight the doors
Opening their brazen folds discover wide   724
Within her ample spaces, o'er the smooth
And level pavement: from the archèd roof
Pendent by subtle magic many a row
Of starry lamps and blazing cressets fed   728
With naphtha and asphaltus yielded light   729
As from a sky. The hasty multitude
Admiring entered, and the work some praise
And some the architect: his hand was known
In heaven by many a towered structure high,

706 **various**] Complex.   707 **strange**] Wonderful.   710 **fabric**] Edifice.
711 **exhalation**] Mist.   712 **symphonies**] Harmonious music; the city is built as
the walls of Thebes were raised by the songs of the legendary musician Amphion.
713 **pilasters**] Columns attached to the walls.   714 **Doric pillars**] The least
ornate and most dignified of the Greek columns: cf. Satan's martial music in the Dorian
mode, l. 550; but note also the elaborate ornamentation of the building as a
whole.   715 **architrave**] The beam resting on the columns that supports the roof;
the lowest section of the entablature.   716 **Cornice or frieze**] The decorative
upper sections of the entablature.   **bossy . . . graven**] Sculptures carved in relief.
717 **fretted**] Ornamented with decorative patterns in relief.   718 **Alcairo**]
Modern Cairo, famous for its luxurious buildings.   720 **Belus**] Babylonian version
of Baal.   **Serapis**] Osiris as god of the underworld.   724 **folds**] 'The leaves of a
folding door' (*OED*).   **discover**] Reveal.   728 **cressets**] Iron baskets used as lan-
terns.   729 **naphtha and asphaltus**] Lamp oil and pitch, fuel for the lamps and
lanterns.

Where sceptred angels held their residence,
And sat as princes, whom the supreme king
Exalted to such power, and gave to rule,
Each in his hierarchy, the orders bright.
Nor was his name unheard or unadored
In ancient Greece; and in Ausonian land   739
Men called him Mulciber; and how he fell   740
From heaven, they fabled, thrown by angry Jove   741
Sheer o'er the crystal battlements; from morn
To noon he fell, from noon to dewy eve,
A summer's day; and with the setting sun
Dropped from the zenith like a falling star,
On Lemnos the Aegaean isle: thus they relate,
Erring; for he with this rebellious rout
Fell along before; nor aught availed him now
To have built in heaven high towers; nor did he scape
By all his engines, but was headlong sent   750
With his industrious crew to build in hell.
Meanwhile the wingèd heralds by command
Of sovereign power, with awful ceremony
And trumpets' sound throughout the host proclaim
A solemn council forthwith to be held
At Pandaemonium, the high capital   756
Of Satan and his peers: their summons called
From every band and squarèd regiment   758
By place or choice the worthiest; they anon
With hundreds and with thousands trooping came
Attended: all access was thronged, the gates
And porches wide, but chief the spacious hall
(Though like a covered field, where champions bold
Wont ride in armed, and at the soldan's chair   764
Defied the best of paynim chivalry   765
To mortal combat or career with lance)   766
Thick swarmed, both on the ground and in the air,
Brushed with the hiss of rustling wings. As bees

---

739 **Ausonian land**] Italy.   740 **Mulciber**] Or Vulcan (the Greek Hephaestos),
smith and artisan of the gods.   740–1 **how . . . fabled**] For Hephaestos' fall see
Iliad, i. 588–95.   750 **engines**] Devices.   756 **Pandaemonium**] Milton's coin-
age from the Greek, meaning 'all the devils'.   758 **squared regiment**] Squadron.
764 **Wont**] Were wont to. **soldan's**] Sultan's.   765 **paynim**] Pagan.   766 **To
. . . lance**] Either a fight to the death or a joust for a prize. **career**] Gallop.

In springtime, when the sun with Taurus rides,   769
Pour forth their populous youth about the hive
In clusters; they among fresh dews and flowers
Fly to and fro, or on the smoothèd plank,
The suburb of their straw-built citadel,
New rubbed with balm, expatiate and confer   774
Their state affairs. So thick the airy crowd
Swarmed and were straitened; till the signal given,
Behold a wonder! they but now who seemed
In bigness to surpass Earth's giant sons
Now less than smallest dwarfs, in narrow room
Throng numberless, like that pygmean race   780
Beyond the Indian mount, or fairy elves,
Whose midnight revels, by a forest side
Or fountain some belated peasant sees,
Or dreams he sees, while overhead the moon
Sits arbitress, and nearer to the earth   785
Wheels her pale course, they on their mirth and dance
Intent, with jocund music charm his ear;
At once with joy and fear his heart rebounds.
Thus incorporeal spirits to smallest forms
Reduced their shapes immense, and were at large,   790
Though without number still amidst the hall
Of that infernal court. But far within
And in their own dimensions like themselves
The great seraphic lords and cherubim
In close recess and secret conclave sat   795
A thousand demigods on golden seats,
Frequent and full. After short silence then   797
And summons read, the great consult began.   798

769 **sun ... rides**] The sun enters Taurus in April.   774 **expatiate**] Both
walk about and talk at length. **confer**] Discuss.   785 **arbitress**] As judge.
795 **close**] Private.   797 **Frequent**] Crowded.   798 **consult**] Consultation.

BOOK II

The Argument

The consultation begun, Satan debates whether another battle be
to be hazarded for the recovery of heaven; some advise it, others
dissuade: a third proposal is preferred, mentioned before by Satan,
to search the truth of that prophecy or tradition in heaven con-
cerning another world, and another kind of creature equal or not
much inferior to themselves, about this time to be created: their
doubt who shall be sent on this difficult search: Satan their chief
undertakes alone the voyage, is honoured and applauded. The
council thus ended, the rest betake them several ways and to several
employments, as their inclinations lead them, to entertain the time
till Satan return. He passes on his journey to hell gates, finds them
shut, and who sat there to guard them, by whom at length they are
opened, and discover to him the great gulf between hell and heaven;   13
with what difficulty he passes through, directed by Chaos, the
power of that place, to the sight of this new world which he sought.   15

HIGH on a throne of royal state, which far
Outshone the wealth of Ormuz and of Ind,   2
Or where the gorgeous East with richest hand
Showers on her kings barbaric pearl and gold,
Satan exalted sat, by merit raised
To that bad eminence; and from despair
Thus high uplifted beyond hope, aspires
Beyond thus high, insatiate to pursue
Vain war with heaven, and by success untaught   9
His proud imaginations thus displayed.
    Powers and dominions, deities of heaven,   11
For since no deep within her gulf can hold
Immortal vigour, though oppressed and fallen,
I give not heaven for lost. From this descent
Celestial virtues rising, will appear   15
More glorious and more dread than from no fall,

---

13 **discover**]. Reveal.   15 **power**]. Ruler.

2 **Ormuz**] An island in the Persian Gulf, a rich trading port. **Ind**] India.
9 **success**] The outcome (with an ironic overtone of the usual meaning).
11 **Powers and dominions**] Two orders of angels, according to St Paul (Colossians
1: 16).   15 **virtues**] Another of Dionysius' orders of angels (see note to i. 324).

And trust themselves to fear no second fate:
Me though just right, and the fixed laws of heaven
Did first create your leader, next free choice,
With what besides, in counsel or in fight,
Hath been achieved of merit, yet this loss   21
Thus far at least recovered, hath much more
Established in a safe unenvied throne
Yielded with full consent. The happier state
In heaven, which follows dignity, might draw
Envy from each inferior; but who here
Will envy whom the highest place exposes   27
Foremost to stand against the thunderer's aim   28
Your bulwark, and condemns to greatest share
Of endless pain? where there is then no good
For which to strive, no strife can grow up there
From faction; for none sure will claim in hell
Precedence, none, whose portion is so small
Of present pain, that with ambitious mind
Will covet more. With this advantage then
To union, and firm faith, and firm accord,
More than can be in heaven, we now return
To claim our just inheritance of old,
Surer to prosper than prosperity
Could have assured us; and by what best way,   40
Whether of open war or covert guile,
We now debate; who can advise, may speak.

    He ceased, and next him Moloch, sceptred king
Stood up, the strongest and the fiercest spirit
That fought in heaven; now fiercer by despair:
His trust was with the eternal to be deemed
Equal in strength, and rather than be less
Cared not to be at all; with that care lost
Went all his fear: of God, or hell, or worse
He recked not, and these words thereafter spake.   50

    My sentence is for open war: of wiles,   51
More unexpert, I boast not: them let those   52
Contrive who need, or when they need, not now.

---

21 **of merit**] By merit.   27 **whom**] Him whom.   28 **the thunderer**]
An epithet for Jupiter.   50 **recked not**] Took no notice. **thereafter**]
Therefore.   51 **sentence**] Judgment.   52 **unexpert**] Inexperienced.

For while they sit contriving, shall the rest,
Millions that stand in arms, and longing wait
The signal to ascend, sit lingering here
Heaven's fugitives, and for their dwelling place
Accept this dark opprobrious den of shame,
The prison of his tyranny who reigns
By our delay? no, let us rather choose   60
Armed with hell flames and fury all at once
O'er heaven's high towers to force resistless way,
Turning our tortures into horrid arms
Against the torturer; when to meet the noise
Of his almighty engine he shall hear   65
Infernal thunder, and for lightning see
Black fire and horror shot with equal rage
Among his angels; and his throne itself
Mixed with Tartarean sulphur, and strange fire,   69
His own invented torments. But perhaps
The way seems difficult and steep to scale
With upright wing against a higher foe.
Let such bethink them, if the sleepy drench   73
Of that forgetful lake benumb not still,   74
That in our proper motion we ascend   75
Up to our native seat: descent and fall
To us is adverse. Who but felt of late
When the fierce foe hung on our broken rear
Insulting, and pursued us through the deep,   79
With what compulsion and laborious flight
We sunk thus low? The ascent is easy then;   81
The event is feared; should we again provoke   82
Our stronger, some worse way his wrath may find   83
To our destruction: if there be in hell
Fear to be worse destroyed: what can be worse
Than to dwell here, driven out from bliss, condemned

---

65 **engine**] War machine.   69 **Tartarean**] Of Tartarus, the classical
hell.   73 **drench**] Soporific drink, the word had its modern meaning in Milton's
time only as a verb, though a slangy or punning usage may be intended.   74 **forget-
ful lake**] The 'oblivious pool' of i. 266.   75 **our proper motion**] The motion that
is naturally ours.   79 **Insulting**] Both exulting and attacking.   81 **The ascent
is easy**] Reversing the sibyl's warning to Aeneas about the descent to hell, '*facilis
descensus Averno*' (implying that the way back, however, is very difficult), *Aeneid*, vi.
126–9.   82 **event**] Outcome.   83 **Our stronger**] He who is stronger than we.

In this abhorrèd deep to utter woe;
Where pain of unextinguishable fire
Must exercise us without hope of end   89
The vassals of his anger, when the scourge
Inexorably, and the torturing hour
Calls us to penance? More destroyed than thus
We should be quite abolished and expire.
What fear we then? what doubt we to incense   94
His utmost ire? which to the height enraged,
Will either quite consume us, and reduce
To nothing this essential, happier far   97
Than miserable to have eternal being:
Or if our substance be indeed divine,
And cannot cease to be, we are at worst
On this side nothing; and by proof we feel   101
Our power sufficient to disturb his heaven,
And with perpetual inroads to alarm,
Though inaccessible, his fatal throne: 104
Which if not victory is yet revenge.

   He ended frowning, and his look denounced   106
Desperate revenge, and battle dangerous
To less than gods. On the other side up rose
Belial, in act more graceful and humane;
A fairer person lost not heaven; he seemed
For dignity composed and high exploit:
But all was false and hollow; though his tongue
Dropped manna, and could make the worse appear   113
The better reason, to perplex and dash
Maturest counsels: for his thoughts were low;
To vice industrious, but to nobler deeds
Timorous and slothful: yet he pleased the ear,
And with persuasive accent thus began.
   I should be much for open war, O peers,
As not behind in hate; if what was urged   120
Main reason to persuade immediate war,

<hr />

89 **exercise**] Afflict; subject to ascetic discipline (leading to the 'penance' of l. 92).
94 **what doubt we**] Why do we hesitate.   97 **essential**] Essence.   100–1 **at worst … nothing**] We are as badly off as we can be, short of annihilation.   **proof**] Experience.   104 **fatal**] Both maintained by fate and dire.   106 **denounced**] Proclaimed.   113 **manna**] Divine sustenance (from the nourishment God provided the Israelites in the wilderness, Exodus 16).

Did not dissuade me most, and seem to cast
Ominous conjecture on the whole success:
When he who most excels in fact of arms,   124
In what he counsels and in what excels
Mistrustful, grounds his courage on despair
And utter dissolution, as the scope   127
Of all his aim, after some dire revenge.
First, what revenge? the towers of heaven are filled
With armèd watch, that render all access
Impregnable; oft on the bordering deep
Encamp their legions, or with obscure wing
Scout far and wide into the realm of night,
Scorning surprise. Or could we break our way
By force, and at our heels all hell should rise
With blackest insurrection, to confound
Heaven's purest light, yet our great enemy
All incorruptible would on his throne
Sit unpolluted, and the ethereal mould   139
Incapable of stain would soon expel
Her mischief, and purge off the baser fire
Victorious. Thus repulsed, our final hope
Is flat despair: we must exasperate
The almighty victor to spend all his rage,
And that must end us, that must be our cure,
To be no more; sad cure; for who would lose,
Though full of pain, this intellectual being,
Those thoughts that wander through eternity,
To perish rather, swallowed up and lost
In the wide womb of uncreated night,   150
Devoid of sense and motion? and who knows,
Let this be good, whether our angry foe
Can give it, or will ever? how he can
Is doubtful; that he never will is sure.
Will he, so wise, let loose at once his ire,
Belike through impotence, or unaware,   156
To give his enemies their wish, and end
Them in his anger, whom his anger saves

---

124 **fact**] Feats.   127 **scope**] Lit. target.   139 **ethereal**] Made of pure fire
(as opposed to the 'baser fire' of l. 141).   156 **Belike**] Doubtless. **impotence**]
Violent passion: the suggestion is sarcastic.

To punish endless? wherefore cease we then?
Say they who counsel war, we are decreed,   *160*
Reserved and destined to eternal woe;
Whatever doing, what can we suffer more,
What can we suffer worse? is this then worst,
Thus sitting, thus consulting, thus in arms?
What when we fled amain, pursued and struck   165
With heaven's afflicting thunder, and besought
The deep to shelter us? this hell then seemed
A refuge from those wounds: or when we lay
Chained on the burning lake? that sure was worse.   169
What if the breath that kindled those grim fires
Awaked should blow them into sevenfold rage
And plunge us in the flames? or from above
Should intermitted vengeance arm again
His red right hand to plague us? what if all   174
Her stores were opened, and this firmament
Of hell should spout her cataracts of fire,
Impendent horrors, threatening hideous fall
One day upon our heads; while we perhaps
Designing or exhorting glorious war,
Caught in a fiery tempest shall be hurled   *180*
Each on his rock transfixed, the sport and prey
Of racking whirlwinds, or for ever sunk
Under yon boiling ocean, wrapped in chains;
There to converse with everlasting groans,   184
Unrespited, unpitied, unreprieved,
Ages of hopeless end; this would be worse.
War therefore, open or concealed, alike
My voice dissuades; for what can force or guile
With him, or who deceive his mind, whose eye   189
Views all things at one view? he from heaven's height
All these our motions vain, sees and derides;   191
Not more almighty to resist our might
Than wise to frustrate all our plots and wiles.

---

165 **What when**] What was it when. **amain**] With all our strength.
169 **Chained on**] Confined to (see i. 210).   174 **red**] Fiery, bloody; 'red right
hand' translates Horace's *rubente dextera*, Jupiter's red right hand afflicting Rome
with the thunderbolts of war (*Odes*, i. ii. 1–4).   184 **converse**] Including its original
meaning, dwell.   188–9 **what can ... With him**] How can force or guile affect
him.   191 **motions**] Proposals.

Shall we then live thus vile, the race of heaven
Thus trampled, thus expelled to suffer here
Chains and these torments? better these than worse
By my advice; since fate inevitable
Subdues us, and omnipotent decree
The victor's will. To suffer, as to do,   199
Our strength is equal, nor the law unjust
That so ordains: this was at first resolved,
If we were wise, against so great a foe
Contending, and so doubtful what might fall.
I laugh, when those who at the spear are bold
And venturous, if that fail them, shrink and fear
What yet they know must follow, to endure
Exile, or ignominy, or bonds, or pain,
The sentence of their conqueror: this is now
Our doom; which if we can sustain and bear,
Our supreme foe in time may much remit
His anger, and perhaps thus far removed
Not mind us not offending, satisfied   212
With what is punished; whence these raging fires
Will slacken, if his breath stir not their flames.
Our purer essence then will overcome
Their noxious vapour, or inured not feel,
Or changed at length, and to the place conformed
In temper and in nature, will receive
Familiar the fierce heat, and void of pain;
This horror will grow mild, this darkness light,   220
Besides what hope the never-ending flight
Of future days may bring, what chance, what change
Worth waiting, since our present lot appears
For happy though but ill, for ill not worst,   224
If we procure not to ourselves more woe.
    Thus Belial with words clothed in reason's garb
Counselled ignoble ease, and peaceful sloth,
Not peace: and after him thus Mammon spake.
    Either to disenthrone the king of heaven
We war, if war be best, or to regain   230

199 **To suffer, as to do**] Passive or active.   212 **Not mind**] Ignore.
220 **light**] Both bright and easy to bear.   224 **For happy**] In degrees of happiness.

Our own right lost: him to unthrone we then
May hope when everlasting fate shall yield
To fickle chance, and Chaos judge the strife:
The former vain to hope argues as vain
The latter: for what place can be for us
Within heaven's bound, unless heaven's lord supreme
We overpower? Suppose he should relent
And publish grace to all, on promise made
Of new subjection; with what eyes could we
Stand in his presence humble, and receive   240
Strict laws imposed, to celebrate his throne
With warbled hymns, and to his godhead sing
Forced hallelujahs; while he lordly sits
Our envied sovereign, and his altar breathes
Ambrosial odours and ambrosial flowers,
Our servile offerings? This must be our task
In heaven, this our delight; how wearisome
Eternity so spent in worship paid
To whom we hate. Let us not then pursue
By force impossible, by leave obtained   250
Unacceptable, though in heaven, our state
Of splendid vassalage, but rather seek
Our own good from ourselves, and from our own
Live to ourselves, though in this vast recess,
Free, and to none accountable, preferring
Hard liberty before the easy yoke
Of servile pomp. Our greatness will appear
Then most conspicuous, when great things of small,
Useful of hurtful, prosperous of adverse
We can create, and in what place soe'er   260
Thrive under evil, and work ease out of pain
Through labour and endurance. This deep world
Of darkness do we dread? How oft amidst
Thick clouds and dark doth heaven's all-ruling sire
Choose to reside, his glory unobscured,
And with the majesty of darkness round
Covers his throne; from whence deep thunders roar
Mustering their rage, and heaven resembles hell?
As he our darkness, cannot we his light

250 **by leave obtained**] If we were granted permission by God.

Imitate when we please? This desert soil
Wants not her hidden lustre, gems and gold;　　　271
Nor want we skill or art, from whence to raise
Magnificence; and what can heaven show more?
Our torments also may in length of time
Become our elements, these piercing fires　　　275
As soft as now severe, our temper changed
Into their temper; which must needs remove　　　277
The sensible of pain. All things invite　　　278
To peaceful counsels, and the settled state
Of order, how in safety best we may
Compose our present evils, with regard　　　281
Of what we are and where, dismissing quite
All thoughts of war: ye have what I advise.
　　He scarce had finished, when such murmur filled
The assembly, as when hollow rocks retain
The sound of blustering winds, which all night long
Had roused the sea, now with hoarse cadence lull
Seafaring men o'erwatched, whose bark by chance　　　288
Or pinnace anchors in a craggy bay
After the tempest: such applause was heard
As Mammon ended, and his sentence pleased,　　　291
Advising peace: for such another field
They dreaded worse than hell: so much the fear
Of thunder and the sword of Michael
Wrought still within them; and no less desire
To found this nether empire, which might rise
By policy, and long process of time,　　　297
In emulation opposite to heaven.
Which when Beelzebub perceived, than whom,
Satan except, none higher sat, with grave
Aspect he rose, and in his rising seemed
A pillar of state; deep on his front engraven　　　302
Deliberation sat and public care;

---

271 **Wants**] Lacks.　　274–5 **Our ... elements**] i.e. we shall truly be in our element; we shall be composed of fire.　276–7 **temper ... temper**] Playing on the senses of tempering steel and of temperament.　278 **The sensible of pain**] What we feel of pain through the senses.　281 **Compose**] Adjust our minds to.　288 **o'erwatched**] Worn out with waking.　291 **sentence**] Opinion. 297 **policy**] Political strategy, with Machiavellian implications.　302 **front**] Forehead or face.

And princely counsel in his face yet shone,
Majestic though in ruin: sage he stood
With Atlantean shoulders fit to bear   306
The weight of mightiest monarchies; his look
Drew audience and attention still as night
Or summer's noontide air, while thus he spake.
   Thrones and imperial powers, offspring of heaven,
Ethereal virtues; or these titles now   311
Must we renounce, and changing style be called   312
Princes of hell? for so the popular vote
Inclines, here to continue, and build up here
A growing empire; doubtless; while we dream,
And know not that the king of heaven hath doomed
This place our dungeon, not our safe retreat
Beyond his potent arm, to live exempt
From heaven's high jurisdiction, in new league
Banded against his throne, but to remain   320
In strictest bondage, though thus far removed,
Under the inevitable curb, reserved
His captive multitude: for he, be sure
In height or depth, still first and last will reign
Sole king, and of his kingdom lose no part
By our revolt, but over hell extend
His empire, and with iron sceptre rule
Us here, as with his golden those in heaven.
What sit we then projecting peace and war?   329
War hath determined us, and foiled with loss
Irreparable; terms of peace yet none
Vouchsafed or sought; for what peace will be given
To us enslaved, but custody severe,
And stripes, and arbitrary punishment   334
Inflicted? and what peace can we return,
But to our power hostility and hate,   336
Untamed reluctance, and revenge though slow,   337
Yet ever plotting how the conqueror least

---

306 **Atlantean**] The Titan Atlas was condemned by Jove to bear the heavens on his shoulders.   310–11 **Thrones ... powers ... virtues**] Angelic orders (see i. 324, ii. 11, and notes).   312 **style**] Title.   329 **What**] Why.   334 **stripes**] Lashes. 336 **to our power**] To the extent of our power.   337 **reluctance**] Resistance, 'the act of struggling against something' (*OED*).

May reap his conquest, and may least rejoice
In doing what we most in suffering feel?
Nor will occasion want, nor shall we need   341
With dangerous expedition to invade
Heaven, whose high walls fear no assault or siege,
Or ambush from the deep. What if we find
Some easier enterprise? There is a place
(If ancient and prophetic fame in heaven
Err not), another world, the happy seat
Of some new race called Man, about this time
To be created like to us, though less
In power and excellence, but favoured more   350
Of him who rules above; so was his will
Pronounced among the gods, and by an oath,
That shook heaven's whole circumference, confirmed.
Thither let us bend all our thoughts, to learn
What creatures there inhabit, of what mould,
Or substance, how endued, and what their power,
And where their weakness, how attempted best,
By force or subtlety: though heaven be shut,
And heaven's high arbitrator sit secure   359
In his own strength, this place may lie exposed
The utmost border of his kingdom, left
To their defence who hold it: here perhaps
Some advantageous act may be achieved
By sudden onset, either with hellfire
To waste his whole creation, or possess
All as our own, and drive as we were driven,
The puny habitants, or if not drive,   367
Seduce them to our party, that their God
May prove their foe, and with repenting hand
Abolish his own works. This would surpass
Common revenge, and interrupt his joy
In our confusion, and our joy upraise   372
In his disturbance; when his darling sons
Hurled headlong to partake with us, shall curse
Their frail original, and faded bliss,

---

341 **want**] Be lacking.   359 **arbitrator**] Judge.   367 **puny**] Lit. 'born
since us' (*puis né*).   372 **confusion**] Destruction.

Faded so soon. Advise if this be worth
Attempting, or to sit in darkness here
Hatching vain empires. Thus Beelzebub
Pleaded his devilish counsel, first devised
By Satan, and in part proposed: for whence,   380
But from the author of all ill could spring
So deep a malice, to confound the race
Of mankind in one root, and earth with hell   383
To mingle and involve, done all to spite   384
The great creator? But their spite still serves
His glory to augment. The bold design
Pleased highly those infernal states, and joy   387
Sparkled in all their eyes; with full assent
They vote: whereat his speech he thus renews.

    Well have ye judged, well ended long debate,
Synod of gods, and like to what ye are,   391
Great things resolved, which from the lowest deep
Will once more lift us up, in spite of fate,
Nearer our ancient seat; perhaps in view
Of those bright confines, whence with neighbouring arms
And opportune excursion we may chance
Re-enter heaven; or else in some mild zone
Dwell not unvisited of heaven's fair light
Secure, and at the brightening orient beam
Purge off this gloom; the soft delicious air,   400
To heal the scar of these corrosive fires
Shall breathe her balm. But first whom shall we send
In search of this new world, whom shall we find
Sufficient? who shall tempt with wandering feet   404
The dark unbottomed infinite abyss
And through the palpable obscure find out
His uncouth way, or spread his airy flight   407
Upborne with indefatigable wings
Over the vast abrupt, ere he arrive   409
The happy isle; what strength, what art can then

379–80 first . . . proposed] See i. 651ff.   383 root] The metaphor is of a family
tree.   384 involve] Entangle, 'beset with difficulty or obscurity' (*OED*).
387 states] Estates, the hierarchy of the realm.   391 Synod] Assembly.
404 tempt] Try, attempt, with overtones of the usual sense.   407 uncouth]
Unknown.   409 abrupt] Chasm (*OED*'s only instance of its use as a noun).
arrive] Reach.

Suffice, or what evasion bear him safe
Through the strict sentries and stations thick
Of angels watching round? Here he had need
All circumspection, and we now no less
Choice in our suffrage; for on whom we send,   415
The weight of all and our last hope relies.

    This said, he sat; and expectation held
His look suspense, awaiting who appeared   418
To second, or oppose, or undertake
The perilous attempt: but all sat mute,
Pondering the danger with deep thoughts; and each
In others' countenance read his own dismay
Astonished: none among the choice and prime   423
Of those heaven-warring champions could be found
So hardy as to proffer or accept
Alone the dreadful voyage; till at last
Satan, whom now transcendent glory raised
Above his fellows, with monarchal pride
Conscious of highest worth, unmoved thus spake.

    O progeny of heaven, empyreal thrones,   430
With reason hath deep silence and demur
Seized us, though undismayed: long is the way
And hard, that out of hell leads up to light;   433
Our prison strong, this huge convex of fire,   434
Outrageous to devour, immures us round   435
Ninefold, and gates of burning adamant   436
Barred over us prohibit all egress.
These passed, if any pass, the void profound
Of unessential night receives him next   439
Wide gaping, and with utter loss of being
Threatens him, plunged in that abortive gulf.   441

---

415 **Choice in our suffrage**] Care in choosing whom we vote for.
418 **suspense**] In suspense.   423 **Astonished**] 'Filled with consternation, dismayed'
(*OED*).   432–3 **long . . . light**] Another echo of the sibyl's words to Aeneas about to
descend to hell; see l. 81.   434 **convex**] Vault.   435 **Outrageous to devour**]
Violently destructive.   436 **adamant**] The hardest substance.   439 **unessential**]
Having no substance, uncreated.   441 **abortive**] Probably not 'causing abortion',
but an adjective derived from the noun, hence monstrous, formless. Alternatively, 'per-
haps Satan thinks of the gulf as a miscarrying womb . . . from which the traveller may
never be born, or which may render him as if unborn' (Fowler). An etymological sense,
'away from birth', hence anti-creative, may also be intended. The word has provoked
much inconclusive editorial debate.

If thence he scape into whatever world,
Or unknown region, what remains him less
Than unknown dangers and as hard escape.
But I should ill become this throne, O peers,
And this imperial sovereignty, adorned
With splendour, armed with power, if aught proposed
And judged of public moment, in the shape   448
Of difficulty or danger could deter
Me from attempting. Wherefore do I assume
These royalties, and not refuse to reign,
Refusing to accept as great a share
Of hazard as of honour, due alike
To him who reigns, and so much to him due
Of hazard more, as he above the rest
High honoured sits? Go therefore mighty powers,
Terror of heaven, though fallen; intend at home,   457
While here shall be our home, what best may ease
The present misery, and render hell
More tolerable; if there be cure or charm
To respite or deceive, or slack the pain
Of this ill mansion: intermit no watch   462
Against a wakeful foe, while I abroad
Through all the coasts of dark destruction seek
Deliverance for us all: this enterprise
None shall partake with me. Thus saying rose
The monarch, and prevented all reply,   467
Prudent, lest from his resolution raised   468
Others among the chief might offer now
(Certain to be refused) what erst they feared;   470
And so refused might in opinion stand
His rivals, winning cheap the high repute
Which he through hazard huge must earn. But they
Dreaded not more the adventure than his voice
Forbidding; and at once with him they rose;
Their rising all at once was as the sound

448 **moment**] Importance.   457 **intend**] Consider.   462 **mansion**] Dwelling.
intermit no watch] Keep uninterrupted watch.   467 **prevented**] Forestalled.
468 **raised**] Made bold.   470 **erst**] At first.

Of thunder heard remote. Towards him they bend
With awful reverence prone; and as a god   478
Extol him equal to the highest in heaven:
Nor failed they to express how much they praised,
That for the general safety he despised
His own: for neither do the spirits damned
Lose all their virtue; lest bad men should boast
Their specious deeds on earth, which glory excites,
Or close ambition varnished o'er with zeal.   485
Thus they their doubtful consultations dark
Ended rejoicing in their matchless chief:
As when from mountain tops the dusky clouds
Ascending, while the north wind sleeps, o'erspread
Heaven's cheerful face, the louring element   490
Scowls o'er the darkened landscape snow, or shower;
If chance the radiant sun with farewell sweet   492
Extend his evening beam, the fields revive,
The birds their notes renew, and bleating herds
Attest their joy, that hill and valley rings.   495
O shame to men! Devil with devil damned
Firm concord holds, men only disagree
Of creatures rational, though under hope
Of heavenly grace: and God proclaiming peace,
Yet live in hatred, enmity, and strife   500
Among themselves, and levy cruel wars,
Wasting the earth, each other to destroy:
As if (which might induce us to accord)
Man had not hellish foes enough besides,
That day and night for his destruction wait.
    The Stygian council thus dissolved; and forth
In order came the grand infernal peers,
Midst came their mighty paramount, and seemed   508
Alone the antagonist of heaven, nor less
Than hell's dread emperor with pomp supreme,
And Godlike imitated state; him round
A globe of fiery seraphim enclosed   512

---

478 awful] Awestruck.   485 close] Secret.   490 louring element] Threat-
ening sky.   492 chance] By chance.   495 that] So that.   508 paramount]
Chief.   512 globe] 'A compact body (of persons)' (*OED*), hence the phalanx.

With bright emblazonry, and horrent arms.   513
Then of their session ended they bid cry
With trumpets' regal sound the great result:
Toward the four winds four speedy cherubim
Put to their mouths the sounding alchemy   517
By herald's voice explained: the hollow abyss
Heard far and wide, and all the host of hell
With deafening shout returned them loud acclaim.
Thence more at ease their minds and somewhat raised   521
By false presumptuous hope, the ranged powers
Disband, and wandering, each his several way
Pursues, as inclination or sad choice
Leads him perplexed, where he may likeliest find
Truce to his restless thoughts, and entertain
The irksome hours, till this great chief return.
Part on the plain, or in the air sublime   528
Upon the wing, or in swift race contend,
As at the Olympian games or Pythian fields;   530
Part curb their fiery steeds, or shun the goal   531
With rapid wheels, or fronted brigades form.   532
As when to warn proud cities war appears
Waged in the troubled sky, and armies rush
To battle in the clouds, before each van   535
Prick forth the airy knights, and couch their spears   536
Till thickest legions close; with feats of arms   537
From either end of heaven the welkin burns.   538
Others with vast Typhoean rage more fell   539
Rend up both rocks and hills, and ride the air
In whirlwind; hell scarce holds the wild uproar.   541

---

513 **emblazonry**] Heraldry. **horrent**] Bristling.   517 **alchemy**] 'A metallic
composition imitating gold', hence 'a trumpet of such metal, or of brass' (*OED*).
521 **raised**] Cheered, made bold.   528 **sublime**] High above.   530 **Pythian
fields**] Near Delphi, where the Pythian games, celebrating Apollo's victory over the
Python, were held.   531 **shun the goal**] Avoid touching the track posts as they
take the turn in their chariots.   532 **fronted**] Facing each other.   535 **van**]
Vanguard.   536 **Prick**] Spur their horses. **couch**] Lower into the attack posi-
tion.   537 **close**] Engage in battle.   538 **welkin**] Sky.   539 **Typhoean**]
Monstrous, from Typhon or Typhoeus (see i. 198–9 and note, and see below,
l. 541). **fell**] fierce, cruel.   541 **whirlwind**] The word for a whirlwind was *typhon*
(not cognate with *typhoon*, but later associated with it).

As when Alcides from Oechalia crowned   542
With conquest, felt the envenomed robe, and tore
Through pain up by the roots Thessalian pines,
And Lichas from the top of Oeta threw   545
Into the Euboic sea. Others more mild,   546
Retreated in a silent valley, sing
With notes angelical to many a harp
Their own heroic deeds and hapless fall
By doom of battle; and complain that fate
Free virtue should enthral to force or chance.
Their song was partial, but the harmony   552
(What could it less when spirits immortal sing?)
Suspended hell, and took with ravishment   554
The thronging audience. In discourse more sweet
(For eloquence the soul, song charms the sense,)
Others apart sat on a hill retired,
In thoughts more elevate, and reasoned high
Of providence, foreknowledge, will and fate,
Fixed fate, free will, foreknowledge absolute,   560
And found no end, in wandering mazes lost.
Of good and evil much they argued then,
Of happiness and final misery,
Passion and apathy, and glory and shame,   564
Vain wisdom all, and false philosophy:
Yet with a pleasing sorcery could charm
Pain for a while or anguish, and excite
Fallacious hope, or arm the obdurèd breast   568
With stubborn patience as with triple steel.
Another part in squadrons and gross bands,   570

---

542 **Alcides**] Hercules (from his grandfather, Alcaeus).   545 **Oeta**] A mountain in
Thessaly, now called Banina.   542–6 **from Oechalia ... Euboic sea**] Returning
victorious from Oechalia, in Laconia, Hercules was brought a gift of the cloak of
the centaur Nessus, whom he had years earlier fought and killed. The cloak, how-
ever, was poisoned, and destroyed him, and in his death agony he hurled Lichas, the
innocent deliverer of the gift, into the sea. See Ovid, *Metamorphoses*, ix. 134 ff.,
Sophocles' *Trachiniae*, and Seneca's *Hercules Furens*. *Euboic* = Euboean; Milton
combines two versions of the story, the dramatists', in which the action takes place on
the island of Euboea, and Ovid's, in which it is in Thessaly.   552 **partial**] In
parts, i.e. harmonized, with a pun on 'prejudiced'.   554 **Suspended**] Enrap-
tured.   564 **apathy**] The Stoic ideal, to be free from passion and unmoved by
suffering.   568 **obdurèd**] Obdurate, 'hardened in wickedness or sin; persistently
impenitent' (*OED*).   570 **gross**] Large.

On bold adventure to discover wide
That dismal world, if any clime perhaps
Might yield them easier habitation, bend
Four ways their flying march, along the banks
Of four infernal rivers that disgorge
Into the burning lake their baleful streams;
Abhorrèd Styx the flood of deadly hate,
Sad Acheron of sorrow, black and deep;
Cocytus, named of lamentation loud
Heard on the rueful stream; fierce Phlegethon   580
Whose waves of torrent fire inflame with rage.
Far off from these a slow and silent stream,
Lethe the river of oblivion rolls   583
Her watery labyrinth, whereof who drinks,
Forthwith his former state and being forgets,
Forgets both joy and grief, pleasure and pain.
Beyond this flood a frozen continent
Lies dark and wild, beat with perpetual storms
Of whirlwind and dire hail, which on firm land
Thaws not, but gathers heap, and ruin seems   590
Of ancient pile; all else deep snow and ice,   591
A gulf profound as that Serbonian bog   592
Betwixt Damietta and Mount Casius old,   593
Where armies whole have sunk: the parching air
Burns frore, and cold performs the effect of fire.   595
Thither by harpy-footed Furies haled,   596
At certain revolutions all the damned   597
Are brought: and feel by turns the bitter change
Of fierce extremes, extremes by change more fierce,
From beds of raging fire to starve in ice   600
Their soft ethereal warmth, and there to pine
Immovable, infixed, and frozen round,
Periods of time, thence hurried back to fire.

577–83 **Abhorrèd Styx ... oblivion**] Etymologizing the names of the rivers of
the classical underworld.   590 **heap**] Into heaps.   591 **pile**] Building.
592 **Serbonian bog**] The quicksands surrounding Lake Serbonis, in Egypt.
593 **Damietta**] A city at the mouth of the Nile.   595 **frore**] Frozen, an archaic
past participle.   596 **harpy-footed Furies**] The harpies, who attacked Aeneas and
his men, had the faces and breasts of young women, the wings and bodies of birds, and
talons for hands (see *Aeneid*, iii. 211ff.). The Furies were the classical agents of divine
retribution.   597 **certain revolutions**] See l. 603.   600 **starve**] Cause to die.

They ferry over this Lethean sound   604
Both to and fro, their sorrow to augment,
And wish and struggle, as they pass, to reach
The tempting stream, with one small drop to lose
In sweet forgetfulness all pain and woe,
All in one moment, and so near the brink;
But fate withstands, and to oppose the attempt
Medusa with gorgonian terror guards   611
The ford, and of itself the water flies
All taste of living wight, as once it fled   613
The lip of Tantalus. Thus roving on   614
In confused march forlorn, the adventurous bands
With shuddering horror pale, and eyes aghast
Viewed first their lamentable lot, and found
No rest: through many a dark and dreary vale
They passed, and many a region dolorous,
O'er many a frozen, many a fiery alp,   620
Rocks, caves, lakes, fens, bogs, dens, and shades of death,
A universe of death, which God by curse
Created evil, for evil only good,
Where all life dies, death lives, and nature breeds,
Perverse, all monstrous, all prodigious things,   625
Abominable, inutterable, and worse
Than fables yet have feigned, or fear conceived,
Gorgons and hydras, and chimeras dire.   628
     Meanwhile the adversary of God and man,
Satan with thoughts inflamed of highest design,
Puts on swift wings, and towards the gates of hell
Explores his solitary flight; sometimes   632
He scours the right hand coast, sometimes the left,
Now shaves with level wing the deep, then soars
Up to the fiery concave towering high.
As when far off at sea a fleet descried
Hangs in the clouds, by equinoctial winds

---

604 **sound**] Strait.   611 **Medusa with gorgonian terror**] Medusa, one of the three gorgons, had snakes for hair and a look so terrible that it turned mortals to stone.   613 **wight**] Person.   614 **Tantalus**] Condemned in hell to suffer intense thirst in a pool whose water was just out of reach.   625 **prodigious**] Unnatural, abnormal.   628 **Gorgons ... hydras ... chimeras**] The hydra was a nine-headed dragon, the chimera breathed fire; for gorgons, see note to l. 611. 632 **Explores**] Tries, puts to proof.

Close sailing from Bengala, or the isles 638
Of Ternate and Tidore, whence merchants bring 639
Their spicy drugs: they on the trading flood
Through the wide Ethiopian to the Cape 641
Ply stemming nightly toward the pole. So seemed 642
Far off the flying fiend: at last appear
Hell bounds high reaching to the horrid roof,
And thrice threefold the gates; three folds were brass, 645
Three iron, three of adamantine rock,
Impenetrable, impaled with circling fire, 647
Yet unconsumed. Before the gates there sat
On either side a formidable shape;
The one seemed woman to the waist, and fair,
But ended foul in many a scaly fold
Voluminous and vast, a serpent armed
With mortal sting: about her middle round 653
A cry of hell hounds never ceasing barked 654
With wide Cerberian mouths full loud, and rung 655
A hideous peal: yet, when they list, would creep, 656
If aught disturbed their noise, into her womb,
And kennel there, yet there still barked and howled,
Within unseen. Far less abhorred than these
Vexed Scylla bathing in the sea that parts
Calabria from the hoarse Trinacrian shore: 661
Nor uglier follow the Night-hag, when called 662
In secret, riding through the air she comes
Lured with the smell of infant blood, to dance
With Lapland witches, while the labouring moon 665
Eclipses at their charms. The other shape,

638 **Bengala**] Bengal: the ships are following the spice route, from India south and west around the Cape of Good Hope.   639 **Ternate and Tidore**] Two of the Moluccas, or Spice Islands, near New Guinea.   641 **Ethiopian**] The Indian Ocean.   642 **stemming**] Making headway.   645 **folds**] Layers.   647 **impaled**] Surrounded.   653 **mortal**] Deadly.   653–4 **about ... hounds**] Milton's figure of Sin is based on the classical Scylla (see further l. 660), a nymph who was changed by the witch Circe into a monster with ferocious dogs sprouting from her lower body.   **cry**] Pack.   655 **Cerberian**] From Cerberus, three-headed watchdog of hell.   656 **list**] Wished.   660–1 **Scylla ... shore**] Scylla ultimately became a dangerous rock off the Sicilian coast   **Trinacrian**] Sicilian.   662 **Night-hag**] The chief witch, or Hecate, goddess of the underworld   **called**] Invoked.   665 **Lapland**] Especially associated with witches   **labouring**] Suffering (because in eclipse, l. 666).

If shape it might be called that shape had none
Distinguishable in member, joint, or limb,
Or substance might be called that shadow seemed,
For each seemed either; black it stood as night,   670
Fierce as ten Furies, terrible as hell,
And shook a dreadful dart; what seemed his head
The likeness of a kingly crown had on.
Satan was now at hand, and from his seat
The monster moving onward came as fast
With horrid strides, hell trembled as he strode.
The undaunted fiend what this might be admired,   - 677
Admired, not feared; God and his son except,
Created thing nought valued he nor shunned;
And with disdainful look thus first began.   680
    Whence and what art thou, execrable shape,
That darest, though grim and terrible, advance
Thy miscreated front athwart my way
To yonder gates? through them I mean to pass,
That be assured, without leave asked of thee:
Retire, or taste thy folly, and learn by proof,   686
Hell-born, not to contend with spirits of heaven.
    To whom the goblin full of wrath replied,   688
Art thou that traitor angel, art thou he,
Who first broke peace in heaven and faith, till then
Unbroken, and in proud rebellious arms
Drew after him the third part of heaven's sons
Conjured against the highest, for which both thou   693
And they outcast from God, are here condemned
To waste eternal days in woe and pain?
And reckon'st thou thyself with spirits of heaven,
Hell-doomed, and breath'st defiance here and scorn
Where I reign king, and to enrage thee more,
Thy king and lord? Back to thy punishment,
False fugitive, and to thy speed add wings,   700
Lest with a whip of scorpions I pursue
Thy lingering, or with one stroke of this dart
Strange horror seize thee, and pangs unfelt before.
    So spake the grisly terror, and in shape,

---

677 **admired**] Wondered.   686 **proof**] Experience.   688 **goblin**] Demon.
693 **Conjured**] Sworn together (Latin *coniuro*).

So speaking and so threatening, grew tenfold
More dreadful and deform: on the other side   706
Incensed with indignation Satan stood
Unterrified, and like a comet burned,
That fires the length of Ophiuchus huge   709
In the Arctic sky, and from his horrid hair   710
Shakes pestilence and war. Each at the head   711
Levelled his deadly aim; their fatal hands
No second stroke intend, and such a frown
Each cast at the other, as when two black clouds
With heaven's artillery fraught, come rattling on
Over the Caspian, then stand front to front
Hovering a space, till winds the signal blow
To join their dark encounter in midair:
So frowned the mighty combatants, that hell
Grew darker at their frown, so matched they stood;   720
For never but once more was either like
To meet so great a foe: and now great deeds
Had been achieved, whereof all hell had rung,
Had not the snaky sorceress that sat
Fast by hell gate, and kept the fatal key,
Risen, and with hideous outcry rushed between.

     O father, what intends thy hand, she cried,
Against thy only son? What fury O son,
Possesses thee to bend that mortal dart
Against thy father's head? and know'st for whom;   730
For him who sits above and laughs the while
At thee ordained his drudge, to execute
Whate'er his wrath, which he calls justice, bids,
His wrath which one day will destroy ye both.

     She spake, and at her words the hellish pest   735
Forbore, then these to her Satan returned:
     So strange thy outcry, and thy words so strange
Thou interposest, that my sudden hand
Prevented spares to tell thee yet by deeds   739

---

706 **deform**] Deformed.   709 **Ophiuchus**] The constellation of the Serpent-Bearer, in the northern sky.   710 **horrid hair**] *Horrid* retains its etymological meaning of 'bristling'; *hair* alludes to the etymology of *comet*, from the Greek for long-haired.   711 **Shakes ... war**] Comets were considered omens of disaster.
735 **pest**] Plague.   739 **spares**] Forbears.

What it intends; till first I know of thee,   *740*
What thing thou art, thus double-formed, and why
In this infernal vale first met thou call'st
Me father, and that phantasm call'st my son?
I know thee not, nor ever saw till now
Sight more detestable than him and thee.
    To whom thus the portress of hell gate replied;
Hast thou forgot me then, and do I seem
Now in thine eye so foul, once deemed so fair
In heaven, when at the assembly, and in sight
Of all the seraphim with thee combined   *750*
In bold conspiracy against heaven's king,
All on a sudden miserable pain
Surprised thee, dim thine eyes, and dizzy swum
In darkness, while thy head flames thick and fast
Threw forth, till on the left side opening wide,
Likest to thee in shape and countenance bright,
Then shining heavenly fair, a goddess armed
Out of thy head I sprung: amazement seized   *758*
All the host of heaven; back they recoiled afraid
At first, and called me Sin, and for a sign
Portentous held me; but familiar grown,   *761*
I pleased, and with attractive graces won
The most averse, thee chiefly, who full oft
Thyself in me thy perfect image viewing
Becam'st enamoured, and such joy thou took'st
With me in secret, that my womb conceived
A growing burden. Meanwhile war arose,
And fields were fought in heaven; wherein remained
(For what could else) to our almighty foe
Clear victory, to our part loss and rout
Through all the empyrean: down they fell
Driven headlong from the pitch of heaven, down   *772*
Into this deep, and in the general fall
I also; at which time this powerful key
Into my hand was given, with charge to keep
These gates for ever shut, which none can pass

757-8 **a goddess ... sprung**] The birth of Sin from the head of Satan parallels
the birth of Athena from the head of Zeus.   761 **Portentous**] Ominous.
772 **pitch**] Height.

Without my opening. Pensive here I sat
Alone, but long I sat not, till my womb
Pregnant by thee, and now excessive grown
Prodigious motion felt and rueful throes.
At last this odious offspring whom thou seest
Thine own begotten, breaking violent way
Tore through my entrails, that with fear and pain   783
Distorted, all my nether shape thus grew
Transformed: but he my inbred enemy
Forth issued, brandishing his fatal dart
Made to destroy: I fled, and cried out Death;
Hell trembled at the hideous name, and sighed
From all her caves, and back resounded Death.
I fled, but he pursued (though more, it seems,   790
Inflamed with lust than rage) and swifter far,
Me overtook his mother all dismayed,
And in embraces forcible and foul
Engendering with me, of that rape begot
These yelling monsters that with ceaseless cry
Surround me, as thou sawest, hourly conceived
And hourly born, with sorrow infinite
To me, for when they list into the womb   798
That bred them they return, and howl and gnaw
My bowels, their repast; then bursting forth
Afresh with conscious terrors vex me round,   801
That rest or intermission none I find.
Before mine eyes in opposition sits
Grim Death my son and foe, who sets them on,
And me his parent would full soon devour
For want of other prey, but that he knows
His end with mine involved; and knows that I
Should prove a bitter morsel, and his bane,
Whenever that shall be; so fate pronounced.
But thou, O father, I forewarn thee, shun   810
His deadly arrow; neither vainly hope
To be invulnerable in those bright arms,
Though tempered heavenly, for that mortal dint,   813
Save he who reigns above, none can resist.

783 that] So that.   798 list] Wish.   801 **conscious terrors**] Terrors born of knowledge.   813 **mortal dint**] Death-dealing blow.

She finished, and the subtle fiend his lore   815
Soon learned, now milder, and thus answered smooth.
Dear daughter, since thou claim'st me for thy sire,
And my fair son here show'st me, the dear pledge
Of dalliance had with thee in heaven, and joys
Then sweet, now sad to mention, through dire change   820
Befallen us unforeseen, unthought of, know
I come no enemy, but to set free
From out this dark and dismal house of pain,
Both him and thee, and all the heavenly host
Of spirits that in our just pretences armed   825
Fell with us from on high: from them I go
This uncouth errand sole, and one for all   827
Myself expose, with lonely steps to tread
The unfounded deep, and through the void immense   829
To search with wandering quest a place foretold
Should be, and, by concurring signs, ere now
Created vast and round, a place of bliss
In the purlieus of heaven, and therein placed   833
A race of upstart creatures, to supply
Perhaps our vacant room, though more removed,   835
Lest heaven surcharged with potent multitude   836
Might hap to move new broils: be this or aught   837
Than this more secret now designed, I haste
To know, and this once known, shall soon return,
And bring ye to the place where thou and Death
Shall dwell at ease, and up and down unseen
Wing silently the buxom air, embalmed   842
With odours; there ye shall be fed and filled
Immeasurably, all things shall be your prey.
He ceased, for both seemed highly pleased, and Death
Grinned horrible a ghastly smile, to hear
His famine should be filled, and blessed his maw   847
Destined to that good hour: no less rejoiced
His mother bad, and thus bespake her sire.

---

815 lore] Lesson.   825 pretences] Claims.   827 uncouth] Unfamiliar, un-
certain.   829 unfounded] Bottomless.   833 purlieus] Outskirts.   835 re-
moved] Distant.   836 surcharged] Overcrowded.   837 hap ... broils]
Chance to precipitate new quarrels.   842 buxom] unresisting, a Spenserian
usage.   embalmed] Balmy, perhaps with an overtone of the usual sense associating
the word with death.   847 famine] Hunger.   maw] Voracious appetite.

The key of this infernal pit by due,   *850*
And by command of heaven's all-powerful king
I keep, by him forbidden to unlock
These adamantine gates; against all force
Death ready stands to interpose his dart,
Fearless to be o'ermatched by living might.
But what owe I to his commands above
Who hates me, and hath hither thrust me down
Into this gloom of Tartarus profound,
To sit in hateful office here confined,   *859*
Inhabitant of heaven, and heavenly-born,
Here in perpetual agony and pain,
With terrors and with clamours compassed round
Of mine own brood, that on my bowels feed:
Thou art my father, thou my author, thou
My being gav'st me; whom should I obey
But thee, whom follow? thou wilt bring me soon
To that new world of light and bliss, among
The gods who live at ease, where I shall reign
At thy right hand voluptuous, as beseems
Thy daughter and thy darling, without end.   *870*
    Thus saying, from her side the fatal key,
Sad instrument of all our woe, she took;
And towards the gate rolling her bestial train,
Forthwith the huge portcullis high updrew,   *874*
Which but her self, not all the Stygian powers
Could once have moved; then in the keyhole turns
The intricate wards, and every bolt and bar   *877*
Of massy iron or solid rock with ease
Unfastens: on a sudden open fly
With impetuous recoil and jarring sound
The infernal doors, and on their hinges grate
Harsh thunder, that the lowest bottom shook
Of Erebus. She opened, but to shut   *883*
Excelled her power; the gates wide open stood,
That with extended wings a bannered host   *885*
Under spread ensigns marching might pass through

859 **office**] Service.   874 **portcullis**] Outer grate.   877 **wards**] The notches
in a key, which correspond to those of the lock and permit it to be opened.
883 **Erebus**] Hell.   885 **That**] So that. **wings**] Flanks of the squadron.

With horse and chariots ranked in loose array;
So wide they stood, and like a furnace mouth
Cast forth redounding smoke and ruddy flame.   889
Before their eyes in sudden view appear
The secrets of the hoary deep, a dark
Illimitable ocean without bound,
Without dimension, where length, breadth, and height,
And time and place are lost; where eldest Night
And Chaos, ancestors of Nature, hold
Eternal anarchy, amidst the noise
Of endless wars, and by confusion stand.
For Hot, Cold, Moist, and Dry, four champions fierce   898
Strive here for mastery, and to battle bring
Their embryon atoms; they around the flag   900
Of each his faction, in their several clans,
Light-armed or heavy, sharp, smooth, swift or slow,
Swarm populous, unnumbered as the sands
Of Barca or Cyrene's torrid soil,   904
Levied to side with warring winds, and poise   905
Their lighter wings. To whom these most adhere,   906
He rules a moment; Chaos umpire sits,
And by decision more embroils the fray
By which he reigns: next him high arbiter
Chance governs all. Into this wild abyss,   910
The womb of nature and perhaps her grave,
Of neither sea, nor shore, nor air, nor fire,
But all these in their pregnant causes mixed
Confus'dly, and which thus must ever fight,
Unless the almighty maker them ordain
His dark materials to create more worlds,
Into this wild abyss the wary fiend
Stood on the brink of hell and looked awhile,
Pondering his voyage; for no narrow frith   919
He had to cross. Nor was his ear less pealed   920
With noises loud and ruinous (to compare

---

889 **redounding**] Overflowing.   898 **Hot ... Dry**] The characteristics of the four humours, corresponding to the four elements of fire, earth, water, and air.   900 **embryon**] As yet unformed.   904 **Barca ... Cyrene**] Cities in the Libyan desert.   905 **poise**] Add weight to.   905–6 **Levied ... wings**] The atoms are used as ballast for the winds.   919 **frith**] Firth, inlet.   920 **pealed**] Deafened.

Great things with small) than when Bellona storms,   922
With all her battering engines bent to raze
Some capital city; or less than if this frame
Of heaven were falling, and these elements
In mutiny had from her axle torn
The steadfast earth. At last his sail-broad vans   927
He spreads for flight, and in the surging smoke
Uplifted spurns the ground, thence many a league
As in a cloudy chair ascending rides   930
Audacious, but that seat soon failing, meets
A vast vacuity: all unawares
Fluttering his pennons vain plumb down he drops   933
Ten thousand fathom deep, and to this hour
Down had been falling, had not by ill chance
The strong rebuff of some tumultuous cloud
Instinct with fire and nitre hurried him   937
As many miles aloft: that fury stayed,
Quenched in a boggy Syrtis, neither sea,   939
Nor good dry land: nigh foundered on he fares,
Treading the crude consistence, half on foot,
Half flying; behoves him now both oar and sail.
As when a griffin through the wilderness   943
With wingèd course o'er hill or moory dale,   944
Pursues the Arimaspian, who by stealth
Had from his wakeful custody purloined
The guarded gold: so eagerly the fiend   947
O'er bog or steep, through straight, rough, dense, or rare,
With head, hands, wings or feet pursues his way,
And swims or sinks, or wades, or creeps, or flies: 950
At length a universal hubbub wild
Of stunning sounds and voices all confused
Borne through the hollow dark assaults his ear
With loudest vehemence: thither he plies,
Undaunted to meet there whatever power

922 **Bellona**] Goddess of war.   927 **vans**] Fans, i.e. wings.   930 **cloudy chair**]
The cloud machinery of masque scenery, in which deities ascended to the stage's
heaven.   933 **pennons**] Feathers, wings.   **plumb**] Directly, like a plumb line.
937 **Instinct**] Infused.   939 **Syrtis**] Dangerous shifting sands on the North African
coast.   943 **griffin**] A fabulous monster with the body of a winged lion and the
head of an eagle.   944 **moory**] Marshy.   945–7 **Pursues . . . gold**] Griffins were
the guardians of hoards of gold, which the Arimaspi, a Scythian tribe, continually
attempted to steal. The well-known story is first told in Herodotus, *Histories*, iii. 16.

Or spirit of the nethermost abyss
Might in that noise reside, of whom to ask
Which way the nearest coast of darkness lies
Bordering on light; when straight behold the throne
Of Chaos, and his dark pavilion spread
Wide on the wasteful deep; with him enthroned   961
Sat sable-vested Night, eldest of things,
The consort of his reign; and by them stood
Orcus and Ades, and the dreaded name   964
Of Demogorgon; Rumour next and Chance,   965
And Tumult and Confusion all embroiled,
And Discord with a thousand various mouths.
      To whom Satan turning boldly, thus. Ye powers
And spirits of this nethermost abyss,
Chaos and ancient Night, I come no spy,   970
With purpose to explore or to disturb
The secrets of your realm, but by constraint
Wandering this darksome desert, as my way
Lies through your spacious empire up to light,
Alone, and without guide, half lost, I seek
What readiest path leads where your gloomy bounds
Confine with heaven; or if some other place   977
From your dominion won, the ethereal king
Possesses lately, thither to arrive
I travel this profound, direct my course;
Directed no mean recompense it brings
To your behoof, if I that region lost,   982
All usurpation thence expelled, reduce
To her original darkness and your sway
(Which is my present journey) and once more
Erect the standard there of ancient Night;
Yours be the advantage all, mine the revenge.
      Thus Satan; and him thus the anarch old   988
With faltering speech and visage incomposed   989

---

961 **wasteful**] Desolate.   964 **Orcus and Ades**] Gods of the underworld.
(Ades = Hades.)   965 **Demogorgon**] The mysterious primal god of pagan myth-
ology, dreadful and unknowable; first mentioned in a late classical gloss on Statius
(the name is perhaps an error for the Platonic Demiurgos, the creator), and described
as the original god by Boccaccio in the *Genealogiae Deorum*.   977 **Confine with**]
Border on (lit. 'share a boundary with').   982 **behoof**] Benefit.   988 **anarch
old**] Chaos.   989 **incomposed**] Discomposed.

Answered. I know thee, stranger, who thou art,   990
That mighty leading angel, who of late
Made head against heaven's king, though overthrown.
I saw and heard, for such a numerous host
Fled not in silence through the frighted deep
With ruin upon ruin, rout on rout,
Confusion worse confounded; and heaven gates
Poured out by millions her victorious bands
Pursuing. I upon my frontiers here
Keep residence; if all I can will serve,
That little which is left so to defend,
Encroached on still through our intestine broils   1001
Weakening the sceptre of old Night: first hell
Your dungeon stretching far and wide beneath;
Now lately heaven and earth, another world
Hung o'er my realm, linked in a golden chain
To that side heaven from whence your legions fell: 1006
If that way be your walk, you have not far;
So much the nearer danger; go and speed;   1008
Havoc and spoil and ruin are my gain.
    He ceased; and Satan stayed not to reply,
But glad that now his sea should find a shore,
With fresh alacrity and force renewed
Springs upward like a pyramid of fire
Into the wild expanse, and through the shock
Of fighting elements, on all sides round
Environed wins his way; harder beset
And more endangered, than when Argo passed
Through Bosphorus, betwixt the jostling rocks: 1018
Or when Ulysses on the larboard shunned   1019
Charybdis, and by the other whirlpool steered.   1020

1001 **intestine**] Internal.   1005–6 **linked . . . heaven**] The notion of the world hanging by a golden chain from the floor of heaven derives originally from Homer (*Iliad*, viii. 23–4), and was greatly elaborated in Platonic and Neoplatonic philosophy. See ll. 1051–2.   1008 **speed**] The word also means 'succeed'.   1017–18 **Argo . . . rocks**] When the Argo, the ship of Jason and the Argonauts, passed through the Bosphorus, it was nearly crushed by the huge floating islands of the Symplegades (see Apollonius Rhodius, *Argonautica*, ii. 552–611).   1019 **larboard**] Port, or left side (as he sailed through the Straits of Messina, between Italy and Sicily). 1020 **Charybdis**] The whirlpool on the Italian side of the Straits, opposite Scylla, the 'other whirlpool' (see *Odyssey*, xii. 73–100, 234–59).

So he with difficulty and labour hard
Moved on, with difficulty and labour he;
But he once past, soon after when man fell,
Strange alteration! Sin and Death amain   1024
Following his track, such was the will of heaven,
Paved after him a broad and beaten way
Over the dark abyss, whose boiling gulf
Tamely endured a bridge of wondrous length
From hell continued reaching the utmost orb
Of this frail world; by which the spirits perverse   *1030*
With easy intercourse pass to and fro
To tempt or punish mortals, except whom
God and good angels guard by special grace.
But now at last the sacred influence
Of light appears, and from the walls of heaven
Shoots far into the bosom of dim night
A glimmering dawn; here nature first begins
Her farthest verge, and Chaos to retire
As from her outmost works a broken foe
With tumult less and with less hostile din,   *1040*
That Satan with less toil, and now with ease
Wafts on the calmer wave by dubious light
And like a weather-beaten vessel holds   1043
Gladly the port, though shrouds and tackle torn;   1044
Or in the emptier waste, resembling air,
Weighs his spread wings, at leisure to behold
Far off the empyreal heaven, extended wide
In circuit, undetermined square or round,   1048
With opal towers and battlements adorned
Of living sapphire, once his native seat;   1050
And fast by hanging in a golden chain   1051
This pendent world, in bigness as a star   1052
Of smallest magnitude close by the moon.
Thither full fraught with mischievous revenge,
Accursed, and in a cursèd hour he hies.

1024 **amain**] At full speed.   1043 **holds**] Approaches.   1044 **shrouds**]
Sails.   1048 **undetermined ... round**] i.e. Satan cannot make out its shape.
1050 **Of**] With.   **living**] 'Native, in its natural condition' (*OED*).   1051 **fast by**]
Beside it.   1052 **This pendent world**] Not the earth, but the whole created
universe.

BOOK III

The Argument

God sitting on his throne sees Satan flying towards this world, then
newly created; shows him to the Son who sat at his right hand;
foretells the success of Satan in perverting mankind; clears his own
justice and wisdom from all imputation, having created man free
and able enough to have withstood his tempter; yet declares his
purpose of grace towards him, in regard he fell not of his own
malice, as did Satan, but by him seduced. The Son of God renders
praises to his father for the manifestation of his gracious purpose
towards man; but God again declares, that grace cannot be extended
toward man without the satisfaction of divine justice; man hath
offended the majesty of God by aspiring to Godhead, and therefore
with all his progeny devoted to death must die, unless someone
can be found sufficient to answer for his offence, and undergo his
punishment. The Son of God freely offers himself a ransom for
man: the Father accepts him, ordains his incarnation, pronounces
his exaltation above all names in heaven and earth; commands all
the angels to adore him; they obey, and hymning to their harps in
full choir, celebrate the Father and the Son. Meanwhile Satan
alights upon the bare convex of this world's outermost orb; where
wandering he first finds a place since called the Limbo of Vanity;
what persons and things fly up thither; thence comes to the gate of
heaven, described ascending by stairs, and the waters above the
firmament that flow about it: his passage thence to the orb of the
sun; he finds there Uriel the regent of that orb, but first changes
himself into the shape of a meaner angel; and pretending a zealous
desire to behold the new creation and man whom God had placed
here, inquires of him the place of his habitation, and is directed;
alights first on Mount Niphates.

> HAIL holy light, offspring of heaven first-born,
> Or of the eternal co-eternal beam
> May I express thee unblamed? since God is light, 3
> And never but in unapproachèd light
> Dwelt from eternity, dwelt then in thee,
> Bright effluence of bright essence increate. 6

2–3 **Or . . . unblamed?**] Or may I, without incurring blame, call you equally eternal
with God? **express**] Describe. **since God is light**] Quoting the First Epistle of
John 1: 5. 6 **effluence**] Radiance. **increate**] Never created.

Or hear'st thou rather pure ethereal stream,   7
Whose fountain who shall tell? before the sun,   8
Before the heavens thou wert, and at the voice
Of God, as with a mantle didst invest   10
The rising world of waters dark and deep,
Won from the void and formless infinite.
Thee I revisit now with bolder wing,
Escaped the Stygian pool, though long detained
In that obscure sojourn, while in my flight
Through utter and through middle darkness borne
With other notes than to the Orphean lyre
I sung of Chaos and eternal Night,   18
Taught by the heavenly Muse to venture down   19
The dark descent, and up to reascend,
Though hard and rare: thee I revisit safe,
And feel thy sovereign vital lamp; but thou
Revisit'st not these eyes, that roll in vain   23
To find thy piercing ray, and find no dawn;
So thick a drop serene hath quenched their orbs,
Or dim suffusion veiled. Yet not the more   26
Cease I to wander where the muses haunt
Clear spring, or shady grove, or sunny hill,
Smit with the love of sacred song; but chief
Thee Sion and the flowery brooks beneath   30
That wash thy hallowed feet, and warbling flow,
Nightly I visit: nor sometimes forget
Those other two equalled with me in fate,
So were I equalled with them in renown,   34
Blind Thamyris, and blind Maeonides,   35

---

7 **hear'st thou rather**] Would you rather be called.   8 **fountain**] Source.
10 **invest**] Envelop.   17–18 **Orphean . . . Night**] The poet Orpheus went to the
underworld and succeeded in recovering his dead wife Eurydice. He was the legendary
founder of the Orphic mystical tradition and a *Hymn to Night* was ascribed to
him.   19 **the heavenly Muse**] Urania, muse of astronomy (see i. 6, and vii. 1).
23 **Revisit'st not these eyes**] Milton had been totally blind since 1652.
25–6 **drop serene . . . suffusion**] Medical terms for Milton's blindness: the *gutta
serena*, in which the eye appears normal, and the cataract, which covers it with an
opaque film.   30 **Sion**] The sacred mountain, source of Hebrew poetry (as opposed
to the Greek spring Helicon and Mount Parnassus).   34 **So were I**] If I
were.   35 **Thamyris**] Legendary bard mentioned by Homer (*Iliad*, ii. 594).
Maeonides] Homer, said to have been born in Maeonia (or Lydia) in Asia Minor.

And Tiresias and Phineus prophets old.   36
Then feed on thoughts, that voluntary move   37
Harmonious numbers; as the wakeful bird   38
Sings darkling, and in shadiest covert hid   39
Tunes her nocturnal note. Thus with the year
Seasons return, but not to me returns
Day, or the sweet approach of even or morn,
Or sight of vernal bloom, or summer's rose,
Or flocks, or herds, or human face divine;
But cloud instead, and ever-during dark
Surrounds me, from the cheerful ways of men
Cut off, and for the book of knowledge fair
Presented with a universal blank
Of nature's works to me expunged and razed,
And wisdom at one entrance quite shut out.   50
So much the rather thou celestial light
Shine inward, and the mind through all her powers
Irradiate, there plant eyes, all mist from thence
Purge and disperse, that I may see and tell
Of things invisible to mortal sight.
    Now had the almighty Father from above,
From the pure empyrean where he sits
High throned above all height, bent down his eye,
His own works and their works at once to view:
About him all the sanctities of heaven   60
Stood thick as stars, and from his sight received   61
Beatitude past utterance; on his right
The radiant image of his glory sat,
His only son; on earth he first beheld
Our two first parents, yet the only two
Of mankind, in the happy garden placed,
Reaping immortal fruits of joy and love,
Uninterrupted joy, unrivalled love
In blissful solitude; he then surveyed
Hell and the gulf between, and Satan there   70

---

36 **Tiresias**] The blind prophet in the Oedipus story. **Phineus**] Blind Thracian
prophet-king.   37 **voluntary**] Freely; of their own volition.   38 **numbers**]
Poetic units, hence verses. **wakeful bird**] The nightingale.   39 **darkling**] In the
dark.   60 **sanctities**] Sacred creatures, the angels.   61 **his sight**] Both from his
eyes, and from seeing him.

Coasting the wall of heaven on this side night
In the dun air sublime, and ready now   72
To stoop with wearied wings, and willing feet   73
On the bare outside of this world, that seemed   /   74
Firm land embosomed without firmament,   75
Uncertain which, in ocean or in air.   76
Him God beholding from his prospect high,
Wherein past, present, future he beholds,
Thus to his only son foreseeing spake.
    Only begotten Son, seest thou what rage
Transports our adversary, whom no bounds
Prescribed, no bars of hell, nor all the chains
Heaped on him there, nor yet the main abyss
Wide interrupt can hold; so bent he seems   84
On desperate revenge, that shall redound
Upon his own rebellious head. And now
Through all restraint broke loose he wings his way
Not far off heaven, in the precincts of light,
Directly towards the new created world,
And man there placed, with purpose to assay
If him by force he can destroy, or worse,
By some false guile pervert; and shall pervert
For man will hearken to his glozing lies,   93
And easily transgress the sole command,
Sole pledge of his obedience: so will fall,
He and his faithless progeny: whose fault?
Whose but his own? ingrate, he had of me   ⚹
All he could have; I made him just and right,
Sufficient to have stood, though free to fall.
Such I created all the ethereal powers   100
And spirits, both them who stood and them who failed;
Freely they stood who stood, and fell who fell.
Not free, what proof could they have given sincere
Of true allegiance, constant faith or love,
Where only what they needs must do, appeared,

72 **sublime**] Aloft.   73 **stoop**] Descend.   74 **outside of this world**] Outer
shell of the universe.   75 **embosomed**] Enclosed. **firmament**] Sky.
76 **Uncertain ... air**] i.e. it is unclear to Satan whether the land is surrounded by
water or air.   84 **interrupt**] 'Forming an interval or breach' (*OED*).   93 **glozing**]
Flattering, cajoling.

Not what they would? what praise could they receive?   106
What pleasure I from such obedience paid,
When will and reason (reason also is choice)
Useless and vain, of freedom both despoiled,
Made passive both, had served necessity,   110
Not me. They therefore as to right belonged,
So were created, nor can justly accuse
Their maker, or their making, or their fate,
As if predestination overruled
Their will, disposed by absolute decree
Or high foreknowledge; they themselves decreed
Their own revolt, not I: if I foreknew,
Foreknowledge had no influence on their fault,
Which had no less proved certain unforeknown.
So without least impulse or shadow of fate,   120
Or aught by me immutably foreseen,
They trespass, authors to themselves in all
Both what they judge and what they choose; for so
I formed them free, and free they must remain,
Till they enthrall themselves: I else must change
Their nature, and revoke the high decree
Unchangeable, eternal, which ordained
Their freedom, they themselves ordained their fall.
The first sort by their own suggestion fell,   129
Self-tempted, self-depraved: man falls deceived
By the other first: man therefore shall find grace,
The other none: in mercy and justice both,
Through heaven and earth, so shall my glory excel,
But mercy first and last shall brightest shine.
    Thus while God spake, ambrosial fragrance filled
All heaven, and in the blessèd spirits elect   136
Sense of new joy ineffable diffused:
Beyond compare the Son of God was seen
Most glorious, in him all his father shone
Substantially expressed, and in his face   140
Divine compassion visibly appeared,

---

106 **would**] Wished to do.   120 **least impulse**] In any way being forced.
129 **first sort**] i.e. the fallen angels. **suggestion**] Temptation.   136 **spirits
elect**] The unfallen angels, who are therefore God's chosen.   140 **Substantially**]
In his substance; i.e. he partakes of the divine nature.

Love without end, and without measure grace,
Which uttering thus he to his father spake.

   O Father, gracious was that word which closed
Thy sovereign sentence, that man should find grace;
For which both heaven and earth shall high extol
Thy praises, with the innumerable sound
Of hymns and sacred songs, wherewith thy throne
Encompassed shall resound thee ever blessed.
For should man finally be lost, should man   *150*
Thy creature late so loved, thy youngest son
Fall circumvented thus by fraud, though joined
With his own folly? that be from thee far,
That far be from thee, Father, who art judge
Of all things made, and judgest only right.
Or shall the adversary thus obtain
His end, and frustrate thine, shall he fulfil
His malice, and thy goodness bring to naught,
Or proud return though to his heavier doom,
Yet with revenge accomplished and to hell   *160*
Draw after him the whole race of mankind,
By him corrupted? or wilt thou thyself
Abolish thy creation, and unmake,
For him, what for thy glory thou hast made?
So should thy goodness and thy greatness both
Be questioned and blasphemed without defence.

   To whom the great creator thus replied.
O Son, in whom my soul hath chief delight,
Son of my bosom, Son who art alone
My word, my wisdom, and effectual might,   *170*
All hast thou spoken as my thoughts are, all
As my eternal purpose hath decreed:
Man shall not quite be lost, but saved who will,
Yet not of will in him, but grace in me   *174*
Freely vouchsafed; once more I will renew
His lapsèd powers, though forfeit and enthralled   *176*
By sin to foul exorbitant desires;   *177*
Upheld by me, yet once more he shall stand

---

170 **effectual might**] My agent, through whom my power takes effect.   174 **of**]
Through.   176 **lapsèd**] Lit. 'fallen'.   177 **exorbitant**] 'Erring, faulty, trans-
gressing' (*OED*).

On even ground against his mortal foe   179
By me upheld, that he may know how frail
His fallen condition is, and to me owe
All his deliverance, and to none but me.
Some I have chosen of peculiar grace
Elect above the rest; so is my will:
The rest shall hear me call, and oft be warned
Their sinful state, and to appease betimes
The incensèd deity, while offered grace
Invites; for I will clear their senses dark,
What may suffice, and soften stony hearts
To pray, repent, and bring obedience due.   190
To prayer, repentance, and obedience due,
Though but endeavoured with sincere intent,
Mine ear shall not be slow, mine eye not shut.
And I will place within them as a guide
My umpire conscience, whom if they will hear,
Light after light well used they shall attain,
And to the end persisting, safe arrive.
This my long sufferance and my day of grace
They who neglect and scorn, shall never taste;
But hard be hardened, blind be blinded more,   200
That they may stumble on, and deeper fall;
And none but such from mercy I exclude.
But yet all is not done; man disobeying,
Disloyal breaks his fealty, and sins   204
Against the high supremacy of heaven,
Affecting godhead, and so losing all,   206
To expiate his treason hath naught left,
But to destruction sacred and devote,   208
He with his whole posterity must die,
Die he or justice must; unless for him
Some other able, and as willing, pay
The rigid satisfaction, death for death.
Say heavenly powers, where shall we find such love,
Which of ye will be mortal to redeem
Man's mortal crime, and just the unjust to save,

---

179 **mortal**] Deadly.   204 **fealty**] Obligation, fidelity: a feudal term.
206 **Affecting godhead**] Assuming divinity.   208 **sacred and devote**] Dedicated
and condemned.

Dwells in all heaven charity so dear?
    He asked, but all the heavenly choir stood mute,
And silence was in heaven: on man's behalf
Patron or intercessor none appeared,   219
Much less that durst upon his own head draw
The deadly forfeiture, and ransom set.
And now without redemption all mankind   222
Must have been lost, adjudged to death and hell
By doom severe, had not the Son of God,   224
In whom the fulness dwells of love divine,
His dearest mediation thus renewed.
    Father, thy word is past, man shall find grace;
And shall grace not find means, that finds her way,
The speediest of thy wingèd messengers,
To visit all thy creatures, and to all
Comes unprevented, unimplored, unsought,   231
Happy for man, so coming; he her aid
Can never seek, once dead in sins and lost;
Atonement for himself or offering meet,   234
Indebted and undone, hath none to bring:
Behold me then, me for him, life for life
I offer, on me let thine anger fall;
Account me man; I for his sake will leave
Thy bosom, and this glory next to thee
Freely put off, and for him lastly die   240
Well pleased, on me let Death wreak all his rage;
Under his gloomy power I shall not long
Lie vanquished; thou hast given me to possess
Life in myself forever, by thee I live,
Though now to Death I yield, and am his due
All that of me can die, yet that debt paid,
Thou wilt not leave me in the loathsome grave
His prey, nor suffer my unspotted soul   248
Forever with corruption there to dwell;
But I shall rise victorious, and subdue
My vanquisher, spoiled of his vaunted spoil;   251
Death his death's wound shall then receive, and stoop

---

219 **Patron**] Protector, advocate.   222 **redemption**] Lit. 'buying back'; compare *ransom*, l. 221.   224 **doom**] Sentence.   231 **unprevented**] Unanticipated. 234 **meet**] Suitable.   248 **unspotted**] Untainted.   251 **spoiled**] Despoiled.

Inglorious, of his mortal sting disarmed.
I through the ample air in triumph high
Shall lead hell captive maugre hell, and show   255
The powers of darkness bound. Thou at the sight
Pleased, out of heaven shalt look down and smile,
While by thee raised I ruin all my foes,
Death last, and with his carcass glut the grave:
Then with the multitude of my redeemed   260
Shall enter heaven long absent, and return,
Father, to see thy face, wherein no cloud
Of anger shall remain, but peace assured,
And reconcilement; wrath shall be no more
Thenceforth, but in thy presence joy entire.

His words here ended, but his meek aspect
Silent yet spake, and breathed immortal love
To mortal men, above which only shone
Filial obedience: as a sacrifice
Glad to be offered, he attends the will   270
Of his great father. Admiration seized
All heaven, what this might mean, and whither tend
Wondering; but soon the almighty thus replied:

O thou in heaven and earth the only peace
Found out for mankind under wrath, O thou
My sole complacence! well thou know'st how dear   276
To me are all my works, nor man the least
Though last created, that for him I spare
Thee from my bosom and right hand, to save,
By losing thee awhile, the whole race lost.
Thou therefore whom thou only canst redeem,
Their nature also to thy nature join;   282
And be thyself man among men on earth,
Made flesh, when time shall be, of virgin seed,
By wondrous birth: be thou in Adam's room   285
The head of all mankind, though Adam's son.
As in him perish all men, so in thee
As from a second root shall be restored,
As many as are restored, without thee none.

255 maugre] In spite of.   270 attends] Both awaits and serves.
276 complacence] Source of pleasure.   281–2 Thou ... join] The syntax is,
'therefore join to thy nature the nature of those whom only thou canst
redeem'.   285 room] Place.

His crime makes guilty all his sons, thy merit
Imputed shall absolve them who renounce   291
Their own both righteous and unrighteous deeds,
And live in thee transplanted, and from thee
Receive new life. So man, as is most just,   294
Shall satisfy for man, be judged and die,
And dying rise, and rising with him raise
His brethren, ransomed with his own dear life.
So heavenly love shall outdo hellish hate
Giving to death, and dying to redeem,   299
So dearly to redeem what hellish hate
So easily destroyed, and still destroys
In those who, when they may, accept not grace.
Nor shalt thou by descending to assume   303
Man's nature, lessen or degrade thine own.
Because thou hast, though throned in highest bliss
Equal to God, and equally enjoying
Godlike fruition, quitted all to save   307
A world from utter loss, and hast been found
By merit more than birthright Son of God,
Found worthiest to be so by being good,   310
Far more than great or high; because in thee
Love hath abounded more than glory abounds,
Therefore thy humiliation shall exalt
With thee thy manhood also to this throne;
Here shalt thou sit incarnate, here shalt reign
Both God and man, Son both of God and man,
Anointed universal king; all power
I give thee, reign for ever, and assume
Thy merits; under thee as head supreme   319
Thrones, princedoms, powers, dominions I reduce: 320
All knees to thee shall bow, of them that bide
In heaven, or earth, or under earth in hell,

---

291 **Imputed**] Assigned, transferred; technical theological language, alluding to the
doctrine of imputed righteousness, whereby Christ's virtue is transferred to Christians
through their faith.   290–4 **His ... life**] Paraphrased from Romans 5: 17–19.
299 **Giving**] Both yielding and giving (Christ) to.   303 **assume**] Take on.
307 **fruition**] 'Enjoyment ... the pleasure arising from possession' (*OED*), possibly
with a pun on *fruit* (cf. i. 1), though the words are etymologically unrelated.   318–19
assume / Thy merits] Take on the honours you merit.   320 **Thrones ...
dominions**] Angelic orders, with *princedoms* replacing its synonym *principalities*.

When thou attended gloriously from heaven
Shalt in the sky appear, and from thee send   324
The summoning archangels to proclaim
Thy dread tribunal: forthwith from all winds   326
The living, and forthwith the cited dead   327
Of all past ages to the general doom   328
Shall hasten, such a peal shall rouse their sleep.
Then all thy saints assembled, thou shalt judge
Bad men and angels, they arraigned shall sink
Beneath thy sentence; hell her numbers full,
Thenceforth shall be forever shut. Meanwhile
The world shall burn, and from her ashes spring
New heaven and earth, wherein the just shall dwell,
And after all their tribulations long
See golden days, fruitful of golden deeds,
With joy and love triumphing, and fair truth.
Then thou thy regal sceptre shalt lay by,
For regal sceptre then no more shall need,   340
God shall be all in all. But all ye gods,   341
Adore him, who to compass all this dies,
Adore the Son, and honour him as me.
    No sooner had the almighty ceased, but all
The multitude of angels with a shout
Loud as from numbers without number, sweet
As from blest voices, uttering joy, heaven rung
With jubilee, and loud hosannas filled   348
The eternal regions: lowly reverent
Towards either throne they bow, and to the ground
With solemn adoration down they cast
Their crowns inwove with amaranth and gold,   352
Immortal amaranth, a flower which once
In Paradise, fast by the tree of life   354
Began to bloom, but soon for man's offence
To heaven removed where first it grew, there grows,

324 ff. The account of judgment and paradise liberally paraphrases Revelation.   326 **from all winds**] i.e. from the four points of the compass.   327 **cited**] Summoned.   328 **doom**] Judgment.   340 **need**] Be needed.   341 **gods**] Angels.   348 **jubilee**] Jubilation.   352 **amaranth**] Lit. 'unwithering', a legendary deathless purple flower; subsequently applied to a large genus of purple-flowered plants and the colour deep purple.   354 **fast by**] Right next to.

And flowers aloft shading the fount of life,
And where the river of bliss through midst of heaven
Rolls o'er Elysian flowers her amber stream;   359
With these that never fade the spirits elect
Bind their resplendent locks inwreathed with beams,
Now in loose garlands thick thrown off, the bright
Pavement that like a sea of jasper shone
Impurpled with celestial roses smiled.
Then crowned again their golden harps they took,
Harps ever tuned, that glittering by their side
Like quivers hung, and with preamble sweet
Of charming symphony they introduce
Their sacred song, and waken raptures high;
No voice exempt, no voice but well could join   370
Melodious part, such concord is in heaven.
      Thee Father first they sung omnipotent,
Immutable, immortal, infinite,
Eternal king; thee author of all being,
Fountain of light, thyself invisible
Amidst the glorious brightness where thou sit'st
Throned inaccessible, but when thou shad'st   377
The full blaze of thy beams, and through a cloud
Drawn round about thee like a radiant shrine,
Dark with excessive bright thy skirts appear,   380
Yet dazzle heaven, that brightest seraphim   381
Approach not, but with both wings veil their eyes.
Thee next they sang of all creation first,
Begotten Son, divine similitude,
In whose conspicuous countenance, without cloud   385
Made visible, the almighty Father shines,
Whom else no creature can behold; on thee
Impressed the effulgence of his glory abides,
Transfused on thee his ample spirit rests.
He heaven of heavens and all the powers therein
By thee created, and by thee threw down

---

359 **Elysian . . . stream**] The river that runs through the Elysian Fields, paradise of
the virtuous and brave (see *Aeneid*, vi. 656–9). **amber**] Connoting both clarity and
beauty.   377 **but**] Except.   380 **bright**] Brightness.   **thy skirts appear**] i.e.
then your robes are visible.   381 **that**] So that.   385 **conspicuous**] Clearly
visible.

The aspiring dominations: thou that day   *392*
Thy father's dreadful thunder didst not spare,
Nor stop thy flaming chariot wheels, that shook
Heaven's everlasting frame, while o'er the necks
Thou drov'st of warring angels disarrayed.
Back from pursuit thy powers with loud acclaim   *397*
Thee only extolled, Son of thy father's might,
To execute fierce vengeance on his foes,
Not so on man; him through their malice fallen,   *400*
Father of mercy and grace, thou didst not doom
So strictly, but much more to pity incline:
No sooner did thy dear and only son
Perceive thee purposed not to doom frail man
So strictly, but much more to pity inclined,
He to appease thy wrath, and end the strife
Of mercy and justice in thy face discerned,
Regardless of the bliss wherein he sat
Second to thee, offered himself to die
For man's offence. O unexampled love,   *410*
Love nowhere to be found less than divine!
Hail, Son of God, saviour of men, thy name
Shall be the copious matter of my song
Henceforth, and never shall my harp thy praise
Forget, nor from thy father's praise disjoin.
    Thus they in heaven, above the starry sphere,
Their happy hours in joy and hymning spent.
Meanwhile upon the firm opacous globe   *418*
Of this round world, whose first convex divides   *419*
The luminous inferior orbs, enclosed   *420*
From Chaos and the inroad of darkness old,
Satan alighted walks: a globe far off
It seemed, now seems a boundless continent
Dark, waste, and wild, under the frown of night
Starless exposed, and ever-threatening storms
Of Chaos blustering round, inclement sky;
Save on that side which from the wall of heaven

392 **aspiring dominations**] Rebel angels.   397 **thy powers**] The loyal angels.
418 **opacous**] Opaque.   419 **first convex**] The outer shell of the created uni-
verse, 'the bare outside of this world' where Satan was about to land at l. 72.
420 **luminous inferior orbs**] The inner spheres of the stars, planets, sun, and moon.

Though distant far some small reflection gains
Of glimmering air less vexed with tempest loud:
Here walked the fiend at large in spacious field.
As when a vulture on Imaus bred,   431
Whose snowy ridge the roving Tartar bounds,
Dislodging from a region scarce of prey
To gorge the flesh of lambs or yeanling kids   434
On hills where flocks are fed, flies toward the springs
Of Ganges or Hydaspes, Indian streams;   436
But in his way lights on the barren plains
Of Sericana, where Chineses drive   438
With sails and wind their cany wagons light:
So on this windy sea of land, the fiend
Walked up and down alone bent on his prey,
Alone, for other creature in this place
Living or lifeless to be found was none,
None yet, but store hereafter from the earth   444
Up hither like aerial vapours flew
Of all things transitory and vain, when sin
With vanity had filled the works of men:
Both all things vain, and all who in vain things
Built their fond hopes of glory or lasting fame,   449
Or happiness in this or the other life;
All who have their reward on earth, the fruits
Of painful superstition and blind zeal,   452
Nought seeking but the praise of men, here find
Fit retribution, empty as their deeds;
All the unaccomplished works of nature's hand,
Abortive, monstrous, or unkindly mixed,   456
Dissolved on earth, fleet hither, and in vain,   457
Till final dissolution, wander here,
Not in the neighbouring moon, as some have dreamed;   459
Those argent fields more likely habitants,   460

431 **Imaus**] The Himalayas.   434 **yeanling**] Newborn.   436 **Hydaspes**]
Now the Jhelum river, a tributary of the Indus.   438 **Sericana**] China; the 'barren
plains' (l. 437) are the Gobi Desert.   444 **store**] Many.   449 **fond**] Foolish.
452 **painful**] Including the sense of laborious.   456 **unkindly**] Unnaturally.
457 **fleet**] Fly.   459 **in . . . dreamed**] Giordano Bruno, Jerome Cardan, and Henry
More had seriously postulated lunar inhabitants, and the idea was satirized by Ariosto,
who located a fool's paradise in the moon in *Orlando Furioso* (1532), and by Ben Jonson's
masque *News from the New World Discovered in the Moon* (1620).   460 **argent**]
Silver.

Translated saints, or middle spirits hold   461
Betwixt the angelical and human kind:
Hither of ill-joined sons and daughters born
First from the ancient world those Giants came   464
With many a vain exploit, though then renowned:
The builders next of Babel on the plain
Of Sennaar, and still with vain design   467
New Babels, had they wherewithal, would build:
Others came single; he who to be deemed
A god, leaped fondly into Aetna flames,   470
Empedocles, and he who to enjoy   471
Plato's Elysium, leaped into the sea,
Cleombrotus, and many more too long,   473
Embryos and idiots, eremites and friars   474
White, black and grey, with all their trumpery.   475
Here pilgrims roam, that strayed so far to seek
In Golgotha him dead, who lives in heaven;   477
And they who to be sure of Paradise
Dying put on the weeds of Dominic,   479
Or in Franciscan think to pass disguised;
They pass the planets seven, and pass the fixed,   481
And that crystalline sphere whose balance weighs
The trepidation talked, and that first moved;   483
And now Saint Peter at heaven's wicket seems   484
To wait them with his keys, and now at foot
Of heaven's ascent they lift their feet, when lo
A violent cross wind from either coast
Blows them transverse ten thousand leagues awry

461 **Translated saints**] Such Old Testament heroes and prophets as Enoch and Elijah, who were transported to heaven.   462–4 **Betwixt . . . came**] Genesis 6: 4 describes how 'the sons of God came in unto the daughters of men', who bore their children, a race of giants. The story is told in more detail in xi. 573–627. 467 **Sennaar**] Shinar; the story is in Genesis 10: 10.   470 **fondly**] Foolishly. 471 **Empedocles**] Sicilian pre-Socratic philosopher (fifth century BC). 473 **Cleombrotus**] A youth said to have drowned himself after reading the *Phaedo*. 474 **eremites**] Hermit friars.   475 **White, black and grey**] Carmelite, Dominican, and Franciscan, from the colour of their habits.   477 **Golgotha**] Site of Christ's crucifixion and burial.   479 **weeds**] Garments.   481 **the fixed**] The sphere of the fixed stars.   482–3 **that crystalline . . . talked**] The crystalline sphere contains the constellation Libra, 'the balance'; this is said to measure the amount of 'trepidation', i.e. irregular motion in the Ptolemaic system.   **talked**] So-called. **that first moved**] The *primum mobile*, the tenth and outermost sphere. 484 **wicket**] Gate; the diminutive term is ironic.

Into the devious air; then might ye see   489
Cowls, hoods and habits with their wearers tossed.
And fluttered into rags, then relics, beads,   491
Indulgences, dispenses, pardons, bulls,   492
The sport of winds: all these upwhirled aloft
Fly o'er the backside of the world far off
Into a limbo large and broad, since called   495
The Paradise of Fools, to few unknown
Long after, now unpeopled, and untrod;
All this dark globe the fiend found as he passed,
And long he wandered, till at last a gleam
Of dawning light turned thitherward in haste   500
His travelled steps; far distant he descries
Ascending by degrees magnificent
Up to the wall of heaven a structure high,
At top whereof, but far more rich appeared
The work as of a kingly palace gate
With frontispiece of diamond and gold   506
Embellished, thick with sparkling orient gems   507
The portal shone, inimitable on earth
By model, or by shading pencil drawn.
The stairs were such as whereon Jacob saw   510
Angels ascending and descending, bands
Of guardians bright, when he from Esau fled
To Padan-Aram in the field of Luz,   513
Dreaming by night under the open sky,
And waking cried, *This is the gate of heaven.*   515
Each stair mysteriously was meant, nor stood   516
There always, but drawn up to heaven sometimes
Viewless, and underneath a bright sea flowed

---

489 **devious**] Both distant and erratic.   491 **beads**] Rosaries.   492 **dispenses**] Dispensations.   **bulls**] Papal decrees.   495 **limbo**] Lit. border region.
506 **frontispiece**] Façade.   507 **orient**] Lustrous, brilliant.   513 **Padan-Aram**] In Syria, where Jacob was fleeing to the protection of his uncle Laban in order to escape Esau's rage.   **Luz**] in the Judaean hills; after the vision Jacob renamed the place Bethel.   510–15 **The stairs . . . heaven**] After Jacob had deceived his father Isaac into giving him the blessing intended for his older brother Esau, and supplanted him as the heir, he had a dream of angels upon a ladder reaching to heaven, and a vision of God promising to make him prosper (Genesis 26–8).   516 **stair**] Step.   **mysteriously**] Symbolically; allegorical interpretations of Jacob's ladder commonly related it to the golden chain of Jupiter (see ii. 1005 and 1051), linking heaven to earth and establishing and justifying the natural and social hierarchies.

Of jasper, or of liquid pearl, whereon
Who after came from earth, sailing arrived,
Wafted by angels, or flew o'er the lake
Rapt in a chariot drawn by fiery steeds.   522
The stairs were then let down, whether to dare
The fiend by easy ascent, or aggravate
His sad exclusion from the doors of bliss.
Direct against which opened from beneath,
Just o'er the blissful seat of Paradise,
A passage down to the earth, a passage wide,
Wider by far than that of after-times
Over Mount Sion, and, though that were large,   530
Over the Promised Land to God so dear,
By which, to visit oft those happy tribes,
On high behests his angels to and fro
Passed frequent, and his eye with choice regard   534
From Paneas the fount of Jordan's flood   535
To Beersaba, where the Holy Land   536
Borders on Egypt and the Arabian shore;
So wide the opening seemed, where bounds were set
To darkness, such as bound the ocean wave.
Satan from hence now on the lower stair   540
That scaled by steps of gold to heaven gate
Looks down with wonder at the sudden view
Of all this world at once. As when a scout
Through dark and desert ways with peril gone
All night; at last by break of cheerful dawn
Obtains the brow of some high-climbing hill,   546
Which to his eye discovers unaware   547
The goodly prospect of some foreign land
First-seen, or some renowned metropolis
With glistering spires and pinnacles adorned,
Which now the rising sun gilds with his beams.
Such wonder seized, though after heaven seen,   552
The spirit malign, but much more envy seized

---

522 **Rapt**] Transported.   534 **choice**] Careful.   535 **Paneas**] Greek name for
the city of Dan, at the source of the Jordan, and the northern boundary
of Canaan.   536 **Beersaba**] Beersheba, the southern boundary.   546 **Obtains**]
Reaches.   547 **discovers**] Reveals.   552 **though after heaven seen**] Though
he had seen heaven.

At sight of all this world beheld so fair.
Round he surveys, and well might, where he stood
So high above the circling canopy
Of night's extended shade; from eastern point
Of Libra to the fleecy star that bears   558
Andromeda far off Atlantic seas   559
Beyond the horizon; then from pole to pole
He views in breadth, and without longer pause
Down right into the world's first region throws   562
His flight precipitant, and winds with ease   563
Through the pure marble air his oblique way   564
Amongst innumerable stars, that shone
Stars distant, but nigh hand seemed other worlds,   566
Or other worlds they seemed, or happy isles,
Like those Hesperian gardens famed of old,   568
Fortunate fields, and groves and flowery vales,
Thrice happy isles, but who dwelt happy there
He stayed not to inquire: above them all
The golden sun in splendour likest heaven
Allured his eye: thither his course he bends
Through the calm firmament; but up or down
By centre, or eccentric, hard to tell,   575
Or longitude, where the great luminary   576
Aloof the vulgar constellations thick,   577
That from his lordly eye keep distance due,
Dispenses light from far; they as they move
Their starry dance in numbers that compute   580
Days, months, and years, towards his all-cheering lamp
Turn swift their various motions, or are turned
By his magnetic beam, that gently warms
The universe, and to each inward part
With gentle penetration, though unseen,

558 Libra . . . star] The constellations of the scales and Aries.   559 Andromeda]
The constellation next to Aries.   562 world's first region] Uppermost region of
the atmosphere.   563 precipitant] Precipitous.   564 marble] The relevant
connotations are cold, smooth, shining.   566 nigh hand] Nearby.   568 Hespe-
rian gardens] The earthly paradise, where the daughters of Hesperus kept the golden
apples of immortality (see Ovid, *Metamorphoses*, iv. 637–8).   575 By centre, or
eccentric] i.e. depending on whether the earth is at the centre of the universe or not:
Milton declines to choose between the Ptolemaic and Copernican systems.   576 lon-
gitude] How far he flew horizontally (as opposed to 'up or down', l. 574).
577 Aloof] Standing apart from.   580 numbers] (Musical) measures.

Shoots invisible virtue even to the deep;   586
So wondrously was set his station bright.
There lands the fiend, a spot like which perhaps
Astronomer in the sun's lucent orb
Through his glazed optic tube yet never saw.   590
The place he found beyond expression bright,
Compared with aught on earth, metal or stone;
Not all parts like, but all alike informed
With radiant light, as glowing iron with fire;
If metal, part seemed gold, part silver clear;   595
If stone, carbuncle most or chrysolite,   596
Ruby or topaz, to the twelve that shone   597
In Aaron's breastplate, and a stone besides   598
Imagined rather oft than elsewhere seen,
That stone, or like to that which here below
Philosophers in vain so long have sought,   601
In vain, though by their powerful art they bind
Volatile Hermes, and call up unbound   603
In various shapes old Proteus from the sea,   604
Drained through a limbeck to his native form.   605
What wonder then if fields and regions here
Breathe forth elixir pure, and rivers run   607
Potable gold, when with one virtuous touch   608
The arch-chemic sun so far from us remote   609
Produces with terrestrial humour mixed   610
Here in the dark so many precious things
Of colour glorious and effect so rare?   612

586 **virtue**] Force.   588–90 **a spot . . . saw**] Galileo had reported his observation
of sunspots in 1613.   595 **clear**] Bright.   596 **carbuncle**] Used for a variety of
red stones, including the garnet and ruby, and also 'applied to a mythical gem said to emit
light in the dark' (*OED*).   **chrysolite**] Used for various green stones, including tourma-
line, zircon, and topaz; the two terms may be in apposition with *Ruby or topaz*, l. 597.
597 **to**] i.e. and so on, to.   598 **Aaron's breastplate**] The ceremonial raiment of
Moses' brother, the high priest. Each stone was inscribed with the name of one of the
twelve tribes (Exodus 28: 17–24).   600–1 **that which . . . sought**] The Philo-
sopher's Stone, which was said by alchemists ('philosophers') to be able to change base
metal into gold.   603 **Hermes**] Or mercury, the crucial element in alchemical
processes.   604 **Proteus**] Sea-god capable of infinite changes of shape.
605 **limbeck**] Chemical retort.   607 **elixir pure**] The final product of the
alchemical process, which would effect the transformation into gold.   608 **Potable**]
Liquid. **virtuous**] Powerful.   609 **arch-chemic**] Archetypical alchemist.
610 **terrestrial humour**] Earthly moisture.   610–12 **Produces . . . glorious**] The
theory was that precious stones are created by the action of the sun's rays penetrating
underground. See vi. 479–81.

Here matter new to gaze the devil met
Undazzled, far and wide his eye commands,
For sight no obstacle found here, nor shade,
But all sunshine, as when his beams at noon
Culminate from the equator, as they now   617
Shot upward still direct, whence no way round
Shadow from body opaque can fall, and the air,
Nowhere so clear, sharpened his visual ray
To objects distant far, whereby he soon
Saw within ken a glorious angel stand,   622
The same whom John saw also in the sun: 623
His back was turned, but not his brightness hid;
Of beaming sunny rays, a golden tiar   625
Circled his head, nor less his locks behind
Illustrious on his shoulders fledge with wings   627
Lay waving round; on some great charge employed
He seemed, or fixed in cogitation deep.
Glad was the spirit impure; as now in hope
To find who might direct his wandering flight
To Paradise the happy seat of man,
His journey's end and our beginning woe.
But first he casts to change his proper shape,   634
Which else might work him danger or delay:
And now a stripling cherub he appears,
Not of the prime, yet such as in his face   637
Youth smiled celestial, and to every limb
Suitable grace diffused, so well he feigned;
Under a coronet his flowing hair
In curls on either cheek played, wings he wore
Of many a coloured plume sprinkled with gold,
His habit fit for speed succinct, and held   643
Before his decent steps a silver wand.   644
He drew not nigh unheard, the angel bright,

617 **Culminate from the equator**] Shine directly overhead, from the celestial
equator (and hence produce no shadows to interfere with Satan's view).   622 **ken**]
Range of vision.   623 **The same whom John saw**] See Revelation 19: 17.
625 **tiar**] Crown.   627 **Illustrious**] Lustrous. **fledge**] Feathered.   634 **casts**]
Both casts about and casts off his present shape.   637 **Not of the prime**] (1) Not
yet mature; (2) not one of the important angels.   643 **succinct**] Girded up, not
voluminous.   644 **decent**] Both graceful and decorous, modest.

Ere he drew nigh, his radiant visage turned,
Admonished by his ear, and straight was known
The archangel Uriel, one of the seven   648
Who in God's presence, nearest to his throne
Stand ready at command, and are his eyes   650
That run through all the heavens, or down to the earth
Bear his swift errands over moist and dry,
O'er sea and land: him Satan thus accosts.

    Uriel, for thou of those seven spirits that stand
In sight of God's high throne, gloriously bright,
The first art wont his great authentic will   656
Interpreter through highest heaven to bring,
Where all his sons thy embassy attend;
And here art likeliest by supreme decree
Like honour to obtain, and as his eye   660
To visit oft this new creation round;
Unspeakable desire to see, and know
All these his wondrous works, but chiefly man,
His chief delight and favour, him for whom
All these his works so wondrous he ordained,
Hath brought me from the choirs of cherubim
Alone thus wandering. Brightest seraph tell
In which of all these shining orbs hath man
His fixèd seat, or fixèd seat hath none,
But all these shining orbs his choice to dwell;   670
That I may find him, and with secret gaze,
Or open admiration him behold
On whom the great creator hath bestowed
Worlds, and on whom hath all these graces poured;
That both in him and all things, as is meet,
The universal maker we may praise;
Who justly hath driven out his rebel foes
To deepest hell, and to repair that loss
Created this new happy race of men
To serve him better: wise are all his ways.   680

    So spake the false dissembler unperceived;
For neither man nor angel can discern
Hypocrisy, the only evil that walks

---

648 **Uriel**] Lit. 'light of God', a cabbalistic name, not in the Bible.
656 **authentic**] Authoritative.

Invisible, except to God alone,
By his permissive will, through heaven and earth:
And oft though wisdom wake, suspicion sleeps
At wisdom's gate, and to simplicity
Resigns her charge, while goodness thinks no ill
Where no ill seems: which now for once beguiled
Uriel, though regent of the sun, and held   690
The sharpest sighted spirit of all in heaven;
Who to the fraudulent imposter foul
In his uprightedness answer thus returned.
Fair angel, thy desire which tends to know   694
The works of God, thereby to glorify
The great work-master, leads to no excess
That reaches blame, but rather merits praise
The more it seems excess, that led thee hither
From thy empyreal mansion thus alone,   699
To witness with thine eyes what some perhaps
Contented with report hear only in heaven:
For wonderful indeed are all his works,
Pleasant to know, and worthiest to be all
Had in remembrance always with delight;
But what created mind can comprehend
Their number, or the wisdom infinite
That brought them forth, but hid their causes deep.
I saw when at his word the formless mass,
This world's material mould, came to a heap:
Confusion heard his voice, and wild uproar   710
Stood ruled, stood vast infinitude confined;
Till at his second bidding darkness fled,   712
Light shone, and order from disorder sprung:
Swift to their several quarters hasted then
The cumbrous elements, earth, flood, air, fire,
And this ethereal quintessence of heaven
Flew upward, spirited with various forms,   717
That rolled orbicular, and turned to stars   718
Numberless, as thou seest, and how they move;
Each had his place appointed, each his course,

---

690 held] Considered.   694 tends] Intends.   699 mansion] Dwelling.
712 his second bidding] God's second command was 'Let there be light.'
717 spirited] Inanimate.   718 orbicular] In a circle.

The rest in circuit walls this universe.
Look downward on that globe whose hither side
With light from hence, though but reflected, shines;
That place is earth the seat of man, that light
His day, which else as the other hemisphere
Night would invade, but there the neighbouring moon
(So call that opposite fair star) her aid
Timely interposes, and her monthly round
Still ending, still renewing, through mid heaven;   729
With borrowed light her countenance triform   730
Hence fills and empties to enlighten the earth,   731
And in her pale dominion checks the night.   732
That spot to which I point is Paradise,
Adam's abode, those lofty shades his bower.
Thy way thou canst not miss, me mine requires.
    Thus said, he turned, and Satan bowing low,
As to superior spirits is wont in heaven,
Where honour due and reverence none neglects,
Took leave, and toward the coast of earth beneath,
Down from the ecliptic, sped with hoped success,   740
Throws his steep flight in many an airy wheel,
Nor stayed, till on Niphates' top he lights.   742

---

729 **still ... still**] Always ... always.   730 **countenance triform**] The
moon has three faces, or phases, the new crescent, the full moon, and the waning
crescent. Its three forms were analogously personified by three goddesses, Diana,
Lucina (or Luna), and Hecate.   731 **Hence**] From here (i.e. the sun).
732 **checks**] Restrains.   740 **ecliptic**] The path of the sun.   742 **Niphates**] A
mountain in Armenia, near the Assyrian border.

BOOK IV

The Argument

Satan now in prospect of Eden, and nigh the place where he must now attempt the bold enterprise which he undertook alone against God and man, falls into many doubts with himself, and many passions, fear, envy, and despair; but at length confirms himself in evil, journeys on to Paradise, whose outward prospect and situation is described, overleaps the bounds, sits in the shape of a cormorant on the tree of life, as highest in the garden to look about him. The garden described; Satan's first sight of Adam and Eve; his wonder at their excellent form and happy state, but with resolution to work their fall; overhears their discourse, thence gathers that the tree of knowledge was forbidden them to eat of, under penalty of death; and thereon intends to found his temptation, by seducing them to transgress: then leaves them awhile, to know further of their state by some other means. Meanwhile Uriel descending on a sunbeam warns Gabriel, who had in charge the gate of Paradise, that some evil spirit had escaped the deep, and passed at noon by his sphere in the shape of a good angel down to Paradise, discovered after by his furious gestures in the mount. Gabriel promises to find him ere morning. Night coming on, Adam and Eve discourse of going to their rest: their bower described; their evening worship. Gabriel drawing forth his bands of night-watch to walk the round of Paradise, appoints two strong angels to Adam's bower, lest the evil spirit should be there doing some harm to Adam or Eve sleeping; there they find him at the ear of Eve, tempting her in a dream, and bring him, though unwilling, to Gabriel; by whom questioned, he scornfully answers, prepares resistance, but hindered by a sign from heaven, flies out of Paradise.

O FOR that warning voice, which he who saw
The Apocalypse heard cry in heaven aloud,
Then when the dragon, put to second rout,   3
Came furious down to be revenged on men,
Woe to the inhabitants on earth! that now,
While time was, our first-parents had been warned   6
The coming of their secret foe, and scaped,

1–3 **which . . . rout**] St John's vision of a new battle in heaven culminating in another defeat of the dragon Satan is in Revelation 12: 3–12.   6 **while time was**] While there was still time.

Haply so scaped his mortal snare; for now
Satan, now first inflamed with rage, came down,
The tempter ere the accuser of mankind,
To wreak on innocent frail man his loss   11
Of that first battle, and his flight to hell:
Yet not rejoicing in his speed, though bold,
Far off and fearless, nor with cause to boast,
Begins his dire attempt, which nigh the birth
Now rolling, boils in his tumultuous breast,
And like a devilish engine back recoils   17
Upon himself; horror and doubt distract
His troubled thoughts, and from the bottom stir
The hell within him, for within him hell
He brings, and round about him, nor from hell
One step no more than from himself can fly
By change of place: now conscience wakes despair   23
That slumbered, wakes the bitter memory
Of what he was, what is, and what must be
Worse; of worse deeds worse sufferings must ensue.
Sometimes towards Eden which now in his view
Lay pleasant, his grieved look he fixes sad,   28
Sometimes towards heaven and the full-blazing sun,
Which now sat high in his meridian tower: 30
Then much revolving, thus in sighs began.   31

   O thou that with surpassing glory crowned,
Look'st from thy sole dominion like the god
Of this new world; at whose sight all the stars
Hide their diminished heads; to thee I call,
But with no friendly voice, and add thy name
O sun, to tell thee how I hate thy beams
That bring to my remembrance from what state
I fell, how glorious once above thy sphere;
Till pride and worse ambition threw me down
Warring in heaven against heaven's matchless king: 41

<hr>

11 wreak] Avenge.   17 **engine**] Cannon.   20–3 **The hell ... place**] As
Mephistopheles tells Faustus in Marlowe's *Doctor Faustus*, I. iii. 76 and II. i. 122–4.
27–8 **Eden ... Lay pleasant**] *Eden* means 'pleasure' in Hebrew.   30 **meridian**]
Noon.   31 **revolving**] Contemplating.   32–41 **O thou ... king**] Milton's
nephew Edward Phillips wrote in his *Life of Milton* that Milton showed him these lines
'several years before the poem was begun' (i.e. in the early 1640s) as the opening speech
of a projected tragedy on the fall.

Ah wherefore! he deserved no such return
From me, whom he created what I was
In that bright eminence, and with his good
Upbraided none; nor was his service hard.
What could be less than to afford him praise,
The easiest recompense, and pay him thanks,
How due! Yet all his good proved ill in me,
And wrought but malice; lifted up so high
I 'sdained subjection, and thought one step higher   50
Would set me highest, and in a moment quit   51
The debt immense of endless gratitude,
So burdensome still paying, still to owe;
Forgetful what from him I still received,   54
And understood not that a grateful mind
By owing owes not, but still pays, at once   56
Indebted and discharged; what burden then?
O had his powerful destiny ordained
Me some inferior angel, I had stood
Then happy; no unbounded hope had raised   60
Ambition. Yet why not? Some other power
As great might have aspired, and me though mean
Drawn to his part; but other powers as great
Fell not, but stand unshaken, from within
Or from without, to all temptations armed.
Hadst thou the same free will and power to stand?
Thou hadst: whom hast thou then or what to accuse,
But heaven's free love dealt equally to all?
Be then his love accursed, since love or hate,
To me alike, it deals eternal woe.   70
Nay cursed be thou; since against his thy will
Chose freely what it now so justly rues.
Me miserable! which way shall I fly
Infinite wrath, and infinite despair?
Which way I fly is hell; myself am hell;
And in the lowest deep a lower deep
Still threatening to devour me opens wide,
To which the hell I suffer seems a heaven.
O then at last relent: is there no place

---

50 'sdained] Disdained.   51 **quit**] Cancel.   53–4 **still**] Always. 56 **still**]
Nevertheless.

Left for repentance, none for pardon left?   *80*

None left but by submission; and that word
Disdain forbids me, and my dread of shame
Among the spirits beneath, whom I seduced
With other promises and other vaunts
Than to submit, boasting I could subdue
The omnipotent. Ay me, they little know
How dearly I abide that boast so vain,   *87*
Under what torments inwardly I groan:
While they adore me on the throne of hell,
With diadem and sceptre high advanced
The lower still I fall, only supreme
In misery; such joy ambition finds.
But say I could repent and could obtain
By act of grace my former state; how soon   *94*
Would height recall high thoughts, how soon unsay
What feigned submission swore: ease would recant
Vows made in pain, as violent and void.
For never can true reconcilement grow
Where wounds of deadly hate have pierced so deep:
Which would but lead me to a worse relapse,   *100*
And heavier fall: so should I purchase dear
Short intermission bought with double smart.
This knows my punisher; therefore as far
From granting he, as I from begging peace:
All hope excluded thus, behold instead
Of us outcast, exiled, his new delight,
Mankind created, and for him this world.
So farewell hope, and with hope farewell fear,
Farewell remorse: all good to me is lost;
Evil be thou my good; by thee at least   *110*
Divided empire with heaven's king I hold
By thee, and more than half perhaps will reign;
As man ere long, and this new world shall know.
    Thus while he spake, each passion dimmed his face
Thrice changed with pale, ire, envy and despair,   *115*
Which marred his borrowed visage, and betrayed

---

87 **dearly**] Painfully. **abide**] Abide by, or await the issue of; suffer, bear.
94 **By act of grace**] By a concession of God's.   114–15 **each passion ... despair**] i.e. each of the three passions brought pallor ('*pale*') to his face.

Him counterfeit, if any eye beheld.
For heavenly minds from such distempers foul   118
Are ever clear. Whereof he soon aware,
Each perturbation smoothed with outward calm,
Artificer of fraud; and was the first
That practised falsehood under saintly show,
Deep malice to conceal, couched with revenge: 123
Yet not enough had practised to deceive
Uriel once warned; whose eye pursued him down
The way he went, and on the Assyrian mount   126
Saw him disfigured, more than could befall
Spirit of happy sort: his gestures fierce
He marked, and mad demeanour, then alone,
As he supposed, all unobserved, unseen.
So on he fares, and to the border comes,
Of Eden, where delicious Paradise,
Now nearer, crowns with her enclosure green,
As with a rural mound the champaign head   134
Of a steep wilderness, whose hairy sides
With thicket overgrown, grotesque and wild,   136
Access denied; and overhead up grew
Insuperable height of loftiest shade,
Cedar, and pine, and fir, and branching palm,
A sylvan scene, and as the ranks ascend   *140*
Shade above shade, a woody theatre
Of stateliest view. Yet higher than their tops
The verdurous wall of Paradise up sprung:
Which to our general sire gave prospect large
Into his nether empire neighbouring round.
And higher than that wall a circling row
Of goodliest trees loaden with fairest fruit,
Blossoms and fruits at once of golden hue
Appeared, with gay enamelled colours mixed: 149
On which the sun more glad impressed his beams
Than in fair evening cloud, or humid bow,   151
When God hath showered the earth; so lovely seemed

. 118 **distempers**] Disorders.   123 **couched**] (Lying) hidden.   126 **the Assyrian mount**] Niphates (see iii. 742).   134 **champaign head**] Open country.   136 **grotesque**] Like a grotto.   149 **enamelled**] Bright.   151 **humid bow**] Rainbow.

That landscape: and of pure now purer air   153
Meets his approach, and to the heart inspires
Vernal delight and joy, able to drive
All sadness but despair: now gentle gales
Fanning their odoriferous wings dispense   157
Native perfumes, and whisper whence they stole
Those balmy spoils. As when to them who sail
Beyond the Cape of Hope, and now are past   160
Mozambique, off at sea north-east winds blow
Sabean odours from the spicy shore   162
Of Araby the blest, with such delay   163
Well pleased they slack their course, and many a league
Cheered with the grateful smell old Ocean smiles.   165
So entertained those odorous sweets the fiend
Who came their bane, though with them better pleased   167
Than Asmodeus with the fishy fume,
That drove him, though enamoured, from the spouse
Of Tobit's son, and with a vengeance sent
From Media post to Egypt, there fast bound.   171
    Now to the ascent of that steep savage hill
Satan had journeyed on, pensive and slow;
But further way found none, so thick entwined,
As one continued brake, the undergrowth   175
Of shrubs and tangling bushes had perplexed   176
All path of man or beast that passed that way:
One gate there only was, and that looked east
On the other side: which when the arch-felon saw
Due entrance he disdained, and in contempt,

---

153 of] From.   157 odoriferous] Scent-bearing.   160 Cape of Hope] Cape
of Good Hope: the ships are travelling the spice route to Asia.   162 Sabean] From
Sheba (modern Yemen), in southern Arabia.   163 Araby the blest] Or *Arabia
Felix*, applied to the main part of the Arabian peninsula and particularly to Yemen.
165 grateful] Gratifying.   Ocean] Oceanus, one of the Titans, father of the rivers
and in Homer the progenitor of the Olympian gods (*Iliad*, xiv. 201ff.).   167 bane]
Poison.   168–71 Asmodeus . . . bound] The story is from the apocryphal Book of
Tobit: Tobit's son Tobias, travelling in Media, in Persia, on the advice of the archangel
Raphael married Sara, whose seven previous husbands had been murdered on their
wedding night by her incubus Asmodeus. Raphael enabled Tobias to escape their fate
by instructing him to burn the heart and liver of a fish, and the smell drove the demon
'into the utmost parts of Egypt, and the angel bound him' (Tobit 8: 3).   post] Quickly
(cf. post-haste).   175 brake] Thicket.   176 had perplexed] Would have
perplexed, rendered impassible.

At one slight bound high overleaped all bound
Of hill or highest wall, and sheer within   182
Lights on his feet. As when a prowling wolf,
Whom hunger drives to seek new haunt for prey,
Watching where shepherds pen their flocks at eve
In hurdled cotes amid the field secure,   186
Leaps o'er the fence with ease into the fold:
Or as a thief bent to unhoard the cash
Of some rich burgher, whose substantial doors,
Cross-barred and bolted fast, fear no assault,
In at the window climbs, or o'er the tiles;
So clomb this first grand thief into God's fold: 192
So since into his church lewd hirelings climb.   193
Thence up he flew, and on the tree of life,
The middle tree and highest there that grew,
Sat like a cormorant; yet not true life
Thereby regained, but sat devising death
To them who lived; nor on the virtue thought   198
Of that life-giving plant, but only used
For prospect, what well used had been the pledge
Of immortality. So little knows
Any, but God alone, to value right
The good before him, but perverts best things
To worst abuse, or to their meanest use.
Beneath him with new wonder now he views
To all delight of human sense exposed
In narrow room nature's whole wealth, yea more,
A heaven on earth, for blissful Paradise
Of God the garden was, by him in the east
Of Eden planted; Eden stretched her line
From Auran eastward to the royal towers   211
Of great Seleucia, built by Grecian kings,   212
Or where the sons of Eden long before

---

182 **sheer**] Entirely.   186 **hurdled cotes**] Fenced shelters.   **secure**] With an
ironic overtone: the sheep are secured, the shepherds too sure of themselves.
192 **clomb**] Climbed; a Spenserian archaism.   193 **lewd**] The original mean-
ing was 'lay or non-clerical', generalized to 'ignorant' and thence to 'wicked,
unprincipled'.   **hirelings**] Mercenaries (i.e. salaried ministers).   198 **virtue**]
Power.   211 **Auran**] Haran, on the eastern boundary of ancient Israel.
212 **Seleucia**] In modern Iraq, on the Tigris.

Dwelt in Telassar: in this pleasant soil   214
His far more pleasant garden God ordained;
Out of the fertile ground he caused to grow
All trees of noblest kind for sight, smell, taste;
And all amid them stood the tree of life,
High eminent, blooming ambrosial fruit
Of vegetable gold; and next to life   220
Our death the tree of knowledge grew fast by,
Knowledge of good bought dear by knowing ill.
Southward through Eden went a river large,
Nor changed his course, but through the shaggy hill
Passed underneath engulfed, for God had thrown
That mountain as his garden mould high raised
Upon the rapid current, which through veins
Of porous earth with kindly thirst up drawn,   228
Rose a fresh fountain, and with many a rill
Watered the garden; thence united fell
Down the steep glade, and met the nether flood,
Which from his darksome passage now appears,
And now divided into four main streams,
Runs diverse, wandering many a famous realm
And country whereof here needs no account,
But rather to tell how, if art could tell,
How from that sapphire fount the crispèd brooks,   237
Rolling on orient pearl and sands of gold,
With mazy error under pendant shades   239
Ran nectar, visiting each plant, and fed
Flowers worthy of Paradise which not nice art   241
In beds and curious knots, but nature boon   242
Poured forth profuse on hill and dale and plain,
Both where the morning sun first warmly smote
The open field, and where the unpierced shade
Embrowned the noontide bowers: thus was this place,
A happy rural seat of various view;
Groves whose rich trees wept odorous gums and balm,
Others whose fruit burnished with golden rind

214 **Telassar**] A city in Eden (2 Kings 19: 12, Isaiah 37: 12).   228 **kindly**]
Natural.   237 **crispèd**] Rippling.   239 **error**] Wandering.   241 **nice**]
Meticulous, delicate.   242 **curious knots**] Complex designs.   **boon**] Bountiful.

Hung amiable, Hesperian fables true,   250
If true, here only, and of delicious taste:
Betwixt them lawns, or level downs, and flocks
Grazing the tender herb, were interposed,
Or palmy hillock, or the flowery lap
Of some irriguous valley spread her store,   255
Flowers of all hue, and without thorn the rose:
Another side, umbrageous grots and caves   257
Of cool recess, o'er which the mantling vine
Lays forth her purple grape, and gently creeps
Luxuriant; meanwhile murmuring waters fall
Down the slope hills, dispersed, or in a lake,
That to the fringèd bank with myrtle crowned,
Her crystal mirror holds, unite their streams.
The birds their choir apply; airs, vernal airs,   264
Breathing the smell of field and grove, attune
The trembling leaves, while universal Pan   266
Knit with the Graces and the Hours in dance   267
Led on the eternal spring. Not that fair field
Of Enna, where Proserpin' gathering flowers
Herself a fairer flower by gloomy Dis
Was gathered, which cost Ceres all that pain
To seek her through the world; nor that sweet grove   272
Of Daphne by Orontes, and the inspired
Castalian spring, might with this Paradise   274
Of Eden strive; nor that Nyseian isle
Girt with the river Triton, where old Cham,
Whom Gentiles Ammon call and Lybian Jove,

---

250 **Hesperian fables**] The golden apples of Hesperus, which conferred immortality.
See iii. 568 and *Comus*, l. 393.   255 **irriguous**] Well-watered.   257 **umbrageous**]
Shady.   264 **apply**] Both join and practise (as in 'applied art').   **airs**] Both breezes
and melodies.   266 **Pan**] God of nature; the word in Greek means 'all'.
267 **Graces ... Hours**] Or Charites and Horae, goddesses respectively of natural
beauty and of the seasons.   269–72 **Enna ... world**] Dis, or Pluto, god of the
underworld, abducted Proserpina, daughter of the grain goddess Ceres, from the
meadow of Enna, in Sicily. Ceres, in mourning, searched for her, and during this time no
crops would grow. Dis agreed to return Proserpina to her mother for half of each year,
and in this period the earth is fertile. The story was considered a pagan analogue to
Eve's fall (Ovid, *Metamorphoses*, v. 391 ff., *Fasti*, iv. 417 ff., and the Homeric *Hymn to
Demeter*).   273–4 **Daphne ... spring**] The grove of Daphne on the river Orontes
in Syria had a spring named for the Castalian Spring of the Muses on Mount Parnassus,
and an oracle of Apollo (hence '*inspired*').

Hid Amalthea and her florid son   278
Young Bacchus from his stepdame Rhea's eye;   279
Nor where Abassin kings their issue guard,   280
Mount Amara, though this by some supposed
True Paradise under the Ethiop line   282
By Nilus' head, enclosed with shining rock,   283
A whole day's journey high, but wide remote
From this Assyrian garden, where the fiend
Saw undelighted all delight, all kind
Of living creatures new to sight and strange:
— Two of far nobler shape erect and tall,
Godlike erect, with native honour clad
In naked majesty seemed lords of all,   290
And worthy seemed, for in their looks divine
The image of their glorious maker shone,
Truth, wisdom, sanctitude severe and pure,
Severe but in true filial freedom placed;   294
Whence true authority in men; though both   295
Not equal, as their sex not equal seemed;
For contemplation he and valour formed,
For softness she and sweet attractive grace,
He for God only, she for God in him:
His fair large front and eye sublime declared   300
Absolute rule; and hyacinthine locks   301
Round from his parted forelock manly hung
Clustering, but not beneath his shoulders broad:
She as a veil down to the slender waist
Her unadornèd golden tresses wore

---

278 **florid**] Ruddy: Bacchus is god of wine.   275–9 **Nyseian . . . eye**] Diodorus
records how Ammon, the son of Saturn and king of Lybia, loved the nymph Amalthea
and had a son, Bacchus, by her. To protect them from the jealousy of his wife Rhea,
he hid them on the island of Nysa, in the River Triton, in modern Tunisia (*Library of
History*, iii. 67 ff.). Ammon was identified by the Romans with Jove, and by Christian
commentators with Noah's son Ham, or Cham in the Vulgate.   280 **Abassin**]
Abyssinian. **issue**] Children.   281–2 **Mount . . . line**] Amara, a sandstone hill in
modern Ethiopia, was thought in Milton's time to be on or near the Equator, the 'Ethiop
line', and sometimes identified with Eden.   283 **Nilus' head**] The source of the
Nile.   294 **filial freedom**] Freedom deriving from their status as God's children.
295 **Whence**] i.e. from God.   300 **front**] Forehead. **sublime**] 'Of lofty . . .
aspect' (*OED*).   301 **hyacinthine locks**] Hair as beautiful as that of Hyacinthus,
the youth loved by Apollo.

Dishevelled, but in wanton ringlets waved   306
As the vine curls her tendrils, which implied
Subjection, but required with gentle sway,
And by her yielded, by him best received,
Yielded with coy submission, modest pride,   310
And sweet reluctant amorous delay.

Nor those mysterious parts were then concealed,   312
Then was not guilty shame, dishonest shame   313
Of nature's works, honour dishonourable,
Sin-bred, how have ye troubled all mankind
With shows instead, mere shows of seeming pure,
And banished from man's life his happiest life,
Simplicity and spotless innocence. —
So passed they naked on, nor shunned the sight
Of God or angel, for they thought no ill: 320
So hand in hand they passed, the loveliest pair
That ever since in love's embraces met,
Adam the goodliest man of men since born
His sons, the fairest of her daughters Eve.   324
Under a tuft of shade that on a green
Stood whispering soft, by a fresh fountain side
They sat them down, and after no more toil
Of their sweet gardening labour than sufficed
To recommend cool zephyr, and made ease   329
More easy, wholesome thirst and appetite
More grateful, to their supper fruits they fell,
Nectarine fruits which the compliant boughs   332
Yielded them, sidelong as they sat recline   333
On the soft downy bank damasked with flowers:
The savoury pulp they chew, and in the rind
Still as they thirsted scoop the brimming stream;
Nor gentle purpose, nor endearing smiles   337

---

306 **wanton**] Here, luxuriant, unrestrained, but the word is most often used pejoratively in the period.   310 **coy**] 'Shyly reserved' (*OED*), perhaps again with an ironic overtone.   312 **mysterious**] Both secret and sacred, as in a religious mystery. 313 **dishonest**] Including the sense 'unchaste'.   323–4 **since . . . sons**] Since his descendants were born (before which time there was no one to compare him with). **her daughters**] i.e. all women.   329 **zephyr**] The west wind.   332 **Nectarine**] Sweet as nectar.   333 **recline**] Reclining.   337 **gentle**] Both kindly and noble. **purpose**] Conversation.

Wanted, nor youthful dalliance as beseems
Fair couple, linked in happy nuptial league,
Alone as they. About them frisking played
All beasts of the earth, since wild, and of all chase   341
In wood or wilderness, forest or den;
Sporting the lion ramped, and in his paw   343
Dandled the kid; bears, tigers, ounces, pards,   344
Gambolled before them, the unwieldy elephant
To make them mirth used all his might, and wreathed
His lithe proboscis; close the serpent sly   347
Insinuating, wove with Gordian twine   348
His braided train, and of his fatal guile   349
Gave proof unheeded; others on the grass
Couched, and now filled with pasture gazing sat,
Or bedward ruminating: for the sun   352
Declined was hasting now with prone career   353
To the Ocean Isles, and in the ascending scale   354
Of heaven the stars that usher evening rose:
When Satan still in gaze, as first he stood,
Scarce thus at length failed speech recovered sad.

    O hell! what do mine eyes with grief behold,
Into our room of bliss thus high advanced   359
Creatures of other mould, earth-born perhaps,
Not spirits, yet to heavenly spirits bright
Little inferior; whom my thoughts pursue
With wonder, and could love, so lively shines
In them divine resemblance, and such grace
The hand that formed them on their shape hath poured.
Ah gentle pair, ye little think how nigh
Your change approaches, when all these delights
Will vanish and deliver ye to woe,
More woe, the more your taste is now of joy;

341 **chase**] Hunting ground.   343 **ramped**] Reared up.   344 **ounces,
pards**] Lynxes (or any similar small wildcats), leopards.   347 **sly**] The word could
mean merely clever or skilful, but the pejorative sense was the primary one by Milton's
time.   348 **Insinuating**] Moving sinuously; like 'sly', with both neutral and
pejorative implications.   **with Gordian twine**] As convoluted as the Gordian knot
(which could not be untied, and was only undone when it was cut by Alexander).
349 **braided**] Tangled, intricate.   352 **ruminating**] Chewing   the   cud.
353 **prone career**] Sinking course.   354 **Ocean Isles**] In the western Atlantic,
identified as the Azores in l. 592.   359 **room**] Place.

Happy, but for so happy ill secured   370
Long to continue, and this high seat your heaven
Ill fenced for heaven to keep out such a foe
As now is entered; yet no purposed foe
To you whom I could pity thus forlorn
Though I unpitied: league with you I seek,
And mutual amity so strait, so close,
That I with you must dwell, or you with me
Henceforth; my dwelling haply may not please
Like this fair Paradise, your sense, yet such
Accept your maker's work; he gave it me,   380
Which I as freely give; hell shall unfold,
To entertain you two, her widest gates,
And send forth all her kings; there will be room,
Not like these narrow limits, to receive,
Your numerous offspring; if no better place,
Thank him who puts me loath to this revenge
On you who wrong me not for him who wronged.
And should I at your harmless innocence
Melt, as I do, yet public reason just,
Honour and empire with revenge enlarged,   390
By conquering this new world, compels me now
To do what else though damned I should abhor.
    So spake the fiend, and with necessity,
The tyrant's plea, excused his devilish deeds.
Then from his lofty stand on that high tree
Down he alights among the sportful herd
Of those four-footed kinds, himself now one,
Now other, as their shape served best his end
Nearer to view his prey, and unespied
To mark what of their state he more might learn   400
By word or action marked: about them round
A lion now he stalks with fiery glare,
Then as a tiger, who by chance hath spied
In some purlieu two gentle fawns at play,   404
Straight couches close, then rising changes oft
His couchant watch, as one who chose his ground
Whence rushing he might surest seize them both

404 **purlieu**] 'A place where one has the right to range at large . . . or which one habitually frequents' (*OED*).

Gripped in each paw: when Adam first of men
To first of women Eve thus moving speech,
Turned him all ear to hear new utterance flow.   410
   Sole partner and sole part of all these joys,   411
Dearer thyself than all; needs must the power
That made us, and for us this ample world
Be infinitely good, and of his good
As liberal and free as infinite,
That raised us from the dust and placed us here
In all this happiness, who at his hand
Have nothing merited, nor can perform
Aught whereof he hath need, he who requires
From us no other service than to keep   420
This one, this easy charge, of all the trees
In Paradise that bear delicious fruit
So various, not to taste that only tree
Of knowledge, planted by the tree of life,
So near grows death to life, what e'er death is,
Some dreadful thing no doubt; for well thou know'st
God hath pronounced it death to taste that tree,
The only sign of our obedience left
Among so many signs of power and rule
Conferred upon us, and dominion given   430
Over all other creatures that possess
Earth, air, and sea. Then let us not think hard
One easy prohibition, who enjoy
Free leave so large to all things else, and choice
Unlimited of manifold delights:
But let us ever praise him, and extol
His bounty, following our delightful task
To prune these growing plants, and tend these flowers,
Which were it toilsome, yet with thee were sweet.
   To whom thus Eve replied. O thou for whom   440
And from whom I was formed flesh of thy flesh,
And without whom am to no end, my guide

---

410 **Turned . . . ear**] The syntax is ambiguous: either Adam's speech compelled
Satan's full attention, or Eve turned fully attentive to Adam ('him' in the latter case
would be dative). The first gives the easier sense, but both constructions are elliptical,
and in any case the confusion of Eve's attention with Satan's may be part of the
point.   411 **sole part**] Unrivalled part, with the additional implication that Eve is
all his joy.

And head, what thou hast said is just and right.
For we to him indeed all praises owe,
And daily thanks, I chiefly who enjoy
So far the happier lot, enjoying thee
Pre-eminent by so much odds, while thou   447
Like consort to thyself canst nowhere find.
That day I oft remember, when from sleep
I first awaked, and found myself reposed   450
Under a shade of flowers, much wondering where
And what I was, whence thither brought, and how.
Not distant far from thence a murmuring sound
Of waters issued from a cave and spread
Into a liquid plain, then stood unmoved
Pure as the expanse of heaven; I thither went
With unexperienced thought, and laid me down
On the green bank, to look into the clear
Smooth lake, that to me seemed another sky.
As I bent down to look, just opposite,   460
A shape within the watery gleam appeared
Bending to look on me, I started back,
It started back, but pleased I soon returned,
Pleased it returned as soon with answering looks
Of sympathy and love; there I had fixed
Mine eyes till now, and pined with vain desire,
Had not a voice thus warned me, What thou seest,
What there thou seest fair creature is thyself,
With thee it came and goes: but follow me,   469
And I will bring thee where no shadow stays   470
Thy coming, and thy soft embraces, he
Whose image thou art, him thou shall enjoy
Inseparably thine, to him shalt bear
Multitudes like thyself, and thence be called
Mother of human race: what could I do,
But follow straight, invisibly thus led?
Till I espied thee, fair indeed and tall,

447 **odds**] 'The amount . . . by which one thing exceeds, or excels . . . another'
(*OED*); like *news*, a plural substantive treated as a singular noun.   460-9 **As . . .
goes**] Recalling Ovid's Narcissus, vainly yearning for his own image reflected in a pool
(*Metamorphoses*, iii. 402 ff.).   470 **shadow stays**] Image awaits.

Under a platan, yet methought less fair,   478
Less winning soft, less amiably mild,
Than that smooth watery image; back I turned,
Thou following cried'st aloud, Return fair Eve,
Whom fly'st thou? Whom thou fly'st, of him thou art,
His flesh, his bone; to give thee being I lent
Out of my side to thee, nearest my heart
Substantial life, to have thee by my side
Henceforth an individual solace dear;   486
Part of my soul I seek thee, and thee claim
My other half: with that thy gentle hand
Seized mine, I yielded, and from that time see
How beauty is excelled by manly grace   490
And wisdom, which alone is truly fair.
    So spake our general mother, and with eyes
Of conjugal attraction unreproved,
And meek surrender, half embracing leaned
On our first father, half her swelling breast
Naked met his under the flowing gold
Of her loose tresses hid: he in delight
Both of her beauty and submissive charms
Smiled with superior love, as Jupiter
On Juno smiles, when he impregns the clouds   500
That shed May flowers; and pressed her matron lip
With kisses pure: aside the devil turned
For envy, yet with jealous leer malign
Eyed them askance, and to himself thus plained.
  — Sight hateful, sight tormenting! thus these two
Emparadised in one another's arms
The happier Eden, shall enjoy their fill
Of bliss on bliss, while I to hell am thrust,
Where neither joy nor love, but fierce desire,
Among our other torments not the least,
Still unfulfilled with pain of longing pines;   511
Yet let me not forget what I have gained
From their own mouths; all is not theirs it seems:
One fatal tree there stands of knowledge called,
Forbidden them to taste: knowledge forbidden?

478 **platan**] Plane tree.   486 **individual**] Inseparable.   500 **impregns**]
Impregnates.   511 **pines**] Torments (me).

Suspicious, reasonless. Why should their Lord
Envy them that? can it be sin to know,
Can it be death? and do they only stand
By ignorance, is that their happy state,
The proof of their obedience and their faith?   520
O fair foundation laid whereon to build
Their ruin! Hence I will excite their minds
With more desire to know, and to reject
Envious commands, invented with design
To keep them low whom knowledge might exalt
Equal with gods; aspiring to be such,
They taste and die: what likelier can ensue?
But first with narrow search I must walk round
This garden, and no corner leave unspied;
A chance but chance may lead where I may meet   530
Some wandering spirit of heaven, by fountain side,
Or in thick shade retired, from him to draw
What further would be learned. Live while ye may,
Yet happy pair; enjoy, till I return,
Short pleasures, for long woes are to succeed. ← Bitter
    So saying, his proud step he scornful turned,   Experience.
But with sly circumspection, and began
Through wood, through waste, o'er hill, o'er dale his roam.
Meanwhile in utmost longitude, where heaven   539
With earth and ocean meets, the setting sun
Slowly descended, and with right aspect
Against the eastern gate of Paradise   542
Levelled his evening rays: it was a rock
Of alabaster, piled up to the clouds,
Conspicuous far, winding with one ascent
Accessible from earth, one entrance high;
The rest was craggy cliff, that overhung
Still as it rose, impossible to climb.   548
Betwixt these rocky pillars Gabriel sat   549
Chief of the angelic guards, awaiting night;
About him exercised heroic games

---

530 **A ... chance**] A bit of mere luck.   539 **in utmost longitude**] At the
greatest distance, 'the ends of the earth'.   541–2 **with ... Against**] i.e. directly
facing.   548 **Still**] Always.   549 **Gabriel**] With Michael, Uriel, and Raphael,
one of the four archangels; the name means 'strength of God'.

The unarmed youth of heaven, but nigh at hand
Celestial armoury, shields, helms, and spears,
Hung high with diamond flaming, and with gold.
Thither came Uriel, gliding through the even
On a sunbeam, swift as a shooting star
In autumn thwarts the night, when vapours fired   557
Impress the air, and shows the mariner
From what point of his compass to beware
Impetuous winds: he thus began in haste.

    Gabriel, to thee thy course by lot hath given
Charge and strict watch that to this happy place
No evil thing approach or enter in;
This day at height of noon came to my sphere
A spirit, zealous, as he seemed, to know
More of the almighty's works, and chiefly man
God's latest image: I described his way   567
Bent all on speed, and marked his airy gait;   568
But in the mount that lies from Eden north,
Where he first lighted, soon discerned his looks
Alien from heaven, with passions foul obscured:
Mine eye pursued him still, but under shade
Lost sight of him; one of the banished crew
I fear, hath ventured from the deep, to raise
New troubles; him thy care must be to find.

    To whom the wingèd warrior thus returned:
Uriel, no wonder if thy perfect sight,
Amid the sun's bright circle where thou sit'st,
See far and wide: in at this gate none pass
The vigilance here placed, but such as come   580
Well known from heaven; and since meridian hour
No creature thence: if spirit of other sort,
So minded, have o'erleaped these earthy bounds
On purpose, hard thou know'st it to exclude
Spiritual substance with corporeal bar.
But if within the circuit of these walks,
In whatsoever shape he lurk, of whom

---

557 thwarts] Both crosses (the literal meaning) and defeats.   vapours fired] Fiery exhalations from the earth, thought to be the cause of shooting stars.   567 described] Descried.   568 gait] Course, bearing.

Thou tell'st, by morrow dawning I shall know.
   So promised he, and Uriel to his charge
Returned on that bright beam, whose point now raised   590
Bore him slope downward to the sun now fallen
Beneath the Azores; whether the bright orb,
Incredible how swift, had thither rolled
Diurnal, or this less voluble earth   594
By shorter flight to the east, had left him there   595
Arraying with reflected purple and gold
The clouds that on his western throne attend:
Now came still evening on, and twilight grey
Had in her sober livery all things clad;
Silence accompanied, for beast and bird,   600
They to their grassy couch, these to their nests
Were slunk, all but the wakeful nightingale;
She all night long her amorous descant sung;   603
Silence was pleased: now glowed the firmament
With living sapphires: Hesperus that led   605
The starry host, rode brightest, till the moon
Rising in clouded majesty, at length
Apparent queen unveiled her peerless light,   608
And o'er the dark her silver mantle threw.
   When Adam thus to Eve: Fair consort, the hour
Of night, and all things now retired to rest
Mind us of like repose, since God hath set   612
Labour and rest, as day and night to men
Successive, and the timely dew of sleep
Now falling with soft slumbrous weight inclines
Our eyelids; other creatures all day long
Rove idle unemployed, and less need rest;
Man hath his daily work of body or mind
Appointed, which declares his dignity,

---

590 **now raised**] The beam points upward because the sun has now moved below the horizon.   594 **Diurnal**] In a single day.   **voluble**] 'Capable of ready rotation on a centre or axis' (*OED*).   592–5 **whether . . . there**] Whether through the movement of the sun or the earth; Milton once again declines to choose between the Ptolemaic and Copernican systems.   600 **Silence accompanied**] Both an absolute construction, for 'silence accompanied evening', and an oxymoron, 'silence was accompanied', by the song of the nightingale of l. 602.   603 **descant**] 'A melodious accompaniment to a simple musical theme' (*OED*).   605 **Hesperus**] The evening star.   608 **Apparent**] Manifest, and playing on 'heir apparent'.   612 **Mind us**] Put us in mind.

And the regard of heaven on all his ways;   620
While other animals unactive range,
And of their doings God takes no account.
Tomorrow ere fresh morning streak the east
With first approach of light, we must be risen,
And at our pleasant labour, to reform
Yon flowery arbours, yonder alleys green,
Our walk at noon, with branches overgrown,
That mock our scant manuring, and require   628
More hands than ours to lop their wanton growth:
Those blossoms also, and those dropping gums,
That lie bestrewn unsightly and unsmooth,
Ask riddance, if we mean to tread with ease;   632
Meanwhile, as nature wills, night bids us rest.

　　To whom thus Eve with perfect beauty adorned.
My author and disposer, what thou bid'st   635
Unargued I obey; so God ordains,
God is thy law, thou mine: to know no more
Is woman's happiest knowledge and her praise.
With thee conversing I forget all time,
All seasons and their change, all please alike.   640
Sweet is the breath of morn, her rising sweet,
With charm of earliest birds; pleasant the sun   642
When first on this delightful land he spreads
His orient beams, on herb, tree, fruit, and flower,
Glistering with dew; fragrant the fertile earth
After soft showers; and sweet the coming on
Of grateful evening mild, then silent night
With this her solemn bird and this fair moon,
And these the gems of heaven, her starry train:
But neither breath of morn when she ascends   650
With charm of earliest birds, nor rising sun
On this delightful land, nor herb, fruit, flower,
Glistering with dew, nor fragrance after showers,

---

628 **manuring**] Cultivation (lit. 'working with the hands').　　632 **Ask riddance**]
Need to be cleared.　　635 **author**] One 'who originates or gives existence'; 'one who
authorizes or instigates'; 'an authority, an informant' (*OED*).　　640 **seasons**] Not
seasonal changes, which began only after the fall, but times of day, as the next eight lines
indicate (usage not recorded in *OED*).　　642 **charm**] Including senses derived from
its double etymology, from Anglo Saxon *cierm*, magic spell, and Latin *carmen*, song.

Nor grateful evening mild, nor silent night
With this her solemn bird, nor walk by moon,
Or glittering starlight without thee is sweet.
But wherefore all night long shine these, for whom
This glorious sight, when sleep hath shut all eyes?
    To whom our general ancestor replied.
Daughter of God and man, accomplished Eve,   *660*
Those have their course to finish, round the earth,
By morrow evening, and from land to land
In order, though to nations yet unborn,
Ministering light prepared, they set and rise;
Lest total darkness should by night regain
Her old possession, and extinguish life
In nature and all things, which these soft fires
Not only enlighten, but with kindly heat
Of various influence foment and warm,   *669*
Temper or nourish, or in part shed down
Their stellar virtue on all kinds that grow
On earth, made hereby apter to receive
Perfection from the sun's more potent ray.
These then, though unbeheld in deep of night,
Shine not in vain, nor think, though men were none,
That heaven would want spectators, God want praise;   *676*
Millions of spiritual creatures walk the earth
Unseen, both when we wake, and when we sleep:
All these with ceaseless praise his works behold
Both day and night: how often from the steep   *680*
Of echoing hill or thicket have we heard
Celestial voices to the midnight air,
Sole, or responsive each to other's note
Singing their great creator: oft in bands
While they keep watch, or nightly rounding walk
With heavenly touch of instrumental sounds
In full harmonic number joined, their songs
Divide the night, and lift our thoughts to heaven.
    Thus talking hand in hand alone they passed
On to their blissful bower; it was a place   *690*
Chosen by the sovereign planter, when he framed
All things to man's delightful use; the roof

---

669 **foment**] 'Cherish with heat' (*OED*).   676 **want . . . want**] Lack . . . lack.

Of thickest covert was inwoven shade
Laurel and myrtle, and what higher grew
Of firm and fragrant leaf; on either side
Acanthus, and each odorous bushy shrub
Fenced up the verdant wall; each beauteous flower,
Iris all hues, roses, and jessamine   698
Reared high their flourished heads between, and wrought   699
Mosaic; underfoot the violet,
Crocus, and hyacinth with rich inlay
Broidered the ground, more coloured than with stone
Of costliest emblem: other creature here   703
Beast, bird, insect, or worm durst enter none;
Such was their awe of man. In shadier bower
More sacred and sequestered, though but feigned,   706
Pan or Silvanus never slept, nor nymph,   707
Nor Faunus haunted. Here in close recess   708
With flowers, garlands, and sweet-smelling herbs
Espousèd Eve decked first her nuptial bed,
And heavenly choirs the hymenean sung,   711
What day the genial angel to our sire   712
Brought her in naked beauty more adorned,
More lovely than Pandora, whom the gods   714
Endowed with all their gifts, and O too like
In sad event, when to the unwiser son   716
Of Japhet brought by Hermes, she ensnared   717
Mankind with her fair looks, to be avenged
On him who had stole Jove's authentic fire.   719
   Thus at their shady lodge arrived, both stood,
Both turned, and under open sky adored
The God that made both sky, air, earth and heaven

---

698 **jessamine**] Jasmine.   699 **flourished**] Flowered.   703 **emblem**] Both inlaid work and symbolic image.   706 **feigned**] Invented (by poets).   707 **Pan ... Sylvanus**] Gods respectively of all nature and of woods and gardens. 708 **Faunus**] Roman farm and forest deity.   711 **hymenean**] Marriage song (from Hymen, god of marriage).   712 **genial**] Presiding over marriage, generative.   714 **Pandora**] Lit. 'all gifts'; the first woman, created at Jove's command and sent with Hermes as a gift for Epimetheus ('hindsight') to avenge the audacity of his brother Prometheus ('foresight'), who had stolen fire from the gods to give to man. Pandora came with a box filled with evils; when Epimetheus opened the box, these were let loose throughout the world.   716 **event**] Outcome.   717 **Japhet**] The Titan Iapetus, father of Prometheus and Epimetheus; he was identified with Noah's son Japhet.   719 **authentic**] Original.

Which they beheld, the moon's resplendent globe
And starry pole: Thou also mad'st the night,   724
Maker omnipotent, and thou the day,
Which we in our appointed work employed
Have finished happy in our mutual help
And mutual love, the crown of all our bliss
Ordained by thee, and this delicious place
For us too large, where thy abundance wants   730
Partakers, and uncropped falls to the ground.
But thou hast promised from us two a race
To fill the earth, who shall with us extol
Thy goodness infinite, both when we wake,
And when we seek, as now, thy gift of sleep.

This said unanimous, and other rites   736
Observing none, but adoration pure
Which God likes best, into their inmost bower
Handed they went; and eased the putting off   739
These troublesome disguises which we wear,
Straight side by side were laid, nor turned I ween
Adam from his fair spouse, nor Eve the rites
Mysterious of connubial love refused: 743
Whatever hypocrites austerely talk
Of purity and place and innocence,
Defaming as impure what God declares
Pure, and commands to some, leaves free to all.   747
Our maker bids increase, who bids abstain   748
But our destroyer, foe to God and man?
Hail wedded love, mysterious law, true source
Of human offspring, sole propriety   751
In Paradise of all things common else.
By thee adulterous lust was driven from men
Among the bestial herds to range, by thee
Founded in reason, loyal, just, and pure,

---

724 pole] Sky, heavens.   730 wants] Lacks.   736 unanimous] Lit. 'with one mind'.   739 Handed] Holding hands.   eased the putting off] Not needing to take off.   743 Mysterious] Sacred.   747 commands to some] In 1 Corinthians 7, marriage is enjoined upon those who otherwise would be unable to avoid fornication (see l. 753).   748 Our ... increase] In Genesis 1: 28.   751 sole propriety] i.e. marriage was the only property exclusively ordained for Adam and Eve in paradise—the relation of husband to wife is conceived as a property relationship.

Relations dear, and all the charities   756
Of father, son, and brother first were known.
Far be it, that I should write thee sin or blame,
Or think thee unbefitting holiest place,
Perpetual fountain of domestic sweets,
Whose bed is undefiled and chaste pronounced,
Present, or past, as saints and patriarchs used.
Here Love his golden shafts employs, here lights   763
His constant lamp, and waves his purple wings,   764
Reigns here and revels; not in the bought smile
Of harlots, loveless, joyless, unendeared,
Casual fruition, nor in court amours
Mixed dance, or wanton masque, or midnight ball,
Or serenade, which the starved lover sings   769
To his proud fair, best quitted with disdain.
These lulled by nightingales embracing slept,
And on their naked limbs the flowery roof
Showered roses, which the morn repaired. Sleep on   773
Blest pair; and O yet happiest if ye seek
No happier state, and know to know no more.

    Now had night measured with her shadowy cone
Halfway uphill this vast sublunar vault,   777
And from their ivory port the cherubim   778
Forth issuing at the accustomed hour stood armed
To their night watches in warlike parade,
When Gabriel to his next in power thus spake.

    Uzziel, half these draw off, and coast the south   782
With strictest watch; these other wheel the north,
Our circuit meets full west. As flame they part
Half wheeling to the shield, half to the spear.   785
From these, two strong and subtle spirits he called   786
That near him stood, and gave them thus in charge.

    Ithuriel and Zephon, with winged speed   788

---

756 **charities**] Natural affections.   763 **Love**] Personified as Cupid. **shafts**] Arrows.   764 **purple**] Imperial, royal; also bright-hued, brilliant, splendid. 769 **starved**] Deprived (of love).   773 **repaired**] Renewed on the branches. 777 **sublunar**] Beneath the moon.   778 **port**] Gate.   782 **Uzziel**] Lit. 'strength of god'; a human name in the Bible, an angel in the cabbalistic tradition.   785 **shield . . . spear**] The sides on which these were held, left and right.   786 **these**] The latter.   788 **Ithuriel and Zephon**] Lit. 'discovery of God' and 'searcher'. Ithuriel is not a biblical name, and the biblical Zephon is not an angel.

Search through this garden, leave unsearched no nook,
But chiefly where those two fair creatures lodge,
Now laid perhaps asleep secure of harm.   791
This evening from the sun's decline arrived
Who tells of some infernal spirit seen   793
Hitherward bent (who could have thought?) escaped
The bars of hell, on errand bad no doubt:
Such where ye find, seize fast, and hither bring.
    So saying, on he led his radiant files,
Dazzling the moon; these to the bower direct
In search of whom they sought: him there they found
Squat like a toad, close at the ear of Eve;   800
Assaying by his devilish art to reach
The organs of her fancy, and with them forge
Illusions as he list, phantasms and dreams,
Or if, inspiring venom, he might taint
The animal spirits that from pure blood arise   805
Like gentle breaths from rivers pure, thence raise
At least distempered, discontented thoughts,
Vain hopes, vain aims, inordinate desires
Blown up with high conceits engendering pride.   809
Him thus intent Ithuriel with his spear
Touched lightly; for no falsehood can endure
Touch of celestial temper, but returns   812
Of force to its own likeness; up he starts   813
Discovered and surprised. As when a spark
Lights on a heap of nitrous powder, laid   815
Fit for the tun some magazine to store   816
Against a rumoured war, the smutty grain   817
With sudden blaze diffused, inflames the air:

791 **secure**] 'Feeling no care or apprehension' (*OED*).   793 **Who**] One who.
805 **animal spirits**] Burton explains the relationship of the bodily spirits: 'The nat-
ural are begotten in the liver, and thence dispersed through the veins . . . The vital
spirits are made in the heart . . . The animal spirits formed of the vital, brought up to
the brain, and diffused by the nerves, to the subordinate members, give sense and
motion to them all' (*Anatomy of Melancholy*, I. i. 2. 2). *Animal* = of the spirit or soul.
809 **high conceits**] Fanciful, excessive conceptions.   812 **celestial temper**] Both
the weapon, tempered in heaven, and Ithurial's angelic nature.   813 **Of force**]
Perforce, necessarily.   815 **nitrous powder**] Gunpowder.   816 **Fit for the
tun**] Ready for storage; *tun* = barrel. **magazine**] Storehouse for explosives.
817 **Against**] In anticipation of. **smutty**] Black; smut is a fungus disease affecting
grain that turns it to black powder.

So started up in his own shape the fiend.
Back stepped those two fair angels half amazed   *820*
So sudden to behold the grisly king;
Yet thus, unmoved with fear, accost him soon.
   Which of those rebel spirits adjudged to hell
Com'st thou, escaped thy prison, and transformed,
Why sat'st thou like an enemy in wait
Here watching at the head of these that sleep?
   Know ye not then said Satan, filled with scorn,
Know ye not me? Ye knew me once no mate
For you, there sitting where ye durst not soar;
Not to know me argues yourselves unknown,   *830*
The lowest of your throng; or if ye know,
Why ask ye, and superfluous begin
Your message, like to end as much in vain?
To whom thus Zephon, answering scorn with scorn.
Think not, revolted spirit, thy shape the same,
Or undiminished brightness, to be known
As when thou stood'st in heaven upright and pure;
That glory then, when thou no more wast good,
Departed from thee, and thou resemblest now
Thy sin and place of doom obscure and foul.   *840*
But come, for thou, be sure, shalt give account
To him who sent us, whose charge is to keep
This place inviolable, and these from harm.
   So spake the cherub, and his grave rebuke
Severe in youthful beauty, added grace
Invincible: abashed the devil stood,
And felt how awful goodness is, and saw
Virtue in her shape how lovely, saw, and pined
His loss; but chiefly to find here observed
His lustre visibly impaired; yet seemed   *850*
Undaunted. If I must contend, said he,
Best with the best, the sender not the sent,
Or all at once; more glory will be won,
Or less be lost. Thy fear, said Zephon bold,
Will save us trial what the least can do
Single against thee wicked, and thence weak.
   The fiend replied not, overcome with rage;
But like a proud steed reined, went haughty on,
Champing his iron curb: to strive or fly

He held it vain; awe from above had quelled   *860*
His heart, not else dismayed. Now drew they nigh
The western point, where those half-rounding guards
Just met, and closing stood in squadron joined
Awaiting next command. To whom their chief
Gabriel from the front thus called aloud.

   O friends, I hear the tread of nimble feet
Hasting this way, and now by glimpse discern
Ithuriel and Zephon through the shade,
And with them comes a third of regal port,
But faded splendour wan; who by his gait   *870*
And fierce demeanour seems the prince of hell,
Not likely to part hence without contest;
Stand firm, for in his look defiance lours.

   He scarce had ended, when those two approached
And brief related whom they brought, where found,
How busied, in what form and posture couched.

   To whom with stern regard thus Gabriel spake.
Why hast thou, Satan, broke the bounds prescribed
To thy transgressions, and disturbed the charge   *879*
Of others, who approve not to transgress
By thy example, but have power and right
To question thy bold entrance on this place;
Employed it seems to violate sleep, and those
Whose dwelling God hath planted here in bliss?

   To whom thus Satan, with contemptuous brow.
Gabriel, thou hadst in heaven the esteem of wise,   *886*
And such I held thee; but this question asked
Puts me in doubt. Lives there who loves his pain?
Who would not, finding way, break loose from hell,
Though thither doomed? Thou wouldst thyself, no doubt,   *890*
And boldly venture to whatever place
Farthest from pain, where thou might'st hope to change
Torment with ease, and soonest recompense
Dole with delight, which in this place I sought;
To thee no reason, who know'st only good,
But evil hast not tried: and wilt object

---

879 **transgressions**] The word includes its etymological sense of crossing bound-
aries.   **charge**] Both the duty and those whom the angels are charged to care for,
Adam and Eve.   886 **hadst ... wise**] Were considered wise.

His will who bound us? Let him surer bar
His iron gates, if he intends our stay
In that dark durance: thus much what was asked.   899
The rest is true, they found me where they say;
But that implies not violence or harm.
    Thus he in scorn. The warlike angel moved,
Disdainfully half smiling thus replied.
O loss of one in heaven to judge of wise,   904
Since Satan fell, whom folly overthrew,
And now returns him from his prison scaped,
Gravely in doubt whether to hold them wise
Or not, who ask what boldness brought him hither
Unlicensed from his bounds in hell prescribed;
So wise he judges it to fly from pain
However, and to scape his punishment.   911
So judge thou still, presumptuous, till the wrath,
Which thou incurr'st by flying, meet thy flight
Sevenfold, and scourge that wisdom back to hell,
Which taught thee yet no better, that no pain
Can equal anger infinite provoked.
But wherefore thou alone? Wherefore with thee
Came not all hell broke loose? Is pain to them
Less pain, less to be fled, or thou than they
Less hardy to endure? Courageous chief,   920
The first in flight from pain, hadst thou alleged
To thy deserted host this cause of flight,
Thou surely hadst not come sole fugitive.
    To which the fiend thus answered frowning stern.
Not that I less endure, or shrink from pain,
Insulting angel, well thou know'st I stood
Thy fiercest, when in battle to thy aid
The blasting vollied thunder made all speed
And seconded thy else not dreaded spear.
But still thy words at random, as before,   930
Argue thy inexperience what behoves
From hard assays and ill successes past
A faithful leader, not to hazard all

---

899 **durance**] Imprisonment. **thus ... asked**] So much for your question.   904 **O ... wise**] 'What a judge of wisdom you are, what a loss to heaven'.   911 **However**] In whatever way he can.   930 **at random**] i.e. missing the point.

Through ways of danger by himself untried,
I therefore, I alone first undertook
To wing the desolate abyss, and spy
This new created world, whereof in hell
Fame is not silent, here in hope to find
Better abode, and my afflicted powers   939
To settle here on earth, or in midair;
Though for possession put to try once more
What thou and thy gay legions dare against;   942
Whose easier business were to serve their Lord
High up in heaven, with songs to hymn his throne,
And practised distances to cringe, not fight.   945
    To whom the warrior angel soon replied.
To say and straight unsay, pretending first
Wise to fly pain, professing next the spy,
Argues no leader but a liar traced,   949
Satan, and couldst thou faithful add? O name,
O sacred name of faithfulness profaned!
Faithful to whom? to thy rebellious crew?
Army of fiends, fit body to fit head;
Was this your discipline and faith engaged,
Your military obedience, to dissolve
Allegiance to the acknowledged power supreme?
And thou sly hypocrite, who now wouldst seem
Patron of liberty, who more than thou
Once fawned, and cringed, and servilely adored
Heaven's awful monarch? wherefore but in hope
To dispossess him, and thy self to reign?
But mark what I aread thee now, avaunt;   962
Fly thither whence thou fled'st: if from this hour
Within these hallowed limits thou appear,
Back to the infernal pit I drag thee chained,
And seal thee so, as henceforth not to scorn
The facile gates of hell too slightly barred.   967
    So threatened he, but Satan to no threats
Gave heed, but waxing more in rage replied.

---

939 **afflicted powers**] Weakened forces—both his own diminished strength and his
crippled army.   942 **gay**] Showy, gaudy.   945 **practised distances**] Keeping a
deferential distance.   947–9 **To say … traced**] Gabriel is mistaken (as he is again
at ll. 1011–12): Satan's two claims do not contradict each other.   962 **aread**] Warn.
avaunt] Begone.   967 **facile**] Easily opened.

Then when I am thy captive talk of chains,
Proud limitary cherub, but ere then　　　　　　971
Far heavier load thyself expect to feel
From my prevailing arm, though heaven's king
Ride on thy wings, and thou with thy compeers,
Used to the yoke, draw'st his triumphant wheels
In progress through the road of heaven star-paved.　　976
　While thus he spake, the angelic squadron bright
Turned fiery red, sharpening in moonèd horns　　978
Their phalanx, and began to hem him round
With ported spears, as thick as when a field　　980
Of Ceres ripe for harvest waving bends　　　　981
Her bearded grove of ears, which way the wind
Sways them; the careful ploughman doubting stands　　983
Lest on the threshing floor his hopeful sheaves
Prove chaff. On the other side Satan alarmed
Collecting all his might dilated stood,
Like Tenerife or Atlas unremoved:　　　　　987
His stature reached the sky, and on his crest
Sat horror plumed; nor wanted in his grasp　　989
What seemed both spear and shield: now dreadful deeds
Might have ensued, nor only Paradise
In this commotion, but the starry cope
Of heaven perhaps, or all the elements
At least had gone to wrack, disturbed and torn
With violence of this conflict, had not soon
The eternal to prevent such horrid fray
Hung forth in heaven his golden scales, yet seen
Betwixt Astrea and the Scorpion sign,　　　　998

---

971 **limitary**] Stationed on the boundary; also, setting limits, and limited.
976 **progress**] Ceremonial procession.　　　978 **moonèd horns**] Formation like the crescent moon.　　　980 **ported spears**] Spears carried 'diagonally across and close to the body, so that the blade is opposite the middle of the left shoulder'; the military command is 'port arms' (*OED*). The point is that the spears therefore are not in the attack position.　　　981 **Ceres**] The grain goddess.　　　983 **careful**] Worried.
987 **Tenerife or Atlas**] Mountains in the Canary Islands and Morocco respectively. **unremoved**] 'Fixed in place, firmly stationed' (*OED*).　　　989 **wanted**] Lacked.　　　997–8 **scales . . . Scorpion**] The constellation Libra, between Virgo and Scorpio; cf. Zeus weighing the fates of Greeks and Trojans (*Iliad*, viii. 69 ff.) and of Achilles and Hector (xxii. 209), and the Virgilian version, Jove weighing Aeneas' and Turnus' fates (*Aeneid*, xii. 725 ff.).　　　**Astrea**] Goddess of justice, who fled from earth after the Golden Age, identified here with the constellation Virgo.

Wherein all things created first he weighed,
The pendulous round earth with balanced air
In counterpoise, now ponders all events,　　　1001
Battles and realms: in these he put two weights
The sequel each of parting and of fight;
The latter quick up flew, and kicked the beam;　　　1004
Which Gabriel spying, thus bespake the fiend.
　　Satan, I know thy strength, and thou know'st mine,
Neither our own but given; what folly then
To boast what arms can do, since thine no more
Than heaven permits, nor mine, though doubled now
To trample thee as mire: for proof look up,　　　1010
And read thy lot in yon celestial sign
Where thou art weighed, and shown how light, how weak,
If thou resist. The fiend looked up and knew　　　1013
His mounted scale aloft: nor more; but fled　　:　1014
Murmuring, and with him fled the shades of night.

1001 **ponders**] Lit. weighs.　　1004 **kicked the beam**] Struck the crossbar.
1011–13 **read . . . resist**] Gabriel misinterprets the sign, which does not weigh Satan
against the angels but fighting against parting, and shows parting to be preferable—for
Gabriel as well as for Satan.　　1013–14 **knew . . . scale**] Satan accepts Gabriel's
interpretation.

BOOK V

The Argument

Morning approached, Eve relates to Adam her troublesome dream;
he likes it not, yet comforts her: they come forth to their day
labours: their morning hymn at the door of their bower. God to
render man inexcusable sends Raphael to admonish him of his
obedience, of his free estate, of his enemy near at hand; who he is,
and why his enemy, and whatever else may avail Adam to know.
Raphael comes down to Paradise, his appearance described, his
coming discerned by Adam afar off sitting at the door of his bower;
he goes out to meet him, brings him to his lodge, entertains him
with the choicest fruits of Paradise got together by Eve; their
discourse at table: Raphael performs his message, minds Adam of
his state and of his enemy; relates at Adam's request who that
enemy is, and how he came to be so, beginning from his first revolt
in heaven, and the occasion thereof; how he drew his legions after
him to the parts of the north, and there incited them to rebel with
him, persuading all but only Abdiel a seraph, who in argument
dissuades and opposes him, then forsakes him.

Now Morn her rosy steps in the eastern clime
Advancing, sowed the earth with orient pearl,
When Adam waked, so customed, for his sleep
Was airy light from pure digestion bred,
And temperate vapours bland, which the only sound
Of leaves and fuming rills, Aurora's fan,   6
Lightly dispersed, and the shrill matin song   7
Of birds on every bough; so much the more
His wonder was to find unwakened Eve
With tresses discomposed, and glowing cheek,
As through unquiet rest: he on his side
Leaning half-raised, with looks of cordial love   12
Hung over her enamoured, and beheld
Beauty, which whether waking or asleep,
Shot forth peculiar graces; then with voice   15
Mild, as when Zephyrus on Flora breathes,   16

---

6 **Aurora**] Goddess of dawn.   5–7 **which . . . dispersed**] i.e. the mere sound of
wind in the leaves and water was enough to wake Adam.   12 **cordial**] Lit. from the
heart.   15 **peculiar**] Special, all its own.   16 **Zephyrus . . . Flora**] The west
wind and the goddess of flowers.

Her hand soft touching, whispered thus. Awake
My fairest, my espoused, my latest found,
Heaven's last best gift, my ever new delight,
Awake, the morning shines, and the fresh field
Calls us, we lose the prime, to mark how spring   21
Our tended plants, how blows the citron grove,   22
What drops the myrrh, and what the balmy reed,   23
How nature paints her colours, how the bee
Sits on the bloom extracting liquid sweet.

    Such whispering waked her, but with startled eye
On Adam, whom embracing, thus she spake.

    O sole in whom my thoughts find all repose,
My glory, my perfection, glad I see
Thy face, and morn returned, for I this night,   30
Such night till this I never passed, have dreamed,
If dreamed, not as I oft am wont, of thee,
Works of day past, or morrow's next design,
But of offence and trouble, which my mind
Knew never till this irksome night; methought
Close at mine ear one called me forth to walk
With gentle voice, I thought it thine; it said,
Why sleep'st thou Eve? now is the pleasant time,
The cool, the silent, save where silence yields
To the night-warbling bird, that now awake
Tunes sweetest his love-laboured song; now reigns   41
Full-orbed the moon, and with more pleasing light
Shadowy sets off the face of things; in vain,
If none regard; heaven wakes with all his eyes,
Whom to behold but thee, nature's desire,
In whose sight all things joy, with ravishment
Attracted by thy beauty still to gaze.   47
I rose as at thy call, but found thee not;
To find thee I directed then my walk;
And on, methought, alone I passed through ways
That brought me on a sudden to the tree
Of interdicted knowledge: fair it seemed,
Much fairer to my fancy than by day:
And as I wondering looked, beside it stood

21 prime] The first morning hour, beginning at six o'clock.   22 blows] Blooms.
23 balmy reed] Balsam.   41 love-laboured] Produced with love.   47 still]
Always.

One shaped and winged like one of those from heaven
By us oft seen; his dewy locks distilled
Ambrosia; on that tree he also gazed;
And O fair plant, said he, with fruit surcharged,
Deigns none to ease thy load and taste thy sweet,
Nor God, nor man; is knowledge so despised?
Or envy, or what reserve forbids to taste?   61
Forbid who will, none shall from me withhold
Longer thy offered good, why else set here?
This said he paused not, but with venturous arm
He plucked, he tasted; me damp horror chilled
At such bold words vouched with a deed so bold: 66
But he thus overjoyed, O fruit divine,
Sweet of thy self, but much more sweet thus cropped,
Forbidden here, it seems, as only fit
For gods, yet able to make gods of men: 70
And why not gods of men, since good, the more
Communicated, more abundant grows,
The author not impaired, but honoured more?
Here, happy creature, fair angelic Eve,
Partake thou also; happy though thou art,
Happier thou mayst be, worthier canst not be:
Taste this, and be henceforth among the gods
Thyself a goddess, not to earth confined,
But sometimes in the air, as we, sometimes
Ascend to heaven, by merit thine, and see   80
What life the gods live there, and such live thou.
So saying, he drew nigh, and to me held,
Even to my mouth of that same fruit held part
Which he had plucked; the pleasant savoury smell
So quickened appetite, that I, methought,
Could not but taste. Forthwith up to the clouds
With him I flew, and underneath beheld
The earth outstretched immense, a prospect wide
And various: wondering at my flight and change
To this high exaltation; suddenly   90
My guide was gone, and I, methought, sunk down,
And fell asleep; but O how glad I waked
To find this but a dream! Thus Eve her night

61 **reserve**] Restriction.   66 **vouched with**] Confirmed by.

Related, and thus Adam answered sad.
   Best image of my self and dearer half,
The trouble of thy thoughts this night in sleep
Affects me equally; nor can I like
This uncouth dream, of evil sprung I fear;   98
Yet evil whence? in thee can harbour none,
Created pure. But know that in the soul
Are many lesser faculties that serve
Reason as chief; among these fancy next   102
Her office holds; of all external things,
Which the five watchful senses represent,
She forms imaginations, airy shapes,
Which reason joining or disjoining, frames
All what we affirm or what deny, and call
Our knowledge or opinion; then retires
Into her private cell when nature rests.   109
Oft in her absence mimic fancy wakes
To imitate her; but misjoining shapes,
Wild work produces oft, and most in dreams,
Ill matching words and deeds long past or late.
Some such resemblances methinks I find
Of our last evening's talk, in this thy dream,
But with addition strange; yet be not sad.
Evil into the mind of god or man
May come and go, so unapproved, and leave
No spot or blame behind: which gives me hope
That what in sleep thou didst abhor to dream,   120
Waking thou never wilt consent to do.
Be not disheartened then, nor cloud those looks
That wont to be more cheerful and serene
Than when fair morning first smiles on the world,
And let us to our fresh employments rise
Among the groves, the fountains, and the flowers
That open now their choicest bosomed smells   127
Reserved from night, and kept for thee in store.
   So cheered he his fair spouse, and she was cheered,

---

98 **uncouth**] Strange, with an overtone of distasteful.   102 **fancy**] Fantasy, in
Renaissance psychology that branch of the imaginative faculty with the power to create
and interpret images.   109 **cell**] Compartment of the brain.   127 **bosomed**]
Hidden.

But silently a gentle tear let fall   *130*
From either eye, and wiped them with her hair;
Two other precious drops that ready stood,
Each in their crystal sluice, he ere they fell
Kissed as the gracious signs of sweet remorse
And pious awe, that feared to have offended.
   So all was cleared, and to the field they haste.
But first from under shady arborous roof,
Soon as they forth were come to open sight
Of day-spring, and the sun, who scarce up risen
With wheels yet hovering o'er the ocean brim,   *140*
Shot parallel to the earth his dewy ray,
Discovering in wide landscape all the east
Of Paradise and Eden's happy plains,
Lowly they bowed adoring, and began
Their orisons, each morning duly paid   145
In various style, for neither various style   146
Nor holy rapture wanted they to praise
Their maker, in fit strains pronounced or sung   148
Unmeditated, such prompt eloquence
Flowed from their lips, in prose or numerous verse,   150
More tuneable than needed lute or harp   151
To add more sweetness, and they thus began.
   These are thy glorious works, parent of good,
Almighty, thine this universal frame,
Thus wondrous fair; thyself how wondrous then!
Unspeakable, who sit'st above these heavens
To us invisible or dimly seen
In these thy lowest works, yet these declare
Thy goodness beyond thought, and power divine:
Speak ye who best can tell, ye sons of light,   *160*
Angels, for ye behold him, and with songs
And choral symphonies, day without night,
Circle his throne rejoicing, ye in heaven,
On earth join all ye creatures to extol
Him first, him last, him midst, and without end.

---

145 **orisons**] Prayers.   146 **various style**] A mixture of styles.   146–8 **neither
. . . maker**] i.e. their prayers included both formal and spontaneous elements.
150 **numerous**] Rhythmical.   151 **tuneable**] Tuneful.

Fairest of stars, last in the train of night,   166
If better thou belong not to the dawn,
Sure pledge of day, that crown'st the smiling morn
With thy bright circlet, praise him in thy sphere
While day arises, that sweet hour of prime.   170
Thou sun, of this great world both eye and soul,
Acknowledge him thy greater, sound his praise
In thy eternal course, both when thou climb'st,
And when high noon hast gained, and when thou fall'st.
Moon, that now meet'st the orient sun, now fly'st
With the fixed stars, fixed in their orb that flies,   176
And ye five other wandering fires that move   177
In mystic dance not without song, resound   178
His praise, who out of darkness called up light.
Air, and ye elements the eldest birth
Of nature's womb, that in quaternion run   181
Perpetual circle, multiform; and mix
And nourish all things, let your ceaseless change
Vary to our great maker still new praise.
Ye mists and exhalations that now rise   185
From hill or steaming lake, dusky or grey,
Till the sun paint your fleecy skirts with gold,
In honour to the world's great author rise,
Whether to deck with clouds the uncoloured sky,
Or wet the thirsty earth with falling showers,
Rising or falling still advance his praise.   191
His praise ye winds, that from four quarters blow,
Breathe soft or loud; and wave your tops, ye pines,
With every plant, in sign of worship wave.
Fountains and ye, that warble, as ye flow,
Melodious murmurs, warbling tune his praise.
Join voices all ye living souls, ye birds,
That singing up to heaven gate ascend,
Bear on your wings and in your notes his praise;

166 **Fairest of stars**] The morning star, called both Venus and Lucifer ('light-bringer').   176 **orb that flies**] Revolving sphere.   177 **five … fires**] The five planets ('other' is a slip on Milton's part, since Venus has already been invoked at l. 166).   178 **not without song**] The music of the spheres.   181 **quaternion**] A group of four.   185 **exhalations**] Vapours.   191 **still**] Ever.

Ye that in waters glide, and ye that walk   200
The earth, and stately tread, or lowly creep;
Witness if I be silent, morn or even,
To hill, or valley, fountain, or fresh shade
Made vocal by my song, and taught his praise.
Hail universal Lord, be bounteous still
To give us only good; and if the night
Have gathered aught of evil or concealed,
Disperse it, as now light dispels the dark.
    So prayed they innocent, and to their thoughts
Firm peace recovered soon and wonted calm.   210
On to their morning's rural work they haste
Among sweet dews and flowers; where any row
Of fruit trees over-woody reached too far
Their pampered boughs, and needed hands to check
Fruitless embraces: or they led the vine
To wed her elm; she spoused about him twines
Her marriageable arms, and with her brings
Her dower the adopted clusters, to adorn
His barren leaves. Them thus employed beheld
With pity heaven's high king, and to him called
Raphael, the sociable spirit, that deigned
To travel with Tobias, and secured
His marriage with the seven-times-wedded maid.   223
    Raphael, said he, thou hear'st what stir on earth
Satan from hell scaped through the darksome gulf
Hath raised in Paradise, and how disturbed
This night the human pair, how he designs
In them at once to ruin all mankind.
Go therefore, half this day as friend with friend
Converse with Adam, in what bower or shade   230
Thou find'st him from the heat of noon retired,
To respite his day-labour with repast,
Or with repose; and such discourse bring on,
As may advise him of his happy state,
Happiness in his power left free to will,
Left to his own free will, his will though free,
Yet mutable; whence warn him to beware

222–3 **Tobias . . . maid**] See iv. 167–71.

He swerve not too secure: tell him withal   238
His danger, and from whom, what enemy
Late fallen himself from heaven, is plotting now
The fall of others from like state of bliss;
By violence, no, for that shall be withstood,
But by deceit and lies; this let him know,
Lest wilfully transgressing he pretend
Surprisal, unadmonished, unforewarned.

    So spake the eternal Father, and fulfilled
All justice: nor delayed the wingèd saint
After his charge received; but from among
Thousand celestial ardours, where he stood   249
Veiled with his gorgeous wings, up springing light
Flew through the midst of heaven; the angelic choirs
On each hand parting, to his speed gave way
Through all the empyreal road; till at the gate
Of heaven arrived, the gate self-opened wide
On golden hinges turning, as by work
Divine the sovereign architect had framed.
From hence, no cloud, or, to obstruct his sight,
Star interposed, however small he sees,
Not unconform to other shining globes,   259
Earth and the garden of God, with cedars crowned
Above all hills. As when by night the glass
Of Galileo, less assured, observes
Imagined lands and regions in the moon:
Or pilot from amidst the Cyclades   264
Delos or Samos first appearing kens   265
A cloudy spot. Down thither prone in flight   266
He speeds, and through the vast ethereal sky
Sails between worlds and worlds, with steady wing
Now on the polar winds, then with quick fan   269
Winnows the buxom air; till within soar   270
Of towering eagles, to all the fowls he seems

---

238 **too secure**] Overconfident of his safety.   249 **ardours**] Effulgent spirits;
biblical usage.   259 **unconform**] Dissimilar.   264 **Cyclades**] An island group
in the Aegean.   265 **Delos**] The central Cycladic island.   **Samos**] An island
north-east of the Cyclades.   **kens**] Perceives.   266 **prone**] Moving downward.
269 **fan**] Wing.   270 **buxom**] Unresisting.   **soar**] The range of altitude.

A phoenix, gazed by all, as that sole bird
When to enshrine his relics in the sun's
Bright temple, to Egyptian Thebes he flies.   274
At once on the eastern cliff of Paradise
He lights, and to his proper shape returns
A seraph winged; six wings he wore, to shade
His lineaments divine; the pair that clad
Each shoulder broad, came mantling o'er his breast
With regal ornament; the middle pair
Girt like a starry zone his waist, and round   281
Skirted his loins and thighs with downy gold
And colours dipped in heaven; the third his feet
Shadowed from either heel with feathered mail
Sky-tinctured grain. Like Maia's son he stood,   285
And shook his plumes, that heavenly fragrance filled
The circuit wide. Straight knew him all the bands
Of angels under watch; and to his state,   288
And to his message high in honour rise;   289
For on some message high they guessed him bound.
Their glittering tents he passed, and now is come
Into the blissful field, through groves of myrrh,
And flowering odours, cassia, nard, and balm;   293
A wilderness of sweets; for nature here
Wantoned as in her prime, and played at will   295
Her virgin fancies, pouring forth more sweet,
Wild above rule or art; enormous bliss.   297
Him through the spicy forest onward come
Adam discerned, as in the door he sat
Of his cool bower, while now the mounted sun
Shot down direct his fervid rays to warm

272–4 **phoenix . . . flies**] The mythical phoenix existed only one at a time; it repro-
duced by immolating itself, and a new phoenix, born from the ashes, flew to the Temple
of the Sun in Heliopolis to offer up the remains to the god (see Ovid, *Metamorphoses*, xv.
391–407). Milton, like other Renaissance writers, identified Heliopolis with the nearby
Egyptian city of Thebes.   281 **zone**] Belt.   285 **Sky-tinctured grain**] Dyed
blue (*grain* was technically crimson dye, but by Milton's time the word also signified any
fast colour).   **Maia's son**] Mercury, the heavenly messenger.   288 **state**] Rank.
289 **message**] The word also meant mission, errand.   293 **cassia**] A plant with a
cinnamon odour.   **nard**] Spikenard, source of a fragrant ointment.   295 **Wantoned**]
Played (innocently)—the word is used of children's games—but with ominous over-
tones.   297 **enormous**] Unfettered (lit. 'outside of the rules'); like *wantoned*, usually
pejorative, but here still innocent: Edenic wildness was superior to postlapsarian art.

Earth's inmost womb, more warmth than Adam needs;
And Eve within, due at her hour prepared
For dinner savoury fruits, of taste to please
True appetite, and not disrelish thirst
Of nectarous draughts between, from milky stream,   306
Berry or grape: to whom thus Adam called.

   Haste hither Eve, and worth thy sight behold
Eastward among those trees, what glorious shape
Comes this way moving; seems another morn   310
Risen on mid-noon; some great behest from heaven
To us perhaps he brings, and will vouchasafe
This day to be our guest. But go with speed,
And what thy stores contain, bring forth and pour
Abundance, fit to honour and receive
Our heavenly stranger; well we may afford
Our givers their own gifts, and large bestow
From large bestowed, where nature multiplies
Her fertile growth, and by disburdening grows
More fruitful, which instructs us not to spare.   320

   To whom thus Eve. Adam, earth's hallowed mould,
Of God inspired, small store will serve, where store,
All seasons, ripe for use hangs on the stalk;
Save what by frugal storing firmness gains   324
To nourish, and superfluous moist consumes:
But I will haste and from each bough and brake,
Each plant and juiciest gourd will pluck such choice
To entertain our angel guest, as he
Beholding shall confess that here on earth
God hath dispensed his bounties as in heaven.   330

   So saying, with dispatchful looks in haste
She turns, on hospitable thoughts intent
What choice to choose for delicacy best,
What order, so contrived as not to mix
Tastes, not well joined, inelegant, but bring
Taste after taste upheld with kindliest change,   336
Bestirs her then, and from each tender stalk
Whatever Earth all-bearing mother yields

---

306 **milky**] Nourishing, juicy, sweet (modifying *Berry or grape* as well as *stream*).   324 **frugal**] Prudent, careful: there is always plenty to eat in Eden, but some food is better if dried.   336 **upheld**] Continued. **kindliest**] Most natural.

In India east or west, or middle shore   339
In Pontus or the Punic coast, or where   340
Alcinous reigned, fruit of all kinds, in coat,   341
Rough, or smooth rind, or bearded husk, or shell
She gathers, tribute large, and on the board
Heaps with unsparing hand; for drink the grape
She crushes, inoffensive must, and meads   345
From many a berry, and from sweet kernels pressed
She tempers dulcet creams, nor these to hold   347
Wants her fit vessels pure, then strews the ground   348
With rose and odours from the shrub unfumed.   349
Meanwhile our primitive great sire, to meet
His godlike guest, walks forth, without more train
Accompanied than with his own complete
Perfections, in himself was all his state,
More solemn than the tedious pomp that waits
On princes, when their rich retinue long
Of horses led, and grooms besmeared with gold
Dazzles the crowd, and sets them all agape.
Nearer his presence Adam though not awed,
Yet with submiss approach and reverence meek,   359
As to a superior nature, bowing low,
     Thus said. Native of heaven, for other place
None can than heaven such glorious shape contain;
Since by descending from the thrones above,
Those happy places thou hast deigned awhile
To want, and honour these, vouchsafe with us   365
Two only, who yet by sovereign gift possess
This spacious ground, in yonder shady bower
To rest, and what the garden choicest bears
To sit and taste, till this meridian heat   369
Be over, and the sun more cool decline.

---

339 **middle shore**] Literally translating Mediterranean.   340 **Pontus**] On the
Black Sea.   **Punic**] Carthaginian, the north-east African coast of the Mediterranean.
341 **Alcinous reigned**] Alcinous ruled the Phaeacians on the legendary island of
Scheria, in the extreme west. Odysseus visited him and saw his superb gardens (*Odyssey*,
vii. 113 ff.).   345 **inoffensive must**] Unfermented grape juice.   **meads**] Drinks
sweetened with honey.   347 **tempers**] Mixes. **dulcet**] Sweet.   348 **Wants**]
Lacks.   349 **unfumed**] Not burned (to produce incense).   359 **submiss**]
Submissive: the diction is formal or legal.   365 **want**] Be parted from.
369 **meridian**] Midday.

Whom thus the angelic virtue answered mild.   371
Adam, I therefore came, nor art thou such
Created, or such place hast here to dwell,
As may not oft invite, though spirits of heaven
To visit thee; lead on then where thy bower
O'ershades; for these mid-hours, till evening rise
I have at will. So to the sylvan lodge
They came, that like Pomona's arbour smiled   378
With flowerets decked and fragrant smells; but Eve
Undecked, save with herself more lovely fair
Than wood-nymph, or the fairest goddess feigned
Of three that in Mount Ida naked strove,   382
Stood to entertain her guest from heaven; no veil
She needed, virtue-proof, no thought infirm   384
Altered her cheek. On whom the angel Hail
Bestowed, the holy salutation used
Long after to blest Mary, second Eve.

Hail mother of mankind, whose fruitful womb
Shall fill the world more numerous with thy sons
Than with these various fruits the trees of God   390
Have heaped this table. Raised of grassy turf
Their table was, and mossy seats had round,
And on her ample square from side to side
All autumn piled, though spring and autumn here
Danced hand in hand. Awhile discourse they hold;   395
No fear lest dinner cool; when thus began   396
Our author. Heavenly stranger, please to taste   397

---

371 **virtue**] Power; also, the Virtues were one of the angelic orders (see i. 128–9 and
ii. 15).   378 **Pomona**] Goddess of fruit.   381–2 **fairest ... strove**] Venus, the
invidious comparison with Eve providing another ominous overtone: the Trojan prince
Paris was chosen to award a golden apple to the fairest of the three goddesses Juno,
Minerva, and Venus. He selected Venus; his reward was the most beautiful woman on
earth, Helen, whom he abducted from her husband Menelaus, and thus precipitated the
Trojan War. The Judgment of Paris took place on Mount Ida (now Kaz Daghi, in
northern Turkey).   384 **virtue-proof**] Taken in context, this must mean 'armed
with virtue'; but the natural interpretation would be 'armed *against* virtue', and Eve
is again being praised in a way that simultaneously calls her virtue into question.
infirm] Irresolute, of weak character.   394–5 **spring ... hand**] As in Spenser's
Garden of Adonis, growth and harvest are simultaneous and perpetual (*Faerie Queene*,
III. vi. 42).   396 **No ... cool**] Miltonic literalism: paradisal meals must be
uncooked, since Adam and Eve learned the use of fire only after the fall (see x. 1078 ff.).
397 **author**] Progenitor.

These bounties which our nourisher, from whom
All perfect good unmeasured out, descends,
To us for food and for delight hath caused
The earth to yield; unsavoury food perhaps
To spiritual natures; only this I know,
That one celestial Father gives to all.
    To whom the angel. Therefore what he gives
(Whose praise be ever sung) to man in part
Spiritual, may of purest spirits be found   406
No ingrateful food: and food alike those pure   407
Intelligential substances require,   408
As doth your rational; and both contain   409
Within them every lower faculty
Of sense, whereby they hear, see, smell, touch, taste,
Tasting concoct, digest, assimilate,   412
And corporeal to incorporeal turn.
For know, whatever was created, needs
To be sustained and fed; of elements
The grosser feeds the purer, earth the sea,
Earth and the sea feed air, the air those fires
Ethereal, and as lowest first the moon;   418
Whence in her visage round those spots, unpurged
Vapours not yet into her substance turned.   420
Nor doth the moon no nourishment exhale
From her moist continent to higher orbs.
The sun that light imparts to all, receives
From all his alimental recompense
In humid exhalations, and at even
Sups with the ocean: though in heaven the trees
Of life ambrosial fruitage bear, and vines
Yield nectar, though from off the boughs each morn
We brush mellifluous dews, and find the ground   429

---

    406 of] By.   407 No ingrateful] i.e. pleasing.   408 Intelligential substances] Angelic intelligences.   409 rational] Contrasted with the pure spiritual ('intelligential') substance of the angels.   412 concoct, digest, assimilate] The three stages of digestion, consisting of the processing of food in the stomach, its conversion to blood, and its incorporation into the body.   418 lowest ... moon] The moon occupied the lowest of the heavenly spheres.   419–20 spots ... turned] The moon's markings here are not elements of the lunar landscape, as in ll. 290–1, but exhalations from earth remaining on the moon's surface, as yet unassimilated.   429 mellifluous] Sweet as honey.

Covered with pearly grain: yet God hath here
Varied his bounty so with new delights,
As may compare with heaven; and to taste
Think not I shall be nice. So down they sat,   433
And to their viands fell, nor seemingly
The angel, nor in mist, the common gloss
Of theologians, but with keen despatch   436
Of real hunger, and concoctive heat   437
To transubstantiate; what redounds, transpires   438
Through spirits with ease; nor wonder; if by fire
Of sooty coal the empiric alchemist   440
Can turn, or holds it possible to turn
Metals of drossiest ore to perfect gold
As from the mine. Meanwhile at table Eve
Ministered naked, and their flowing cups
With pleasant liquors crowned: O innocence   445
Deserving Paradise! if ever, then,
Then had the sons of God excuse to have been
Enamoured at that sight; but in those hearts
Love unlibidinous reigned, nor jealousy
Was understood, the injured lover's hell.   450

    Thus when with meats and drinks they had sufficed,
Not burdened nature, sudden mind arose
In Adam, not to let the occasion pass
Given him by this great conference to know
Of things above his world, and of their being
Who dwell in heaven, whose excellence he saw
Transcend his own so far, whose radiant forms
Divine effulgence, whose high power so far
Exceeded human, and his wary speech

---

433 **nice**] 'Fastidious, difficult to please' (*OED*).   434–6 **nor ... theologians**]
i.e. angels are material beings: Milton rejects the orthodox view, which holds that angels
are immaterial but assume slightly material bodies to converse with mortals (as, for
example, in Donne's 'Air and Angels', l. 3).   437 **concoctive heat**] Digestive
energy.   438 **transubstantiate**] Turn one substance into another, with a pun on
the theological sense, the Roman Catholic doctrine of the Eucharist, which Milton and
the Reformers rejected. **redounds**] Is excessive.   440 **empiric**] Experimental,
usually with pejorative implications—the noun was a term for a charlatan or quack. But
since Milton's point about the angels depends on the validity of the analogy, the com-
parison reveals either a belief in the authenticity of empiric alchemy or an unacknow-
ledged ambivalence about angelic transubstantiation.   445 **crowned**] Filled to
overflowing.

Thus to the empyreal minister he framed.   460
　　Inhabitant with God, now know I well
Thy favour, in this honour done to man,
Under whose lowly roof thou hast vouchsafed
To enter, and these earthly fruits to taste,
Food not of angels, yet accepted so,
As that more willingly thou couldst not seem
At heaven's high feasts to have fed: yet what compare?   467
　　To whom the winged hierarch replied.   468
O Adam, one almighty is, from whom
All things proceed, and up to him return,
If not depraved from good, created all
Such to perfection, one first matter all,   472
Indued with various forms, various degrees
Of substance, and in things that live, of life;
But more refined, more spiritous, and pure,
As nearer to him placed or nearer tending
Each in their several active spheres assigned,
Till body up to spirit work, in bounds
Proportioned to each kind. So from the root   479
Springs lighter the green stalk, from thence the leaves
More airy, last the bright consummate flower   481
Spirits odorous breathes: flowers and their fruit
Man's nourishment, by gradual scale sublimed   483
To vital spirits aspire, to animal,
To intellectual, give both life and sense,   485
Fancy and understanding, whence the soul
Reason receives, and reason is her being,
Discursive, or intuitive; discourse   488
Is oftest yours, the latter most is ours,
Differing but in degree, of kind the same.
Wonder not then, what God for you saw good
If I refuse not, but convert, as you,
To proper substance; time may come when men   493

---

467 **what compare?**] How can they be comparable?   468 **hierarch**] Archangel (lit. 'holy leader').   472 **one first matter**] i.e. the world was created not *ex nihilo*, out of nothing, but of an original essential matter.   478–9 **bounds . . . kind**] Stages appropriate to each form of life.   481 **consummate**] Perfected.   483 **sublimed**] Refined; an alchemical term.   484–5 **vital . . . intellectual**] The three kinds of fluids that enable and control the bodily and intellectual functions.   488 **Discursive**] Through the reasoning process.   493 **proper**] My own.

With angels may participate, and find
No inconvenient diet, nor too light fare:
And from these corporal nutriments perhaps
Your bodies may at last turn all to spirit,
Improved by tract of time, and winged ascend   498
Ethereal, as we, or may at choice
Here or in heavenly paradises dwell;
If ye be found obedient, and retain
Unalterably firm his love entire
Whose progeny you are. Meanwhile enjoy
Your fill what happiness this happy state
Can comprehend, incapable of more.
    To whom the patriarch of mankind replied,
O favourable spirit, propitious guest,
Well hast thou taught the way that might direct
Our knowledge, and the scale of nature set
From centre to circumference, whereon   510
In contemplation of created things
By steps we may ascend to God. But say,
What meant that caution joined, *If ye be found
Obedient?* Can we want obedience then   514
To him, or possibly his love desert
Who formed us from the dust, and placed us here
Full to the utmost measure of what bliss
Human desires can seek or apprehend?
    To whom the angel. Son of heaven and earth,
Attend: that thou art happy, owe to God;   520
That thou continuest such, owe to thyself,
That is, to thy obedience; therein stand.
This was that caution given thee; be advised.
God made thee perfect, not immutable;
And good he made thee, but to persevere
He left it in thy power, ordained thy will
By nature free, not overruled by fate
Inextricable, or strict necessity;
Our voluntary service he requires,
Not our necessitated, such with him   530
Finds no acceptance, nor can find, for how
Can hearts, not free, be tried whether they serve

498 **tract**] Length.   514 **want**] Lack.

Willing or no, who will but what they must
By destiny, and can no other choose?
Myself and all the angelic host that stand
In sight of God enthroned, our happy state
Hold, as you yours, while our obedience holds;
On other surety none; freely we serve,
Because we freely love, as in our will
To love or not; in this we stand or fall: *540*
And some are fallen, to disobedience fallen,
And so from heaven to deepest hell; O fall
From what high state of bliss into what woe!
   To whom our great progenitor. Thy words
Attentive, and with more delighted ear,
Divine instructor, I have heard, than when
Cherubic songs by night from neighbouring hills
Aerial music send: nor knew I not
To be both will and deed created free;
Yet that we never shall forget to love   *550*
Our maker, and obey him whose command
Single, is yet so just, my constant thoughts
Assured me, and still assure: though what thou tell'st
Hath passed in heaven, some doubt within me move,
But more desire to hear, if thou consent,
The full relation, which must needs be strange,
Worthy of sacred silence to be heard;   557
And we have yet large day, for scarce the sun
Hath finished half his journey, and scarce begins
His other half in the great zone of heaven.
   Thus Adam made request, and Raphael
After short pause assenting, thus began.
   High matter thou enjoin'st me, O prime of men,
Sad task and hard, for how shall I relate
To human sense the invisible exploits
Of warring spirits; how without remorse   566
The ruin of so many glorious once
And perfect while they stood; how last unfold
The secrets of another world, perhaps

557 **Worthy . . . silence**] Translating Horace's '*sacro digna silentio*', referring to the attentiveness of the spirits in the underworld to the songs of Sappho and Alcaeus (*Odes*, II. xiii. 29).   566 **remorse**] Sorrow, compassion.

Not lawful to reveal? Yet for thy good   570
This is dispensed, and what surmounts the reach
Of human sense, I shall delineate so,
By likening spiritual to corporal forms,
As may express them best, though what if earth
Be but the shadow of heaven, and things therein
Each to other like, more than on earth is thought?   576
  As yet this world was not, and Chaos wild
Reigned where these heavens now roll, where earth now rests
Upon her centre poised, when on a day
(For time, though in eternity, applied
To motion, measures all things durable   581
By present, past, and future) on such day
As heaven's great year brings forth, the empyreal host   583
Of angels by imperial summons called,
Innumerable before the almighty's throne
Forthwith from all the ends of heaven appeared
Under their hierarchs in orders bright:
Ten thousand thousand ensigns high advanced,
Standards, and gonfalons twixt van and rear   589
Stream in the air, and for distinction serve
Of hierarchies, of orders, and degrees;
Or in their glittering tissues bear emblazed
Holy memorials, acts of zeal and love   593
Recorded eminent. Thus when in orbs
Of circuit inexpressible they stood,
Orb within orb, the Father infinite,
By whom in bliss embosomed sat the Son,
Amidst as from a flaming mount, whose top
Brightness had made invisible, thus spake.
  Hear all ye angels, progeny of light,   600
Thrones, dominations, princedoms, virtues, powers,

574–6 **earth . . . like**] The Platonic doctrine that earth is formed on the model of
heaven and that what we perceive as real is merely a shadow of the divine is from
Republic, x; but Milton's materialist version stresses the likeness of earth to heaven, not
their differences.   581 **things durable**] Things that last at all, that have any exten-
sion in time.   583 **great year**] The period when an entire cycle of the heavens is
completed, and the heavenly bodies have returned to their original positions;
Plato's estimate of its length is unclear, but is usually given as 36,000 years (*Timaeus*,
39D).   589 **gonfalons**] Banners. **van**] Front.   593 **memorials**] Records,
commemorations.

Hear my decree, which unrevoked shall stand.
This day I have begot whom I declare
My only son, and on this holy hill   604
Him have anointed, whom ye now behold
At my right hand; your head I him appoint;
And by myself have sworn to him shall bow
All knees in heaven, and shall confess him Lord:
Under his great vicegerent reign abide   609
United as one individual soul   610
Forever happy: him who disobeys
Me disobeys, breaks union, and that day
Cast out from God and blessèd vision, falls
Into utter darkness, deep engulfed, his place
Ordained without redemption, without end.
   So spake the omnipotent, and with his words
All seemed well pleased, all seemed, but were not all.
That day, as other solemn days, they spent
In song and dance about the sacred hill,
Mystical dance, which yonder starry sphere
Of planets and of fixed in all her wheels
Resembles nearest, mazes intricate,
Eccentric intervolved, yet regular   623
Then most, when most irregular they seem,
And in their motions harmony divine
So smooths her charming tones, that God's own ear
Listens delighted. Evening now approached
(For we have also our evening and our morn,
We ours for change delectable, not need)
Forthwith from dance to sweet repast they turn   630
Desirous; all in circles as they stood,
Tables are set, and on a sudden piled
With angels' food, and rubied nectar flows
In pearl, in diamond, and massy gold,
Fruit of delicious vines, the growth of heaven.
On flowers reposed, and with fresh flowerets crowned,

603–4 **This . . . son**] The begetting on 'this day' is metaphorical, alluding to Psalm
2: 6 ff.   609 **vicegerent**] Deputized, exercising God's authority.   610 **indi-
vidual**] Inseparable.   623 **Eccentric**] Slightly irregular; a technical astronomical
term for an off-centre stellar motion (see note to viii. 83).   **intervolved**] Intertwined.

They eat, they drink, and in communion sweet
Quaff immortality and joy, secure
Of surfeit where full measure only bounds
Excess, before the all bounteous king, who showered   640
With copious hand, rejoicing in their joy.
Now when ambrosial night with clouds exhaled
From that high mount of God, whence light and shade
Spring both, the face of brightest heaven had changed
To grateful twilight (for night comes not there
In darker veil) and roseate dews disposed   646
All but the unsleeping eyes of God to rest,
Wide over all the plain, and wider far
Than all this globous earth in plain outspread,
(Such are the courts of God) the angelic throng
Dispersed in bands and files their camp extend
By living streams among the trees of life,
Pavilions numberless, and sudden reared,
Celestial tabernacles, where they slept
Fanned with cool winds, save those who in their course
Melodious hymns about the sovereign throne
Alternate all night long: but not so waked
Satan, so call him now, his former name   658
Is heard no more in heaven; he of the first,
If not the first archangel, great in power,
In favour and pre-eminence, yet fraught
With envy against the Son of God, that day
Honoured by his great father, and proclaimed
Messiah king anointed, could not bear   664
Through pride that sight, and thought himself impaired.   665
Deep malice thence conceiving and disdain,
Soon as midnight brought on the dusky hour
Friendliest to sleep and silence, he resolved
With all his legions to dislodge, and leave   669
Unworshipped, unobeyed the throne supreme

637–40 **They ... showered**] In the first (1667) edition, these lines read, 'They eat,
they drink, and with refection sweet | Are filled, before the all bounteous king,
who showered'.   646 **roseate**] Rose-scented, punning on *ros*, Latin for 'dew'.
658 **his former name**] Lucifer, according to Isaiah 14: 12.   664 **anointed**] Liter-
ally translating 'messiah'.   665 **impaired**] Damaged, injured.   669 **dislodge**]
Both move (himself) and displace (God's throne, l. 670).

Contemptuous, and his next subordinate   671
Awakening, thus to him in secret spake.
    Sleep'st thou companion dear, what sleep can close
Thy eyelids? and rememb'rest what decree
Of yesterday, so late hath passed the lips
Of heaven's almighty. Thou to me thy thoughts
Wast wont, I mine to thee was wont to impart;
Both waking we were one; how then can now
Thy sleep dissent? new laws thou seest imposed;
New laws from him who reigns, new minds may raise   680
In us who serve, new counsels, to debate
What doubtful may ensue, more in this place
To utter is not safe. Assemble thou
Of all those myriads which we lead the chief;
Tell them that by command, ere yet dim night
Her shadowy cloud withdraws, I am to haste,
And all who under me their banners wave,
Homeward with flying march where we possess
The quarters of the north, there to prepare
Fit entertainment to receive our king   690
The great Messiah, and his new commands,
Who speedily through all the hierarchies
Intends to pass triumphant, and give laws.
    So spake the false archangel, and infused
Bad influence into the unwary breast
Of his associate; he together calls,
Or several one by one, the regent powers,   697
Under him regent, tells, as he was taught,
That the most high commanding, now ere night,
Now ere dim night had disencumbered heaven,
The great hierarchal standard was to move;
Tells the suggested cause, and casts between
Ambiguous words and jealousies, to sound
Or taint integrity; but all obeyed
The wonted signal, and superior voice
Of their great potentate; for great indeed
His name, and high was his degree in heaven;
His countenance, as the morning star that guides   708

671 his next subordinate] Identified as Beelzebub in i. 79–81.   697 several]
Separately.   708 morning star] Lucifer, lit. 'light-bringer'.

The starry flock, allured them, and with lies
Drew after him the third part of heaven's host:
Meanwhile the eternal eye, whose sight discerns
Abstrusest thoughts, from forth his holy mount   712
And from within the golden lamps that burn
Nightly before him, saw without their light
Rebellion rising, saw in whom, how spread
Among the sons of morn, what multitudes
Were banded to oppose his high decree;
And smiling to his only son thus said.

    Son, thou in whom my glory I behold
In full resplendence, heir of all my might,
Nearly it now concerns us to be sure   721
Of our omnipotence, and with what arms
We mean to hold what anciently we claim
Of deity or empire, such a foe
Is rising, who intends to erect his throne
Equal to ours, throughout the spacious north;
Nor so content, hath in his thought to try
In battle, what our power is, or our right.
Let us advise, and to this hazard draw   729
With speed what force is left, and all employ
In our defence, lest unawares we lose
This our high place, our sanctuary, our hill.

    To whom the Son with calm aspect and clear
Lightning divine, ineffable, serene,
Made answer. Mighty Father, thou thy foes
Justly hast in derision, and secure   736
Laugh'st at their vain designs and tumults vain,
Matter to me of glory, whom their hate
Illustrates, when they see all regal power   739
Given me to quell their pride, and in event   740
Know whether I be dextrous to subdue   741
Thy rebels, or be found the worst in heaven.

    So spake the Son, but Satan with his powers

---

712 **Abstrusest**] Most hidden.   721 **Nearly**] Significantly, intimately.
729 **advise**] Deliberate, consider together.   736 **Justly ... derision**] Alluding to
God's laughter in Psalm 2: 4.   739 **Illustrates**] Used in its literal sense of 'renders
illustrious'.   740 **in event**] In the outcome.   741 **dextrous**] Capable, alluding
to his place *ad dextram*, at God's right hand.

Far was advanced on wingèd speed, an host
Innumerable as the stars of night,
Or stars of morning, dewdrops, which the sun
Impearls on every leaf and every flower.
Regions they passed, the mighty regencies
Of seraphim and potentates and thrones   749
In their triple degrees, regions to which   750
All thy dominion, Adam, is no more
Than what this garden is to all the earth,
And all the sea, from one entire globose
Stretched into longitude; which having passed   754
At length into the limits of the north
They came, and Satan to his royal seat
High on a hill, far blazing, as a mount
Raised on a mount, with pyramids and towers
From diamond quarries hewn, and rocks of gold,
The palace of great Lucifer, (so call
That structure in the dialect of men
Interpreted) which not long after, he
Affecting all equality with God,   763
In imitation of that mount whereon
Messiah was declared in sight of heaven,
The Mountain of the Congregation called;   766
For thither he assembled all his train,
Pretending so commanded to consult
About the great reception of their king,
Thither to come, and with calumnious art   770
Of counterfeited truth thus held their ears.
    Thrones, dominations, princedoms, virtues, powers,
If these magnific titles yet remain
Not merely titular, since by decree
Another now hath to himself engrossed
All power, and us eclipsed under the name
Of king anointed, for whom all this haste
Of midnight march, and hurried meeting here,
This only to consult how we may best

749 **potentates**] Angelic powers, one of the orders of angels.   750 **triple degrees**] Alluding to Dionysius' system of angelic hierarchies; see i. 134.   **to**] In comparison with.   753–4 **globose ... longitude**] Flattened sphere (as in maps drawn on Mercator's projection).   763 **Affecting**] Claiming, aspiring to.   766 **The ... called**] For Lucifer's inauguration of his holy mountain see Isaiah 14: 13.

With what may be devised of honours new   *780*
Receive him coming to receive from us
Knee-tribute yet unpaid, prostration vile,
Too much to one, but double how endured,
To one and to his image now proclaimed?
But what if better counsels might erect
Our minds and teach us to cast off this yoke?
Will ye submit your necks, and choose to bend
The supple knee? Ye will not, if I trust   *788*
To know ye right, or if ye know yourselves
Natives and sons of heaven possessed before
By none, and if not equal all, yet free,
Equally free; for orders and degrees
Jar not with liberty, but well consist.   *793*
Who can in reason then or right assume
Monarchy over such as live by right
His equals, if in power and splendour less,
In freedom equal? or can introduce
Law and edict on us, who without law
Err not, much less for this to be our lord,
And look for adoration to the abuse   *800*
Of those imperial titles which assert
Our being ordained to govern, not to serve?
    Thus far his bold discourse without control
Had audience, when among the seraphim
Abdiel, than whom none with more zeal adored   *805*
The Deity, and divine commands obeyed,
Stood up, and in a flame of zeal severe
The current of his fury thus opposed.
    O argument blasphemous, false and proud!
Words which no ear ever to hear in heaven   *810*
Expected, least of all from thee, ingrate
In place thyself so high above thy peers.
Canst thou with impious obloquy condemn
The just decree of God, pronounced and sworn,
That to his only son by right endued
With regal sceptre, every soul in heaven
Shall bend the knee, and in that honour due

---

788 **supple**] Lit. 'submissive', suppliant.   793 **well consist**] Are fully consistent.
805 **Abdiel**] Lit. 'Servant of God'; not an angel in the Bible.

Confess him rightful king? Unjust thou say'st
Flatly unjust, to bind with laws the free,
And equal over equals to let reign,
One over all with unsucceeded power.   821
Shalt thou give law to God, shalt thou dispute
With him the points of liberty, who made
Thee what thou art, and formed the powers of heaven
Such as he pleased, and circumscribed their being?
Yet by experience taught we know how good,
And of our good, and of our dignity
How provident he is, how far from thought
To make us less, bent rather to exalt
Our happy state under one head more near   830
United. But to grant it thee unjust,
That equal over equals monarch reign:
Thyself though great and glorious dost thou count,
Or all angelic nature joined in one,
Equal to him begotten son, by whom
As by his word the mighty Father made
All things, even thee, and all the spirits of heaven
By him created in their bright degrees,
Crowned them with glory, and to their glory named
Thrones, dominations, princedoms, virtues, powers,   840
Essential powers, nor by his reign obscured,
But more illustrious made, since he the head
One of our number thus reduced becomes,
His laws our laws, all honour to him done
Returns our own. Cease then this impious rage,
And tempt not these; but hasten to appease
The incensèd Father, and the incensèd Son,
While pardon may be found in time besought.
    So spake the fervent angel, but his zeal
None seconded, as out of season judged,   850
Or singular and rash, whereat rejoiced
The apostate, and more haughty thus replied.
That we were formed then say'st thou? and the work
Of secondary hands, by task transferred
From Father to his son? strange point and new!
Doctrine which we would know whence learned: who saw

821 **unsucceeded**] Eternal, with no successor.

When this creation was? rememb'rest thou
Thy making, while the maker gave thee being?
We know no time when we were not as now;
Know none before us, self-begot, self-raised
By our own quickening power, when fatal course   861
Had circled his full orb, the birth mature
Of this our native heaven, ethereal sons.
Our puissance is our own, our own right hand
Shall teach us highest deeds, by proof to try
Who is our equal: then thou shalt behold
Whether by supplication we intend
Address, and to begirt the almighty throne
Beseeching or besieging. This report,
These tidings carry to the anointed king;   870
And fly, ere evil intercept thy flight.

    He said, and as the sound of waters deep
Hoarse murmur echoed to his words applause
Through the infinite host, nor less for that
The flaming seraph fearless, though alone
Encompassed round with foes, thus answered bold.

    O alienate from God, O spirit accursed,
Forsaken of all good; I see thy fall
Determined, and thy hapless crew involved
In this perfidious fraud, contagion spread   880
Both of thy crime and punishment: henceforth
No more be troubled how to quit the yoke
Of God's Messiah; those indulgent laws
Will not be now vouchsafed, other decrees
Against thee are gone forth without recall;
That golden sceptre which thou didst reject
Is now an iron rod to bruise and break
Thy disobedience. Well thou didst advise,
Yet not for thy advice or threats I fly
These wicked tents devoted, lest the wrath   890
Impendent, raging into sudden flame`
Distinguish not: for soon expect to feel
His thunder on thy head, devouring fire.
Then who created thee lamenting learn,

---

861 **fatal**] Ordained by fate, inevitable.   890 **devoted**] 'Formally or surely
consigned to evil; doomed' (*OED*).   **lest**] i.e. but rather lest.

When who can uncreate thee thou shalt know.
  So spake the seraph Abdiel faithful found,
Among the faithless, faithful only he;
Among innumerable false, unmoved,
Unshaken, unseduced, unterrified
His loyalty he kept, his love, his zeal;
Nor number, nor example with him wrought   901
To swerve from truth, or change his constant mind
Though single. From amidst them forth he passed,
Long way through hostile scorn, which he sustained
Superior, nor of violence feared aught;
And with retorted scorn his back he turned   906
On those proud towers to swift destruction doomed.

901 **with him wrought**] Persuaded him.   906 **with retorted scorn**] Having returned their scorn.

BOOK VI

The Argument

Raphael continues to relate how Michael and Gabriel were sent
forth to battle against Satan and his angels. The first fight described:
Satan and his powers retire under night: he calls a council, invents
devilish engines, which in the second day's fight put Michael and
his angels to some disorder; but they at length pulling up mountains
overwhelmed both the force and machines of Satan: yet the tumult
not so ending, God on the third day sends Messiah his son, for
whom he had reserved the glory of that victory: he in the power
of his father coming to the place, and causing all his legions to stand
still on either side, with his chariot and thunder driving into the
midst of his enemies, pursues them unable to resist towards the
wall of heaven; which opening, they leap down with horror and
confusion into the place of punishment prepared for them in the
deep: Messiah returns with triumph to his father.

ALL night the dreadless angel unpursued
Through heaven's wide champaign held his way, till Morn,   2
Waked by the circling Hours, with rosy hand   3
Unbarred the gates of light. There is a cave
Within the mount of God, fast by his throne,   5
Where light and darkness in perpetual round
Lodge and dislodge by turns, which makes through heaven
Grateful vicissitude, like day and night;   8
Light issues forth, and at the other door
Obsequious darkness enters, till her hour   10
To veil the heaven, though darkness there might well
Seem twilight here; and now went forth the morn
Such as in highest heaven, arrayed in gold
Empyreal, from before her vanished night,
Shot through with orient beams: when all the plain
Covered with thick embattled squadrons bright,   16
Chariots and flaming arms, and fiery steeds
Reflecting blaze on blaze, first met his view:

---

2 **champaign**] Plain.   3 **Hours**] The Horae, goddesses of the seasons and
gatekeepers of heaven (see *Iliad*, v. 749 and Spenser, *Faerie Queene*, VII. vii. 45).
5 **fast by**] Next to.   8 **vicissitude**] Change.   10 **Obsequious**] Obedient, with
an overtone of its literal sense, 'following'.   16 **embattled**] Ready for battle.

War he perceived, war in procinct, and found   19
Already known what he for news had thought
To have reported: gladly then he mixed
Among those friendly powers who him received
With joy and acclamations loud, that one
That of so many myriads fallen, yet one
Returned not lost: on to the sacred hill
They led him high applauded, and present
Before the seat supreme; from whence a voice
From midst a golden cloud thus mild was heard.
 Servant of God, well done, well hast thou fought   29
The better fight, who single hast maintained
Against revolted multitudes the cause
Of truth, in word mightier than they in arms;
And for the testimony of truth has borne
Universal reproach, far worse to bear
Than violence: for this was all thy care
To stand approved in sight of God, though worlds
Judged thee perverse: the easier conquest now
Remains thee, aided by this host of friends,
Back on thy foes more glorious to return
Than scorned thou didst depart, and to subdue   40
By force, who reason for their law refuse,
Right reason for their law, and for their king
Messiah, who by right of merit reigns.
Go Michael of celestial armies prince,
And thou in military prowess next
Gabriel, lead forth to battle these my sons
Invincible, lead forth my armed saints
By thousands and by millions ranged for fight;
Equal in number to that godless crew
Rebellious, them with fire and hostile arms   50
Fearless assault, and to the brow of heaven
Pursuing drive them out from God and bliss,
Into their place of punishment, the gulf
Of Tartarus, which ready opens wide
His fiery chaos to receive their fall.
 So spake the sovereign voice, and clouds began

19 **procinct**] Readiness. 29 **Servant of God**] Translating 'Abdiel'.

To darken all the hill, and smoke to roll
In dusky wreaths, reluctant flames, the sign   58
Of wrath awaked: nor with less dread the loud
Ethereal trumpet from on high gan blow:
At which command the powers militant,
That stood for heaven, in mighty quadrate joined   62
Of union irresistible, moved on
In silence their bright legions, to the sound
Of instrumental harmony that breathed
Heroic ardour to adventurous deeds
Under their godlike leaders, in the cause
Of God and his Messiah. On they move
Indissolubly firm; nor obvious hill,   69
Nor straitening vale, nor wood, nor stream divides   70
Their perfect ranks; for high above the ground
Their march was, and the passive air upbore
Their nimble tread, as when the total kind
Of birds in orderly array on wing
Came summoned over Eden to receive
Their names of thee; so over many a tract
Of heaven they marched, and many a province wide
Tenfold the length of this terrene: at last   78
Far in th' horizon to the north appeared
From skirt to skirt a fiery region, stretched   80
In battailous aspect, and nearer view
Bristled with upright beams innumerable
Of rigid spears, and helmets thronged, and shields
Various, with boastful argument portrayed,   84
The banded powers of Satan hasting on
With furious expedition; for they weened   86
That selfsame day by fight, or by surprise
To win the mount of God, and on his throne
To set the envier of his state, the proud
Aspirer, but their thoughts proved fond and vain   90
In the mid-way: though strange to us it seemed
At first, that angel should with angel war,

---

58 **reluctant**] With an overtone of its literal sense, 'struggling, writhing'.
62 **quadrate**] Square formation.   69 **obvious**] Lit. 'in the way'.   70 **straiten-
ing**] Narrowly confining.   78 **terrene**] Earth.   80 **skirt to skirt**] End to end.
84 **argument**] Heraldic emblems.   86 **expedition**] Speed.   90 **fond**] Foolish.

And in fierce hosting meet, who wont to meet   93
So oft in festivals of joy and love
Unanimous, as sons of one great sire
Hymning the eternal Father: but the shout
Of battle now began, and rushing sound
Of onset ended soon each milder thought.
High in the midst exalted as a god
The apostate in his sun-bright chariot sat   100
Idol of majesty divine, enclosed
With flaming cherubim, and golden shields;
Then lighted from his gorgeous throne, for now
'Twixt host and host but narrow space was left,
A dreadful interval, and front to front
Presented stood in terrible array
Of hideous length: before the cloudy van,   107
On the rough edge of battle ere it joined,
Satan with vast and haughty strides advanced,
Came towering, armed in adamant and gold;   110
Abdiel that sight endured not, where he stood
Among the mightiest, bent on highest deeds,
And thus his own undaunted heart explores.
     O heaven! that such resemblance of the highest
Should yet remain, where faith and realty   115
Remain not; wherefore should not strength and might
There fail where virtue fails, or weakest prove
Where boldest; though to sight unconquerable?   118
His puissance, trusting in the almighty's aid,
I mean to try, whose reason I have tried   120
Unsound and false; nor is it aught but just,
That he who in debate of truth hath won,
Should win in arms, in both disputes alike
Victor; though brutish that contest and foul,
When reason hath to deal with force, yet so
Most reason is that reason overcome.   126
     So pondering, and from his armèd peers
Forth stepping opposite, halfway he met

---

93 **hosting**] Enmity.   107 **cloudy**] Ominous.   **van**] Vanguard.   110 **adamant**]
A mythical substance of impenetrable hardness.   115 **realty**] Sincerity, honesty; re-
ality.   118 **to sight**] Seemingly.   120 **tried**] Tested (and found).   126 **Most
reason is**] It is most reasonable.

His daring foe, at this prevention more   129
Incensed, and thus securely him defied.   130
   Proud, art thou met? Thy hope was to have reached
The height of thy aspiring unopposed,
The throne of God unguarded, and his side
Abandoned at the terror of thy power
Or potent tongue; fool, not to think how vain
Against the omnipotent to rise in arms;
Who out of smallest things could without end
Have raised incessant armies to defeat
Thy folly; or with solitary hand
Reaching beyond all limit at one blow
Unaided could have finished thee, and whelmed   141
Thy legions under darkness; but thou seest
All are not of thy train; there be who faith   143
Prefer, and piety to God, though then
To thee not visible, when I alone
Seemed in thy world erroneous to dissent
From all: my sect thou seest, now learn too late   147
How few sometimes may know, when thousands err.
   Whom the grand foe with scornful eye askance
Thus answered. Ill for thee, but in wished hour
Of my revenge, first sought for thou return'st
From flight, seditious angel, to receive
Thy merited reward, the first assay   153
Of this right hand provoked, since first that tongue
Inspired with contradiction durst oppose
A third part of the gods, in synod met   156
Their deities to assert, who while they feel
Vigour divine within them, can allow
Omnipotence to none. But well thou com'st
Before thy fellows, ambitious to win
From me some plume, that thy success may show   161

---

129 **prevention**] 'The action of ... baffling or stopping another person in the execution of his designs' (*OED*).   130 **securely**] Confidently.   141 **whelmed**] Overthrown and buried.   143 **who**] Those who.   147 **sect**] Abdiel ironically applies the royalist term for religious schismatics to himself.   153 **assay**] Trial. 156 **synod**] Assembly.   161 **thy success**] How you succeed: 'success' means, literally, simply the outcome of an action, whether good or bad; but given its more usual sense, Satan's usage is unintentionally ironic.

Destruction to the rest: this pause between   162
(Unanswered lest thou boast) to let thee know;   163
At first I thought that liberty and heaven
To heavenly souls had been all one; but now
I see that most through sloth had rather serve,
Ministering spirits, trained up in feast and song;
Such hast thou armed, the minstrelsy of heaven,   168
Servility with freedom to contend,
As both their deeds compared this day shall prove.
    To whom in brief thus Abdiel stern replied.
Apostate, still thou err'st, nor end wilt find
Of erring, from the path of truth remote:
Unjustly thou deprav'st it with the name   174
Of servitude to serve whom God ordains,
Or nature; God and nature bid the same,
When he who rules is worthiest, and excels
Them whom he governs. This is servitude,
To serve the unwise, or him who hath rebelled
Against his worthier, as thine now serve thee,
Thyself not free, but to thyself enthralled;
Yet lewdly dar'st our ministering upbraid.   182
Reign thou in hell thy kingdom, let me serve
In heaven God ever blessed, and his divine
Behests obey, worthiest to be obeyed;
Yet chains in hell, not realms expect: meanwhile
From me returned, as erst thou saidst, from flight,
This greeting on thy impious crest receive.
    So saying, a noble stroke he lifted high,
Which hung not, but so swift with tempest fell   190
On the proud crest of Satan, that no sight,
Nor motion of swift thought, less could his shield
Such ruin intercept: ten paces huge
He back recoiled; the tenth on bended knee
His massy spear upstayed; as if on earth
Winds underground or waters forcing way

162 **pause between**] i.e. between our meeting and your destruction.   163 (**Un-answered . . . boast**)] Lest you boast that I was unable to answer you.   168 **min-strelsy**] Minstrels; cognate with 'ministering', l. 167.   174 **deprav'st**] Distorts, perverts.   182 **lewdly**] Combining the senses of foolishly and wickedly.

Sidelong, had pushed a mountain from his seat
Half sunk with all his pines. Amazement seized
The rebel thrones, but greater rage to see
Thus foiled their mightiest, ours joy filled, and shout,   200
Presage of victory and fierce desire
Of battle: whereat Michael bid sound
The archangel trumpet; through the vast of heaven
It sounded, and the faithful armies rung
Hosanna to the highest: nor stood at gaze
The adverse legions, nor less hideous joined
The horrid shock: now storming fury rose,
And clamour such as heard in heaven till now
Was never, arms on armour clashing brayed
Horrible discord, and the madding wheels   210
Of brazen chariots raged; dire was the noise
Of conflict; overhead the dismal hiss
Of fiery darts in flaming volleys flew,
And flying vaulted either host with fire.
So under fiery cope together rushed   215
Both battles main, with ruinous assault   216
And inextinguishable rage; all heaven
Resounded, and had earth been then, all earth
Had to her centre shook. What wonder? when
Millions of fierce encountering angels fought
On either side, the least of whom could wield
These elements, and arm him with the force
Of all their regions: how much more of power
Army against army numberless to raise
Dreadful combustion warring, and disturb,   225
Though not destroy, their happy native seat;
Had not the eternal king omnipotent
From his stronghold of heaven high overruled
And limited their might; though numbered such   229
As each divided legion might have seemed
A numerous host, in strength each armèd hand

---

210 **madding**] Furiously whirling.   215 **cope**] Sky.   216 **battles main**]
Both mighty troops and the bulk or main body of both armies; also, a 'main battle' is
'a pitched battle, as opposed to mere skirmishing' (*OED*).   225 **combustion**]
Conflict.   229 **numbered such**] So numerous.

A legion; led in fight, yet leader seemed
Each warrior single as in chief, expert   233
When to advance, or stand, or turn the sway
Of battle, open when, and when to close
The ridges of grim war; no thought of flight,
None of retreat, no unbecoming deed
That argued fear; each on himself relied,
As only in his arm the moment lay   239
Of victory; deeds of eternal fame
Were done, but infinite: for wide was spread
That war and various; sometimes on firm ground
A standing fight, then soaring on main wing   243
Tormented all the air; all air seemed then
Conflicting fire: long time in even scale
The battle hung; till Satan, who that day
Prodigious power had shown, and met in arms
No equal, ranging through the dire attack
Of fighting seraphim confused, at length
Saw where the sword of Michael smote, and felled
Squadrons at once, with huge two-handed sway   251
Brandished aloft the horrid edge came down
Wide wasting; such destruction to withstand
He hasted, and opposed the rocky orb
Of tenfold adamant, his ample shield
A vast circumference: at his approach
The great archangel from his warlike toil
Surceased, and glad as hoping here to end
Intestine war in heaven, the arch foe subdued   259
Or captive dragged in chains, with hostile frown
And visage all inflamed first thus began.
    Author of evil, unknown till thy revolt,
Unnamed in heaven, now plenteous, as thou seest
These acts of hateful strife, hateful to all,
Though heaviest by just measure on thyself
And thy adherents: how hast thou disturbed
Heaven's blessèd peace, and into nature brought
Misery, uncreated till the crime

232–3 leader ... chief] Every single warrior seemed like a leader.   239 As]
if.   moment] Deciding factor.   243 main] Powerful.   251 sway] Swinging
motion.   259 Intestine war] Civil war.

Of thy rebellion? how hast thou instilled
Thy malice into thousands, once upright   270
And faithful, now proved false. But think not here
To trouble holy rest; heaven casts thee out
From all her confines. Heaven the seat of bliss
Brooks not the works of violence and war.
Hence then, and evil go with thee along
Thy offspring, to the place of evil, hell,
Thou and thy wicked crew; there mingle broils,
Ere this avenging sword begin thy doom,
Or some more sudden vengeance winged from God
Precipitate thee with augmented pain.   280
    So spake the prince of angels; to whom thus
The adversary. Nor think thou with wind
Of airy threats to awe whom yet with deeds
Thou canst not. Hast thou turned the least of these
To flight, or if to fall, but that they rise
Unvanquished, easier to transact with me
That thou shouldst hope, imperious, and with threats
To chase me hence? err not that so shall end   288
The strife which thou call'st evil, but we style
The strife of glory: which we mean to win,
Or turn this heaven itself into the hell
Thou fablest, here however to dwell free,
If not to reign: meanwhile thy utmost force,
And join him named Almighty to thy aid,
I fly not, but have sought thee far and nigh.
    They ended parle, and both addressed for fight   296
Unspeakable; for who, though with the tongue
Of angels, can relate, or to what things
Liken on earth conspicuous, that may lift
Human imagination to such height   300
Of godlike power: for likest gods they seemed,
Stood they or moved, in stature, motion, arms
Fit to decide the empire of great heaven.
Now waved their fiery swords, and in the air
Made horrid circles; two broad suns their shields
Blazed opposite, while expectation stood

---

288 **err not**] Do not mistakenly believe.   296 **parle**] Parley.   **addressed**]
Prepared.

In horror; from each hand with speed retired
Where erst was thickest fight, the angelic throng,   308
And left large field, unsafe within the wind
Of such commotion, such as to set forth
Great things by small, if nature's concord broke,
Among the constellations war were sprung,
Two planets rushing from aspect malign   313
Of fiercest opposition in mid sky,
Should combat, and their jarring spheres confound.
Together both with next to almighty arm,
Uplifted imminent one stroke they aimed
That might determine, and not need repeat,   318
As not of power, at once; nor odds appeared   319
In might or swift prevention; but the sword   320
Of Michael from the armoury of God
Was given him tempered so, that neither keen
Nor solid might resist that edge: it met
The sword of Satan with steep force to smite
Descending, and in half cut sheer, nor stayed,
But with swift wheel reverse, deep entering sheared
All his right side; then Satan first knew pain,
And writhed him to and fro convolved; so sore
The griding sword with discontinuous wound   329
Passed through him, but the ethereal substance closed
Not long divisible, and from the gash
A stream of nectarous humour issuing flowed   332
Sanguine, such as celestial spirits may bleed,   333
And all his armour stained erewhile so bright.
Forthwith on all sides to his aid was run
By angels many and strong, who interposed
Defence, while others bore him on their shields
Back to his chariot; where it stood retired
From off the files of war; there they him laid
Gnashing for anguish and despite and shame   340
To find himself not matchless, and his pride

---

308 **erst**] Formerly.   313 **aspect malign**] Opposed positions (hence shedding evil influence).   318 **determine**] Decide the outcome.   **repeat**] Be repeated.
319 **As ... once**] It would not have been possible to repeat such a blow right away.   320 **prevention**] Anticipation.   329 **griding**] Cutting.   **discontinuous wound**] The technical medical term for an open wound.   332 **humour**] Fluid.   333 **Sanguine**] Red, and analogous to blood in mortals.

Humbled by such rebuke, so far beneath
His confidence to equal God in power.
Yet soon he healed; for spirits that live throughout
Vital in every part, not as frail man
In entrails, heart or head, liver or reins,   346
Cannot but by annihilating die;
Nor in their liquid texture mortal wound
Receive, no more than can the fluid air:
All heart they live, all head, all eye, all ear,
All intellect, all sense, and as they please,
They limb themselves, and colour, shape or size
Assume, as likes them best, condense or rare.   353
   Meanwhile in other parts like deeds deserved
Memorial, where the might of Gabriel fought,
And with fierce ensigns pierced the deep array
Of Moloch furious king, who him defied,
And at his chariot wheels to drag him bound
Threatened, nor from the holy one of heaven
Refrained his tongue blasphemous; but anon
Down cloven to the waist, with shattered arms
And uncouth pain fled bellowing. On each wing   362
Uriel and Raphael his vaunting foe,   363
Though huge, and in a rock of diamond armed,
Vanquished Adramelec, and Asmadai,   365
Two potent thrones, that to be less than gods
Disdained, but meaner thoughts learned in their flight,
Mangled with ghastly wounds through plate and mail,
Nor stood unmindful Abdiel to annoy   369
The atheist crew, but with redoubled blow   370
Ariel and Arioch, and the violence   371

346 **reins**] Kidneys.   353 **condense or rare**] Dense or airy.   362 **uncouth**]
(Hitherto) unknown.   362–3 **On . . . foe**] i.e. each had his foe. Raphael describes
his own actions without identifying himself.   365 **Adramelec**] Adramelech,
Babylonian sun god (2 Kings 17: 31).   **Asmadai**] The evil spirit Asmodeus of the
Tobit story; see iv. 168.   369 **annoy**] Harass, injure.   370 **atheist**] Lit. 'god-
less'.   371 **Ariel**] Though in the Bible this is an epithet for Jerusalem (lit. 'lion of
God', Isaiah 29: 1), in the cabbalistic tradition it is the name of an evil angel, formerly a
pagan god. The name also appears as a spirit of earth in many magical texts, e.g. H. C.
Agrippa's *De Occulta Philosophia* (Shakespeare's airy spirit is apparently without prece-
dent).   **Arioch**] Lit. 'lion-like'; a king against whom Abraham fought (Genesis 14),
and a Babylonian captain hostile to the Jews (Daniel 2: 14). But Milton seems to be
relying on Renaissance demonology, in which the name is that of a vengeful spirit.

Of Ramiel scorched and blasted overthrew.   372
I might relate of thousands, and their names
Eternize here on earth; but those elect
Angels contented with their fame in heaven
Seek not the praise of men: the other sort
In might though wondrous and in acts of war,
Nor of renown less eager, yet by doom
Cancelled from heaven and sacred memory,
Nameless in dark oblivion let them dwell.
For strength from truth divided and from just,
Illaudable, naught merits but dispraise   382
And ignominy, yet to glory aspires
Vainglorious, and through infamy seeks fame:
Therefore eternal silence be their doom.
    And now their mightiest quelled, the battle swerved,
With many an inroad gored; deformèd rout
Entered, and foul disorder; all the ground
With shivered armour strewn, and on a heap
Chariot and charioteer lay overturned
And fiery foaming steeds; what stood, recoiled
O'er-wearied, through the faint Satanic host
Defensive scarce, or with pale fear surprised,   393
Then first with fear surprised and sense of pain
Fled ignominious, to such evil brought
By sin of disobedience, till that hour
Not liable to fear or flight or pain.
Far otherwise the inviolable saints
In cubic phalanx firm advanced entire,
Invulnerable, impenetrably armed:
Such high advantages their innocence
Gave them above their foes, not to have sinned,
Not to have disobeyed; in fight they stood
Unwearied, unobnoxious to be pained   404
By wound, though from their place by violence moved.
    Now night her course began, and over heaven
Inducing darkness, grateful truce imposed,

---

372 **Ramiel**] 'Thunder of God', not a biblical name; an evil angel in the pseud-epigraphic Book of Enoch, and the name of a devil in various cabbalistic texts.
382 **Illaudable**] Not worthy of praise.   393 **Defensive scarce**] Hardly able to
defend themselves.   404 **unobnoxious**] Lit. 'not subject to injury'.

And silence on the odious din of war:
Under her cloudy covert both retired,
Victor and vanquished: on the foughten field   410
Michael and his angels prevalent   411
Encamping, placed in guard their watches round,
Cherubic waving fires: on the other part
Satan with his rebellious disappeared,
Far in the dark dislodged, and void of rest,
His potentates to council called by night;
And in the midst thus undismayed began.

   O now in danger tried, now known in arms
Not to be overpowered, companions dear,
Found worthy not of liberty alone,
Too mean pretence, but what we more affect,   421
Honour, dominion, glory, and renown,
Who have sustained one day in doubtful fight
(And if one day, why not eternal days?)
What heaven's lord had powerfullest to send
Against us from about his throne, and judged
Sufficient to subdue us to his will,
But proves not so: then fallible, it seems,
Of future we may deem him, though till now   429
Omniscient thought. True is, less firmly armed,
Some disadvantage we endured and pain,
Till now not known, but known as soon contemned,
Since now we find this our empyreal form
Incapable of mortal injury
Imperishable, and though pierced with wound,
Soon closing, and by native vigour healed.
Of evil then so small as easy think
The remedy; perhaps more valid arms,
Weapons more violent, when next we meet,
May serve to better us, and worse our foes,   440
Or equal what between us made the odds,
In nature none: if other hidden cause
Left them superior, while we can preserve
Unhurt our minds, and understanding sound,

---

410 **foughten field**] Battlefield.   411 **prevalent**] Having prevailed, victorious.
421 **mean pretence**] Modest ambition, but with an overtone of the modern sense.
affect] Aim at; 'put on a false appearance of' (*OED*).   429 **Of future**] In future.

Due search and consultation will disclose.
　He sat; and in the assembly next upstood
Nisroch, of principalities the prime;   447
As one he stood escaped from cruel fight,
Sore toiled, his riven arms to havoc hewn,
And cloudy in aspect thus answering spake.
Deliverer from new lords, leader to free
Enjoyment of our right as gods; yet hard
For gods, and too unequal work we find
Against unequal arms to fight in pain,
Against unpained, impassive; from which evil   455
Ruin must needs ensue; for what avails
Valour or strength, though matchless, quelled with pain
Which all subdues, and makes remiss the hands   458
Of mightiest. Sense of pleasure we may well
Spare out of life perhaps, and not repine,
But live content, which is the calmest life:
But pain is perfect misery, the worst
Of evils, and excessive, overturns
All patience. He who therefore can invent
With what more forcible we may offend   465
Our yet unwounded enemies, or arm
Ourselves with like defence, to me deserves
No less than for deliverance what we owe.
　Whereto with look composed Satan replied.
Not uninvented that, which thou aright
Believ'st so main to our success, I bring;
Which of us who beholds the bright surface
Of this ethereous mould whereon we stand,
This continent of spacious heaven, adorned
With plant, fruit, flower ambrosial, gems and gold,
Whose eye so superficially surveys
These things, as not to mind from whence they grow   477
Deep underground, materials dark and crude,
Of spiritous and fiery spume, till touched
With heaven's ray, and tempered they shoot forth
So beauteous, opening to the ambient light.

---

447 **Nisroch**] An Assyrian god in 2 Kings 19: 37.　　455 **impassive**] Not subject
to pain.　　458 **remiss**] Weak.　　465 **offend**] Attack.　　477 **mind**] Remember.

These in their dark nativity the deep
Shall yield us pregnant with infernal flame,
Which into hollow engines long and round
Thick-rammed, at the other bore with touch of fire   485
Dilated and infuriate shall send forth
From far with thundering noise among our foes
Such implements of mischief as shall dash
To pieces, and o'erwhelm whatever stands
Adverse, that they shall fear we have disarmed
The thunderer of his only dreaded bolt.
Nor long shall be our labour, yet ere dawn,
Effect shall end our wish. Meanwhile revive;
Abandon fear; to strength and counsel joined
Think nothing hard, much less to be despaired.
He ended, and his words their drooping cheer   496
Enlightened, and their languished hope revived.
The invention all admired, and each, how he
To be the inventor missed, so easy it seemed
Once found, which yet unfound most would have thought   500
Impossible: yet haply of thy race
In future days, if malice should abound,
Someone intent on mischief, or inspired
With devilish machination might devise
Like instrument to plague the sons of men
For sin, on war and mutual slaughter bent.
Forthwith from council to the work they flew,
None arguing stood, innumerable hands
Were ready, in a moment up they turned
Wide the celestial soil, and saw beneath
The originals of nature in their crude   511
Conception; sulphurous and nitrous foam
They found, they mingled, and with subtle art,
Concocted and adusted they reduced   514
To blackest grain, and into store conveyed:
Part hidden veins digged up (nor hath this earth
Entrails unlike) of mineral and stone,

---

485 **touch**] Both contact and touch-powder, fine gunpowder.   496 **cheer**]
Spirits.   511 **originals**] Basic elements.   514 **Concocted and adusted**]
Heated and dried, alchemical processes.

Whereof to found their engines and their balls   518
Of missive ruin; part incentive reed   519
Provide, pernicious with one touch to fire.   520
So all ere day-spring, under conscious night   521
Secret they finished, and in order set,
With silent circumspection unespied.
Now when fair morn orient in heaven appeared   524
Up rose the victor angels, and to arms
The matin trumpet sung: in arms they stood
Of golden panoply, refulgent host,
Soon banded; others from the dawning hills
Looked round, and scouts each coast light-armèd scour,
Each quarter, to descry the distant foe,   530
Where lodged, or whither fled, or if for fight,
In motion or in halt: him soon they met
Under spread ensigns moving nigh, in slow
But firm battalion; back with speediest sail
Zophiel, of cherubim the swiftest wing,   535
Came flying, and in midair aloud thus cried.
   Arm, warriors, arm for fight, the foe at hand,
Whom fled we thought, will save us long pursuit
This day, fear not his flight; so thick a cloud
He comes, and settled in his face I see
Sad resolution and secure: let each   541
His adamantine coat gird well, and each
Fit well his helm, gripe fast his orbèd shield,
Borne even or high, for this day will pour down,
If I conjecture aught, no drizzling shower,
But rattling storm of arrows barbed with fire.
So warned he them aware themselves, and soon
In order, quit of all impediment;
Instant without disturb they took alarm,   549
And onward move embattled; when behold
Not distant far with heavy pace the foe

518 **found**] Cast (as in a foundry). **engines**] War machines, specifically cannons. 519 **missive**] Missile. **incentive**] Igniting. 520 **pernicious**] The word, from two separate Latin roots, means both swift and destructive. 521 **conscious**] Both aware and guilty; but also indicating their own unnatural wakefulness. 524 **orient**] Both bright and rising. 535 **Zophiel**] Lit. 'spy of God'; not a biblical name. 541 **Sad**] Serious. **secure**] Confident. 549 **took alarm**] Responded to the alarm, or call to battle.

Approaching gross and huge; in hollow cube
Training his devilish enginery, impaled   553
On every side with shadowing squadrons deep,
To hide the fraud. At interview both stood   555
Awhile, but suddenly at head appeared
Satan: and thus was heard commanding loud.

   Vanguard, to right and left the front unfold;
That all may see who hate us, how we seek
Peace and composure, and with open breast   560
Stand ready to receive them, if they like
Our overture, and turn not back perverse;
But that I doubt, however witness heaven,
Heaven witness thou anon, while we discharge
Freely our part; ye who appointed stand
Do as you have in charge, and briefly touch
What we propound, and loud that all may hear.

   So scoffing in ambiguous words, he scarce   568
Had ended; when to right and left the front
Divided, and to either flank retired.

Which to our eyes discovered new and strange,   571
A triple mounted row of pillars laid
On wheels (for like to pillars most they seemed
Or hollowed bodies made of oak or fir,
With branches lopped, in wood or mountain felled)
Brass, iron, stony mould, had not their mouths   576
With hideous orifice gapèd on us wide,
Portending hollow truce; at each behind   578
A seraph stood, and in his hand a reed
Stood waving tipped with fire; while we suspense,   580
Collected stood within our thoughts amused,   581
Not long, for sudden all at once their reeds
Put forth, and to a narrow vent applied

---

553 **Training**] Drawing behind.   **impaled**] Surrounded, fenced in.   555 **in-
terview**]   Mutual   view.   560 **composure**]   Composition,   settlement.
568 **ambiguous words**] Calling attention to the miltary puns in ll. 560-7, including, in
addition to 'composure', 'breast' (heart and the front line of the company), 'overture'
(opening of negotiations and aperture, orifice), 'discharge' (perform and fire off),
'appointed' (chosen and equipped), 'have in charge' (have been charged to do and are
ready to fire, as a loaded weapon), and 'touch' (mention and ignite).   571 **discovered**]
Revealed.   576 **mould**] Moulded out of (brass, etc.).   578 **hollow**] False.
580 **suspense**] Suspended, in suspense.   581 **amused**] Bemused, puzzled.

With nicest touch. Immediate in a flame,
But soon obscured with smoke, all heaven appeared,
From those deep throated engines belched, whose roar
Embowelled with outrageous noise the air,
And all her entrails tore, disgorging foul
Their devilish glut, chained thunderbolts and hail   589
Of iron globes, which on the victor host
Levelled, with such impetuous fury smote,
That whom they hit, none on their feet might stand,
Though standing else as rocks, but down they fell
By thousands, angel on archangel rolled;
The sooner for their arms, unarmed they might
Have easily as spirits evaded swift
By quick contraction or remove; but now   597
Foul dissipation followed and forced rout;   598
Nor served it to relax their serried files.
What should they do? If on they rushed, repulse
Repeated, and indecent overthrow   601
Doubled, would render them yet more despised,
And to their foes a laughter; for in view
Stood ranked of seraphim another row
In posture to displode their second tire   605
Of thunder: back defeated to return
They worse abhorred. Satan beheld their plight,
And to his mates thus in derision called.

O friends, why come not on these victors proud?
Erewhile they fierce were coming, and when we,   610
To entertain them fair with open front
And breast, (what could we more?) propounded terms
Of composition, straight they changed their minds,
Flew off, and into strange vagaries fell,
As they would dance, yet for a dance they seemed
Somewhat extravagant and wild, perhaps
For joy of offered peace: but I suppose
If our proposals once again were heard
We should compel them to a quick result.
To whom thus Belial in like gamesome mood,   620

589 **chained thunderbolts**] Satan's troops are using chain shot, cannonballs linked together with chains.   597 **quick contraction or remove**] Quickly diminishing their size or departing.   598 **dissipation**] Dispersal.   601 **indecent**] Shameful.   605 **displode ... tire**] Fire ... volley.

Leader, the terms we sent were terms of weight,
Of hard contents, and full of force urged home,
Such as we might perceive amused them all,   623
And stumbled many; who receives them right,   624
Had need from head to foot well understand;   625
Not understood, this gift they have besides,
They show us when our foes walk not upright.
  So they among themselves in pleasant vein
Stood scoffing, heightened in their thoughts beyond
All doubt of victory, eternal might   630
To match with their inventions they presumed
So easy, and of his thunder made a scorn,
And all his host derided, while they stood
Awhile in trouble; but they stood not long,
Rage prompted them at length, and found them arms
Against such hellish mischief fit to oppose.
Forthwith (behold the excellence, the power
Which God hath in his mighty angels placed)
Their arms away they threw, and to the hills
(For earth hath this variety from heaven
Of pleasure situate in hill and dale)
Light as the lightning glimpse they ran, they flew,
From their foundations loosening to and fro
They plucked the seated hills with all their load,   644
Rocks, waters, woods, and by the shaggy tops
Up lifting bore them in their hands: amaze,
Be sure, and terror seized the rebel host,
When coming towards them so dread they saw
The bottom of the mountains upward turned,
Till on those cursèd engines' triple-row
They saw them whelmed, and all their confidence
Under the weight of mountains buried deep,
Themselves invaded next, and on their heads
Main promontories flung, which in the air   654
Came shadowing, and oppressed whole legions armed,
Their armour helped their harm, crushed in and bruised
Into their substance pent, which wrought them pain

---

  623 **amused**] Baffled.   624 **stumbled**] Caused to stumble.   625 **under-
stand**] Both comprehend and support themselves.   644 **seated**] Fixed.
654 **Main**] Whole.

Implacable, and many a dolorous groan,
Long struggling underneath, ere they could wind
Out of such prison, though spirits of purest light,
Purest at first, now gross by sinning grown.
The rest in imitation to like arms
Betook them, and the neighbouring hills uptore;
So hills amid the air encountered hills
Hurled to and fro with jaculation dire,   665
That underground they fought in dismal shade;
Infernal noise; war seemed a civil game
To this uproar; horrid confusion heaped   668
Upon confusion rose: and now all heaven
Had gone to wrack, with ruin overspread,
Had not the almighty Father where he sits
Shrined in his sanctuary of heaven secure,
Consulting on the sum of things, foreseen   673
This tumult, and permitted all, advised: 674
That his great purpose he might so fulfil,
To honour his anointed son avenged
Upon his enemies, and to declare
All power on him transferred: whence to his son
The assessor of his throne he thus began.   679

   Effulgence of my glory, Son beloved,
Son in whose face invisible is beheld
Visibly, what by deity I am,
And in whose hand what by decree I do,
Second omnipotence, two days are past,
Two days, as we compute the days of heaven,
Since Michael and his powers went forth to tame
These disobedient; sore hath been their fight,
As likeliest was, when two such foes met armed;
For to themselves I left them, and thou know'st,
Equal in their creation they were formed,
Save what sin hath impaired, which yet hath wrought
Insensibly, for I suspend their doom;   692
Whence in perpetual fight they needs must last

---

  665 **jaculation**] Throwing.   668 **To**] Compared with.   673 **Consulting**]
Deliberating. **foreseen**] Having foreseen.   674 **advised**] Advisedly, in full
knowledge.   679 **assessor**] 'One who sits beside; hence one who shares another's
rank, position or dignity' (*OED*).   692 **Insensibly**] Imperceptibly.

Endless, and no solution will be found:
War wearied hath performed what war can do,
And to disordered rage let loose the reins,
With mountains as with weapons armed, which makes
Wild work in heaven, and dangerous to the main.   698
Two days are therefore past, the third is thine;
For thee I have ordained it, and thus far
Have suffered, that the glory may be thine   701
Of ending this great war, since none but thou
Can end it. Into thee such virtue and grace
Immense I have transfused, that all may know
In heaven and hell thy power above compare,
And this perverse commotion governed thus,
To manifest thee worthiest to be heir
Of all things, to be heir and to be king
By sacred unction, thy deservèd right.   709
Go then thou mightiest in thy father's might,
Ascend my chariot, guide the rapid wheels
That shake heaven's basis, bring forth all my war,
My bow and thunder, my almighty arms
Gird on, and sword upon thy puissant thigh;
Pursue these sons of darkness, drive them out
From all heaven's bounds into the utter deep:
There let them learn, as likes them, to despise
God and Messiah his anointed king.
    He said, and on his son with rays direct
Shone full, he all his father full expressed   720
Ineffably into his face received,
And thus the filial Godhead answering spake.
    O Father, O supreme of heavenly thrones,
First, highest, holiest, best, thou always seek'st
To glorify thy son, I always thee,
As is most just; this I my glory account,
My exaltation, and my whole delight,
That thou in me well pleased, declar'st thy will
Fulfilled, which to fulfil is all my bliss.
Sceptre and power, thy giving, I assume,   730
And gladlier shall resign, when in the end
Thou shalt be all in all, and I in thee

698 **main**] Whole.   701 **suffered**] Permitted.   709 **unction**] Anointing.

Forever, and in me all whom thou lov'st:
But whom thou hat'st, I hate, and can put on
Thy terrors, as I put thy mildness on,
Image of thee in all things; and shall soon,
Armed with thy might, rid heaven of these rebelled,
To their prepared ill mansion driven down
To chains of darkness, and the undying worm,
That from thy just obedience could revolt,   *740*
Whom to obey is happiness entire.
Then shall thy saints unmixed, and from the impure
Far separate, circling thy holy mount
Unfeignèd hallelujahs to thee sing,
Hymns of high praise, and I among them chief.
So said, he o'er his sceptre bowing, rose
From the right hand of glory where he sat,
And the third sacred morn began to shine
Dawning through heaven: forth rushed with whirlwind sound
The chariot of paternal deity,
Flashing thick flames, wheel within wheel undrawn,
Itself instinct with spirit, but convoyed   752
By four cherubic shapes, four faces each
Had wondrous, as with stars their bodies all
And wings were set with eyes, with eyes the wheels
Of beryl, and careering fires between;
Over their heads a crystal firmament,
Whereon a sapphire throne, inlaid with pure
Amber, and colours of the showery arch.   759
He in celestial panoply all armed
Of radiant urim, work divinely wrought,   761
Ascended, at his right hand Victory
Sat, eagle-winged, beside him hung his bow
And quiver with three-bolted thunder stored,
And from about him fierce effusion rolled
Of smoke and bickering flame, and sparkles dire;   766
Attended with ten thousand thousand saints,
He onward came, far off his coming shone,

752 **instinct**] Impelled.   749–59 For the source of Milton's chariot in the whirlwind see Ezekiel 1: 4 ff.   761 **urim**] The mystical stones incorporated, along with the *thummim*, into the breastplate of Aaron the High Priest (see iii. 597–8 and Exodus 28: 30).   766 **bickering**] Flashing.

And twenty thousand (I their number heard)
Chariots of God, half on each hand were seen:
He on the wings of cherub rode sublime   771
On the crystalline sky, in sapphire throned.

Illustrious far and wide, but by his own   773
First seen, them unexpected joy surprised,
When the great ensign of Messiah blazed
Aloft by angels borne, his sign in heaven:
Under whose conduct Michael soon reduced   777
His army, circumfused on either wing,   778
Under their head embodied all in one.   779

Before him power divine his way prepared;
At his command the uprooted hills retired
Each to his place, they heard his voice and went
Obsequious, heaven his wonted face renewed,   783
And with fresh flowerets hill and valley smiled.

This saw his hapless foes but stood obdured,   785
And to rebellious fight rallied their powers
Insensate, hope conceiving from despair.   787
In heavenly spirits could such perverseness dwell?   788
But to convince the proud what signs avail,
Or wonders move the obdurate to relent?
They hardened more by what might most reclaim,
Grieving to see his glory, at the sight
Took envy, and aspiring to his height,   793
Stood re-embattled fierce, by force or fraud
Weening to prosper, and at length prevail
Against God and Messiah, or to fall
In universal ruin last, and now
To final battle drew, disdaining flight,
Or faint retreat; when the great Son of God
To all his host on either hand thus spake.   800
     Stand still in bright array ye saints, here stand

---

771 **sublime**] Including its literal sense, aloft.   773 **Illustrious**] Luminous,
clearly manifest.   777 **reduced**] Lit. 'led back'.   778 **circumfused**] Diffused.
wing] Flank.   779 **embodied . . . one**] Regrouped into a single body, or *corps*.
783 **Obsequious**] Obedient; however the word had its pejorative connotations by
Milton's time.   785 **obdured**] Hardened.   787 **Insensate**] Senselessly.
788 **In . . . dwell?**] Paraphrasing Virgil's wonder at Juno's implacable enmity toward
Aeneas, *Aeneid*, i. 11.   793 **height**] Milton's form, as always, is 'highth'; the line is
not a rhyme in seventeenth-century English.

Ye angels armed, this day from battle rest;
Faithful hath been your warfare, and of God
Accepted, fearless in his righteous cause,
And as ye have received, so have ye done
Invincibly; but of this cursèd crew
The punishment to other hand belongs,
Vengeance is his, or whose he sole appoints;
Number to this day's work is not ordained
Nor multitude, stand only and behold   810
God's indignation on these godless poured
By me, not you but me they have despised,
Yet envied; against me is all their rage,
Because the Father, to whom in heaven supreme
Kingdom and power and glory appertains,
Hath honoured me according to his will.
Therefore to me their doom he hath assigned;
That they may have their wish, to try with me
In battle which the stronger proves, they all,
Or I alone against them, since by strength
They measure all, of other excellence
Not emulous, nor care who them excels;
Nor other strife with them do I vouchsafe.   823
    So spake the Son, and into terror changed
His countenance too severe to be beheld
And full of wrath bent on his enemies.
At once the four spread out their starry wings   827
With dreadful shade contiguous, and the orbs
Of his fierce chariot rolled, as with the sound
Of torrent floods, or of a numerous host.
He on his impious foes right onward drove,
Gloomy as night; under his burning wheels
The steadfast empyrean shook throughout,
All but the throne itself of God. Full soon
Among them he arrived; in his right hand
Grasping ten thousand thunders, which he sent   836
Before him, such as in their souls infixed

809–10 **Number . . . multitude**] i.e. Christ alone will be the agent of God's venge-
ance.   823 **vouchsafe**] 'Condescend to engage in' (*OED*).   827 **the four**] The
'cherubic shapes' of l. 753.   836 **thunders**] Thunderbolts.

Plagues; they astonished all resistance lost,   838
All courage; down their idle weapons dropped;
O'er shields and helms, and helmèd heads he rode
Of thrones and mighty seraphim prostrate,
That wished the mountains now might be again
Thrown on them as a shelter from his ire.
Nor less on either side tempestuous fell
His arrows, from the fourfold-visaged four,   845
Distinct with eyes, and from the living wheels   846
Distinct alike with multitude of eyes;
One spirit in them ruled, and every eye
Glared lightning, and shot forth pernicious fire   849
Among the accursed, that withered all their strength,
And of their wonted vigour left them drained,
Exhausted, spiritless, afflicted, fallen.
Yet half his strength he put not forth, but checked
His thunder in mid-volley, for he meant
Not to destroy, but root them out of heaven:
The overthrown he raised, and as a herd
Of goats or timorous flock together thronged
Drove them before him thunderstruck, pursued
With terrors and with furies to the bounds
And crystal wall of heaven, which opening wide,
Rolled inward, and a spacious gap disclosed
Into the wasteful deep; the monstrous sight   862
Struck them with horror backward, but far worse
Urged them behind; headlong themselves they threw
Down from the verge of heaven, eternal wrath
Burnt after them to the bottomless pit.
    Hell heard the unsufferable noise, hell saw
Heaven ruining from heaven and would have fled
Affrighted; but strict fate had cast too deep
Her dark foundations, and too fast had bound.   870
Nine days they fell; confounded Chaos roared,
And felt tenfold confusion in their fall
Through his wild anarchy, so huge a rout
Encumbered him with ruin: hell at last

---

838 **Plagues**] Scourges (lit. 'wounds').   845 **fourfold-visaged four**] See
ll. 753–4.   846 **Distinct**] Decorated.   849 **pernicious**] Both swift and
destructive.   862 **wasteful**] Desolate.

Yawning received them whole, and on them closed,
Hell their fit habitation fraught with fire
Unquenchable, the house of woe and pain.
Disburdened heaven rejoiced, and soon repaired
Her mural breach, returning whence it rolled.
Sole victor from the expulsion of his foes   880
Messiah his triumphal chariot turned:
To meet him all his saints, who silent stood
Eyewitnesses of his almighty acts,
With jubilee advanced; and as they went,
Shaded with branching palm, each order bright,
Sung triumph, and him sung victorious king,
Son, heir, and Lord, to him dominion given,
Worthiest to reign: he celebrated rode
Triumphant through mid-heaven, into the courts
And temple of his mighty father throned   890
On high: who into glory him received,
Where now he sits at the right hand of bliss.
    Thus measuring things in heaven by things on earth
At thy request, and that thou mayst beware
By what is past, to thee I have revealed
What might have else to human race been hid;
The discord which befell, and war in heaven
Among the angelic powers, and the deep fall
Of those too high aspiring, who rebelled
With Satan, he who envies now thy state,   900
Who now is plotting how he may seduce
Thee also from obedience, that with him
Bereaved of happiness thou mayst partake
His punishment, eternal misery;
Which would be all his solace and revenge,
As a despite done against the most high,
Thee once to gain companion of his woe.
But listen not to his temptations, warn
Thy weaker; let it profit thee to have heard   909
By terrible example the reward
Of disobedience; firm they might have stood,
Yet fell; remember, and fear to transgress.

909 **weaker**] Weaker vessel, alluding to 1 Peter 3: 7, 'honour unto the wife, as unto the weaker vessel'.

BOOK VII

The Argument

Raphael at the request of Adam relates how and wherefore this world was first created; that God, after the expelling of Satan and his angels out of heaven, declared his pleasure to create another world and other creatures to dwell therein; sends his son with glory and attendance of angels to perform the work of creation in six days: the angels celebrate with hymns the performance thereof, and his re-ascension into heaven.

DESCEND from heaven Urania, by that name   1
If rightly thou art called, whose voice divine
Following, above the Olympian hill I soar,   3
Above the flight of Pegasean wing.   4
The meaning, not the name I call: for thou
Nor of the muses nine, nor on the top
Of old Olympus dwell'st, but heavenly born,
Before the hills appeared, or fountain flowed,
Thou with eternal wisdom didst converse,   9
Wisdom thy sister, and with her didst play
In presence of the almighty Father, pleased
With thy celestial song. Up led by thee
Into the heaven of heavens I have presumed,
An earthly guest, and drawn empyreal air,
Thy tempering; with like safety guided down   15
Return me to my native element:
Lest from this flying steed unreined, (as once
Bellerophon, though from a lower clime)   18

---

1 **Urania**] Classical muse of astronomy, but here used in a more literal sense: the name means 'heavenly', from Greek *ouranos*, the sky, and Milton invokes 'The meaning, not the name' (l. 5).   3 **Olympian hill**] Olympus, a favourite haunt of the muses and the home of the classical gods.   4 **Pegasean wing**] The winged horse Pegasus, who created the muses' sacred fountain Hippocrene by stamping his hoof on Mount Helicon, and was therefore associated with poetic inspiration. His rider was Bellerophon (l. 18).   9 **converse**] The word retains its literal meaning, 'dwell'.   15 **Thy tempering**] Tempered by you.   17–18 **as once Bellerophon**] Bellerophon attempted to fly to heaven on Pegasus, and Zeus punished him by sending a gadfly to sting the horse and cause it to throw its rider; though he survived his fall he lived out his last years, according to the mythographers, in blindness and alone (hence perhaps Milton's choice of him as an appropriate heroic model).

Dismounted, on the Aleian field I fall   19
Erroneous there to wander and forlorn.   20
Half yet remains unsung, but narrower bound
Within the visible diurnal sphere;   22
Standing on earth, not rapt above the pole,   23
More safe I sing with mortal voice, unchanged
To hoarse or mute, though fallen on evil days,
On evil days though fallen, and evil tongues;   26
In darkness, and with dangers compassed round,   27
And solitude; yet not alone, while thou
Visit'st my slumbers nightly, or when morn
Purples the east: still govern thou my song,
Urania, and fit audience find, though few.
But drive far off the barbarous dissonance
Of Bacchus and his revellers, the race   33
Of that wild rout that tore the Thracian bard
In Rhodope, where woods and rocks had ears   35
To rapture, till the savage clamour drowned   36
Both harp and voice; nor could the muse defend   37
Her son. So fail not thou, who thee implores: 38
For thou art heavenly, she an empty dream.

    Say goddess, what ensued when Raphael,
The affable archangel, had forewarned
Adam by dire example to beware
Apostasy, by what befell in heaven
To those apostates, lest the like befall

---

19 **Aleian field**] In Lycia, in modern Turkey, where Bellerophon fell.
20 **Erroneous**] Lit. 'wandering'.   22 **visible diurnal sphere**] The visible universe, which revolves diurnally, or daily, around the earth.   23 **rapt**] Transported.
25–6 **though fallen . . . tongues**] Milton, as an important spokesman for the revolution, was under attack in the last year of the Commonwealth, and in danger of arrest and indictment after the restoration of the monarchy in 1660.   27 **In darkness**] Milton had been totally blind since 1652.   33 **Bacchus**] The Greek Dionysus, god of wine, theatre, and ecstatic poetry, patron of the legendary poet Orpheus, but also leader of the 'barbarous . . . rout' of Bacchantes, his murderers.   35 **Rhodope**] A Thracian mountain.   35–6 **woods . . . rapture**] According to Ovid, nature was so entranced with Orpheus' songs that not only the animals but the rocks and trees stopped to listen, and wept at his fate.   37 **muse**] Calliope, muse of epic poetry and mother of Orpheus.   34–8 **Thracian bard . . . son**] Orpheus had offended the Bacchantes by spurning women after the death of his wife Eurydice and his failure to bring her back from Hades. Instead he turned to boys, and was credited with the introduction of pederasty into Greece. In revenge, the Thracian maenads attacked him and tore him to pieces. See *Metamorphoses*, xi. 1ff., and *Lycidas*, ll. 58–63.

In Paradise to Adam or his race,
Charged not to touch the interdicted tree,
If they transgress, and slight that sole command,
So easily obeyed amid the choice
Of all tastes else to please their appetite,
Though wandering. He with his consorted Eve   50
The story heard attentive, and was filled
With admiration, and deep muse to hear   52
Of things so high and strange, things to their thought
So unimaginable as hate in heaven,
And war so near the peace of God in bliss
With such confusion: but the evil soon
Driven back redounded as a flood on those
From whom it sprung, impossible to mix
With blessedness. Whence Adam soon repealed   59
The doubts that in his heart arose: and now
Led on, yet sinless, with desire to know
What nearer might concern him, how this world
Of heaven and earth conspicuous first began,   63
When, and whereof created, for what cause,
What within Eden or without was done
Before his memory, as one whose drought
Yet scarce allayed still eyes the current stream,   67
Whose liquid murmur heard new thirst excites,
Proceeded thus to ask his heavenly guest.

    Great things, and full of wonder in our ears,
Far differing from this world, thou hast revealed
Divine interpreter, by favour sent
Down from the empyrean to forewarn
Us timely of what might else have been our loss,
Unknown, which human knowledge could not reach:
For which to the infinitely good we owe
Immortal thanks, and his admonishment
Receive with solemn purpose to observe
Immutably his sovereign will, the end
Of what we are. But since thou hast vouchsafed   80
Gently for our instruction to impart

---

50 **consorted**] Associated, leagued, united as consorts.   52 **admiration**]
Wonder.   59 **repealed**] Abandoned (lit. 'called back').   63 **conspicuous**]
Visible (as opposed to the world of God and the angels beyond the visible spheres).
67 **current**] Running.

Things above earthly thought, which yet concerned
Our knowing, as to highest wisdom seemed,
Deign to descend now lower, and relate
What may no less perhaps avail us known,
How first began this heaven which we behold
Distant so high, with moving fires adorned
Innumerable, and this which yields or fills
All space, the ambient air wide interfused
Embracing round this florid earth, what cause   90
Moved the creator in his holy rest
Through all eternity so late to build
In chaos, and the work begun, how soon
Absolved, if unforbid thou mayst unfold   94
What we, not to explore the secrets ask
Of his eternal empire, but the more
To magnify his works, the more we know.
And the great light of day yet wants to run
Much of his race though steep, suspense in heaven   99
Held by thy voice, thy potent voice he hears,
And longer will delay to hear thee tell
His generation, and the rising birth   102
Of nature from the unapparent deep: 103
Or if the star of evening and the moon
Haste to thy audience, night with her will bring
Silence, and sleep listening to thee will watch,   106
Or we can bid his absence, till thy song
End, and dismiss thee ere the morning shine.
    Thus Adam his illustrious guest besought:
    And thus the godlike angel answered mild.
This also thy request with caution asked
Obtain: though to recount almighty works
What words or tongue of seraph can suffice,
Or heart of man suffice to comprehend?
Yet what thou canst attain, which best may serve
To glorify the maker, and infer   116
Thee also happier, shall not be withheld

---

90 **florid**] Flourishing, beautiful; lit. 'full of flowers'.   94 **Absolved**]
Completed.   99 **suspense**] Both suspended and attentive.   102 **His generation**]
How he was created.   103 **unapparent**] Invisible.   106 **watch**] Stay
awake.   116 **infer**] Render.

Thy hearing, such commission from above
I have received, to answer thy desire
Of knowledge within bounds; beyond abstain
To ask, nor let thine own inventions hope   121
Things not revealed, which the invisible king,
Only omniscient, hath suppressed in night,
To none communicable in earth or heaven:
Enough is left besides to search and know.
But knowledge is as food, and needs no less
Her temperance over appetite, to know
In measure what the mind may well contain,
Oppresses else with surfeit, and soon turns
Wisdom to folly, as nourishment to wind.
    Know then, that after Lucifer from heaven
(So call him, brighter once amidst the host   132
Of angels, than that star the stars among)   133
Fell with his flaming legions through the deep
Into his place, and the great Son returned
Victorious with his saints, the omnipotent
Eternal Father from his throne beheld
Their multitude, and to his son thus spake.
 — At least our envious foe hath failed, who thought
All like himself rebellious, by whose aid
This inaccessible high strength, the seat
Of deity supreme, us dispossessed,   142
He trusted to have seized, and into fraud   143
Drew many, whom their place knows here no more;
Yet far the greater part have kept, I see,
Their station, heaven yet populous retains
Number sufficient to possess her realms
Though wide, and this high temple to frequent
With ministeries due and solemn rites:
But lest his heart exalt him in the harm
Already done, to have dispeopled heaven
My damage fondly deemed, I can repair   152
That detriment, if such it be to lose

---

121 **inventions**] Speculations, inventiveness.   132 **So call him**] Satan lost his
original name Lucifer ('light-bringer') after his rebellion; see v. 658.   133 **that star**]
Lucifer is the name of Venus as the morning star.   142 **us dispossessed**] Once he
had dispossessed us.   143 **into fraud**] i.e. into his own fraud.   152 **fondly**]
Foolishly.

Self-lost, and in a moment will create
Another world, out of one man a race
Of men innumerable, there to dwell,
Not here, till by degrees of merit raised
They open to themselves at length the way
Up hither, under long obedience tried,
And earth be changed to heaven, and heaven to earth,
One kingdom, joy and union without end.
Meanwhile inhabit lax, ye powers of heaven,   162
And thou my word, begotten Son, by thee
This I perform, speak thou, and be it done:
My overshadowing spirit and might with thee
I send along, ride forth, and bid the deep
Within appointed bounds be heaven and earth,
Boundless the deep, because I am who fill
Infinitude, nor vacuous the space.
Though I uncircumscribed myself retire,   170
And put not forth my goodness, which is free
To act or not, necessity and chance
Approach not me, and what I will is fate.
  So spake the almighty, and to what he spake
His word, the filial Godhead, gave effect.
Immediate are the acts of God, more swift
Than time or motion, but to human ears
Cannot without process of speech be told,
So told as earthly notion can receive.   179
Great triumph and rejoicing was in heaven
When such was heard declared the almighty's will;
Glory they sung to the most high, good will
To future men, and in their dwellings peace:
Glory to him whose just avenging ire
Had driven out the ungodly from his sight
And th' habitations of the just; to him
Glory and praise, whose wisdom had ordained
Good out of evil to create, instead
Of spirits malign a better race to bring
Into their vacant room, and thence diffuse   190
His good to worlds and ages infinite.

---

162 **inhabit lax**] Spread out, relax.   179 **earthly notion**] Human understanding.

So sang the hierarchies: meanwhile the Son
On his great expedition now appeared,
Girt with omnipotence, with radiance crowned
Of majesty divine, sapience and love
Immense, and all his father in him shone.
About his chariot numberless were poured
Cherub and seraph, potentates and thrones,
And virtues, wingèd spirits, and chariots winged,
From the armoury of God, where stand of old   200
Myriads between two brazen mountains lodged
Against a solemn day, harnessed at hand,
Celestial equipage; and now came forth
Spontaneous, for within them spirit lived,
Attendant on their Lord: heaven opened wide
Her ever during gates, harmonious sound
On golden hinges moving, to let forth
The king of glory in his powerful word
And spirit coming to create new worlds.
On heavenly ground they stood, and from the shore
They viewed the vast immeasurable abyss
Outrageous as a sea, dark, wasteful, wild,   212
Up from the bottom turned by furious winds
And surging waves, as mountains to assault
Heaven's height, and with the centre mix the pole.
    Silence, ye troubled waves, and thou deep, peace,
Said then the omnific word, your discord end: 217
    Nor stayed, but on the wings of cherubim
Uplifted, in paternal glory rode
Far into chaos, and the world unborn;
For chaos heard his voice: him all his train
Followed in bright procession to behold
Creation, and the wonders of his might.
Then stayed the fervid wheels, and in his hand   224
He took the golden compasses, prepared
In God's eternal store, to circumscribe
This universe, and all created things:
One foot he centred, and the other turned
Round through the vast profundity obscure,

---

212 **Outrageous**] Both enormous and violent.   217 **omnific**] All-creating;
apparently a Miltonic coinage.   224 **fervid**] Burning (cf. vi. 832).

And said, Thus far extend, thus far thy bounds,   230
This be thy just circumference, O world.
Thus God the heaven created, thus the earth,
Matter unformed and void: darkness profound
Covered the abyss: but on the watery calm
His brooding wings the spirit of God outspread,
And vital virtue infused, and vital warmth   236
Throughout the fluid mass, but downward purged
The black tartareous cold infernal dregs   238
Adverse to life: then founded, then conglobed   239
Like things to like, the rest to several place
Disparted, and between spun out the air,
And earth self balanced on her centre hung.

    Let there be light, said God, and forthwith light   243
Ethereal, first of things, quintessence pure
Sprung from the deep, and from her native east
To journey through the airy gloom began,
Sphered in a radiant cloud, for yet the sun
Was not; she in a cloudy tabernacle
Sojourned the while. God saw the light was good;
And light from darkness by the hemisphere   250
Divided: light the day, and darkness night
He named. Thus was the first day even and morn:
Nor passed uncelebrated, nor unsung
By the celestial choirs, when orient light
Exhaling first from darkness they beheld;
Birth day of heaven and earth; with joy and shout
The hollow universal orb they filled,
And touched their golden harps, and hymning praised
God and his works, creator him they sung,
Both when first evening was, and when first morn.   260

    Again, God said, Let there be firmament
Amid the waters, and let it divide
The waters from the waters: and God made
The firmament, expanse of liquid, pure,
Transparent, elemental air, diffused
In circuit to the uttermost convex

---

236 **virtue**] Power.   238 **tartareous**] Gritty, crusty, with an overtone of
Tartarus, the classical hell.   239 **founded**] Gave shape to.   **conglobed**] Made into
globes or spheres.   243 ff The account of creation paraphrases Genesis 1: 4–8.

Of this great round: partition firm and sure,
The waters underneath from those above
Dividing: for as earth, so he the world
Built on circumfluous waters calm, in wide
Crystalline ocean, and the loud misrule
Of Chaos far removed, lest fierce extremes
Contiguous might distemper the whole frame: 273
And Heaven he named the firmament: so even
And morning chorus sung the second day.
   The earth was formed, but in the womb as yet
Of waters, embryon immature involved,   277
Appeared not: over all the face of earth
Main ocean flowed, not idle, but with warm   279
Prolific humour softening all her globe,   280
Fermented the great mother to conceive,
Satiate with genial moisture, when God said   282
Be gathered now ye waters under heaven
Into one place, and let dry land appear.
Immediately the mountains huge appear
Emergent, and their broad bare backs upheave
Into the clouds, their tops ascend the sky:
So high as heaved the tumid hills, so low   288
Down sunk a hollow bottom broad and deep,
Capacious bed of waters: thither they
Hasted with glad precipitance, uprolled
As drops on dust conglobing from the dry;   292
Part rise in crystal wall, or ridge direct,
For haste; such flight the great command impressed
On the swift floods: as armies at the call
Of trumpet (for of armies thou hast heard)
Troop to their standard, so the watery throng,
Wave rolling after wave, where way they found,
If steep, with torrent rapture, if through plain,   299
Soft ebbing; nor withstood them rock or hill,
But they, or underground, or circuit wide

---

273 **distemper**] Disturb the order of.   277 **embryon**] Embryo.   **involved**]
Lit. 'enveloped, surrounded'.   279 **Main**] Mighty; 'said of a considerable uninter-
rupted stretch of land or water' (*OED*).   280 **Prolific humour**] Fertile liquid.
282 **genial**] Generative.   288 **tumid**] Swollen.   292 **conglobing**] Becoming
spheres.   299 **rapture**] Forceful movement.

With serpent error wandering, found their way,   302
And on the washy ooze deep channels wore;
Easy, ere God had bid the ground be dry,
All but within those banks, where rivers now
Stream, and perpetual draw their humid train.
The dry land, earth, and the great receptacle
Of congregated waters he called seas:
And saw that it was good, and said, Let the earth
Put forth the verdant grass, herb yielding seed,
And fruit tree yielding fruit after her kind;
Whose seed is in herself upon the earth.   312
He scarce had said, when the bare earth, till then
Desert and bare, unsightly, unadorned,
Brought forth the tender grass whose verdure clad
Her universal face with pleasant green,
Then herbs of every leaf, that sudden flowered
Opening their various colours, and made gay
Her bosom smelling sweet: and these scarce blown,
Forth flourished thick the clustering vine, forth crept
The swelling gourd, up stood the corny reed   321
Embattled in her field: and the humble shrub,   322
And bush with frizzled hair implicit: last   323
Rose as in dance the stately trees, and spread
Their branches hung with copious fruit; or gemmed   325
Their blossoms: with high woods the hills were crowned,
With tufts the valleys and each fountain side,
With borders long the rivers. That earth now
Seemed like to heaven, a seat where gods might dwell,
Or wander with delight, and love to haunt   330
Her sacred shades: though God had yet not rained
Upon the earth, and man to till the ground
None was, but from the earth a dewy mist
Went up and watered all the ground, and each
Plant of the field, which ere it was in the earth

302 **serpent error**] Winding like a serpent.   307–12 **The dry land . . . earth**]
The account follows Genesis 1: 10 ff.   321 **swelling**] Bentley's emendation for the
first and second editions' 'smelling' (cf. l. 319) has been almost universally
accepted.   322 **humble**] 'Of plants: low-growing' (*OED*), but including the sug-
gestion of a natural hierarchy analogous to the social hierarchy.   323 **implicit**]
Tangled.   325 **gemmed**] Budded.

God made, and every herb, before it grew
On the green stem; God saw that it was good.
So even and morn recorded the third day.
    Again the almighty spake: Let there be lights   339
High in the expanse of heaven to divide
The day from night; and let them be for signs,
For seasons, and for days, and circling years,
And let them be for lights as I ordain
Their office in the firmament of heaven
To give light on the earth; and it was so.
And God made two great lights, great for their use
To man, the greater to have rule by day,
The less by night altern: and made the stars,   348
And set them in the firmament of heaven
To illuminate the earth, and rule the day
In their vicissitude, and rule the night,   351
And light from darkness to divide. God saw,
Surveying his great work, that it was good:
For of celestial bodies first the sun
A mighty sphere he framed, unlightsome first,
Though of ethereal mould: then formed the moon
Globose, and every magnitude of stars,
And sowed with stars the heaven thick as a field:
Of light by far the greater part he took,
Transplanted from her cloudy shrine, and placed   360
In the sun's orb, made porous to receive
And drink the liquid light, firm to retain
Her gathered beams, great palace now of light.
Hither as to their fountain other stars
Repairing, in their golden urns draw light,
And hence the morning planet gilds her horns;   366
By tincture or reflection they augment   367
Their small peculiar, though from human sight   368
So far remote, with diminution seen.

---

339 ff. The account depends on Genesis 1: 14–18.   348 **altern**] Alternately.
351 **vicissitude**] Alternation.   360 **cloudy shrine**] See l. 248.   366 **morning
. . . horns**] Venus was known, most recently through Galileo's observations, to have
phases, like the moon; 'her' is Milton's emendation of the first edition's 'his', referring
to Lucifer as the morning star.   367 **tincture**] Absorption (of the sun's light).
368 **small peculiar**] Own small light.

First in his east the glorious lamp was seen,
Regent of day, and all th' horizon round
Invested with bright rays, jocund to run
His longitude through heaven's high road: the grey
Dawn, and the Pleiades before him danced   374
Shedding sweet influence: less bright the moon,
But opposite in levelled west was set
His mirror, with full face borrowing her light   377
From him, for other light she needed none
In that aspect, and still that distance keeps
Till night, then in the east her turn she shines,
Revolved on heaven's great axle, and her reign
With thousand lesser lights dividual holds,   382
With thousand thousand stars, that then appeared
Spangling the hemisphere: then first adorned
With their bright luminaries that set and rose,
Glad evening and glad morn crowned the fourth day.

   And God said, Let the waters generate
Reptile with spawn abundant, living soul:
And let fowl fly above the earth, with wings
Displayed on the open firmament of heaven.   390
And God created the great whales, and each
Soul living, each that crept, which plenteously
The waters generated by their kinds,
And every bird of wing after his kind;
And saw that it was good, and blessed them, saying,
Be fruitful, multiply, and in the seas
And lakes and running streams the waters fill;
And let the fowl be multiplied on the earth.   398
Forthwith the sounds and seas, each creek and bay
With fry innumerable swarm, and shoals
Of fish that with their fins and shining scales
Glide under the green wave, in schools that oft
Bank the mid-sea: part single or with mate   403
Graze the seaweed their pasture, and through groves
Of coral stray, or sporting with quick glance

374 **Pleiades**] The seven daughters of Atlas, who were transformed into the con-
stellation of seven stars in Taurus.   377 **His**] The sun's.   382 **dividual**]
Shared.   387–98 **And God said . . . earth**] The account paraphrases Genesis
1: 20–3.   403 **Bank**] Make a bank in (because they are so numerous).

Show to the sun their waved coats dropped with gold,   406
Or in their pearly shells at ease, attend   407
Moist nutriment, or under rocks their food
In jointed armour watch: on smooth the seal,   409
And bended dolphins play: part huge of bulk
Wallowing unwieldy, enormous in their gait
Tempest the ocean: there leviathan   412
Hugest of living creatures, on the deep
Stretched like a promontory sleeps or swims,
And seems a moving land, and at his gills   415
Draws in, and at his trunk spouts out a sea.
Meanwhile the tepid caves, and fens and shores
Their brood as numerous hatch, from the egg that soon
Bursting with kindly rupture forth disclosed   419
Their callow young, but feathered soon and fledge   420
They summed their pens, and soaring the air sublime   421
With clang despised the ground, under a cloud   422
In prospect; there the eagle and the stork   423
On cliffs and cedar tops their eyries build:
Part loosely wing the region, part more wise
In common, ranged in figure wedge their way,   426
Intelligent of seasons, and set forth   427
Their airy caravan high over seas
Flying, and over lands with mutual wing
Easing their flight; so steers the prudent crane
Her annual voyage, borne on winds; the air
Floats, as they pass, fanned with unnumbered plumes: 432
From branch to branch the smaller birds with song
Solaced the woods, and spread their painted wings
Till even, nor then the solemn nightingale
Ceased warbling, but all night tuned her soft lays:
Others on silver lakes and rivers bathed
Their downy breast: the swan with archèd neck

---

406 **dropped**] Spotted, a heraldic usage.   407 **attend**] Await.   409 **smooth**]
Calm water.   412 **Tempest**] Make stormy.   412–15 **leviathan . . . land**] The
great sea creature has not yet become Satanic (see i. 200 ff.).   419 **kindly**] Natural.
420 **callow**] Unfledged, not ready to fly.   **fledge**] Fledged.   421 **summed their
pens**] Had all their feathers.   422 **clang**] From Latin *clangor*, the harsh cry of a
bird.   422–3 **under . . . prospect**] Viewed from below ('in prospect') the earth
seemed under a cloud (so numerous were the birds).   426 **ranged . . . way**] Fly in a
wedge-shaped formation.   427 **Intelligent**] Aware.   432 **Floats**] Undulates.

Between her white wings mantling proudly, rows   439
Her state with oary feet: yet oft they quit   440
The dank, and rising on stiff pennons, tower   441
The mid aerial sky: others on ground
Walked firm; the crested cock whose clarion sounds
The silent hours, and the other whose gay train   444
Adorns him, coloured with the florid hue
Of rainbows and starry eyes. The waters thus
With fish replenished, and the air with fowl,
Evening and morn solemnized the fifth day.
   The sixth, and of creation last arose
With evening harps and matin, when God said,
Let the earth bring forth soul living in her kind,   451
Cattle and creeping things, and beast of the earth,
Each in their kind. The earth obeyed, and straight
Opening her fertile womb teemed at a birth   454
Innumerous living creatures, perfect forms,   455
Limbed and full grown: out of the ground up rose
As from his lair the wild beast where he wons   457
In forest wild, in thicket, brake, or den;
Among the trees in pairs they rose, they walked:
The cattle in the fields and meadows green:
Those rare and solitary, these in flocks
Pasturing at once, and in broad herds upsprung.
The grassy clods now calved, now half appeared   463
The tawny lion, pawing to get free
His hinder parts, then springs as broke from bonds,
And rampant shakes his brinded mane; the ounce,   466
The leopard, and the tiger, as the mole
Rising, the crumbled earth above them threw
In hillocks; the swift stag from underground
Bore up his branching head: scarce from his mould
Behemoth biggest born of earth upheaved   471

---

   439 **mantling**]   Forming   a   mantle.   440 **state**]   Dignified   bearing.
441 **dank**] Water.   444 **the other**] The peacock.   451 **soul**] Bentley's emend-
ation of the first and second editions' 'Fowle' and 'Foul' has been universally
accepted.   454 **teemed ... birth**] Bore in a single delivery.   455 **perfect**]
Complete.   457 **wons**] Dwells.   463 **clods**] Earth.   466 **brinded**] Brindled
(streaked or flecked). **ounce**] Lynx.   471 **Behemoth**] A huge biblical beast
mentioned in Job 40: 15, usually identified in Milton's time as the elephant.

His vastness: fleeced the flocks and bleating rose,
As plants: ambiguous between sea and land   473
The river horse and scaly crocodile.   474
At once came forth whatever creeps the ground,
Insect or worm; those waved their limber fans
For wings, and smallest lineaments exact
In all the liveries decked of summer's pride
With spots of gold and purple, azure and green:
These as a line their long dimension drew,
Streaking the ground with sinuous trace; not all
Minims of nature; some of serpent kind   482
Wondrous in length and corpulence involved   483
Their snaky folds, and added wings. First crept   484
The parsimonious emmet, provident   485
Of future, in small room large heart enclosed,
Pattern of just equality perhaps
Hereafter, joined in her popular tribes
Of commonalty: swarming next appeared   489
The female bee that feeds her husband drone
Deliciously, and builds her waxen cells
With honey stored: the rest are numberless,
And thou their natures know'st, and gav'st them names,
Needless to thee repeated; nor unknown
The serpent subtlest beast of all the field,
Of huge extent sometimes, with brazen eyes
And hairy mane terrific, though to thee   497
Not noxious, but obedient at thy call.
Now heaven in all her glory shone, and rolled
Her motions, as the great first mover's hand
First wheeled their course; earth in her rich attire
Consummate lovely smiled; air, water, earth,   502
By fowl, fish, beast, was flown, was swum, was walked
Frequent; and of the sixth day yet remained;   504

---

473 **ambiguous**] Amphibious.   474 **river horse**] Literally translating hippopo-
tamus.   482 **Minims**] Smallest creatures.   483 **involved**] Coiled.   484 **added
wings**] i.e. some serpents were winged before the fall.   485 **parsimonious
emmet**] Thrifty ant.   487–9 **Pattern . . . commonality**] i.e. the ants may serve as
a model for future democratic societies.   497 **mane terrific**] Recalling Virgil's
account of the splendid sea-serpents coming to destroy Laöcoön (*Aeneid*, ii. 203–7).
502 **Consummate**] Completed.   504 **Frequent**] In great numbers.

There wanted yet the masterwork, the end   505
Of all yet done; a creature who not prone
And brute as other creatures, but endued
With sanctity of reason, might erect
His stature, and upright with front serene   509
Govern the rest, self-knowing, and from thence
Magnanimous to correspond with heaven,   511
But grateful to acknowledge whence his good
Descends, thither with heart and voice and eyes
Directed in devotion, to adore
And worship God supreme, who made him chief
Of all his works: therefore the omnipotent
Eternal Father (for where is not he
Present) thus to his son audibly spake.
    Let us make now man in our image, man
In our similitude, and let them rule   520
Over the fish and fowl of sea and air,
Beast of the field, and over all the earth,
And every creeping thing that creeps the ground.
This said, he formed thee, Adam, thee O man
Dust of the ground, and in thy nostrils breathed
The breath of life; in his own image he
Created thee, in the image of God
Express, and thou becam'st a living soul.   528
Male he created thee, but thy consort
Female for race; then blessed mankind, and said,
Be fruitful, multiply, and fill the earth,
Subdue it, and throughout dominion hold
Over fish of the sea, and fowl of the air,
And every living thing that moves on the earth.   534
Wherever thus created, for no place
Is yet distinct by name, thence, as thou know'st
He brought thee into this delicious grove,
This garden, planted with the trees of God,
Delectable both to behold and taste;
And freely all their pleasant fruit for food

---

505 end] Both completion and object.   509 front] Brow.   511 **Magnani-
mous**] Lit. 'great-souled'; magnanimity was the Aristotelian virtue to be aspired to
by monarchs.   528 **Express**] Exact.   519–34 **Let ... earth**] Adapted from
Genesis 1: 26–8 and 2: 7.

Gave thee, all sorts are here that all the earth yields,
Variety without end; but of the tree
Which tasted works knowledge of good and evil,
Thou mayst not; in the day thou eat'st, thou diest;   544
Death is the penalty imposed, beware,
And govern well thy appetite, lest Sin
Surprise thee, and her black attendant Death.
Here finished he, and all that he had made
Viewed, and behold all was entirely good;
So even and morn accomplished the sixth day:
Yet not till the creator from his work
Desisting, though unwearied, up returned
Up to the heaven of heavens his high abode,   553
Thence to behold this new created world
The addition of his empire, how it showed
In prospect from his throne, how good how fair,
Answering his great idea. Up he rode   557
Followed with acclamation and the sound
Symphonious of ten thousand harps that tuned   559
Angelic harmonies: the earth, the air
Resounded, (thou remember'st, for thou heard'st)
The heavens and all the constellations rung,
The planets in their station listening stood,
While the bright pomp ascended jubilant.   564
Open, ye everlasting gates, they sung,
Open, ye heavens, your living doors; let in
The great creator from his work returned
Magnificent, his six days' work, a world;
Open, and henceforth oft; for God will deign
To visit oft the dwellings of just men   570
Delighted, and with frequent intercourse
Thither will send his wingèd messengers
On errands of supernal grace. So sung
The glorious train ascending: he through heaven,
That opened wide her blazing portals, led
To God's eternal house direct the way,

542–4 **but ... diest**] The proscription of the tree of knowledge and the warning
of the death penalty are in Genesis 2: 16–17.   553 **heaven of heavens**] Highest
heaven.   557 **Answering**] Corresponding to.   559 **Symphonious**] Harmon-
ious. **tuned**] Performed.   564 **pomp**] 'A triumphal or ceremonial procession'
(*OED*).

A broad and ample road, whose dust is gold
And pavement stars, as stars to thee appear,
Seen in the galaxy, that Milky Way
Which nightly as a circling zone thou seest
Powdered with stars. And now on earth the seventh   *580*
Evening arose in Eden, for the sun
Was set, and twilight from the east came on,
Forerunning night; when at the holy mount
Of heaven's high-seated top, the imperial throne
Of Godhead, fixed for ever firm and sure,
The filial power arrived, and sat him down
With his great father, for he also went
Invisible, yet stayed (such privilege
Hath omnipresence) and the work ordained,   *590*
Author and end of all things, and from work
Now resting, blessed and hallowed the seventh day,
As resting on that day from all his work,
But not in silence holy kept; the harp
Had work and rested not, the solemn pipe,
And dulcimer, all organs of sweet stop,
All sounds on fret by string or golden wire   597
Tempered soft tunings; intermixed with voice
Choral or unison: of incense clouds
Fuming from golden censers hid the mount.
Creation and the six days' acts they sung,
Great are thy works, Jehovah, infinite
Thy power; what thought can measure thee or tongue
Relate thee; greater now in thy return
Than from the giant angels; thee that day   605
Thy thunders magnified; but to create
Is greater than created to destroy.
Who can impair thee, mighty king, or bound
Thy empire? Easily the proud attempt
Of spirits apostate and their counsels vain
Thou hast repelled, while impiously they thought
Thee to diminish, and from thee withdraw

597 **sounds on fret**] Sounds determined by fingering the frets, or bars, that regulate
the notes on the finger-boards of lutes and similar instruments. **string**] Gut.
605 **giant angels**] Satan's rebellion, as often in the period, is a version of the attempt
by the Giants to overthrow Jove.

The number of thy worshippers. Who seeks
To lessen thee, against his purpose serves
To manifest the more thy might: his evil
Thou usest, and from thence creat'st more good.
Witness this new-made world, another heaven
From heaven gate not far, founded in view
On the clear hyaline, the glassy sea;   619
Of amplitude almost immense, with stars   620
Numerous, and every star perhaps a world
Of destined habitation; but thou know'st
Their seasons: among these the seat of men,
Earth with her nether ocean circumfused,
Their pleasant dwelling place. Thrice happy men,
And sons of men, whom God hath thus advanced,
Created in his image, there to dwell
And worship him, and in reward to rule
Over his works, on earth, in sea, or air,
And multiply a race of worshippers   630
Holy and just: thrice happy if they know
Their happiness, and persevere upright.
    So sung they, and the empyrean rung,
With hallelujahs: thus was Sabbath kept.
And thy request think now fulfilled, that asked
How first this world and face of things began,   636
And what before thy memory was done
From the beginning, that posterity
Informed by thee might know; if else thou seek'st
Aught, not surpassing human measure, say.

619 **hyaline**] Transliterating the Greek word for 'glassy', and referring to the 'sea of glass like unto crystal' before God's throne in Revelation 4: 6.   620 **immense**] Infinite (lit. 'unmeasurable').   636 **face**] Appearance.

BOOK VIII

The Argument

Adam inquires concerning celestial motions, is doubtfully answered, and exhorted to search rather things more worthy of knowledge: Adam assents, and still desirous to detain Raphael, relates to him what he remembered since his own creation, his placing in Paradise, his talk with God concerning solitude and fit society, his first meeting and nuptials with Eve, his discourse with the angel thereupon; who after admonitions repeated departs.

THE angel ended, and in Adam's ear
So charming left his voice, that he awhile   2
Thought him still speaking, still stood fixed to hear;
Then as new waked thus gratefully replied.   4
What thanks sufficient, or what recompense
Equal have I to render thee, divine
Historian, who thus largely hast allayed
The thirst I had of knowledge, and vouchsafed
This friendly condescension to relate   9
Things else by me unsearchable, now heard
With wonder, but delight, and, as is due,
With glory attributed to the high
Creator; something yet of doubt remains,
Which only thy solution can resolve.
When I behold this goodly frame, this world
Of heaven and earth consisting, and compute
Their magnitudes, this earth a spot, a grain,
An atom, with the firmament compared
And all her numbered stars, that seem to roll
Spaces incomprehensible (for such
Their distance argues and their swift return
Diurnal) merely to officiate light   22

---

2 **charming**] Including its literal sense 'spell-binding'.   1–4 **The angel ... replied**] These lines were added in the 1674 edition, when the 10-book poem became 12; l. 4 originally read, 'To whom thus Adam gratefully replied.'   9 **condescension**] The sense is certainly positive ('affability to one's inferiors, with courteous disregard of difference of rank': *OED*); but the word had started to have its modern pejorative sense by the 1640s. Cf. l. 649 below.   22 **officiate**] Supply, with a religious overtone from its literal meaning, perform a divine service.

Round this opacous earth, this punctual spot,   23
One day and night; in all their vast survey
Useless besides, reasoning I oft admire,   25
How nature wise and frugal could commit
Such disproportions, with superfluous hand
So many nobler bodies to create,
Greater so manifold to this one use,
For aught appears, and on their orbs impose
Such restless revolution day by day
Repeated, while the sedentary earth,   32
That better might with far less compass move,
Served by more noble than herself, attains
Her end without least motion, and receives
As tribute such a sumless journey brought   36
Of incorporeal speed, her warmth and light;   37
Speed, to describe whose swiftness number fails.

   So spake our sire, and by his countenance seemed
Entering on studious thoughts abstruse, which Eve
Perceiving where she sat retired in sight,
With lowliness majestic from her seat,
And grace that won who saw to wish her stay,
Rose, and went forth among her fruits and flowers,
To visit how they prospered, bud and bloom,   45
Her nursery; they at her coming sprung   46
And touched by her fair tendance gladlier grew.   47
Yet went she not, as not with such discourse
Delighted, or not capable her ear
Of what was high: such pleasure she reserved,
Adam relating, she sole auditress;
Her husband the relater she preferred
Before the angel, and of him to ask
Chose rather; he, she knew would intermix
Grateful digressions, and solve high dispute
With conjugal caresses, from his lip
Not words alone pleased her. O when meet now

---

23 **opacous**] Dark.   **punctual**] Tiny (like a point).   25 **admire**] Wonder.
32 **sedentary**] Motionless.   36 **sumless**] Immeasurable.   37 **Of incorporeal
speed**] With the swiftness of the spirit (since nothing physical could move so
quickly), as in l. 110, 'speed almost spiritual'.   45 **visit**] 'Inspect or examine'
(*OED*); the etymological meaning is 'see'.   46 **Her nursery**] The objects of her
care.   47 **tendance**] Tending.

Such pairs, in love and mutual honour joined?
With goddess-like demeanour forth she went;
Not unattended, for on her as queen
A pomp of winning graces waited still,   61
And from about her shot darts of desire
Into all eyes to wish her still in sight.
And Raphael now to Adam's doubt proposed
Benevolent and facile thus replied.   65
    To ask or search I blame thee not, for heaven
Is as the book of God before thee set,
Wherein to read his wondrous works, and learn
His seasons, hours, or days, or months, or years:
This to attain, whether heaven move or earth,   70
Imports not, if thou reckon right, the rest
From man or angel the great architect
Did wisely to conceal, and not divulge
His secrets to be scanned by them who ought
Rather admire; or if they list to try
Conjecture, he his fabric of the heavens
Hath left to their disputes, perhaps to move
His laughter at their quaint opinions wide   78
Hereafter, when they come to model heaven
And calculate the stars, how they will wield
The mighty frame, how build, unbuild, contrive
To save appearances, how gird the sphere   82
With centric and eccentric scribbled o'er,   83
Cycle and epicycle, orb in orb: 84
Already by thy reasoning this I guess,
Who art to lead thy offspring, and supposest
That bodies bright and greater should not serve
The less not bright, nor heaven such journeys run,
Earth sitting still, when she alone receives
The benefit: consider first, that great

---

61 **pomp**] Procession. **still**] Always.   65 **facile**] 'Affable, courteous' (*OED*); the word did not yet have its pejorative implications.   78 **wide**] Erring.   82 **To save appearances**] Like 'to save the phenomena', a standard term for attempts to reconcile observed celestial phenomena with astronomical theory.   83 **centric and eccentric**] Orbits with the earth at the centre and off-centre respectively: eccentric spheres were a necessary element in both Ptolemaic and Copernican explanations of celestial motion.   84 **epicycle**] A smaller orbit, whose centre is on the circumference of the main orbit; also essential to Ptolemaic and Copernican theories.

Or bright infers not excellence: the earth   91
Though, in comparison of heaven, so small,
Nor glistering, may of solid good contain
More plenty than the sun that barren shines,
Whose virtue on itself works no effect,
But in the fruitful earth; there first received
His beams, unactive else, their vigour find.
Yet not to earth are those bright luminaries
Officious, but to thee earth's habitant.   99
And for the heaven's wide circuit, let it speak
The maker's high magnificence, who built
So spacious, and his line stretched out so far;
That man may know he dwells not in his own;
An edifice too large for him to fill,
Lodged in a small partition, and the rest
Ordained for uses to his Lord best known.
The swiftness of those circles attribute,
Though numberless, to his omnipotence,
That to corporeal substances could add
Speed almost spiritual; me thou think'st not slow,   110
Who since the morning hour set out from heaven
Where God resides, and ere midday arrived
In Eden, distance inexpressible
By numbers that have name. But this I urge,
Admitting motion in the heavens, to show
Invalid that which thee to doubt it moved;
Not that I so affirm, though so it seem
To thee who hast thy dwelling here on earth.
God to remove his ways from human sense,
Placed heaven from earth so far, that earthly sight,   120
If it presume, might err in things too high,
And no advantage gain. What if the sun
Be centre to the world, and other stars
By his attractive virtue and their own   124
Incited, dance about him various rounds?
Their wandering course now high, now low, then hid,   126
Progressive, retrograde, or standing still,

91 **infers**] 'Implies' (*OED*); the modern distinction had not yet developed.
99 **Officious**] Dutiful.   124 **attractive   virtue**] Power   of   attraction.
126 **wandering course**] Etymologizing 'planet', from the Greek for 'wanderer'.

In six thou seest, and what if seventh to these
The planet earth, so steadfast though she seem,
Insensibly three different motions move?   130
Which else to several spheres thou must ascribe,
Moved contrary with thwart obliquities,   132
Or save the sun his labour, and that swift
Nocturnal and diurnal rhomb supposed,   134
Invisible else above all stars, the wheel
Of day and night; which needs not thy belief,
If earth industrious of her self fetch day
Travelling east, and with her part averse
From the sun's beam meet night, her other part
Still luminous by his ray. What if that light
Sent from her through the wide transpicuous air,   141
To the terrestrial moon be as a star   142
Enlightening her by day, as she by night
This earth? reciprocal, if land be there,
Fields and inhabitants: her spots thou seest
As clouds, and clouds may rain, and rain produce
Fruits in her softened soil, for some to eat
Allotted there; and other suns perhaps
With their attendant moons thou wilt descry
Communicating male and female light,   150
Which two great sexes animate the world,
Stored in each orb perhaps with some that live.
For such vast room in nature unpossessed
By living soul, desert and desolate,
Only to shine, yet scarce to contribute
Each orb a glimpse of light, conveyed so far
Down to this habitable, which returns
Light back to them, is obvious to dispute.   158

130 **three different motions**] The daily rotation, the yearly rotation around the sun, and the rotation of the earth's axis itself.   132 **thwart obliquities**] The spheres moving 'athwart' each other in the Ptolemaic system.   134 **Nocturnal . . . rhomb**] The outermost tenth sphere, or *primum mobile*, which in Ptolemaic astronomy revolved around the universe.   141 **transpicuous**] Transparent.   142 **terrestrial moon**] Raphael suggests that the moon is another earth, with 'fields and inhabitants' (l. 145).   150 **male . . . light**] The light of the sun is conceived as male, that of the moon female, just as in mythology the sun was a god, Apollo, the moon a goddess, Diana.   158 **obvious**] 'Exposed or open' (*OED*). Milton himself debated the point as a Cambridge undergraduate in his Seventh Prolusion.

But whether thus these things, or whether not,
Whether the sun predominant in heaven
Rise on the earth, or earth rise on the sun,
He from the east his flaming road begin,
Or she from west her silent course advance
With inoffensive pace that spinning sleeps   164
On her soft axle, while she paces even,
And bears thee soft with the smooth air along,
Solicit not thy thoughts with matters hid,   167
Leave them to God above, him serve and fear;
Of other creatures, as him pleases best,
Wherever placed, let him dispose: joy thou
In what he gives to thee, this Paradise
And thy fair Eve; heaven is for thee too high
To know what passes there; be lowly wise:
Think only what concerns thee and thy being;
Dream not of other worlds, what creatures there
Live, in what state, condition or degree,
Contented that thus far hath been revealed
Not of earth only but of highest heaven.
    To whom thus Adam cleared of doubt, replied.
How fully hast thou satisfied me, pure
Intelligence of heaven, angel serene,   181
And freed from intricacies, taught to live,
The easiest way, nor with perplexing thoughts
To interrupt the sweet of life, from which
God hath bid dwell far off all anxious cares,
And not molest us, unless we our selves
Seek them with wandering thoughts, and notions vain.
But apt the mind or fancy is to rove
Unchecked, and of her roving is no end;
Till warned, or by experience taught, she learn,
That not to know at large of things remote
From use, obscure and subtle, but to know
That which before us lies in daily life,
Is the prime wisdom, what is more, is fume,   194

---

164 **inoffensive**]   Harmless,   not   dangerous.   167 **Solicit**]   Disturb.
180–1 **pure / Intelligence**] Angelic creature.   194 **fume**] 'Something comparable
to smoke or vapour as being unsubstantial, transient, imaginary' (*OED*).

Or emptiness, or fond impertinence,   195
And renders us in things that most concern
Unpractised, unprepared, and still to seek.   197
Therefore from this high pitch let us descend
A lower flight, and speak of things at hand
Useful, whence haply mention may arise
Of something not unseasonable to ask
By sufferance, and thy wonted favour deigned.
Thee I have heard relating what was done
Ere my remembrance: now hear me relate
My story, which perhaps thou hast not heard;
And day is yet not spent; till then thou seest
How subtly to detain thee I devise,
Inviting thee to hear while I relate,
Fond, were it not in hope of thy reply:
For while I sit with thee, I seem in heaven,   210
And sweeter thy discourse is to my ear
Than fruits of palm-tree pleasantest to thirst
And hunger both, from labour, at the hour
Of sweet repast; they satiate, and soon fill,
Though pleasant, but thy words with grace divine
Imbued, bring to their sweetness no satiety.
    To whom thus Raphael answered heavenly meek.
Nor are thy lips ungraceful, sire of men,
Nor tongue ineloquent; for God on thee
Abundantly his gifts hath also poured   220
Inward and outward both, his image fair:
Speaking or mute all comeliness and grace
Attends thee, and each word, each motion forms.
Nor less think we in heaven of thee on earth
Than of our fellow servant, and inquire
Gladly into the ways of God with man:
For God we see hath honoured thee, and set
On man his equal love: say therefore on;
For I that day was absent, as befell,
Bound on a voyage uncouth and obscure,   230
Far on excursion toward the gates of hell;

195 **fond impertinence**] Foolish irrelevance ('impertinence' did not yet have its modern sense of 'taking liberties').   197 **still to seek**] Always searching. 230 **uncouth**] Strange, unfamiliar.

Squared in full legion (such command we had)
To see that none thence issued forth a spy,
Or enemy, while God was in his work,
Lest he incensed at such eruption bold,
Destruction with creation might have mixed.
Not that they durst without his leave attempt,
But us he sends upon his high behests
For state, as sovereign king, and to inure   239
Our prompt obedience. Fast we found, fast shut
The dismal gates, and barricadoed strong;
But long ere our approaching heard within
Noise, other than the sound of dance or song,
Torment, and loud lament, and furious rage.
Glad we returned up to the coasts of light
Ere Sabbath evening: so we had in charge.
But thy relation now; for I attend,   247
Pleased with thy words no less than thou with mine.
    So spake the godlike power, and thus our sire.
For man to tell how human life began
Is hard; for who himself beginning knew?
Desire with thee still longer to converse
Induced me. As new waked from soundest sleep
Soft on the flowery herb I found me laid
In balmy sweat, which with his beams the sun
Soon dried, and on the reeking moisture fed.   256
Straight toward heaven my wondering eyes I turned,
And gazed awhile the ample sky, till raised
By quick instinctive motion up I sprung,
As thitherward endeavouring, and upright
Stood on my feet; about me round I saw
Hill, dale, and shady woods, and sunny plains,
And liquid lapse of murmuring streams; by these,   263
Creatures that lived, and moved, and walked, or flew,
Birds on the branches warbling; all things smiled,
With fragrance and with joy my heart o'erflowed.
My self I then perused, and limb by limb
Surveyed, and sometimes went, and sometimes ran   268

239 **state**] Dignity.   **inure**] Exercise, make habitual.   247 **relation**] Story.
256 **reeking**] Vaporous (without its modern pejorative sense).   263 **lapse**]
Lapping, flow.   268 **went**] Walked.

With supple joints, and lively vigour led:
But who I was, or where, or from what cause,
Knew not; to speak I tried, and forthwith spake,
My tongue obeyed and readily could name
Whate'er I saw. Thou sun, said I, fair light,
And thou enlightened earth, so fresh and gay,
Ye hills and dales, ye rivers, woods, and plains,
And ye that live and move, fair creatures, tell,
Tell, if ye saw, how came I thus, how here?
Not of myself; by some great maker then,
In goodness and in power pre-eminent;
Tell me, how may I know him, how adore,   280
From whom I have that thus I move and live,
And feel that I am happier than I know.
While thus I called, and strayed I knew not whither,
From where I first drew air, and first beheld
This happy light, when answer none returned,
On a green shady bank profuse of flowers
Pensive I sat me down; there gentle sleep
First found me, and with soft oppression seized
My drowsèd sense, untroubled, though I thought
I then was passing to my former state   290
Insensible, and forthwith to dissolve:
When suddenly stood at my head a dream,
Whose inward apparition gently moved
My fancy to believe I yet had being,
And lived: one came, methought, of shape divine,
And said, Thy mansion wants thee, Adam, rise,   296
First man, of men innumerable ordained
First father, called by thee I come thy guide
To the garden of bliss, thy seat prepared.   299
So saying, by the hand he took me raised,
And over fields and waters, as in air
Smooth sliding without step, last led me up
A woody mountain; whose high top was plain,
A circuit wide, enclosed, with goodliest trees
Planted, with walks, and bowers, that what I saw
Of earth before scarce pleasant seemed. Each tree

296 **mansion**] Dwelling (not necessarily a building). **wants**] Lacks.
299 **seat**] Residence.

Loaden with fairest fruit that hung to the eye
Tempting, stirred in me sudden appetite
To pluck and eat; whereat I waked, and found
Before mine eyes all real, as the dream   310
Had lively shadowed: here had new begun
My wandering, had not he who was my guide
Up hither, from among the trees appeared
Presence divine. Rejoicing, but with awe
In adoration at his feet I fell
Submiss: he reared me, and Whom thou sought'st I am,   316
Said mildly, Author of all this thou seest
Above, or round about thee or beneath.
This Paradise I give thee, count it thine
To till and keep, and of the fruit to eat:
Of every tree that in the garden grows
Eat freely with glad heart; fear here no dearth:
But of the tree whose operation brings
Knowledge of good and ill, which I have set
The pledge of thy obedience and thy faith,
Amid the garden by the tree of life,
Remember what I warn thee, shun to taste,
And shun the bitter consequence: for know,
The day thou eat'st thereof, my sole command
Transgressed, inevitably thou shalt die;   330
From that day mortal, and this happy state
Shalt lose, expelled from hence into a world
Of woe and sorrow. Sternly he pronounced
The rigid interdiction, which resounds
Yet dreadful in mine ear, though in my choice
Not to incur; but soon his clear aspect
Returned and gracious purpose thus renewed.   337
Not only these fair bounds, but all the earth
To thee and to thy race I give; as lords
Possess it, and all things that therein live,
Or live in sea, or air, beast, fish, and fowl.
In sign whereof each bird and beast behold
After their kinds; I bring them to receive
From thee their names, and pay thee fealty

316 **Submiss**] Submissive.   320–30 **To till ... die**] Paraphrasing Genesis 2:
15–17.   337 **purpose**] Matter, discourse.

With low subjection; understand the same
Of fish within their watery residence,
Not hither summoned, since they cannot change
Their element to draw the thinner air.
As thus he spake, each bird and beast behold
Approaching two and two, these cowering low   *350*
With blandishment, each bird stooped on his wing.
I named them, as they passed, and understood
Their nature, with such knowledge God endued
My sudden apprehension: but in these
I found not what methought I wanted still;
And to the heavenly vision thus presumed.
   O by what name, for thou above all these,
Above mankind, or aught than mankind higher,
Surpassest far my naming, how may I
Adore thee, author of this universe,   *360*
And all this good to man, for whose well being
So amply, and with hands so liberal
Thou hast provided all things: but with me
I see not who partakes. In solitude
What happiness, who can enjoy alone,
Or all enjoying, what contentment find?
Thus I presumptuous; and the vision bright,
As with a smile more brightened, thus replied.
   What call'st thou solitude, is not the earth
With various living creatures, and the air
Replenished, and all these at thy command   *371*
To come and play before thee, know'st thou not
Their language and their ways, they also know,
And reason not contemptibly; with these
Find pastime, and bear rule; thy realm is large.
So spake the universal Lord, and seemed
So ordering. I with leave of speech implored,
And humble deprecation thus replied.
   Let not my words offend thee, heavenly power,
My maker, be propitious while I speak.   *380*
Hast thou not made me here thy substitute,
And these inferior far beneath me set?
Among unequals what society

371 **Replenished**] 'Abundantly stocked' (*OED*).

Can sort, what harmony or true delight?
Which must be mutual, in proportion due
Given and received; but in disparity
The one intense, the other still remiss   387
Cannot well suit with either, but soon prove
Tedious alike: of fellowship I speak
Such as I seek, fit to participate
All rational delight, wherein the brute
Cannot be human consort; they rejoice
Each with their kind, lion with lioness;
So fitly them in pairs thou hast combined;
Much less can bird with beast, or fish with fowl
So well converse, nor with the ox the ape;   396
Worse then can man with beast, and least of all.
Whereto the almighty answered, not displeased.
A nice and subtle happiness I see   399
Thou to thy self proposest, in the choice
Of thy associates, Adam, and wilt taste
No pleasure, though in pleasure, solitary.   402
What think'st thou then of me, and this my state,
Seem I to thee sufficiently possessed
Of happiness, or not? who am alone
From all eternity, for none I know
Second to me or like, equal much less.
How have I then with whom to hold converse
Save with the creatures which I made, and those
To me inferior, infinite descents   410
Beneath what other creatures are to thee?
    He ceased, I lowly answered. To attain
The height and depth of thy eternal ways
All human thoughts come short, supreme of things;
Thou in thyself art perfect, and in thee
Is no deficience found; not so is man,
But in degree, the cause of his desire
By conversation with his like to help,

---

387 **intense . . . still remiss**] High-tuned . . . always weak or low (continuing the
musical metaphor of tighter and more slack strings on an instrument).   396 **con-
verse**] 'Consort, keep company' (*OED*); the original senses include 'dwell' and
'have sexual intercourse'; cf. 1. 418.   399 **nice**] Delicate, fastidious.   402 **in
pleasure**] Eden etymologically means 'pleasure'.

Or solace his defects. No need that thou
Shouldst propagate, already infinite;
And through all numbers absolute, though one;   421
But man by number is to manifest
His single imperfection, and beget   423
Like of his like, his image multiplied,
In unity defective, which requires   425
Collateral love, and dearest amity.
Thou in thy secrecy although alone,
Best with thy self accompanied, seek'st not
Social communication, yet so pleased,
Canst raise thy creature to what height thou wilt
Of union or communion, deified;
I by conversing cannot these erect   432
From prone, nor in their ways complacence find.   433
Thus I emboldened spake, and freedom used
Permissive, and acceptance found, which gained   435
This answer from the gracious voice divine.

   Thus far to try thee, Adam, I was pleased,
And find thee knowing not of beasts alone,
Which thou hast rightly named, but of thyself,
Expressing well the spirit within thee free,   *440*
My image, not imparted to the brute,
Whose fellowship therefore unmeet for thee
Good reason was thou freely shouldst dislike,
And be so minded still; I, ere thou spak'st,
Knew it not good for man to be alone,
And no such company as then thou saw'st
Intended thee, for trial only brought,
To see how thou couldst judge of fit and meet:
What next I bring shall please thee, be assured,
Thy likeness, thy fit help, thy other self,
Thy wish exactly to thy heart's desire.
   He ended, or I heard no more, for now
My earthly by his heavenly overpowered,   453

---

   421 **through ... absolute**] Both 'perfect in all your parts' and 'containing all
numbers in your unity'.   423 **His single imperfection**] His incomplete-
ness in being single.   425 **unity**] Singleness.   432 **these**] The animals.
433 **complacence**] Pleasure, satisfaction.   435 **Permissive**] Which was permit-
ted.   453 **earthly**] i.e. earthly nature.

Which it had long stood under, strained to the height
In that celestial colloquy sublime,
As with an object that excels the sense,
Dazzled and spent, sunk down, and sought repair
Of sleep, which instantly fell on me, called
By nature as in aid, and closed mine eyes.
Mine eyes he closed, but open left the cell
Of fancy my internal sight, by which
Abstract as in a trance methought I saw,   462
Though sleeping, where I lay, and saw the shape
Still glorious before whom awake I stood;
Who stooping opened my left side, and took
From thence a rib, with cordial spirits warm,   466
And life-blood streaming fresh; wide was the wound,
But suddenly with flesh filled up and healed:
The rib he formed and fashioned with his hands;
Under his forming hands a creature grew,
Manlike, but different sex, so lovely fair,
That what seemed fair in all the world, seemed now
Mean, or in her summed up, in her contained
And in her looks, which from that time infused
Sweetness into my heart, unfelt before,
And into all things from her air inspired   476
The spirit of love and amorous delight.
She disappeared, and left me dark, I waked
To find her, or forever to deplore
Her loss, and other pleasures all abjure:
When out of hope, behold her, not far off,   481
Such as I saw her in my dream, adorned
With what all earth or heaven could bestow
To make her amiable: on she came,
Led by her heavenly maker, though unseen,
And guided by his voice, nor uninformed
Of nuptial sanctity and marriage rites:
Grace was in all her steps, heaven in her eye,
In every gesture dignity and love.

---

462 **Abstract**] From a distance, carried away.   466 **cordial**] Vital (lit. 'from the heart').   476 **air**] (1) Demeanour; (2) breath; the latter sense is continued in 'inspired', lit. 'breathed in'.   481 **out of hope**] Hopeless.

I overjoyed could not forbear aloud.   490
    This turn hath made amends; thou hast fulfilled
Thy words, creator bounteous and benign,
Giver of all things fair, but fairest this
Of all thy gifts, nor enviest. I now see   494
Bone of my bone, flesh of my flesh, myself
Before me; woman is her name, of man
Extracted; for this cause he shall forego
Father and mother, and to his wife adhere;
And they shall be one flesh, one heart, one soul.   499
    She heard me thus, and though divinely brought,
Yet innocence and virgin modesty,
Her virtue and the conscience of her worth,   502
That would be wooed, and not unsought be won,
Not obvious, not obtrusive, but retired,   504
The more desirable, or to say all,
Nature herself, though pure of sinful thought,
Wrought in her so, that seeing me, she turned;
I followed her, she what was honour knew,
And with obsequious majesty approved   509
My pleaded reason. To the nuptial bower
I led her blushing like the morn: all heaven,
And happy constellations on that hour
Shed their selectest influence; the earth
Gave sign of gratulation, and each hill;   514
Joyous the birds; fresh gales and gentle airs
Whispered it to the woods, and from their wings   516
Flung rose, flung odours from the spicy shrub,
Disporting, till the amorous bird of night   518
Sung spousal, and bid haste the evening star
On his hilltop, to light the bridal lamp.
Thus I have told thee all my state, and brought
My story to the sum of earthly bliss
Which I enjoy, and must confess to find

---

  490 **aloud**] Speaking aloud.   494 **enviest**] i.e. 'you do not begrudge me the gift'.   495–9 **Bone . . . soul**] Paraphrasing Genesis 3: 23–4, repeated in Matthew 19: 4–6 and Mark 10: 6–8.   502 **conscience**] Consciousness.   504 **obvious**] Flaunting herself.   509 **obsequious**] Compliant, dutiful; the word had just begun to acquire its modern pejorative sense.   514 **gratulation**] Rejoicing.   516 **their wings**] Those of the personified airs.   518 **bird of night**] Nightingale.

In all things else delight indeed, but such
As used or not, works in the mind no change,
Nor vehement desire, these delicacies   526
I mean of taste, sight, smell, herbs, fruits, and flowers,
Walks, and the melody of birds; but here
Far otherwise, transported I behold,   529
Transported touch; here passion first I felt,
Commotion strange, in all enjoyments else
Superior and unmoved, here only weak
Against the charm of beauty's powerful glance.   533
Or nature failed in me, and left some part
Not proof enough such object to sustain,   535
Or from my side subducting, took perhaps   536
More than enough; at least on her bestowed
Too much of ornament, in outward show
Elaborate, of inward less exact.   539
For well I understand in the prime end
Of nature her the inferior, in the mind
And inward faculties, which most excel,
In outward also her resembling less
His image who made both, and less expressing
The character of that dominion given
O'er other creatures; yet when I approach
Her loveliness, so absolute she seems
And in her self complete, so well to know
Her own, that what she wills to do or say,
Seems wisest, virtuousest, discreetest, best;   550
All higher knowledge in her presence falls
Degraded, wisdom in discourse with her
Loses discountenanced, and like folly shows;
Authority and reason on her wait,
As one intended first, not after made
Occasionally; and to consummate all,   556
Greatness of mind and nobleness their seat

526 **vehement**] Lit. 'deprived of mind' (in contrast with l. 525).   529 **transported**] Ecstatic.   533 **charm**] Spell.   535 **proof**] Combining the senses of experienced and armed. **sustain**] Withstand.   536 **subducting**] Removing.   539 **exact**] Perfect; cf. ix. 1017.   550 **discreetest**] Most discerning, showing best judgment.   556 **Occasionally**] For an occasion, i.e. to satisfy Adam's desire for a companion.

Build in her loveliest, and create an awe
About her, as a guard angelic placed.
To whom the angel with contracted brow.
　Accuse not nature, she hath done her part;
Do thou but thine, and be not diffident   562
Of wisdom, she deserts thee not, if thou
Dismiss not her, when most thou need'st her nigh,
By attributing overmuch to things
Less excellent, as thou thy self perceiv'st.
For what admir'st thou, what transports thee so,
An outside? fair no doubt, and worthy well
Thy cherishing, thy honouring, and thy love,
Not thy subjection: weigh with her thyself;   570
Then value: ofttimes nothing profits more
Than self esteem, grounded on just and right
Well managed; of that skill the more thou know'st,
The more she will acknowledge thee her head,
And to realities yield all her shows:
Made so adorn for thy delight the more,   576
So awful, that with honour thou mayst love   577
Thy mate, who sees when thou art seen least wise.
But if the sense of touch whereby mankind
Is propagated seem such dear delight
Beyond all other, think the same vouchsafed
To cattle and each beast; which would not be
To them made common and divulged, if aught
Therein enjoyed were worthy to subdue
The soul of man, or passion in him move.
What higher in her society thou find'st
Attractive, human, rational, love still;
In loving thou dost well, in passion not,
Wherein true love consists not; love refines
The thoughts, and heart enlarges, hath his seat   590
In reason, and is judicious, is the scale
By which to heavenly love thou mayst ascend,
Not sunk in carnal pleasure, for which cause
Among the beasts no mate for thee was found.

---

562 **diffident**] Mistrustful.　　576 **adorn**] Adorned (cf. 'elaborate', l. 539); the adjective is apparently Milton's coinage.　　577 **awful**] Awe-inspiring.

To whom thus half abashed Adam replied.
Neither her outside formed so fair, nor aught
In procreation common to all kinds
(Though higher of the genial bed by far,   598
And with mysterious reverence I deem)
So much delights me as those graceful acts,
Those thousand decencies that daily flow
From all her words and actions mixed with love
And sweet compliance, which declare unfeigned
Union of mind, or in us both one soul;
Harmony to behold in wedded pair
More grateful than harmonious sound to the ear.
Yet these subject not; I to thee disclose   607
What inward thence I feel, not therefore foiled,   608
Who meet with various objects, from the sense
Variously representing; yet still free   610
Approve the best, and follow what I approve.
To love thou blam'st me not, for love thou say'st
Leads up to heaven, is both the way and guide;
Bear with me then, if lawful what I ask;
Love not the heavenly spirits, and how their love
Express they, by looks only, or do they mix
Irradiance, virtual or immediate touch?   617
     To whom the angel with a smile that glowed
Celestial rosy red, love's proper hue,
Answered. Let it suffice thee that thou know'st
Us happy, and without love no happiness.
Whatever pure thou in the body enjoy'st
(And pure thou wert created) we enjoy
In eminence, and obstacle find none   624
Of membrane, joint, or limb, exclusive bars:
Easier than air with air, if spirits embrace,
Total they mix, union of pure with pure
Desiring; nor restrained conveyance need   628

---

598 **genial**] Relating to generation, hence nuptial.   607 **subject not**] Do
not make me subject to her.   608 **foiled**] Overcome.   609–10 **from . . .
representing**] Variously presented to me by my senses.   617 **virtual**] 'In essence
or effect, though not formally or actually' (*OED*).   **immediate**] Through actual
contact (to make love by looks would be virtual, to 'mix irradiance' would be
immediate).   624 **In eminence**] To the highest degree.   628 **restrained
conveyance**] Restrictions on the manner of expression.

As flesh to mix with flesh, or soul with soul.
But I can now no more; the parting sun
Beyond the earth's green cape and verdant isles   631
Hesperian sets, my signal to depart.   632
Be strong, live happy, and love, but first of all
Him whom to love is to obey, and keep
His great command; take heed lest passion sway
Thy judgment to do aught, which else free will
Would not admit; thine and of all thy sons
The weal or woe in thee is placed; beware.
I in thy persevering shall rejoice,
And all the blessed: stand fast; to stand or fall   640
Free in thine own arbitrament it lies.
Perfect within, no outward aid require;
And all temptation to transgress repel.
    So saying, he arose; whom Adam thus
Followed with benediction. Since to part,
Go heavenly guest, ethereal messenger,
Sent from whose sovereign goodness I adore.
Gentle to me and affable hath been
Thy condescension, and shall be honoured ever
With grateful memory: thou to mankind   650
Be good and friendly still, and oft return.
    So parted they, the angel up to heaven
From the thick shade, and Adam to his bower.

---

631 **verdant isles**] The Cape Verde Isles, off West Africa.   632 **Hesperian**] In the west.

BOOK IX

The Argument

Satan having compassed the earth, with meditated guile returns as a mist by night into Paradise, enters into the serpent sleeping. Adam and Eve in the morning go forth to their labours, which Eve proposes to divide in several places, each labouring apart: Adam consents not, alleging the danger, lest that enemy, of whom they were forewarned, should attempt her found alone: Eve loath to be thought not circumspect or firm enough, urges her going apart, the rather desirous to make trial of her strength; Adam at last yields: the serpent finds her alone; his subtle approach, first gazing, then speaking, with much flattery extolling Eve above all other creatures. Eve wondering to hear the serpent speak, asks how he attained to human speech and such understanding not till now; the serpent answers, that by tasting of a certain tree in the garden he attained both to speech and reason, till then void of both: Eve requires him to bring her to that tree, and finds it to be the tree of knowledge forbidden: the serpent now grown bolder, with many wiles and arguments induces her at length to eat; she pleased with the taste deliberates awhile whether to impart thereof to Adam or not, at last brings him of the fruit, relates what persuaded her to eat thereof: Adam at first amazed, but perceiving her lost, resolves through vehemence of love to perish with her; and extenuating the trespass eats also of the fruit: the effects thereof in them both; they seek to cover their nakedness; then fall to variance and accusation of one another.

> No MORE of talk where God or angel guest
> With man, as with his friend, familiar used   2
> To sit indulgent, and with him partake
> Rural repast, permitting him the while
> Venial discourse unblamed: I now must change   5
> Those notes to tragic; foul distrust, and breach
> Disloyal on the part of man, revolt,
> And disobedience: on the part of heaven
> Now alienated, distance and distaste,

---

2 **familiar**] Including the sense of familial.   5 **Venial**] Pardonable (not 'permissible' or 'blameless', as the *OED* claims (*s.v.* 3), in which case 'unblamed' would make no sense): the implication is that Adam is at fault (e.g. for his inquisitiveness about astronomy), but not seriously.

Anger and just rebuke, and judgment given,
That brought into this world a world of woe,
Sin and her shadow Death, and Misery
Death's harbinger: sad task, yet argument   13
Not less but more heroic than the wrath
Of stern Achilles on his foe pursued   15
Thrice fugitive about Troy wall; or rage   16
Of Turnus for Lavinia disespoused,   17
Or Neptune's ire or Juno's, that so long
Perplexed the Greek and Cytherea's son;   19
If answerable style I can obtain   20
Of my celestial patroness, who deigns   21
Her nightly visitation unimplored,
And dictates to me slumbering, or inspires
Easy my unpremeditated verse:
Since first this subject for heroic song
Pleased me long choosing, and beginning late;   26
Not sedulous by nature to indite   27
Wars, hitherto the only argument   28
Heroic deemed, chief mastery to dissect   29
With long and tedious havoc fabled knights
In battles feigned; the better fortitude   31
Of patience and heroic martyrdom
Unsung; or to describe races and games,
Or tilting furniture, emblazoned shields,   34
Impresas quaint, caparisons and steeds;   35
Bases and tinsel trappings, gorgeous knights   36
At joust and tournament; then marshalled feast

13 **argument**] Subject.   15 **his foe**] Hector.   16 **fugitive**] Fleeing; for
Achilles' pursuit of and victory over Hector see *Iliad*, xxii.   16–17 **rage ...
disespoused**] Lavinia, the daughter of the king of Latium, was betrothed to Turnus,
King of the Rutuli. Her father Latinus, however, in deference to a divine warning
that he should marry her to a stranger, gave her to Aeneas instead, thus precipitating
hostility and conflict between the Rutuli and the Trojans (*Aeneid*, vii).   19 **the
Greek ... son**] Odysseus and Aeneas, son of Venus or Cytherea, so-called from
her association with the island of Cythera.   20 **answerable**] Appropriate.
21 **celestial patroness**] Urania, muse of astronomy (see vii. 1 ff.).   25–6 **this ...
late**] Milton's earliest sketches for *Paradise Lost* were written in the early 1640s, as the
subject of a drama.   27 **sedulous**] Eager, diligent.   28 **argument**] Subject
matter.   29 **dissect**] Analyse.   31 **feigned**] Invented, as in the *Faerie Queene*.
34 **tilting furniture**] Jousting weapons.   35 **Impresas quaint**] Complex
heraldic symbols.   **caparisons**] Ornamental coverings for horses.   36 **Bases**]
Cloth coverings for horses.

Served up in hall with sewers, and seneschals;   38
The skill of artifice or office mean,
Not that which justly gives heroic name
To person or to poem. Me of these
Nor skilled nor studious, higher argument
Remains, sufficient of itself to raise
That name, unless an age too late, or cold   44
Climate, or years damp my intended wing
Depressed, and much they may, if all be mine,
Not hers who brings it nightly to my ear.
      The sun was sunk, and after him the star
Of Hesperus, whose office is to bring   49
Twilight upon the earth, short arbiter
Twixt day and night, and now from end to end
Night's hemisphere had veiled the horizon round:
When Satan who late fled before the threats
Of Gabriel out of Eden, now improved   54
In meditated fraud and malice, bent
On man's destruction, maugre what might hap   56
Of heavier on himself, fearless returned.
By night he fled, and at midnight returned
From compassing the earth, cautious of day,
Since Uriel regent of the sun descried
His entrance, and forewarned the cherubim
That kept their watch; thence full of anguish driven,
The space of seven continued nights he rode
With darkness, thrice the equinoctial line
He circled, four times crossed the car of Night   65
From pole to pole, traversing each colure;   66
On the eighth returned, and on the coast averse
From entrance or cherubic watch, by stealth
Found unsuspected way. There was a place,
Now not, though sin, not time, first wrought the change,

---

38 **sewers, and seneschals**] The sewer (lit. 'seater') 'superintended the arrange-
ment of the table, the seating of the guests, and the tasting and serving of the
meal' (*OED*); the seneschal was the major-domo, or chief steward of the house-
hold.   44 **That name**] Of epic.   49 **Hesperus**] Venus as the evening
star.   54 **improved**] 'Increased, aggravated' (*OED*).   56 **maugre**] Despite.
64–5 **thrice . . . circled**] Satan circles the earth at the equator, keeping ahead of the
sun and thereby remaining in darkness.   66 **colure**] The colures are two longi-
tudinal circles intersecting at right angles at the poles and dividing the ecliptic into
four equal parts.

Where Tigris at the foot of Paradise
Into a gulf shot underground, till part
Rose up a fountain by the tree of life;
In with the river sunk, and with it rose
Satan involved in rising mist, then sought
Where to lie hid; sea he had searched and land
From Eden over Pontus, and the pool   77
Maeotis, up beyond the river Ob;   78
Downward as far antarctic; and in length
West from Orontes to the ocean barred   80
At Darien, thence to the land where flows   81
Ganges and Indus: thus the orb he roamed
With narrow search; and with inspection deep
Considered every creature, which of all
Most opportune might serve his wiles, and found
The serpent subtlest beast of all the field.
Him after long debate, irresolute
Of thoughts revolved, his final sentence chose
Fit vessel, fittest imp of fraud, in whom
To enter, and his dark suggestions hide   90
From sharpest sight: for in the wily snake,
Whatever sleights none would suspicious mark,
As from his wit and native subtlety
Proceeding, which in other beasts observed
Doubt might beget of diabolic power   95
Active within beyond the sense of brute.
Thus he resolved, but first from inward grief
His bursting passion into plaints thus poured:
    O earth, how like to heaven, if not preferred
More justly, seat worthier of gods, as built
With second thoughts, reforming what was old!
For what god after better worse would build?
Terrestrial heaven, danced round by other heavens
That shine, yet bear their bright officious lamps,   104
Light above light, for thee alone, as seems,
In thee concentring all their precious beams

77 **Pontus**] The Black Sea.   78 **Maeotis**] The Sea of Azov.   **river Ob**] In the Siberian Arctic.   80 **Orontes**] A river in Lebanon, Syria, and Turkey. 81 **Darien**] Panama.   90 **suggestions**] Temptations to evil.   95 **Doubt**] Suspicion.   104 **officious**] Dutiful, though here perhaps with its modern pejorative overtone.

Of sacred influence: as God in heaven
Is centre, yet extends to all, so thou
Centring receiv'st from all those orbs; in thee,
Not in themselves, all their known virtue appears
Productive in herb, plant, and nobler birth
Of creatures animate with gradual life   112
Of growth, sense, reason, all summed up in man.
With what delight could I have walked thee round,
If I could joy in aught, sweet interchange
Of hill, and valley, rivers, woods and plains,
Now land, now sea, and shores with forest crowned,
Rocks, dens, and caves; but I in none of these
Find place or refuge; and the more I see
Pleasures about me, so much more I feel
Torment within me, as from the hateful siege   121
Of contraries; all good to me becomes
Bane, and in heaven much worse would by my state,
But neither here seek I, no nor in heaven
To dwell, unless by mastering heaven's supreme;
Nor hope to be myself less miserable
By what I seek, but others to make such
As I, though thereby worse to me redound:
For only in destroying I find ease
To my relentless thoughts; and him destroyed,   130
Or won to what may work his utter loss,
For whom all this was made, all this will soon
Follow, as to him linked in weal or woe,
In woe then; that destruction wide may range:
To me shall be the glory sole among
The infernal powers, in one day to have marred
What he almighty styled, six nights and days
Continued making, and who knows how long
Before had been contriving, though perhaps
Not longer than since I in one night freed   140
From servitude inglorious well-nigh half
The angelic name, and thinner left the throng
Of his adorers: he to be avenged
And to repair his numbers thus impaired,

112 **gradual**] Gradated, in stages.   121 **siege**] Both seat and attack.

Whether such virtue spent of old now failed   145
More angels to create, if they at least
Are his created, or to spite us more,   147
Determined to advance into our room   148
A creature formed of earth, and him endow,
Exalted from so base original,   150
With heavenly spoils, our spoils: what he decreed
He effected; man he made, and for him built
Magnificent this world, and earth his seat,
Him lord pronounced, and, O indignity!
Subjected to his service angel wings,
And flaming ministers to watch and tend
Their earthy charge: of these the vigilance
I dread, and to elude, thus wrapped in mist
Of midnight vapour glide obscure, and pry
In every bush and brake, where hap may find   160
The serpent sleeping, in whose mazy folds
To hide me, and the dark intent I bring.
O foul descent! that I who erst contended
With gods to sit the highest, am now constrained
Into a beast, and mixed with bestial slime,
This essence to incarnate and imbrute,
That to the height of deity aspired;
But what will not ambition and revenge
Descend to? Who aspires must down as low
As high he soared, obnoxious first or last
To basest things. Revenge, at first though sweet,   171
Bitter ere long back on itself recoils;
Let it; I reck not, so it light well aimed,   173
Since higher I fall short, on him who next   174
Provokes my envy, this new favourite
Of heaven, this man of clay, son of despite,
Whom us the more to spite his maker raised
From dust: spite then with spite is best repaid.
    So saying, through each thicket dank or dry,
Like a black mist low creeping, he held on   180

145 **virtue**] Power.   146–7 **if ... created**] i.e. if the angels are not self-created, or did not always exist; cf. v. 860.   148 **room**] Place.   150 **original**] Origin. 170–1 **obnoxious ... To**] Exposed to harm from; the modern sense was apparently not yet in use.   173 **reck**] Care.   174 **higher**] i.e. when I aim at God.

His midnight search, where soonest he might find
The serpent: him fast sleeping soon he found
In labyrinth of many a round self-rolled,
His head the midst, well stored with subtle wiles:
Not yet in horrid shade or dismal den,
Nor nocent yet, but on the grassy herb   186
Fearless unfeared he slept: in at his mouth
The devil entered, and his brutal sense,   188
In heart or head, possessing soon inspired
With act intelligential; but his sleep
Disturbed not, waiting close the approach of morn.   191
Now whenas sacred light began to dawn
In Eden on the humid flowers, that breathed
Their morning incense, when all things that breathe,
From the earth's great altar send up silent praise
To the creator, and his nostrils fill
With grateful smell, forth came the human pair   197
And joined their vocal worship to the choir
Of creatures wanting voice, that done, partake   199
The season, prime for sweetest scents and airs:
Then commune how that day they best may ply
Their growing work: for much their work outgrew
The hands' dispatch of two, gardening so wide.
And Eve first to her husband thus began.

　　Adam, well may we labour still to dress
This garden, still to tend plant, herb and flower,
Our pleasant task enjoined, but till more hands
Aid us, the work under our labour grows,
Luxurious by restraint; what we by day   209
Lop overgrown, or prune, or prop, or bind,
One night or two with wanton growth derides   211
Tending to wild. Thou therefore now advise
Or hear what to my mind first thoughts present,
Let us divide our labours, thou where choice
Leads thee, or where most needs, whether to wind

---

186 **Nor nocent**] Both not harmful and innocent.　　188 **brutal**] Animal.
191 **close**] Secretly.　　197 **grateful**] Including the meaning 'pleasing'.
199 **wanting**] Lacking.　　209 **Luxurious**] Luxuriant, though the word was most
commonly pejorative, and must have such an overtone here.　　211 **wanton**]
Unrestrained; like *luxurious* above, with pejorative overtones.

The woodbine round this arbour, or direct
The clasping ivy where to climb, while I
In yonder spring of roses intermixed   218
With myrtle, find what to redress till noon: 219
For while so near each other thus all day
Our task we choose, what wonder if so near
Looks intervene and smiles, or object new
Casual discourse draw on, which intermits
Our day's work brought to little, though begun
Early, and the hour of supper comes unearned.
　　To whom mild answer Adam thus returned.
Sole Eve, associate sole, to me beyond
Compare above all living creatures dear,
Well hast thou motioned, well thy thoughts employed   229
How we might best fulfil the work which here
God hath assigned us, nor of me shalt pass
Unpraised: for nothing lovelier can be found
In woman, than to study household good,
And good works in her husband to promote.
Yet not so strictly hath our Lord imposed
Labour, as to debar us when we need
Refreshment, whether food, or talk between,
Food of the mind, or this sweet intercourse
Of looks and smiles, for smiles from reason flow,
To brute denied, and are of love the food,   240
Love not the lowest end of human life.
For not to irksome toil, but to delight
He made us, and delight to reason joined.
These paths and bowers doubt not but our joint hands
Will keep from wilderness with ease, as wide
As we need walk, till younger hands ere long
Assist us: but if much converse perhaps
Thee satiate, to short absence I could yield.
For solitude sometimes is best society,
And short retirement urges sweet return.   250
But other doubt possesses me, lest harm
Befall thee severed from me; for thou know'st
What hath been warned us, what malicious foe

218 **spring**] Grove.　　219 **redress**] 'Set upright again' (*OED*).　　229 **motioned**]
Suggested.

Envying our happiness, and of his own
Despairing, seeks to work us woe and shame
By sly assault; and somewhere nigh at hand
Watches, no doubt, with greedy hope to find
His wish and best advantage, us asunder,
Hopeless to circumvent us joined, where each
To other speedy aid might lend at need;   260
Whether his first design be to withdraw
Our fealty from God, or to disturb
Conjugal love, than which perhaps no bliss
Enjoyed by us excites his envy more;
Or this, or worse, leave not the faithful side   265
That gave thee being, still shades thee and protects.
The wife, where danger or dishonour lurks,
Safest and seemliest by her husband stays,
Who guards her, or with her the worst endures.

   To whom the virgin majesty of Eve,   270
As one who loves, and some unkindness meets,
With sweet austere composure thus replied.

   Offspring of heaven and earth, and all earth's lord,
That such an enemy we have, who seeks
Our ruin, both by thee informed I learn,
And from the parting angel overheard
As in a shady nook I stood behind,
Just then returned at shut of evening flowers.
But that thou shouldst my firmness therefore doubt
To God or thee, because we have a foe   280
May tempt it, I expected not to hear.
His violence thou fear'st not, being such,
As we, not capable of death or pain,
Can either not receive, or can repel.
His fraud is then thy fear, which plain infers
Thy equal fear that my firm faith and love
Can by his fraud be shaken or seduced;
Thoughts, which how found they harbour in thy breast
Adam, misthought of her to thee so dear?

   To whom with healing words Adam replied.   290
Daughter of God and man, immortal Eve,

---

265 **Or . . . worse**] Whether his intention be this or something worse.   270 **virgin**]
Innocent.

For such thou art, from sin and blame entire: 292
Not diffident of thee do I dissuade
Thy absence from my sight, but to avoid
The attempt itself, intended by our foe.
For he who tempts, though in vain, at least asperses   296
The tempted with dishonour foul, supposed
Not incorruptible of faith, not proof
Against temptation: thou thyself with scorn
And anger wouldst resent the offered wrong,
Though ineffectual found: misdeem not then,
If such affront I labour to avert
From thee alone, which on us both at once
The enemy, though bold, will hardly dare,
Or daring, first on me the assault shall light.
Nor thou his malice and false guile contemn;
Subtle he needs must be, who could seduce
Angels, nor think superfluous others' aid.
I from the influence of thy looks receive
Access in every virtue, in thy sight   310
More wise, more watchful, stronger, if need were
Of outward strength; while shame, thou looking on,
Shame to be overcome or over-reached
Would utmost vigour raise, and raised unite.
Why shouldst not thou like sense within thee feel
When I am present, and thy trial choose
With me, best witness of thy virtue tried.
    So spake domestic Adam in his care
And matrimonial love; but Eve, who thought
Less attributed to her faith sincere,   320
Thus her reply with accent sweet renewed.
    If this be our condition, thus to dwell
In narrow circuit straitened by a foe,
Subtle or violent, we not endued
Single with like defence, wherever met,
How are we happy, still in fear of harm?   326
But harm precedes not sin: only our foe
Tempting affronts us with his foul esteem
Of our integrity: his foul esteem

292 **entire**]   'Free   from   reproach,   unblemished,   blameless'   (*OED*).
296 **asperses**] Slanders.   310 **Access**] Increase.   326 **still**] Always

Sticks no dishonour on our front, but turns   330
Foul on himself; then wherefore shunned or feared
By us? who rather double honour gain
From his surmise proved false, find peace within,
Favour from heaven, our witness from the event.   334
And what is faith, love, virtue unassayed
Alone, without exterior help sustained?
Let us not then suspect our happy state
Left so imperfect by the maker wise,
As not secure to single or combined.
Frail is our happiness, if this be so,   340
And Eden were no Eden thus exposed.
    To whom thus Adam fervently replied.
O woman, best are all things as the will
Of God ordained them, his creating hand
Nothing imperfect or deficient left
Of all that he created, much less man,
Or aught that might his happy state secure,
Secure from outward force; within himself
The danger lies, yet lies within his power:
Against his will he can receive no harm.
But God left free the will, for what obeys
Reason, is free, and reason he made right,
But bid her well beware, and still erect,   353
Lest by some fair-appearing good surprised
She dictate false, and misinform the will
To do what God expressly hath forbid.
Not then mistrust, but tender love enjoins,
That I should mind thee oft, and mind thou me.   358
Firm we subsist, yet possible to swerve,
Since reason not impossibly may meet
Some specious object by the foe suborned,   361
And fall into deception unaware,
Not keeping strictest watch, as she was warned.
Seek not temptation then, which to avoid
Were better, and most likely if from me
Thou sever not: trial will come unsought.

---

330 **front**] Lit. 'face', but punning on 'affronts', l. 328.   334 **event**] Outcome.
353 **still erect**] Always alert.   358 **mind**] Both remind, admonish, and pay
attention to.   361 **specious**] Deceptively attractive.

Wouldst thou approve thy constancy, approve   367
First thy obedience; the other who can know,
Not seeing thee attempted, who attest?
But if thou think, trial unsought may find
Us both securer than thus warned thou seem'st,   371
Go; for thy stay, not free, absents thee more;
Go in thy native innocence, rely
On what thou hast of virtue, summon all,
For God towards thee hath done his part, do thine.

    So spake the patriarch of mankind, but Eve
Persisted, yet submiss, though last, replied.

    With thy permission then, and thus forewarned
Chiefly by what thy own last reasoning words
Touched only, that our trial, when least sought,   380
May find us both perhaps far less prepared,
The willinger I go, nor much expect
A foe so proud will first the weaker seek;
So bent, the more shall shame him his repulse.

    Thus saying, from her husband's hand her hand
Soft she withdrew, and like a wood-nymph light
Oread or dryad, or of Delia's train,   387
Betook her to the groves, but Delia's self
In gait surpassed and goddess-like deport,
Though not as she with bow and quiver armed,   390
But with such gardening tools as art yet rude,
Guiltless of fire had formed, or angels brought.   392
To Pales, or Pomona thus adorned,   393
Likeliest she seemed, Pomona when she fled
Vertumnus, or to Ceres in her prime,   395
Yet virgin of Proserpina from Jove.   396
Her long with ardent look his eye pursued
Delighted, but desiring more her stay.
Oft he to her his charge of quick return

---

367 **approve**] Prove, test.   371 **securer**] Less careful.   387 **Oread or dryad**]
Mountain or wood nymph. **Delia**] Diana, so called from her birthplace on
Delos.   390 **bow and quiver**] Diana was goddess of the hunt.   392 **Guiltless**]
Innocent, without experience.   393 **Pales**] Goddess of pastures. **Pomona**]
Goddess of orchards.   395 **Vertumnus**] More properly Vortumnus, god of gardens,
who presided over the changes of the year. Variously disguised, he pursued and wooed
Pomona, ultimately successfully; see *Metamorphoses*, xiv. 628 ff.   **Ceres**] Goddess of
agriculture (cf. iv. 268 ff.).   396 **Proserpina**] Child of Ceres by Jove.

Repeated, she to him as oft engaged   400
To be returned by noon amid the bower,
And all things in best order to invite
Noontide repast, or afternoon's repose.
O much deceived, much failing, hapless Eve,
Of thy presumed return! event perverse!   405
Thou never from that hour in Paradise
Found'st either sweet repast, or sound repose;
Such ambush hid among sweet flowers and shades
Waited with hellish rancour imminent
To intercept thy way, or send thee back
Despoiled of innocence, of faith, of bliss.
For now, and since first break of dawn the fiend,
Mere serpent in appearance, forth was come,   413
And on his quest, where likeliest he might find
The only two of mankind, but in them
The whole included race, his purposed prey.
In bower and field he sought, where any tuft
Of grove or garden-plot more pleasant lay,
Their tendance or plantation for delight,   419
By fountain or by shady rivulet
He sought them both, but wished his hap might find
Eve separate, he wished, but not with hope
Of what so seldom chanced, when to his wish,
Beyond his hope, Eve separate he spies,
Veiled in a cloud of fragrance, where she stood,
Half spied, so thick the roses bushing round
About her glowed, oft stooping to support
Each flower of slender stalk, whose head though gay
Carnation, purple, azure, or specked with gold,
Hung drooping unsustained, them she upstays
Gently with myrtle band, mindless the while,   431
Herself, though fairest unsupported flower,
From her best prop so far, and storm so nigh.
Nearer he drew, and many a walk traversed
Of stateliest covert, cedar, pine, or palm,
Then voluble and bold, now hid, now seen   436

---

405 **event perverse**] Evil outcome.   413 **Mere**] Wholly a.   419 **Their tendance**] The object of their care.   431 **mindless**] Both unaware and inattentive (cf. l. 358).   436 **voluble**] Undulating.

Among thick-woven arborets and flowers   437
Embordered on each bank, the hand of Eve: 438
Spot more delicious than those gardens feigned
Or of revived Adonis, or renowned   440
Alcinous, host of old Laertes' son,   441
Or that, not mystic, where the sapient king   442
Held dalliance with his fair Egyptian spouse.   443
Much he the place admired, the person more.
As one who long in populous city pent,
Where houses thick and sewers annoy the air,
Forth issuing on a summer's morn to breathe
Among the pleasant villages and farms
Adjoined, from each thing met conceives delight,
The smell of grain, or tedded grass, or kine,   450
Or dairy, each rural sight, each rural sound;
If chance with nymph-like step fair virgin pass,
What pleasing seemed, for her now pleases more,   453
She most, and in her look sums all delight.
Such pleasure took the serpent to behold
This flowery plat, the sweet recess of Eve   456
Thus early, thus alone; her heavenly form
Angelic, but more soft, and feminine,
Her graceful innocence, her every air
Of gesture or least action overawed   460
His malice, and with rapine sweet bereaved
His fierceness of the fierce intent it brought:
That space the evil one abstracted stood

437 **arborets**] Shrubs.   438 **hand**] Handiwork.   439–40 **gardens** ...
Adonis] Adonis was the lover of Venus. When hunting he was killed by a boar, and
Venus made the anemone (or in some versions the rose) spring from his blood. After his
death, in response to the pleas of both Venus and Proserpina, Jove restored him to life
and allowed him to live half the year with each—the myth, like that of Proserpina
herself, was from the earliest times said to allude to the cycles of the crops. The Garden
of Adonis became a proverbial expression for the swift passing of earthly beauty;
however, in Spenser's version of the tale, it is the secret garden where Adonis and
Venus make love, a place of 'perpetual spring and harvest' (*Faerie Queene*, III.
vi. 29).   441 **Alcinous ... son**] Homer describes the visit of Odysseus, son of
Laertes, to Alcinous, king of the Phaeacians, and his marvellous gardens, in *Odyssey*, vii.
112 ff.; cf. above, v. 341.   442 **not mystic**] Real, not fabled or allegorical. **sapient
king**] Solomon.   443 **Egyptian spouse**] Solomon married the daughter of Pharaoh
(1 Kings 3: 1); for Solomon's garden see Song of Solomon 6: 2.   450 **tedded**] Cut
and dried, for use as hay. **kine**] Cattle.   453 **for**] Because of.   456 **plat**] Plot
of ground.

From his own evil, and for the time remained
Stupidly good, of enmity disarmed,
Of guile, of hate, of envy, of revenge;
But the hot hell that always in him burns,
Though in mid-heaven, soon ended his delight,
And tortures him now more, the more he sees
Of pleasure not for him ordained: then soon
Fierce hate he recollects, and all his thoughts
Of mischief, gratulating, thus excites.   472

    Thoughts, whither have ye led me, with what sweet
Compulsion thus transported to forget
What hither brought us, hate, not love, nor hope
Of Paradise for hell, hope here to taste   476
Of pleasure, but all pleasure to destroy,
Save what is in destroying, other joy
To me is lost. Then let me not let pass
Occasion which now smiles, behold alone
The woman, opportune to all attempts,   481
Her husband, for I view far round, not nigh,
Whose higher intellectual more I shun,   483
And strength, of courage haughty, and of limb   484
Heroic built, though of terrestrial mould,
Foe not informidable, exempt from wound,
I not; so much hath hell debased, and pain
Enfeebled me, to what I was in heaven.   488
She fair, divinely fair, fit love for gods,
Not terrible, though terror be in love
And beauty, not approached by stronger hate,
Hate stronger, under show of love well feigned,
The way which to her ruin now I tend.

    So spake the enemy of mankind, enclosed
In serpent, inmate bad, and toward Eve
Addressed his way, not with indented wave,
Prone on the ground, as since, but on his rear,
Circular base of rising folds, that towered
Fold above fold a surging maze, his head

---

472 **gratulating**] Rejoicing.　　476 **for**] In exchange for.　　481 **opportune**]
Open, conveniently located.　　483 **intellectual**] Intellect.　　484 **haughty**]
Lofty, high-minded.　　488 **to**] In comparison with.

Crested aloft, and carbuncle his eyes;   500
With burnished neck of verdant gold, erect
Amidst his circling spires, that on the grass   502
Floated redundant: pleasing was his shape,   503
And lovely, never since of serpent kind
Lovelier, not those that in Illyria changed
Hermione and Cadmus, or the god   506
In Epidaurus; nor to which transformed   507
Ammonian Jove, or Capitoline was seen,
He with Olympias, this with her who bore
Scipio the height of Rome. With tract oblique   510
At first, as one who sought access, but feared
To interrupt, sidelong he works his way.
As when a ship by skilful steersman wrought
Nigh river's mouth or foreland, where the wind
Veers oft, as oft so steers, and shifts her sail;
So varied he, and of his tortuous train
Curled many a wanton wreath in sight of Eve,
To lure her eye; she busied heard the sound
Of rustling leaves, but minded not, as used
To such disport before her through the field,
From every beast, more duteous at her call,
Than at Circean call the herd disguised.   522
He bolder now, uncalled before her stood;
But as in gaze admiring: oft he bowed
His turret crest, and sleek enamelled neck,
Fawning, and licked the ground whereon she trod.
His gentle dumb expression turned at length
The eye of Eve to mark his play; he glad
Of her attention gained, with serpent tongue

---

500 **carbuncle**] 'A mythical gem said to emit light in the dark' (*OED*).
502 **spires**] Coils.   503 **redundant**] The word had the senses of both 'wavelike'
and 'copious'.   505-6 **those ... Cadmus**] For the metamorphosis of Harmonia (or
Hermione) and Cadmus into serpents see *Metamorphoses*, iv. 563 ff.   506-7 **god ...
Epidaurus**] Aesculapius, god of healing, who appeared in his shrine at Epidaurus in
the form of a serpent (*Metamorphoses*, xv. 760-4).   508-10 **Ammonian ... Scipio**]
Jupiter Ammon made love to Olympias, the mother of Alexander the Great, in the form
of a serpent, as Jupiter Capitolinus (so named from his shrine on the Capitoline in
Rome) did to the mother of the Roman hero Scipio Africanus. **height of Rome**]
Greatest Roman. **tract**] Path, course.   522 **at ... disguised**] The sorceress
Circe transformed her victims into fawning animals (*Odyssey*, x. 212-19).

Organic, or impulse of vocal air,   530
His fraudulent temptation thus began.
    Wonder not, sovereign mistress, if perhaps
Thou canst, who art sole wonder, much less arm
Thy looks, the heaven of mildness, with disdain,
Displeased that I approach thee thus, and gaze
Insatiate, I thus single, nor have feared
Thy awful brow, more awful thus retired.
Fairest resemblance of thy maker fair,
Thee all things living gaze on, all things thine
By gift, and thy celestial beauty adore   540
With ravishment beheld, there best beheld
Where universally admired; but here
In this enclosure wild, these beasts among,
Beholders rude, and shallow to discern
Half what in thee is fair, one man except,
Who sees thee? (and what is one?) who shouldst be seen
A goddess among gods, adored and served
By angels numberless, thy daily train.
    So glozed the tempter, and his proem tuned;   549
Into the heart of Eve his words made way,
Though at the voice much marvelling; at length
Not unamazed she thus in answer spake.
What may this mean? Language of man pronounced
By tongue of brute, and human sense expressed?
The first at least of these I thought denied
To beasts, whom God on their creation-day
Created mute to all articulate sound;
The latter I demur, for in their looks   558
Much reason, and in their actions oft appears.
Thee, serpent, subtlest beast of all the field
I knew, but not with human voice endued;
Redouble then this miracle, and say,
How cam'st thou speakable of mute, and how
To me so friendly grown above the rest
Of brutal kind, that daily are in sight?

---

530 **Organic**] Being used as an organ or instrument (of speech, because snakes have
no vocal chords). **impulse ... air**] Impelling the air to make the sounds of
speech. 549 **glozed**] Flattered. 558 **demur**] Am doubtful about.

Say, for such wonder claims attention due.
    To whom the guileful tempter thus replied.
Empress of this fair world, resplendent Eve,
Easy to me it is to tell thee all
What thou command'st, and right thou shouldst be obeyed: *570*
I was at first as other beasts that graze
The trodden herb, of abject thoughts and low,
As was my food, nor aught but food discerned
Or sex, and apprehended nothing high:
Till on a day roving the field, I chanced
A goodly tree far distant to behold
Loaden with fruit of fairest colours mixed,
Ruddy and gold: I nearer drew to gaze;
When from the boughs a savoury odour blown,
Grateful to appetite, more pleased my sense   580
Than smell of sweetest fennel, or the teats   581
Of ewe or goat dropping with milk at even,
Unsucked of lamb or kid, that tend their play.
To satisfy the sharp desire I had
Of tasting those fair apples, I resolved
Not to defer; hunger and thirst at once,   586
Powerful persuaders, quickened at the scent
Of that alluring fruit, urged me so keen.
About the mossy trunk I wound me soon,
For high from ground the branches would require   *590*
Thy utmost reach or Adam's: round the tree
All other beasts that saw, with like desire
Longing and envying stood, but could not reach.
Amid the tree now got, where plenty hung
Tempting so nigh, to pluck and eat my fill
I spared not, for such pleasure till that hour
At feed or fountain never had I found.
Sated at length, ere long I might perceive
Strange alteration in me, to degree
Of reason in my inward powers, and speech
Wanted not long, though to this shape retained.   601
Thenceforth to speculations high or deep

---

580 **Grateful**] Pleasing.   581 **fennel ... teats**] Snakes were said to be especially fond of fennel, and of milk sucked directly from the teat.   586 **defer**] Delay.   601 **Wanted**] Lacked.

I turned my thoughts, and with capacious mind
Considered all things visible in heaven,
Or earth, or middle, all things fair and good;   605
But all that fair and good in thy divine
Semblance, and in thy beauty's heavenly ray
United I beheld; no fair to thine
Equivalent or second, which compelled
Me thus, though importune perhaps, to come
And gaze, and worship thee of right declared
Sovereign of creatures, universal dame.
    So talked the spirited sly snake; and Eve
Yet more amazed unwary thus replied.
    Serpent, thy overpraising leaves in doubt
The virtue of that fruit, in thee first proved: 616
But say, where grows the tree, from hence how far?
For many are the trees of God that grow
In Paradise, and various, yet unknown
To us, in such abundance lies our choice,
As leaves a greater store of fruit untouched,
Still hanging incorruptible, till men
Grow up to their provision, and more hands   623
Help to disburden nature of her birth.   624
    To whom the wily adder, blithe and glad.
Empress, the way is ready, and not long,
Beyond a row of myrtles, on a flat,
Fast by a fountain, one small thicket past
Of blowing myrrh and balm; if thou accept   629
My conduct, I can bring thee thither soon.
    Lead then, said Eve. He leading swiftly rolled
In tangles, and made intricate seem straight,
To mischief swift. Hope elevates, and joy
Brightens his crest, as when a wandering fire,
Compact of unctuous vapour, which the night   635
Condenses, and the cold environs round,

---

605 **middle**] The air between.   616 **virtue**] Combining the meanings of power,
innate excellence, and nature.   **proved**] Tested.   623 **their provision**] What they
provide.   624 **birth**] Milton uses 'bearth', an etymologizing spelling not in normal
usage, but appropriate to trees which 'bear' fruit.   629 **blowing**] Blooming.
635 **Compact ... vapour**] Composed of oily gases; referring to the *ignis fatuus*, or
will-o'-the-wisp.

Kindled through agitation to a flame,
Which oft, they say, some evil spirit attends
Hovering and blazing with delusive light,
Misleads the amazed night-wanderer from his way   640
To bogs and mires, and oft through pond or pool,
There swallowed up and lost, from succour far.
So glistered the dire snake, and into fraud
Led Eve our credulous mother, to the tree
Of prohibition, root of all our woe;
Which when she saw, thus to her guide she spake.
— Serpent, we might have spared our coming hither,
Fruitless to me, though fruit be here to excess,
The credit of whose virtue rest with thee,
Wondrous indeed, if cause of such effects.   650
But of this tree we may not taste nor touch;
God so commanded, and left that command
Sole daughter of his voice; the rest, we live
Law to our selves, our reason is our law.
— To whom the tempter guilefully replied.
Indeed? hath God then said that of the fruit
Of all these garden trees ye shall not eat,
Yet lords declared of all in earth or air?
— To whom thus Eve yet sinless. Of the fruit
Of each tree in the garden we may eat,   660
But of the fruit of this fair tree amidst
The garden, God hath said, Ye shall not eat
Thereof, nor shall ye touch it, lest ye die.
She scarce had said, though brief, when now more bold
The tempter, but with show of zeal and love
To man, and indignation at his wrong,
New part puts on, and as to passion moved,
Fluctuates disturbed, yet comely and in act   668
Raised, as of some great matter to begin.
As when of old some orator renowned
In Athens or free Rome, where eloquence
Flourished, since mute, to some great cause addressed,
Stood in himself collected, while each part,
Motion, each act won audience ere the tongue,
Sometimes in height began, as no delay

668 **Fluctuates**] Changes his aspect.

Of preface brooking through his zeal of right.　　676
So standing, moving, or to height upgrown
The tempter all impassioned thus began.

O sacred, wise, and wisdom-giving plant,
Mother of science, now I feel thy power　　680
Within me clear, not only to discern
Things in their causes, but to trace the ways
Of highest agents, deemed however wise.
Queen of this universe, do not believe
Those rigid threats of death; ye shall not die:
How should ye? by the fruit? it gives you life
To knowledge: by the threatener? look on me,　　687
Me who have touched and tasted, yet both live,
And life more perfect have attained than fate
Meant me, by venturing higher than my lot.
Shall that be shut to man, which to the beast
Is open? or will God incense his ire
For such a petty trespass, and not praise
Rather your dauntless virtue, whom the pain
Of death denounced, whatever thing death be,　　695
Deterred not from achieving what might lead
To happier life, knowledge of good and evil;
Of good, how just? of evil, if what is evil
Be real, why not known, since easier shunned?
God therefore cannot hurt ye, and be just;　　700
Not just, not God; not feared then, nor obeyed:
Your fear itself of death removes the fear.
Why then was this forbid? Why but to awe,
Why but to keep ye low and ignorant,
His worshipper; he knows that in the day
Ye eat thereof, your eyes that seem so clear,
Yet are but dim, shall perfectly be then
Opened and cleared, and ye shall be as gods,
Knowing both good and evil as they know.
That ye should be as gods, since I as man,　　710
Internal man, is but proportion meet,

675–6 **Sometimes ... brooking**] i.e. began at the height of the argument, without any preface.　680 **science**] Knowledge.　685–7 **ye ... knowledge**] Paraphrasing Genesis 3: 4–5. **To knowledge**] Eventuating in knowledge. 695 **denounced**] Threatened.

I of brute human, ye of human gods.
So ye shall die perhaps, by putting off
Human, to put on gods, death to be wished,
Though threatened, which no worse than this can bring.
And what are gods that man may not become
As they, participating godlike food?   717
The gods are first, and that advantage use
On our belief, that all from them proceeds;
I question it, for this fair earth I see,
Warmed by the sun, producing every kind,
Them nothing: if they all things, who enclosed   722
Knowledge of good and evil in this tree,
That whoso eats thereof, forthwith attains
Wisdom without their leave? and wherein lies
The offence, that man should thus attain to know?
What can your knowledge hurt him, or this tree
Impart against his will if all be his?
Or is it envy, and can envy dwell
In heavenly breasts? these, these and many more
Causes import your need of this fair fruit.
Goddess humane, reach then, and freely taste.   732

  He ended, and his words replete with guile
Into her heart too easy entrance won:
Fixed on the fruit she gazed, which to behold
Might tempt alone, and in her ears the sound
Yet rung of his persuasive words, impregned   737
With reason, to her seeming, and with truth;
Meanwhile the hour of noon drew on, and waked
An eager appetite, raised by the smell
So savoury of that fruit, which with desire,
Inclinable now grown to touch or taste,   742
Solicited her longing eye; yet first
Pausing a while, thus to her self she mused.

  Great are thy virtues, doubtless, best of fruits,
Though kept from man, and worthy to be admired,
Whose taste, too long forborne, at first assay

---

717 **participating**] Partaking of.   722 **they**] 'Produce' understood.   732
humane] Both benevolent and human: the spellings were not yet fully distinguished
in the seventeenth century.   737 **impregned**] Impregnated.   742 **Inclinable**]
Inclined, disposed.

Gave elocution to the mute, and taught
The tongue not made for speech to speak thy praise:
Thy praise he also who forbids thy use,   750
Conceals not from us, naming thee the tree
Of knowledge, knowledge both of good and evil;
Forbids us then to taste, but his forbidding
Commends thee more, while it infers the good   754
By thee communicated, and our want:
For good unknown, sure is not had, or had
And yet unknown, is as not had at all.
In plain then, what forbids he but to know,   758
Forbids us good, forbids us to be wise?
Such prohibitions bind not. But if death
Bind us with after-bands, what profits then
Our inward freedom? In the day we eat
Of this fair fruit, our doom is, we shall die.
How dies the serpent? he hath eaten and lives,
And knows, and speaks, and reasons, and discerns,
Irrational till then. For us alone
Was death invented? or to us denied
This intellectual food, for beasts reserved?
For beasts it seems: yet that one beast which first
Hath tasted, envies not, but brings with joy
The good befallen him, author unsuspect,   771
Friendly to man, far from deceit or guile.
What fear I then, rather what know to fear
Under this ignorance of good and evil,
Of God or death, of law or penalty?
Here grows the cure of all, this fruit divine,
Fair to the eye, inviting to the taste,
Of virtue to make wise: what hinders then
To reach, and feed at once both body and mind?
    So saying, her rash hand in evil hour   780
Forth reaching to the fruit, she plucked, she ate:
Earth felt the wound, and nature from her seat
Sighing through all her works gave signs of woe,
That all was lost. Back to the thicket slunk
The guilty serpent, and well might, for Eve

754 infers] Implies.   758 In plain] In plain words.   771 author
unsuspect] Trustworthy authority.

Intent now wholly on her taste, naught else
Regarded, such delight till then, as seemed,
In fruit she never tasted, whether true
Or fancied so, through expectation high
Of knowledge, nor was godhead from her thought.
Greedily she engorged without restraint,
And knew not eating death: satiate at length,
And heightened as with wine, jocund and boon,   793
Thus to herself she pleasingly began.

   O sovereign, virtuous, precious of all trees
In Paradise, of operation blessed
To sapience, hitherto obscured, infamed,   797
And thy fair fruit let hang, as to no end
Created; but henceforth my early care,
Not without song, each morning, and due praise
Shall tend thee, and the fertile burden ease
Of thy full branches offered free to all;
Till dieted by thee I grow mature
In knowledge, as the gods who all things know;
Though others envy what they cannot give;
For had the gift been theirs, it had not here
Thus grown. Experience, next to thee I owe,
Best guide; not following thee, I had remained
In ignorance, thou open'st wisdom's way,
And giv'st access, though secret she retire.   *810*
And I perhaps am secret; heaven is high,
High and remote to see from thence distinct
Each thing on earth; and other care perhaps
May have diverted from continual watch
Our great forbidder, safe with all his spies
About him. But to Adam in what sort
Shall I appear? shall I to him make known
As yet my change, and give him to partake
Full happiness with me, or rather not,
But keep the odds of knowledge in my power
Without copartner? so to add what wants   821
In female sex, the more to draw his love,

---

  793 **boon**] Jovial.   797 **To sapience**] In producing knowledge, with a pun on the etymological meaning of sapience, 'taste' (*sapere*, taste, know). **infamed**] Slandered.
821 **wants**] Is wanting.

And render me more equal, and perhaps,
A thing not undesirable, sometime
Superior; for inferior who is free?
This may be well: but what if God have seen,
And death ensue? then I shall be no more,
And Adam wedded to another Eve,
Shall live with her enjoying, I extinct;
A death to think. Confirmed then I resolve,   *830*
Adam shall share with me in bliss or woe:
So dear I love him, that with him all deaths
I could endure, without him live no life.
  So saying, from the tree her step she turned,
But first low reverence done, as to the power
That dwelt within, whose presence had infused
Into the plant sciential sap, derived   837
From nectar, drink of gods. Adam the while
Waiting desirous her return, had wove
Of choicest flowers a garland to adorn
Her tresses, and her rural labours crown,
As reapers oft are wont their harvest queen.
Great joy he promised to his thoughts, and new
Solace in her return, so long delayed;
Yet oft his heart, divine of something ill,   845
Misgave him; he the faltering measure felt;   846
And forth to meet her went, the way she took
That morn when first they parted; by the tree
Of knowledge he must pass, there he her met,
Scarce from the tree returning; in her hand
A bough of fairest fruit that downy smiled,
New gathered, and ambrosial smell diffused.
To him she hasted, in her face excuse
Came prologue, and apology to prompt,
Which with bland words at will she thus addressed.
  Hast thou not wondered, Adam, at my stay?
Thee I have missed, and thought it long, deprived
Thy presence, agony of love till now
Not felt, nor shall be twice, for never more
Mean I to try, what rash untried I sought,   *860*

837 **sciential**] Endowed with or bestowing knowledge.   845 **divine of**]
Divining.   846 **faltering measure**] Of his heart, which 'misgave him'.

The pain of absence from thy sight. But strange
Hath been the cause, and wonderful to hear:
This tree is not as we are told, a tree
Of danger tasted, nor to evil unknown
Opening the way, but of divine effect
To open eyes, and make them gods who taste;
And hath been tasted such: the serpent wise,
Or not restrained as we, or not obeying,
Hath eaten of the fruit, and is become,
Not dead, as we are threatened, but thenceforth   *870*
Endued with human voice and human sense,
Reasoning to admiration, and with me
Persuasively hath so prevailed, that I
Have also tasted, and have also found
The effects to correspond, opener mine eyes,
Dim erst, dilated spirits, ampler heart,   *876*
And growing up to godhead; which for thee
Chiefly I sought, without thee can despise.
For bliss, as thou hast part, to me is bliss,
Tedious, unshared with thee, and odious soon.
Thou therefore also taste, that equal lot
May join us, equal joy, as equal love;
Lest thou not tasting, different degree
Disjoin us, and I then too late renounce
Deity for thee, when fate will not permit.
    Thus Eve with countenance blithe her story told;
But in her cheek distemper flushing glowed.   *887*
On the other side, Adam, soon as he heard
The fatal trespass done by Eve, amazed,
Astonied stood and blank, while horror chill   *890*
Ran through his veins, and all his joints relaxed;
From his slack hand the garland wreathed for Eve
Down dropped, and all the faded roses shed:
Speechless he stood and pale, till thus at length
First to himself he inward silence broke.   → *presentation*
    O fairest of creation, last and best   *of consciousness*
Of all God's works, creature in whom excelled
Whatever can to sight or thought be formed,

876 **erst**] Formerly.   887 **distemper**] Disorder, intoxication.   890 **Astonied**]
Stunned (lit. 'turned to stone').   **blank**] Speechless, nonplussed, helpless.

Holy, divine, good, amiable or sweet!
How art thou lost, how on a sudden lost,
Defaced, deflowered, and now to death devote?   901
Rather how hast thou yielded to transgress
The strict forbiddance, how to violate
The sacred fruit forbidden! some cursed fraud
Of enemy hath beguiled thee, yet unknown,
And me with thee hath ruined, for with thee
Certain my resolution is to die;
How can I live without thee, how forgo
Thy sweet converse and love so dearly joined,
To live again in these wild woods forlorn?   910
Should God create another Eve, and I
Another rib afford, yet loss of thee
Would never from my heart; no no, I feel
The link of nature draw me: flesh of flesh,
Bone of my bone thou art, and from thy state
Mine never shall be parted, bliss or woe. —

   So having said, as one from sad dismay
Recomforted, and after thoughts disturbed
Submitting to what seemed remediless,
Thus in calm mood his words to Eve he turned.   920
   Bold deed thou hast presumed, adventurous Eve,
And peril great provoked, who thus hath dared
Had it been only coveting to eye
That sacred fruit, sacred to abstinence,
Much more to taste it under ban to touch.
But past who can recall, or done undo?
Not God omnipotent, nor fate, yet so
Perhaps thou shalt not die, perhaps the fact   928
Is not so heinous now, foretasted fruit,
Profaned first by the serpent, by him first
Made common and unhallowed ere our taste;
Nor yet on him found deadly, he yet lives,
Lives, as thou saidst, and gains to live as man
Higher degree of life, inducement strong
To us, as likely tasting to attain
Proportional ascent, which cannot be

901 **devote**] Condemned.   928 **fact**] Crime, the most usual seventeenth-century sense.

But to be gods, or angels demigods.
Nor can I think that God, creator wise,
Though threatening, will in earnest so destroy
Us his prime creatures, dignified so high,   *940*
Set over all his works, which in our fall,
For us created, needs with us must fail,
Dependent made; so God shall uncreate,
Be frustrate, do, undo, and labour lose,
Not well conceived of God, who though his power
Creation could repeat, yet would be loath
Us to abolish, lest the adversary
Triumph and say, Fickle their state whom God
Most favours, who can please him long; me first
He ruined, now mankind; whom will he next?
Matter of scorn, not to be given the foe,   *951*
However I with thee have fixed my lot,
Certain to undergo like doom, if death   *953*
Consort with thee, death is to me as life;
So forcible within my heart I feel
The bond of nature draw me to my own,
My own in thee, for what thou art is mine;
Our state cannot be severed, we are one,
One flesh; to lose thee were to lose my self.
    So Adam, and thus Eve to him replied.   *960*
O glorious trial of exceeding love,
Illustrious evidence, example high!
Engaging me to emulate, but short
Of thy perfection, how shall I attain,
Adam, from whose dear side I boast me sprung,
And gladly of our union hear thee speak,
One heart, one soul in both; whereof good proof
This day affords, declaring thee resolved,
Rather than death or aught than death more dread
Shall separate us, linked in love so dear,   *970*
To undergo with me one guilt, one crime,
If any be, of tasting this fair fruit,
Whose virtue, for of good still good proceeds,
Direct, or by occasion hath presented

---

951 **Matter ... foe**] 'He would not give the enemy grounds for contempt.'
953 **Certain**] Resolved (Lat. *certus*).

This happy trial of thy love, which else
So eminently never had been known.
Were it I thought death menaced would ensue
This my attempt, I would sustain alone
The worst, and not persuade thee rather die
Deserted, than oblige thee with a fact   980
Pernicious to thy peace, chiefly assured
Remarkably so late of thy so true,
So faithful love unequalled; but I feel
Far otherwise the event, not death, but life   984
Augmented, opened eyes, new hopes, new joys,
Taste so divine, that what of sweet before
Hath touched my sense, flat seems to this, and harsh.   987
On my experience, Adam, freely taste,
And fear of death deliver to the winds.
     So saying, she embraced him, and for joy
Tenderly wept, much won that he his love
Had so ennobled, as of choice to incur
Divine displeasure for her sake, or death.
In recompense (for such compliance bad
Such recompense best merits) from the bough
She gave him of that fair enticing fruit
With liberal hand: he scrupled not to eat
Against his better knowledge, not deceived,
But fondly overcome with female charm.   999
Earth trembled from her entrails, as again
In pangs, and nature gave a second groan,
Sky loured and muttering thunder, some sad drops
Wept at completing of the mortal sin
Original; while Adam took no thought,
Eating his fill, nor Eve to iterate
Her former trespass feared, the more to soothe
Him with her loved society, that now
As with new wine intoxicated both
They swim in mirth, and fancy that they feel
Divinity within them breeding wings   1010
Wherewith to scorn the earth: but that false fruit

---

980 oblige thee] Make you subject to a penalty, involve you in guilt.   fact] Deed.
984 event] Outcome.   987 to] In comparison with.   999 fondly] Foolishly.

Far other operation first displayed,
Carnal desire inflaming, he on Eve
Began to cast lascivious eyes, she him
As wantonly repaid; in lust they burn:
Till Adam thus gan Eve to dalliance move.   1016
   Eve, now I see thou art exact of taste,
And elegant, of sapience no small part,   1018
Since to each meaning savour we apply,   1019
And palate call judicious; I the praise
Yield thee, so well this day thou hast purveyed.
Much pleasure we have lost, while we abstained
From this delightful fruit, nor known till now
True relish, tasting; if such pleasure be
In things to us forbidden, it might be wished,
For this one tree had been forbidden ten.
But come, so well refreshed, now let us play,
As meet is, after such delicious fare;   1028
For never did thy beauty since the day
I saw thee first and wedded thee, adorned
With all perfections, so inflame my sense
With ardour to enjoy thee, fairer now
Than ever, bounty of this virtuous tree.
   So said he, and forbore not glance or toy   1034
Of amorous intent, well understood
Of Eve, whose eye darted contagious fire.
Her hand he seized, and to a shady bank,
Thick overhead with verdant roof embowered
He led her nothing loath; flowers were the couch,
Pansies, and violets, and asphodel,
And hyacinth, earth's freshest softest lap.
There they their fill of love and love's disport
Took largely, of their mutual guilt the seal,
The solace of their sin, till dewy sleep
Oppressed them, wearied with their amorous play.
Soon as the force of that fallacious fruit,
That with exhilarating vapour bland   1047

1016 **dalliance**] Sport, trifling, with implications of wanton or lascivious flirtation.
1018 **elegant**] Refined.   1019 **each meaning**] Of 'taste', judgment, and savour;
cf. l. 797, above.   1028 **meet**] Appropriate.   1034 **toy**] 'Light caress' (*OED*).
1047 **bland**] 'Pleasing to the senses' (*OED*).

About their spirits had played, and inmost powers
Made err, was now exhaled, and grosser sleep
Bred of unkindly fumes, with conscious dreams   1050
Encumbered, now had left them, up they rose
As from unrest, and each the other viewing,
Soon found their eyes how opened, and their minds
How darkened; innocence, that as a veil
Had shadowed them from knowing ill, was gone,
Just confidence, and native righteousness
And honour from about them, naked left
To guilty shame he covered, but his robe
Uncovered more, so rose the Danite strong   1059
Herculean Samson from the harlot-lap
Of Philistean Dalilah, and waked   1061
Shorn of his strength, they destitute and bare   1062
Of all their virtue: silent, and in face
Confounded long they sat, as stricken mute,
Till Adam, though not less than Eve abashed,
At length gave utterance to these words constrained.
    O Eve, in evil hour thou didst give ear
To that false worm, of whomsoever taught
To counterfeit man's voice, true in our fall,
False in our promised rising; since our eyes   *1070*
Opened we find indeed, and find we know
Both good and evil, good lost, and evil got,
Bad fruit of knowledge, if this be to know,
Which leaves us naked thus, of honour void,
Of innocence, of faith, of purity,
Our wonted ornaments now soiled and stained,
And in our faces evident the signs
Of foul concupiscence; whence evil store;   1078
Even shame, the last of evils; of the first
Be sure then. How shall I behold the face
Henceforth of God or angel, erst with joy   1081
And rapture so oft beheld? those heavenly shapes

1050 **unkindly**] Both unnatural and immoral. **conscious**] Guilty.   1059 **Danite**]
Samson was from the tribe of Dan.   1061 **Dalilah**] Milton uses a variant of the
Vulgate form Dalila.   1059–62 **so rose . . . strength**] For Delilah's treachery in
cutting off Samson's hair see Judges 16.   1078 **evil store**] A multitude of evils.
1081 **erst**] Formerly.

Will dazzle now this earthly, with their blaze
Insufferably bright. O might I here
In solitude live savage, in some glade
Obscured, where highest woods impenetrable
To star or sunlight, spread their umbrage broad
And brown as evening: cover me ye pines,
Ye cedars, with innumerable boughs
Hide me, where I may never see them more.   1090
But let us now, as in bad plight, devise
What best may for the present serve to hide
The parts of each from other, that seem most
To shame obnoxious, and unseemliest seen,   1094
Some tree whose broad smooth leaves together sewed,
And girded on our loins, may cover round
Those middle parts, that this newcomer, shame,
There sit not, and reproach us as unclean.
    So counselled he, and both together went
Into the thickest wood, there soon they chose
The fig-tree, not that kind for fruit renowned,   1101
But such as at this day to Indians known
In Malabar or Deccan spreads her arms
Branching so broad and long, that in the ground
The bended twigs take root, and daughters grow
About the mother tree, a pillared shade
High overarched, and echoing walks between;
There oft the Indian herdsman shunning heat
Shelters in cool, and tends his pasturing herds
At loopholes cut through thickest shade: those leaves
They gathered, broad as Amazonian targe,   1111
And with what skill they had, together sewed,
To gird their waist, vain covering if to hide
Their guilt and dreaded shame; O how unlike
To that first naked glory. Such of late
Columbus found the American so girt
With feathered cincture, naked else and wild
Among the trees on isles and woody shores.

1094 **obnoxious**] Exposed (to evil or harm).   1101 **fig-tree**] The banyan, or
ficus Indica.   1111 **Amazonian targe**] The shields of Amazons: Milton found the
simile (and the 'loopholes' of the previous line) in the description of the banyan in
Gerard's *Herbal* (1597), 1330.

Thus fenced, and as they thought, their shame in part
Covered, but not at rest or ease of mind,   *1120*
They sat them down to weep, nor only tears
Rained at their eyes, but high winds worse within
Began to rise, high passions, anger, hate,
Mistrust, suspicion, discord, and shook sore
Their inward state of mind, calm region once
And full of peace, now tossed and turbulent:
For understanding ruled not, and the will
Heard not her lore, both in subjection now
To sensual appetite, who from beneath
Usurping over sovereign reason claimed   *1130*
Superior sway: from thus distempered breast,
Adam, estranged in look and altered style,
Speech intermitted thus to Eve renewed.

    Would thou hadst hearkened to my words, and stayed
With me, as I besought thee, when that strange
Desire of wandering this unhappy morn,
I know not whence possessed thee; we had then
Remained still happy, not as now, despoiled
Of all our good, shamed, naked, miserable.
Let none henceforth seek needless cause to approve   *1140*
The faith they owe; when earnestly they seek   *1141*
Such proof, conclude, they then begin to fail.

    To whom soon moved with touch of blame thus Eve.
What words have passed thy lips, Adam severe,
Imput'st thou that to my default, or will
Of wandering, as thou call'st it, which who knows
But might as ill have happened thou being by,
Or to thy self perhaps: hadst thou been there,
Or here the attempt, thou couldst not have discerned
Fraud in the serpent, speaking as he spake;   *1150*
No ground of enmity between us known,
Why he should mean me ill, or seek to harm.
Was I to have never parted from thy side?
As good have grown there still a lifeless rib.
Being as I am, why didst not thou the head
Command me absolutely not to go,

1140 **approve**] Test, demonstrate.   1141 **owe**] Either possess, or are obliged
to render.

Going into such danger as thou saidst?
Too facile then thou didst not much gainsay,
Nay didst permit, approve, and fair dismiss.
Hadst thou been firm and fixed in thy dissent,   *1160*
Neither had I transgressed, nor thou with me.
    To whom then first incensed Adam replied,
Is this the love, is this the recompense
Of mine to thee, ingrateful Eve, expressed
Immutable when thou wert lost, not I,   *1165*
Who might have lived and joyed immortal bliss,
Yet willingly chose rather death with thee:
And am I now upbraided, as the cause
Of thy transgressing? not enough severe,
It seems, in thy restraint: what could I more?
I warned thee, I admonished thee, foretold
The danger, and the lurking enemy
That lay in wait; beyond this had been force,
And force upon free will hath here no place.
But confidence then bore thee on, secure   *1175*
Either to meet no danger, or to find
Matter of glorious trial; and perhaps
I also erred in overmuch admiring
What seemed in thee so perfect, that I thought
No evil durst attempt thee, but I rue   *1180*
That error now, which is become my crime,
And thou the accuser. Thus it shall befall
Him who to worth in women overtrusting
Lets her will rule; restraint she will not brook,
And left to herself, if evil thence ensue,
She first his weak indulgence will accuse.
    Thus they in mutual accusation spent
The fruitless hours, but neither self-condemning,
And of their vain contest appeared no end.

1164–5 **expressed / Immutable**] (My love) which I declared was unalterable.
1175 **secure**] Over-confident.

BOOK X

The Argument

Man's transgression known, the guardian angels forsake Paradise, and return up to heaven to approve their vigilance, and are approved, God declaring that the entrance of Satan could not be by them prevented. He sends his son to judge the transgressors, who descends and gives sentence accordingly; then in pity clothes them both, and re-ascends. Sin and Death sitting till then at the gates of hell, by wondrous sympathy feeling the success of Satan in this new world, and the sin by man there committed, resolve to sit no longer confined in hell, but to follow Satan their sire up to the place of man: to make the way easier from hell to this world to and fro, they pave a broad highway or bridge over Chaos, according to the track that Satan first made; then preparing for earth, they meet him proud of his success returning to hell; their mutual gratulation. Satan arrives at Pandaemonium, in full assembly relates with boasting his success against man; instead of applause is entertained with a general hiss by all his audience, transformed with himself also suddenly into serpents, according to his doom given in Paradise; then deluded with a show of the forbidden tree springing up before them, they greedily reaching to take of the fruit, chew dust and bitter ashes. The proceedings of Sin and Death; God foretells the final victory of his son over them, and the renewing of all things; but for the present commands his angels to make several alterations in the heavens and elements. Adam more and more perceiving his fallen condition heavily bewails, rejects the condolement of Eve; she persists and at length appeases him: then to evade the curse likely to fall on their offspring, proposes to Adam violent ways which he approves not, but conceiving better hope, puts her in mind of the late promise made them, that her seed should be revenged on the serpent, and exhorts her with him to seek peace of the offended Deity, by repentance and supplication.

> MEANWHILE the heinous and despiteful act
> Of Satan done in Paradise, and how
> He in the serpent, had perverted Eve,
> Her husband she, to taste the fatal fruit,
> Was known in heaven; for what can scape the eye
> Of God all-seeing, or deceive his heart
> Omniscient, who in all things wise and just,
> Hindered not Satan to attempt the mind

Of man, with strength entire, and free will armed,
Complete to have discovered and repulsed   10
Whatever wiles of foe or seeming friend.
For still they knew, and ought to have still remembered   12
The high injunction not to taste that fruit,
Whoever tempted; which they not obeying,
Incurred, what could they less, the penalty,
And manifold in sin, deserved to fall.
Up into heaven from Paradise in haste
The angelic guards ascended, mute and sad
For man, for of his state by this they knew,   19
Much wondering how the subtle fiend had stolen
Entrance unseen. Soon as the unwelcome news
From earth arrived at heaven gate, displeased
All were who heard, dim sadness did not spare
That time celestial visages, yet mixed
With pity, violated not their bliss.
About the new-arrived, in multitudes
The ethereal people ran, to hear and know
How all befell: they towards the throne supreme
Accountable made haste to make appear   29
With righteous plea, their utmost vigilance,
And easily approved; when the most high   31
Eternal Father from his secret cloud,
Amidst in thunder uttered thus his voice.

　　Assembled angels, and ye powers returned
From unsuccessful charge, be not dismayed,
Nor troubled at these tidings from the earth,
Which your sincerest care could not prevent,
Foretold so lately what would come to pass,
When first this tempter crossed the gulf from hell.
I told ye then he should prevail and speed   40
On his bad errand, man should be seduced
And flattered out of all, believing lies
Against his maker; no decree of mine
Concurring to necessitate his fall,
Or touch with lightest moment of impulse

---

10 **Complete**] Fully able.　　12 **still**] Always.　　19 **by this**] By this time.
28–9 **they . . . Accountable**] i.e. those who were responsible (for the vigilance of l. 30).
31 **approved**] Justified, vindicated (modifying *vigilance*).　　40 **speed**] Succeed.

His free will, to her own inclining left
In even scale. But fallen he is, and now
What rests but that the mortal sentence pass   48
On his transgression, death denounced that day,   49
Which he presumes already vain and void,
Because not yet inflicted, as he feared,
By some immediate stroke; but soon shall find
Forbearance no acquittance ere day end.   53
Justice shall not return as bounty scorned.   54
But whom send I to judge them? whom but thee
Vicegerent Son, to thee I have transferred
All judgment, whether in heaven, or earth, or hell.
Easy it might be seen that I intend
Mercy colleague with justice, sending thee
Man's friend, his mediator, his designed   60
Both ransom and redeemer voluntary,
And destined man himself to judge man fallen.

So spake the Father, and unfolding bright
Toward the right hand his glory, on the Son
Blazed forth unclouded deity; he full
Resplendent all his father manifest
Expressed, and thus divinely answered mild.

Father eternal, thine is to decree,
Mine both in heaven and earth to do thy will
Supreme, that thou in me thy son beloved   70
Mayst ever rest well pleased. I go to judge
On earth these thy transgressors, but thou know'st,
Whoever judged, the worst on me must light,
When time shall be, for so I undertook
Before thee; and not repenting, this obtain
Of right, that I may mitigate their doom
On me derived, yet I shall temper so   77
Justice with mercy, as may illustrate most   78
Them fully satisfied, and thee appease.   79
Attendance none shall need, nor train, where none   80
Are to behold the judgment, but the judged,

48 rests] Remains.   49 denounced] Formally proclaimed (as 'the mortal
sentence').   53 acquittance] Acquittal.   54 Justice . . . return as] My justice
must not be repaid with (but the syntax is curiously obscure as God justifies himself).
77 On me derived] Diverted on to me.   78 illustrate] Show.   79 Them]
Both justice and mercy (l. 78) and Adam and Eve.   80 train] Attendants.

Those two; the third best absent is condemned,   82
Convict by flight, and rebel to all law   83
Conviction to the serpent none belongs.   84
　　Thus saying, from his radiant seat he rose
Of high collateral glory: him thrones and powers,
Princedoms, and dominations ministrant
Accompanied to heaven gate, from whence
Eden and all the coast in prospect lay.
Down he descended straight; the speed of gods
Time counts not, though with swiftest minutes winged.
Now was the sun in western cadence low   92
From noon, and gentle airs due at their hour
To fan the earth now waked, and usher in
The evening cool when he from wrath more cool
Came the mild judge and intercessor both
To sentence man: the voice of God they heard   97
Now walking in the garden, by soft winds
Brought to their ears, while day declined, they heard,
And from his presence hid themselves among
The thickest trees, both man and wife, till God
Approaching, thus to Adam called aloud.
　　Where art thou Adam, wont with joy to meet
My coming seen far off? I miss thee here,
Not pleased, thus entertained with solitude,
Where obvious duty erewhile appeared unsought:
Or come I less conspicuous, or what change
Absents thee, or what chance detains? Come forth.
He came, and with him Eve, more loath, though first
To offend, discountenanced both, and discomposed;   110
Love was not in their looks, either to God
Or to each other, but apparent guilt,
And shame, and perturbation, and despair,
Anger, and obstinacy, and hate, and guile.
Whence Adam faltering long, thus answered brief.
　　I heard thee in the garden, and of thy voice

---

82 **the third**] Satan.   83 **Convict**] Convicted.   84 **Conviction**] In the legal sense, a formal determination of guilt.   **none belongs**] Is not appropriate to.   92 **cadence**] Setting, sinking, with an overtone of the musical sense— cf. 'airs', l. 93.   97 **voice of God**] As viceregent, Christ speaks with God's voice, and is called God throughout the scene.

Afraid, being naked, hid myself. To whom
The gracious judge without revile replied.　　　　　　118
　　My voice thou oft hast heard, and hast not feared,
But still rejoiced, how is it now become
So dreadful to thee? that thou art naked, who
Hath told thee? hast thou eaten of the tree
Whereof I gave thee charge thou shouldst not eat?
　　To whom thus Adam sore beset replied.
O heaven! in evil strait this day I stand
Before my judge, either to undergo
My self the total crime, or to accuse
My other self, the partner of my life;
Whose failing, while her faith to me remains,
I should conceal, and not expose to blame　　　　　　130
By my complaint; but strict necessity
Subdues me, and calamitous constraint
Lest on my head both sin and punishment,
However insupportable, be all
Devolved; though should I hold my peace, yet thou
Wouldst easily detect what I conceal.
This woman whom thou mad'st to be my help,
And gav'st me as thy perfect gift, so good,
So fit, so acceptable, so divine,
That from her hand I could suspect no ill,　　　　　　140
And what she did, whatever in itself,
Her doing seemed to justify the deed;
She gave me of the tree, and I did eat.
　　To whom the sovereign presence thus replied.
Was she thy God, that her thou didst obey
Before his voice, or was she made thy guide,
Superior, or but equal, that to her
Thou didst resign thy manhood, and the place
Wherein God set thee above her made of thee,
And for thee, whose perfection far excelled　　　　　　150
Hers in all real dignity: adorned
She was indeed, and lovely to attract
Thy love, not thy subjection, and her gifts
Were such as under government well seemed,
Unseemly to bear rule, which was thy part

118 **revile**] Abuse.

And person, hadst thou known thyself aright.   156
   So having said, he thus to Eve in few: 157
Say woman, what is this which thou hast done?
   To whom sad Eve with shame nigh overwhelmed,
Confessing soon, yet not before her judge
Bold or loquacious, thus abashed replied.
   The serpent me beguiled and I did eat.
   Which when the Lord God heard, without delay
To judgment he proceeded on the accused
Serpent though brute, unable to transfer
The guilt on him who made him instrument
Of mischief, and polluted from the end   167
Of his creation; justly then accursed,
As vitiated in nature: more to know
Concerned not man (since he no further knew)
Nor altered his offence; yet God at last
To Satan first in sin his doom applied,
Though in mysterious terms, judged as then best:
And on the serpent thus his curse let fall.
   Because thou hast done this, thou art accursed
Above all cattle, each beast of the field;
Upon thy belly grovelling thou shalt go,
And dust shalt eat all the days of thy life.
Between thee and the woman I will put
Enmity, and between thine and her seed;   180
Her seed shall bruise thy head, thou bruise his heel.
   So spake this oracle, then verified
When Jesus son of Mary second Eve,
Saw Satan fall like lightning down from heaven,   184
Prince of the air; then rising from his grave
Spoiled principalities and powers, triumphed
In open show, and with ascension bright   187
Captivity led captive through the air,   188

155–6 **part / And person**] Theatrical terms, role and character.   157 **in few**] In few words.   165–7 **unable . . . mischief**] Since the serpent cannot speak, he cannot accuse Satan; and hence the first instance of God's justice after the fall is the condemnation of the only wholly innocent party to the crime. Milton undertakes no mitigation of the biblical account in Genesis 3: 14–15, though he acknowledges its 'mysterious terms' (l. 173).   184 **Saw . . . heaven**] Jesus reports Satan's fall in Luke 10: 18. 186–7 **Spoiled . . . show**] Cf. St Paul's account of Christ's victory, Colossians 2:15.   187–8 **with ascension . . . captive**] Alluding to Psalm 68: 18.

The realm itself of Satan long usurped,
Whom he shall tread at last under our feet;   *190*
Even he who now foretold his fatal bruise,
And to the woman thus his sentence turned.
    Thy sorrow I will greatly multiply
By thy conception; children thou shalt bring
In sorrow forth, and to thy husband's will
Thine shall submit, he over thee shall rule.
    On Adam last thus judgment he pronounced.
Because thou hast hearkened to the voice of thy wife,
And eaten of the tree concerning which
I charged thee, saying: Thou shalt not eat thereof,   *200*
Cursed is the ground for thy sake, thou in sorrow
Shalt eat thereof all the days of thy life;
Thorns also and thistles it shall bring thee forth
Unbid, and thou shalt eat the herb of the field,
In the sweat of thy face shalt thou eat bread,
Till thou return unto the ground, for thou
Out of the ground wast taken, know thy birth,
For dust thou art, and shalt to dust return.   *208*
    So judged he man, both judge and saviour sent,
And the instant stroke of death denounced that day   *210*
Removed far off; then pitying how they stood
Before him naked to the air, that now
Must suffer change, disdained not to begin
Thenceforth the form of servant to assume,
As when he washed his servants' feet so now   *215*
As father of his family he clad
Their nakedness with skins of beasts, or slain,
Or as the snake with youthful coat repaid;   *218*
And thought not much to clothe his enemies:
Nor he their outward only with the skins
Of beasts, but inward nakedness, much more
Opprobrious, with his robe of righteousness,

198–208 The passage quotes Genesis 3: 17–19 almost verbatim.   210 **denounced**]
Pronounced (as a judge passing a sentence).   215 **washed . . . feet**] Jesus washes his
disciples' feet in John 13: 5.   217–18 **or slain . . . repaid**] Milton offers alternative
possibilities for the source of the first clothing, a subject on which the scripture gives no
guidance: either Christ killed animals for their pelts, or the animals sloughed off their
skins as snakes do.   **repaid**] recompensed (for losing its skin).

Arraying covered from his father's sight.
To him with swift ascent he up returned,
Into his blissful bosom reassumed
In glory as of old, to him appeased
All, though all-knowing, what had passed with man
Recounted, mixing intercession sweet.
Meanwhile ere thus was sinned and judged on earth,
Within the gates of hell sat Sin and Death,
In counterview within the gates, that now   231
Stood open wide, belching outrageous flame
Far into Chaos, since the fiend passed through,
Sin opening, who thus now to Death began.

    O son, why sit we here each other viewing
Idly, while Satan our great author thrives
In other worlds, and happier seat provides
For us his offspring dear? It cannot be
But that success attends him; if mishap,
Ere this he had returned, with fury driven
By his avengers, since no place like this
Can fit his punishment, or their revenge.   242
Methinks I feel new strength within me rise,
Wings growing, and dominion given me large
Beyond this deep; whatever draws me on,
Or sympathy, or some connatural force   246
Powerful at greatest distance to unite
With secret amity things of like kind
By secretest conveyance. Thou my shade   249
Inseparable must with me along:
For Death from Sin no power can separate.
But lest the difficulty of passing back
Stay his return perhaps over this gulf
Impassable, impervious, let us try
Adventurous work, yet to thy power and mine
Not unagreeable, to found a path
Over this main from hell to that new world   257
Where Satan now prevails, a monument

---

231 **In counterview**] Opposite each other.   241–2 **no place . . . fit**] i.e. no other
place is so suitable.   246 **Or . . . or**] Whether . . . or.   **connatural force**] Innate
force linking us.   249 **conveyance**] Communication.   257 **main**] The ocean of
Chaos: see ii. 919.

Of merit high to all the infernal host,
Easing their passage hence, for intercourse,   260
Or transmigration, as their lot shall lead.   261
Nor can I miss the way, so strongly drawn
By this new-felt attraction and instinct.
    Whom thus the meagre shadow answered soon.
Go whither fate and inclination strong
Leads thee, I shall not lag behind, nor err
The way, thou leading, such a scent I draw
Of carnage, prey innumerable, and taste
The savour of death from all things there that live:
Nor shall I to the work thou enterprisest
Be wanting, but afford thee equal aid.
    So saying, with delight he snuffed the smell   272
Of mortal change on earth. As when a flock
Of ravenous fowl, though many a league remote,
Against the day of battle, to a field,   275
Where armies lie encamped, come flying, lured
With scent of living carcasses designed   277
For death, the following day, in bloody fight.
So scented the grim feature, and upturned   279
His nostril wide into the murky air,
Sagacious of his quarry from so far.   281
Then both from out hell gates into the waste
Wide anarchy of Chaos damp and dark
Flew diverse, and with power (their power was great)   284
Hovering upon the waters; what they met
Solid or slimy, as in raging sea
Tossed up and down, together crowded drove
From each side shoaling towards the mouth of hell.   288
As when two polar winds blowing adverse
Upon the Cronian sea, together drive   290
Mountains of ice, that stop the imagined way   291
Beyond Petsora eastward, to the rich   292

---

260 **intercourse**] Coming and going.   261 **transmigration**] Permanent emigration.   272 **snuffed**] Inhaled.   275 **Against**] In anticipation of. 277 **designed**] Designated.   279 **feature**] Form, creature.   281 **Sagacious**] On the scent, 'acute in . . . the sense of smell' (*OED*).   284 **diverse**] In different directions.   288 **shoaling**] Crowded.   290 **Cronian sea**] Arctic Ocean (from Cronos, or Saturn, the oldest and therefore the coldest of the gods).   291 **the imagined way**] The fabled northern passage to Asia.   292 **Petsora**] Or Pechora, Siberian river.

Cathayan coast. The aggregated soil
Death with his mace petrific, cold and dry,   294
As with a trident smote, and fixed as firm   295
As Delos floating once; the rest his look   296
Bound with Gorgonian rigor not to move,   297
And with asphaltic slime; broad as the gate,   298
Deep to the roots of hell the gathered beach
They fastened, and the mole immense wrought on   300
Over the foaming deep high arched, a bridge
Of length prodigious joining to the wall   302
Immovable of this now fenceless world   303
Forfeit to Death; from hence a passage broad,
Smooth, easy, inoffensive down to hell.   305
So, if great things to small may be compared,
Xerxes, the liberty of Greece to yoke,
From Susa his Memnonian palace high   308
Came to the sea, and over Hellespont   309
Bridging his way, Europe with Asia joined,
And scourged with many a stroke the indignant waves.   311
Now had they brought the work by wondrous art
Pontifical, a ridge of pendent rock   313
Over the vexed abyss, following the track   314
Of Satan, to the selfsame place where he
First lighted from his wing, and landed safe
From out of Chaos to the outside bare
Of this round world: with pins of adamant   318

---

294 **petrific**] That turns things to stone.   295 **trident**] The three-pronged
weapon of Neptune.   296 **Delos floating**] When Leto, or Latona, was pregnant
by Jupiter, Neptune created the floating island of Delos as a haven for her from the anger
of Juno, and there she gave birth to the twins Apollo and Diana. Jupiter later anchored
the island among the Cyclades.   297 **Gorgonian rigor**] The look of the gorgons
turned people to stone.   298 **asphaltic slime**] Pitch, used by the devils in the con-
struction of Pandaemonium (i. 729).   300 **mole**] Massive pier.   302 **wall**] The
outer shell of the universe (see ii. 1029–30).   303 **fenceless**] Defenceless.
305 **inoffensive**] Without obstacles.   308 **Susa**] The biblical Shushan, in Persia,
Xerxes' winter capital.   **Memnonian**]. Susa was founded by Tithonus, the lover of
Aurora, whose son Memnon was the first king.   309 **Hellespont**] The Dardanelles,
the Turkish strait connecting the Sea of Marmara with the Aegean, and the dividing
line between Europe and Asia.   307–11 **Xerxes . . . waves**] When a storm des-
troyed the bridge of ships that Xerxes had created across the Hellespont, he ordered the
sea to be beaten.   313 **Pontifical**] Lit. 'bridge-making'.   314 **vexed**] Stormy.
318 **adamant**] The mythical substance of impenetrable hardness.

And chains they made all fast, too fast they made
And durable; and now in little space
The confines met of empyrean heaven   321
And of this world, and on the left hand hell
With long reach interposed; three several ways
In sight, to each of these three places led.
And now their way to earth they had descried,
To Paradise first tending, when behold
Satan in likeness of an angel bright
Betwixt the Centaur and the Scorpion steering   328
His zenith, while the sun in Aries rose:
Disguised he came, but those his children dear
Their parent soon discerned, though in disguise.
He after Eve seduced, unminded slunk   332
Into the wood fast by, and changing shape
To observe the sequel, saw his guileful act
By Eve, though all unweeting, seconded
Upon her husband, saw their shame that sought
Vain covertures; but when he saw descend
The Son of God to judge them terrified
He fled, not hoping to escape, but shun
The present, fearing guilty what his wrath   340
Might suddenly inflict; that past, returned
By night, and listening where the hapless pair
Sat in their sad discourse, and various plaint,
Thence gathered his own doom, which understood
Not instant, but of future time. With joy
And tidings fraught, to hell he now returned,
And at the brink of Chaos, near the foot
Of this new wondrous pontifice, unhoped   348
Met who to meet him came, his offspring dear.
Great joy was at their meeting, and at sight
Of that stupendous bridge his joy increased.
Long he admiring stood, till Sin, his fair
Enchanting daughter, thus the silence broke.
    O parent, these are thy magnific deeds,
Thy trophies, which thou view'st as not thine own,
Thou art their author and prime architect:

---

321 **confines**] Boundaries.   328 **Centaur ... Scorpion**] The constellations
Sagittarius and Scorpio.   332 **unminded**] Unnoticed.   348 **pontifice**] Bridge.

For I no sooner in my heart divined,
My heart, which by a secret harmony
Still moves with thine, joined in connection sweet,
That thou on earth hadst prospered, which thy looks   *360*
Now also evidence, but straight I felt
Though distant from thee worlds between, yet felt
That I must after thee with this thy son;
Such fatal consequence unites us three:
Hell could no longer hold us in her bounds,
Nor this unvoyageable gulf obscure
Detain from following thy illustrious track.
Thou hast achieved our liberty, confined
Within hell gates till now, thou us empowered
To fortify thus far, and overlay   370
With this portentous bridge the dark abyss.   371
Thine now is all this world, thy virtue hath won   372
What thy hands builded not, thy wisdom gained
With odds what war hath lost, and fully avenged   374
Our foil in heaven; here thou shalt monarch reign,   375
There didst not; there let him still victor sway,
As battle hath adjudged, from this new world
Retiring, by his own doom alienated,   378
And henceforth monarchy with thee divide
Of all things parted by the empyreal bounds,
His quadrature, from thy orbicular world,   381
Or try thee now more dangerous to his throne.   382
   Whom thus the prince of darkness answered glad.
Fair daughter, and thou son and grandchild both,   384
High proof ye now have given to be the race
Of Satan (for I glory in the name,
Antagonist of heaven's almighty king)   387
Amply have merited of me, of all

---

370 **fortify**] Grow strong; also making the bridge strong.   371 **portentous**]
Both ominous and prodigious.   372 **virtue**] Strength, valour, with an ironic
overtone of the moral sense.   374 **odds**] Advantage.   375 **foil**] Defeat.
378 **doom**] Sentence.   381 **quadrature**] Heaven is here conceived as a square,
apparently on the authority of Revelation 21: 16, where the New Jerusalem is described
as 'four-square'. In ii. 1048, however, heaven in Satan's view was 'undeter-
mined square or round'.   382 **try thee**] Find you to be.   384 **son and
grandchild**] Because Death is the child of Satan's incest with his daughter
Sin.   387 **Antagonist**] Literally translating Satan.

The infernal empire, that so near heaven's door
Triumphal with triumphal act have met,   390
Mine with this glorious work, and made one realm
Hell and this world, one realm, one continent
Of easy thoroughfare. Therefore while I
Descend through darkness, on your road with ease
To my associate powers, them to acquaint
With these successes, and with them rejoice,
You two this way, among these numerous orbs
All yours, right down to Paradise descend;
There dwell and reign in bliss, thence on the earth
Dominion exercise and in the air,   400
Chiefly on man, sole lord of all declared,
Him first make sure your thrall, and lastly kill.
My substitutes I send ye, and create
Plenipotent on earth, of matchless might   404
Issuing from me: on your joint vigour now
My hold of this new kingdom all depends,
Through Sin to Death exposed by my exploit.
If your joint power prevails, the affairs of hell
No detriment need fear, go and be strong.
    So saying he dismissed them, they with speed
Their course through thickest constellations held
Spreading their bane; the blasted stars looked wan,
And planets, planet-struck, real eclipse   413
Then suffered. The other way Satan went down
The causeway to hell gate; on either side
Disparted Chaos over-built exclaimed,
And with rebounding surge the bars assailed,
That scorned his indignation: through the gate,   418
Wide open and unguarded, Satan passed,
And all about found desolate; for those
Appointed to sit there, had left their charge,
Flown to the upper world; the rest were all
Far to the inland retired, about the walls
Of Pandaemonium, city and proud seat

---

404 **Plenipotent**] Deputies with full authority, parallel with Christ as God's agent
on earth.   413 **planet-struck**] Stricken by their malignant influence as they wander
through the heavens: 'planet struck' = suffering from the unfavourable astrological
influence of a malignant planet.   **real eclipse**] i.e. not merely apparent, a function of
the view of the heavens from earth.   418 **his**] Chaos's.

Of Lucifer, so by allusion called,
Of that bright star to Satan paragoned.   426
There kept their watch the legions, while the grand
In council sat, solicitous what chance   428
Might intercept their emperor sent, so he
Departing gave command, and they observed.
As when the Tartar from his Russian foe
By Astrakhan over the snowy plains   432
Retires, or Bactrian sophy from the horns   433
Of Turkish crescent, leaves all waste beyond   434
The realm of Aladule, in his retreat   435
To Tauris or Casbeen. So these the late   436
Heaven-banished host, left desert utmost hell   437
Many a dark league, reduced in careful watch   438
Round their metropolis, and now expecting
Each hour their great adventurer from the search
Of foreign worlds: he through the midst unmarked,
In show plebeian angel militant   442
Of lowest order, passed; and from the door
Of that Plutonian hall, invisible   444
Ascended his high throne, which under state   445
Of richest texture spread, at the upper end
Was placed in regal lustre. Down awhile
He sat, and round about him saw unseen:
At last as from a cloud his fulgent head   449
And shape star-bright appeared, or brighter, clad
With what permissive glory since his fall
Was left him, or false glitter: all amazed
At that so sudden blaze the Stygian throng
Bent their aspect, and whom they wished beheld,
Their mighty chief returned: loud was the acclaim:
Forth rushed in haste the great consulting peers,

---

426 **paragoned**] Compared (in Isaiah 14: 12: 'How art thou fallen from heaven, Lucifer, son of the morning').   428 **solicitous**] Apprehensive about.   432 **Astrakhan**] Tartar city on the Volga, near the Caspian Sea. 433 **Bactrian Sophy**] The Persian Shah.   433–4 **horns ... crescent**] Both the Turks' insignia and their battle array.   435 **Aladule**] Armenia.   436 **Tauris or Casbeen**] Tabriz, Kazvin, both in northern Iran.   437 **left ... hell**] Left the outermost reaches of hell deserted.   438 **reduced**] Retreated.   442 **show**] Appearance.   444 **Plutonian**] Underworld (from Pluto, the classical god of the underworld).   445 **state**] Canopy.   449 **fulgent**] Radiant.

Raised from their dark divan, and with like joy   457
Congratulant approached him, who with hand
Silence, and with these words attention won.

   Thrones, dominations, princedoms, virtues, powers,
For in possession such, not only of right,
I call ye and declare ye now, returned
Successful beyond hope, to lead ye forth
Triumphant out of this infernal pit
Abominable, accursed, the house of woe,
And dungeon of our tyrant: now possess,
As lords, a spacious world, to our native heaven
Little inferior, by my adventure hard
With peril great achieved. Long were to tell
What I have done, what suffered, with what pain   470
Voyaged the unreal, vast, unbounded deep
Of horrible confusion, over which
By Sin and Death a broad way now is paved
To expedite your glorious march; but I
Toiled out my uncouth passage, forced to ride   475
The untractable abyss, plunged in the womb
Of unoriginal Night and Chaos wild,   477
That jealous of their secrets fiercely opposed   478
My journey strange, with clamorous uproar
Protesting fate supreme; thence how I found
The new created world, which fame in heaven   481
Long had foretold, a fabric wonderful
Of absolute perfection, therein man
Placed in a paradise, by our exile
Made happy: him by fraud I have seduced
From his creator, and the more to increase
Your wonder, with an apple; he thereat
Offended, worth your laughter, hath given up
Both his belovèd man and all his world,
To Sin and Death a prey, and so to us,   490
Without our hazard, labour, or alarm,
To range in, and to dwell, and over man
To rule, as over all he should have ruled.

457 **divan**] Council; originally the Turkish privy council.   475 **uncouth**]
Both strange and solitary.   477 **unoriginal**] Eternal, without any origin.
478 **fiercely opposed**] In fact, Night offered no opposition, and Chaos aided Satan:
see ii. 990–1009.   481 **fame**] Rumour.

True is, me also he hath judged, or rather
Me not, but the brute serpent in whose shape
Man I deceived: that which to me belongs,
Is enmity, which he will put between
Me and mankind; I am to bruise his heel;
His seed, when is not set, shall bruise my head: 499
A world who would not purchase with a bruise,
Or much more grievous pain? Ye have the account
Of my performance: what remains, ye gods,
But up and enter now into full bliss.

    So having said, a while he stood, expecting
Their universal shout and high applause
To fill his ear, when contrary he hears
On all sides, from innumerable tongues
A dismal universal hiss, the sound
Of public scorn; he wondered, but not long
Had leisure, wondering at himself now more;
His visage drawn he felt to sharp and spare,
His arms clung to his ribs, his legs entwining
Each other, till supplanted down he fell   513
A monstrous serpent on his belly prone,
Reluctant, but in vain, a greater power   515
Now ruled him, punished in the shape he sinned,
According to his doom: he would have spoke,   517
But hiss for hiss returned with forkèd tongue
To forkèd tongue, for now were all transformed
Alike, to serpents all as accessories
To his bold riot: dreadful was the din   521
Of hissing through the hall, thick swarming now
With complicated monsters head and tail,   523
Scorpion and asp, and amphisbaena dire,   524
Cerastes horned, hydrus, and ellops drear,   525
And dipsas (not so thick swarmed once the soil   526
Bedropped with blood of Gorgon, or the isle   527

    499 **when is not set**] The time is not yet determined.   513 **supplanted**] Over-
thrown (lit. 'tripped up').   515 **Reluctant**] Lit. 'struggling'.   517 **his doom**]
Both   Satan's   fate   and   God's   judgment.   521 **riot**]   Rebellion.
523 **complicated**] Intertwined.   524 **amphisbaena**] A fabulous serpent with a
head at either end.   525 **Cerastes**] A four-horned serpent. **hydrus and ellops**]
Water snakes.   526 **dipsas**] A mythical snake whose bite caused violent
thirst.   526–7 **soil . . . Gorgon**] After Perseus slew Medusa, serpents sprang from
the blood that dropped from her severed head.

Ophiusa) but still greatest he the midst,   528
Now dragon grown, larger than whom the sun   529
Engendered in the Pythian vale on slime,
Huge Python, and his power no less he seemed   531
Above the rest still to retain; they all
Him followed issuing forth to the open field,
Where all yet left of that revolted rout
Heaven-fallen, in station stood or just array,   535
Sublime with expectation when to see   536
In triumph issuing forth their glorious chief;
They saw, but other sight instead, a crowd
Of ugly serpents; horror on them fell,
And horrid sympathy; for what they saw,
They felt themselves now changing; down their arms,
Down fell both spear and shield, down they as fast,
And the dire hiss renewed, and the dire form
Catched by contagion, like in punishment,
As in their crime. Thus was the applause they meant,
Turned to exploding hiss, triumph to shame   546
Cast on themselves from their own mouths. There stood
A grove hard by, sprung up with this their change,
His will who reigns above, to aggravate
Their penance, laden with fair fruit, like that
Which grew in Paradise, the bait of Eve
Used by the tempter: on that prospect strange
Their earnest eyes they fixed, imagining
For one forbidden tree a multitude
Now risen, to work them further woe or shame;
Yet parched with scalding thirst and hunger fierce,
Though to delude them sent, could not abstain,
But on they rolled in heaps, and up the trees
Climbing, sat thicker than the snaky locks
That curled Megaera: greedily they plucked   560
The fruitage fair to sight, like that which grew

528 **Ophiusa**] Lit. 'snake-filled', an ancient name for Rhodes and several other Greek islands.   529 **whom**] Him whom.   529–31 **the sun . . . Python**] For the birth of the great Python from the slime of the universal flood, see *Metamorphoses*, i. 438–40.   535 **in . . . array**] At their posts, or in review formation.   536 **Sublime**] Raised up.   546 **exploding**] With an overtone of its etymological meaning, 'driving them off the stage' (from *explaudo*, the opposite of *plaudo*, applaud).   560 **Megaera**] One of the three avenging Furies.

Near that bituminous lake where Sodom flamed;
This more delusive, not the touch, but taste
Deceived; they fondly thinking to allay
Their appetite with gust, instead of fruit   565
Chewed bitter ashes, which the offended taste
With spattering noise rejected: oft they assayed,
Hunger and thirst constraining, drugged as oft,   568
With hatefulest disrelish writhed their jaws
With soot and cinders filled; so oft they fell
Into the same illusion, not as man
Whom they triumphed once lapsed. Thus were they plagued   572
And worn with famine, long and ceaseless hiss,
Till their lost shape, permitted, they resumed,
Yearly enjoined, some say, to undergo
This annual humbling certain numbered days,
To dash their pride, and joy for man seduced.
However some tradition they dispersed
Among the heathen of their purchase got,   579
And fabled how the serpent, whom they called
Ophion with Eurynome, the wide-   581
Encroaching Eve perhaps, had first the rule
Of high Olympus, thence by Saturn driven
And Ops, ere yet Dictaean Jove was born.   584
Meanwhile in Paradise the hellish pair
Too soon arrived, Sin there in power before,   586
Once actual, now in body, and to dwell   587
Habitual habitant; behind her Death
Close following pace for pace, not mounted yet
On his pale horse; to whom Sin thus began.   590
    Second of Satan sprung, all-conquering Death,
What think'st thou of our empire now, though earned

---

565 **gust**] Relish.   568 **drugged**] Nauseated, a usage apparently originating with
Milton.   571–2 **not . . . lapsed**] Implying both that unlike man, they fell over and over
again, and that man, once he had fallen, was not deceived again by 'the same illu-
sion'. **triumphed**] Triumphed over.   579 **purchase**] Plunder.   581 **Ophion
with Eurynome**] The original king and queen of Olympus; Ophion means 'serpent',
Eurynome 'wide-ruling' (hence 'the wide-encroaching Eve').   584 **Ops**] Or Rhea,
wife of Saturn. **Dictaean**] From Dicte, the mountain in Crete where Jupiter was
raised.   586 **in power**] Potentially.   587 **Once actual**] Once sin has been
committed: 'actual sin' is the theological term for a willed sinful act, as opposed to the
general human condition of original sin—in the case of Adam and Eve, these are the
same.   589–90 **mounted . . . horse**] For Death on his pale horse, see Revelation 6: 8.

With travail difficult, not better far
Than still at hell's dark threshold to have sat watch,
Unnamed, undreaded, and thy self half starved?
    Whom thus the Sin-born monster answered soon.
To me, who with eternal famine pine,
Alike is hell, or Paradise, or heaven,
There best, where most with ravin I may meet;   599
Which here, though plenteous, all too little seems
To stuff this maw, this vast unhide-bound corpse.   601
    To whom the incestuous mother thus replied.
Thou therefore on these herbs, and fruits, and flowers
Feed first, on each beast next, and fish, and fowl,
No homely morsels, and whatever thing
The scythe of time mows down, devour unspared,
Till I in man residing through the race,
His thoughts, his looks, words, actions all infect,
And season him thy last and sweetest prey.
    This said, they both betook them several ways,   610
Both to destroy, or unimmortal make
All kinds, and for destruction to mature
Sooner or later; which the almighty seeing,
From his transcendent seat the saints among,
To those bright orders uttered thus his voice.
    See with what heat these dogs of hell advance
To waste and havoc yonder world, which I
So fair and good created, and had still
Kept in that state, had not the folly of man
Let in these wasteful furies, who impute   620
Folly to me, so doth the prince of hell
And his adherents, that with so much ease
I suffer them to enter and possess
A place so heavenly, and conniving seem   624
To gratify my scornful enemies,
That laugh, as if transported with some fit
Of passion, I to them had quitted all,   627
At random yielded up to their misrule;
And know not that I called and drew them thither

---

599 **ravin**] Prey.   601 **unhide-bound**] Shapeless, not bound or limited in size
by any outer skin (see ii. 667).   624 **conniving**] Lit. 'winking, shutting the eyes',
with implications of complicity.   627 **quitted**] Given over.

My hell-hounds, to lick up the draff and filth   630
Which man's polluting sin with taint hath shed
On what was pure, till crammed and gorged, nigh burst
With sucked and glutted offal, at one sling
Of thy victorious arm, well-pleasing Son,
Both Sin, and Death, and yawning grave at last
Through Chaos hurled, obstruct the mouth of hell
Forever, and seal up his ravenous jaws.
Then heaven and earth renewed shall be made pure
To sanctity that shall receive no stain:
Till then the curse pronounced on both precedes.   640

    He ended, and the heavenly audience loud
Sung hallelujah, as the sound of seas,
Through multitude that sung: Just are thy ways,
Righteous are thy decrees on all thy works;
Who can extenuate thee? Next, to the Son,   645
Destined restorer of mankind, by whom
New heaven and earth shall to the ages rise,
Or down from heaven descend. Such was their song,
While the creator calling forth by name
His mighty angels gave them several charge,
As sorted best with present things. The sun   651
Had first his precept so to move, so shine,
As might affect the earth with cold and heat
Scarce tolerable, and from the north to call
Decrepit winter, from the south to bring
Solstitial summer's heat. To the blank moon   656
Her office they prescribed, to the other five   657
Their planetary motions and aspects   658
In sextile, square, and trine, and opposite,
Of noxious efficacy, and when to join   660
In synod unbenign, and taught the fixed   661
Their influence malignant when to shower,
Which of them rising with the sun, or falling,
Should prove tempestuous: to the winds they set

630 **draff**] Dregs.   640 **precedes**] i.e. God's curse takes precedence until Christ's victory.   645 **extenuate**] Diminish.   651 **sorted best with**] Was most appropriate to.   656 **blank**] Pale, white (French *blanc*).   657 **the other five**] i.e. planets.   658 **aspects**] Astrological positions, the *sextile*, *square*, *trine*, and *opposite* of l. 659.   660 **noxious efficacy**] In these four positions, the planets were said to have harmful effects on earth.   661 **synod**] Conjunction.   **fixed**] i.e. stars.

Their corners, when with bluster to confound   665
Sea, air, and shore, the thunder when to roll
With terror through the dark aerial hall.
Some say he bid his angels turn askance
The poles of earth twice ten degrees and more
From the sun's axle; they with labour pushed
Oblique the centric globe: some say the sun   671
Was bid turn reins from the equinoctial road   672
Like distant breadth to Taurus with the Seven   673
Atlantic Sisters, and the Spartan Twins   674
Up to the tropic Crab; thence down amain   675
By Leo and the Virgin and the Scales,   676
As deep as Capricorn, to bring in change
Of seasons to each clime; else had the spring
Perpetual smiled on earth with vernant flowers,   679
Equal in days and nights, except to those   680
Beyond the polar circles; to them day
Had unbenighted shone, while the low sun
To recompense his distance, in their sight
Had rounded still the horizon, and not known
Or east or west, which had forbid the snow
From cold Estotiland, and south as far   686
Beneath Magellan. At that tasted fruit   687
The sun, as from Thyestean banquet, turned
His course intended; else how had the world   689
Inhabited, though sinless, more than now,

664-5 **winds ... corners**] Alluding to the notion that the winds blow from the four
corners of the earth.   671 **centric globe**] Earth.   672 **equinoctial road**]
Equator.   673 **Like distant breadth**] A similar distance.   673-4 **Taurus ...
Sisters**] In spring, the sun reaches Taurus, which includes the stars of the Pleiades, or
Seven Sisters, daughters of Atlas, hence 'Atlantic'.   **Spartan twins**] Gemini, the twins
Castor and Pollux.   675 **tropic Crab**] Tropic of Cancer.   676 **Virgin ...
Scales**] The constellations Virgo and Libra.   679 **vernant flowers**] Flowers spe-
cific to spring.   668-80 To account for the prelapsarian 'eternal spring', Milton
assumes that before the fall the sun's course coincided with the celestial equator. Alter-
native explanations are given for its present course, moving between the tropics of
Cancer in the spring and Capricorn in the autumn, and the consequent change of the
seasons: if the universe is heliocentric, the earth was tilted on its axis; if geocentric, the
sun changed its route.   686 **Estotiland**] In northern Labrador.   687 **Magel-
lan**] The Straits of Magellan, below South America.   688-9 **sun ... intended**]
Thyestes seduced the wife of his brother Atreus. In revenge, Atreus killed Thyestes'
sons and served their flesh to their unsuspecting father at a banquet. In Seneca's
Thyestes the sun is represented as turning aside in horror (ll. 776 ff.).

Avoided pinching cold and scorching heat?
These changes in the heavens, though slow, produced
Like change on sea and land, sideral blast,   693
Vapour, and mist, and exhalation hot,
Corrupt and pestilent: now from the north
Of Norumbega, and the Samoed shore   696
Bursting their brazen dungeon, armed with ice
And snow and hail and stormy gust and flaw,   698
Boreas, and Caecias and Argestes loud   699
And Thrascias rend the woods and seas upturn;
With adverse blast upturns them from the south
Notus and Afer black with thunderous clouds
From Serraliona; thwart of these as fierce   703
Forth rush the levant and the ponent winds   704
Eurus and Zephyr, with their lateral noise,
Sirocco, and Libecchio, thus began   706
Outrage from lifeless things; but Discord first
Daughter of Sin, among the irrational,
Death introduced through fierce antipathy:
Beast now with beast gan war, and fowl with fowl,   710
And fish with fish; to graze the herb all leaving,
Devoured each other; nor stood much in awe
Of man but fled him, or with countenance grim
Glared on him passing: these were from without
The growing miseries, which Adam saw
Already in part, though hid in gloomiest shade,
To sorrow abandoned, but worse felt within,
And in a troubled sea of passion tossed,
Thus to disburden sought with sad complaint.

O miserable of happy! is this the end   720
Of this new glorious world, and me so late
The glory of that glory, who now become
Accursed of blessed, hide me from the face
Of God, whom to behold was then my height

---

693 **sideral blast**] Evil influence from the stars.   696 **Norumbega**] Roughly,
northern New England and Nova Scotia. **Samoed**] Siberian.   698 **flaw**] Wind
squall.   699 ff. **Boreas ... Caecias, etc**] Names of the various winds.
703 **Serraliona**] Sierra Leone. **thwart**] i.e. blowing across the north–south winds
from east and west.   704 **Levant ... ponent**] East and west (lit. 'rising and
setting', hence from the directions of sunrise and sunset).   706 **Sirocco, and
Libecchio**] Italian names for south-east and south-west winds respectively.

Of happiness: yet well, if here would end
The misery, I deserved it, and would bear
My own deservings; but this will not serve;
All that I eat or drink, or shall beget,
Is propagated curse. O voice once heard   729
Delightfully, *Increase and multiply*,
Now death to hear! for what can I increase
Or multiply, but curses on my head?
Who of all ages to succeed, but feeling
The evil on him brought by me, will curse
My head, Ill fare our ancestor impure,
For this we may thank Adam; but his thanks
Shall be the execration; so besides
Mine own that bide upon me, all from me   738
Shall with a fierce reflux on me redound,
On me as on their natural centre light
Heavy, though in their place. O fleeting joys
Of Paradise, dear bought with lasting woes!
Did I request thee, maker, from my clay
To mould me man, did I solicit thee
From darkness to promote me, or here place
In this delicious garden? as my will
Concurred not to my being, it were but right
And equal to reduce me to my dust,   748
Desirous to resign, and render back
All I received, unable to perform
Thy terms too hard, by which I was to hold
The good I sought not. To the loss of that,
Sufficient penalty, why hast thou added
The sense of endless woes? inexplicable
Thy justice seems; yet to say truth, too late,
I thus contest; then should have been refused
Those terms whatever, when they were proposed:
Thou didst accept them; wilt thou enjoy the good,
Then cavil the conditions? and though God
Made thee without thy leave, what if thy son   *760*
Prove disobedient, and reproved, retort,
Wherefore didst thou beget me? I sought it not:

---

729 **Is propagated curse**] Extends the curse.   738 **Mine own**] Curses.
748 **equal**] Just.

Wouldst thou admit for his contempt of thee
That proud excuse? yet him not thy election,   764
But natural necessity begot.
God made thee of choice his own, and of his own   766
To serve him, thy reward was of his grace,
Thy punishment then justly is at his will.
Be it so, for I submit, his doom is fair,
That dust I am, and shall to dust return: 770
O welcome hour whenever! why delays
His hand to execute what his decree
Fixed on this day? why do I overlive,
Why am I mocked with death, and lengthened out
To deathless pain? how gladly would I meet
Mortality my sentence, and be earth
Insensible, how glad would lay me down
As in my mother's lap? there I should rest
And sleep secure; his dreadful voice no more
Would thunder in my ears, no fear of worse
To me and to my offspring would torment me
With cruel expectation. Yet one doubt
Pursues me still, lest all I cannot die,   783
Lest that pure breath of life, the spirit of man
Which God inspired, cannot together perish
With this corporeal clod; then in the grave,
Or in some other dismal place who knows
But I shall die a living death? O thought
Horrid, if true! yet why? it was but breath
Of life that sinned; what dies but what had life
And sin? the body properly hath neither.
All of me then shall die: let this appease
The doubt, since human reach no further knows.
For though the Lord of all be infinite,
Is his wrath also? be it, man is not so,   795
But mortal doomed. How can he exercise
Wrath without end on man whom death must end?
Can he make deathless death? that were to make
Strange contradiction, which to God himself
Impossible is held, as argument

764 election] Choice.   766 of choice] By choice.   783 all I cannot] I
cannot entirely.   795 be it] Even if it is.

Of weakness, not of power. Will he draw out,
For anger's sake, finite to infinite
In punished man, to satisfy his rigour
Satisfied never; that were to extend
His sentence beyond dust and nature's law,
By which all causes else according still
To the reception of their matter act,
Not to the extent of their own sphere. But say   808
That death be not one stroke, as I supposed,
Bereaving sense, but endless misery
From this day onward, which I feel begun
Both in me, and without me, and so last
To perpetuity; ay me, that fear
Comes thundering back with dreadful revolution
On my defenceless head; both death and I
Am found eternal, and incorporate both,   816
Nor I on my part single, in me all   817
Posterity stands cursed: fair patrimony
That I must leave ye, sons; O were I able
To waste it all my self, and leave ye none!
So disinherited how would ye bless
Me now your curse! Ah, why should all mankind
For one man's fault thus guiltless be condemned,
If guiltless? But from me what can proceed,
But all corrupt, both mind and will depraved,
Not to do only, but to will the same
With me? how can they then acquitted stand
In sight of God? Him after all disputes
Forced I absolve: all my evasions vain,
And reasonings, though through mazes, lead me still   830
But to my own conviction: first and last
On me, me only, as the source and spring
Of all corruption, all the blame lights due;
So might the wrath. Fond wish! couldst thou support   834

806–8 all . . . sphere] Adam uses a scholastic argument, which holds that 'an agent's action is limited by the recipient's capacity to be acted upon; so although God's wrath might be infinite, the fact that man is finite means that there must be a limit to his suffering' (J. Martin Evans, *Paradise Lost Books 9 and 10*, 1973).   816 **incorporate**] Both embodied, and together in one body.   817 **Nor . . . single**] Nor am I only a single body either.   834 **So . . . wrath**] 'I wish the wrath would also', or 'perhaps the wrath will also'.

That burden heavier than the earth to bear,
Than all the world much heavier, though divided
With that bad woman? Thus what thou desir'st
And what thou fear'st, alike destroys all hope
Of refuge, and concludes thee miserable
Beyond all past example and future,   *840*
To Satan only like both crime and doom.
O conscience, into what abyss of fears
And horrors hast thou driven me; out of which
I find no way, from deep to deeper plunged!

      Thus Adam to himself lamented loud
Through the still night, not now, as ere man fell,
Wholesome and cool, and mild, but with black air
Accompanied, with damps and dreadful gloom,
Which to his evil conscience represented
All things with double terror: on the ground
Outstretched he lay, on the cold ground, and oft
Cursed his creation, death as oft accused
Of tardy execution, since denounced   *853*
The day of his offence. Why comes not death,
Said he, with one thrice acceptable stroke
To end me? Shall truth fail to keep her word,
Justice divine not hasten to be just?
But death comes not at call, justice divine
Mends not her slowest pace for prayers or cries.
O woods, O fountains, hillocks, dales and bowers,   *860*
With other echo late I taught your shades
To answer, and resound far other song.
Whom thus afflicted when sad Eve beheld,
Desolate where she sat, approaching nigh
Soft words to his fierce passion she assayed:
But her with stern regard he thus repelled.

      Out of my sight, thou serpent, that name best   *867*
Befits thee with him leagued, thyself as false
And hateful; nothing wants, but that thy shape,   *869*
Like his, and colour serpentine may show
Thy inward fraud, to warn all creatures from thee

---

853 **denounced**] Proclaimed.   867 **thou serpent**] It had been noted as early as
the ancient rabbinic commentators that the name Eve is related to old Semitic words,
e.g. in Phoenician and Aramaic, for 'serpent'.   869 **wants**] Is missing.

Henceforth; lest that too heavenly form, pretended
To hellish falsehood, snare them. But for thee   873
I had persisted happy, had not thy pride
And wand'ring vanity, when least was safe,
Rejected my forewarning, and disdained
Not to be trusted, longing to be seen
Though by the devil himself, him overweening
To over-reach, but with the serpent meeting   879
Fooled and beguiled, by him thou, I by thee,
To trust thee from my side, imagined wise,
Constant, mature, proof against all assaults,
And understood not all was but a show
Rather than solid virtue, all but a rib
Crooked by nature, bent, as now appears,
More to the part sinister from me drawn,   886
Well if thrown out, as supernumerary
To my just number found. O why did God,   888
Creator wise, that peopled highest heaven
With spirits masculine, create at last
This novelty on earth, this fair defect
Of nature, and not fill the world at once
With men as angels without feminine,
Or find some other way to generate
Mankind? this mischief had not then befallen,
And more that shall befall, innumerable
Disturbances on earth through female snares,
And strait conjunction with this sex: for either   898
He never shall find out fit mate, but such
As some misfortune brings him, or mistake,
Or whom he wishes most shall seldom gain
Through her perverseness, but shall see her gained
By a far worse, or if she love, withheld
By parents, or his happiest choice too late
Shall meet, already linked and wedlock-bound

872–3 **pretended / To**] 'Feigned by', with overtones of its etymological sense 'held out [e.g. as a screen] before'.   878–9 **him ... over-reach**] Arrogantly thinking to outsmart him.   886 **part sinister**] Left side, with ominous overtones. 887–8 **supernumerary ... number**] Some commentators, including Calvin, argued that Eve was created from an extra rib, since Adam was created perfect.   898 **strait conjunction**] Close connection: *conjunction* was used in the period for both the marriage union and sexual intercourse.

To a fell adversary, his hate or shame:
Which infinite calamity shall cause
To human life, and household peace confound.

He added not, and from her turned, but Eve
Not so repulsed, with tears that ceased not flowing,   *910*
And tresses all disordered, at his feet
Fell humble, and embracing them, besought
His peace, and thus proceeded in her plaint.

Forsake me not thus, Adam, witness heaven
What love sincere, and reverence in my heart
I bear thee, and unweeting have offended,
Unhappily deceived; thy suppliant
I beg, and clasp thy knees; bereave me not,
Whereon I live, thy gentle looks, thy aid,
Thy counsel in this uttermost distress,
My only strength and stay: forlorn of thee,   *920*
Whither shall I betake me, where subsist?
While yet we live, scarce one short hour perhaps,
Between us two let there be peace, both joining,
As joined in injuries, one enmity
Against a foe by doom express assigned us,   *926*
That cruel serpent: on me exercise not
Thy hatred for this misery befallen,
On me already lost, me than thyself
More miserable; both have sinned, but thou
Against God only, I against God and thee,
And to the place of judgment will return,
There with my cries importune heaven, that all
The sentence from thy head removed may light
On me, sole cause to thee of all this woe,
Me me only just object of his ire.

She ended weeping, and her lowly plight,
Immovable till peace obtained from fault
Acknowledged and deplored, in Adam wrought
Commiseration; soon his heart relented   *940*
Towards her, his life so late and sole delight,
Now at his feet submissive in distress,
Creature so fair his reconcilement seeking,
His counsel whom she had displeased, his aid;

926 **doom express**] Christ's sentence, delivered at ll. 179–80.

As one disarmed, his anger all he lost,
And thus with peaceful words upraised her soon.
   Unwary, and too desirous, as before,
So now of what thou know'st not, who desir'st
The punishment all on thyself; alas,
Bear thine own first, ill able to sustain   950
His full wrath whose thou feel'st as yet least part,
And my displeasure bear'st so ill. If prayers
Could alter high decrees, I to that place
Would speed before thee, and be louder heard,
That on my head all might be visited,
Thy frailty and infirmer sex forgiven,
To me committed and by me exposed.
But rise, let us no more contend, nor blame
Each other, blamed enough elsewhere, but strive
In offices of love, how we may lighten   960
Each other's burden in our share of woe;
Since this day's death denounced, if aught I see,
Will prove no sudden, but a slow-paced evil,
A long day's dying to augment our pain,
And to our seed (O hapless seed!) derived.   965
   To whom thus Eve, recovering heart, replied.
Adam, by sad experiment I know
How little weight my words with thee can find,
Found so erroneous, thence by just event
Found so unfortunate; nevertheless,
Restored by thee, vile as I am, to place
Of new acceptance, hopeful to regain
Thy love, the sole contentment of my heart
Living or dying, from thee I will not hide
What thoughts in my unquiet breast are risen,
Tending to some relief of our extremes,
Or end, though sharp and sad, yet tolerable,
As in our evils, and of easier choice.   978
If care of our descent perplex us most,   979
Which must be born to certain woe, devoured
By death at last, and miserable it is
To be to others cause of misery,

---

965 **derived**] Passed down.   978 **As ... evils**] In evils such as ours.
979 **descent**] Descendants.

Our own begotten, and of our loins to bring
Into this cursèd world a woeful race,
That after wretched life must be at last
Food for so foul a monster, in thy power
It lies, yet ere conception to prevent
The race unblest, to being yet unbegot.
Childless thou art, childless remain: so death   989
Shall be deceived his glut, and with us two   990
Be forced to satisfy his ravenous maw.
But if thou judge it hard and difficult,
Conversing, looking, loving, to abstain   993
From love's due rights, nuptial embraces sweet,
And with desire to languish without hope,
Before the present object languishing   996
With like desire, which would be misery
And torment less than none of what we dread,
Then both ourselves and seed at once to free
From what we fear for both, let us make short,   1000
Let us seek death, or he not found, supply
With our own hands his office on ourselves;
Why stand we longer shivering under fears,
That show no end but death, and have the power,
Of many ways to die the shortest choosing,
Destruction with destruction to destroy.
    She ended here, or vehement despair
Broke off the rest; so much of death her thoughts
Had entertained, as dyed her cheeks with pale.
But Adam with such counsel nothing swayed,   1010
To better hopes his more attentive mind
Labouring had raised, and thus to Eve replied.
    Eve, thy contempt of life and pleasures seems
To argue in thee something more sublime
And excellent than what thy mind contemns;
But self-destruction therefore sought, refutes

---

989 **so death**] In the first five editions, these words appear at the beginning of the following line. All editors have moved it back to regularize the metre, with the exception of Fowler, who argues that 'the line division . . . is perhaps intended to mime first the deficiency of childlessness . . . then the glut denied to Death.' 990 **deceived**] Cheated of.   993 **Conversing**] Lit. 'cohabiting'.   996 **present object**] Object in your presence, i.e. Eve.   1000 **make short**] Be quick.

That excellence thought in thee, and implies,
Not thy contempt, but anguish and regret
For loss of life and pleasure overloved.
Or if thou covet death, as utmost end   1020
Of misery, so thinking to evade
The penalty pronounced, doubt not but God
Hath wiselier armed his vengeful ire than so
To be forestalled; much more I fear lest death
So snatched will not exempt us from the pain
We are by doom to pay; rather such acts
Of contumacy will provoke the highest   1027
To make death in us live: then let us seek
Some safer resolution, which methinks
I have in view, calling to mind with heed
Part of our sentence, that thy seed shall bruise
The serpent's head; piteous amends, unless
Be meant, whom I conjecture, our grand foe
Satan, who in the serpent hath contrived
Against us this deceit: to crush his head
Would be revenge indeed; which will be lost
By death brought on ourselves, or childless days
Resolved, as thou proposest; so our foe
Shall scape his punishment ordained, and we
Instead shall double ours upon our heads.   1040
No more be mentioned then of violence
Against ourselves, and wilful barrenness,
That cuts us off from hope, and savours only
Rancour and pride, impatience and despite,
Reluctance against God and his just yoke   1045
Laid on our necks. Remember with what mild
And gracious temper he both heard and judged
Without wrath or reviling; we expected
Immediate dissolution, which we thought
Was meant by death that day, when lo, to thee
Pains only in child-bearing were foretold,
And bringing forth, soon recompensed with joy,
Fruit of thy womb: on me the curse aslope   1053
Glanced on the ground, with labour I must earn

1027 **contumacy**]   Wilful   disobedience.   1045 **Reluctance**]   Resistance.
1053 **aslope**] Falling aslant, missing its true mark.

My bread; what harm? Idleness had been worse;
My labour will sustain me; and lest cold
Or heat should injure us, his timely care
Hath unbesought provided, and his hands
Clothed us unworthy, pitying while he judged;
How much more, if we pray him, will his ear   *1060*
Be open, and his heart to pity incline,
And teach us further by what means to shun
The inclement seasons, rain, ice, hail and snow,
Which now the sky with various face begins
To show us in this mountain, while the winds
Blow moist and keen, shattering the graceful locks
Of these fair spreading trees; which bids us seek
Some better shroud, some better warmth to cherish   1068
Our limbs benumbed, ere this diurnal star   1069
Leave cold the night, how we his gathered beams   1070
Reflected, may with matter sere foment,   1071
Or by collision of two bodies grind
The air attrite to fire, as late the clouds   1073
Jostling or pushed with winds rude in their shock
Tine the slant lightning, whose thwart flame driven down   1075
Kindles the gummy bark of fir or pine,
And sends a comfortable heat from far,
Which might supply the sun: such fire to use   1078
And what may else be remedy or cure
To evils which our own misdeeds have wrought,
He will instruct us praying, and of grace
Beseeching him, so as we need not fear   1082
To pass commodiously this life, sustained
By him with many comforts, till we end
In dust, our final rest and native home.
What better can we do, than to the place
Repairing where he judged us, prostrate fall
Before him reverent, and there confess
Humbly our faults, and pardon beg, with tears
Watering the ground, and with our sighs the air

1068 **shroud**] Shelter. **cherish**] Keep warm, comfort.   1069 **this diurnal star**] The sun.   1070 **how**] Seek how.   1071 **with . . . foment**] Kindle in dry matter (*fire*, l. 1073).   1073 **attrite**] By friction.   1075 **Tine**] Ignite. **thwart**] Slanting.   1078 **supply**] Replace.   1081–2 **of . . . him**] Asking him for grace.

Frequenting, sent from hearts contrite, in sign   1091
Of sorrow unfeigned, and humiliation meek.
Undoubtedly he will relent and turn
From his displeasure; in whose look serene,
When angry most he seemed and most severe,
What else but favour, grace, and mercy shone?
   So spake our father penitent, nor Eve
Felt less remorse: they forthwith to the place
Repairing where he judged them prostrate fell
Before him reverent, and both confessed   1100
Humbly their faults, and pardon begged, with tears
Watering the ground, and with their sighs the air
Frequenting, sent from hearts contrite, in sign
Of sorrow unfeigned, and humiliation meek.

1091 **Frequenting**] Filling.

BOOK XI

The Argument

The Son of God presents to his father the prayers of our first parents now repenting, and intercedes for them: God accepts them, but declares that they must no longer abide in Paradise; sends Michael with a band of cherubim to dispossess them; but first to reveal to Adam future things: Michael's coming down. Adam shows to Eve certain ominous signs; he discerns Michael's approach, goes out to meet him: the angel denounces their departure. Eve's lamentation. Adam pleads, but submits: the angel leads him up to a high hill, sets before him in vision what shall happen till the flood.

THUS they in lowliest plight repentant stood
Praying, for from the mercy-seat above
Prevenient grace descending had removed   3
The stony from their hearts, and made new flesh
Regenerate grow instead, that sighs now breathed
Unutterable, which the spirit of prayer
Inspired, and winged for heaven with speedier flight
Than loudest oratory: yet their port
Not of mean suitors, nor important less
Seemed their petition, than when the ancient pair
In fables old, less ancient yet than these,
Deucalion and chaste Pyrrha to restore
The race of mankind drowned, before the shrine
Of Themis stood devout. To heaven their prayers   14
Flew up, nor missed the way, by envious winds
Blown vagabond or frustrate: in they passed
Dimensionless through heavenly doors; then clad   17
With incense, where the golden altar fumed,
By their great intercessor, came in sight
Before the Father's throne: them the glad Son

---

3 **Prevenient grace**] The grace that precedes and makes possible repentance. 12–14 **Deucalion ... devout**] Deucalion was the Noah of Greek myth. He and his wife Pyrrha were instructed by the oracle of Themis, goddess of Justice, to repopulate the earth after the universal flood by throwing stones behind them, from which grew men and women; see *Metamorphoses*, i. 321–80.   17 **Dimensionless**] Non-corporeal, immaterial.

Presenting, thus to intercede began.
    See Father, what first fruits on earth are sprung
From thy implanted grace in man, these sighs
And prayers, which in this golden censer, mixed
With incense, I thy priest before thee bring,
Fruits of more pleasing savour from thy seed
Sown with contrition in his heart, than those
Which his own hand manuring all the trees   28
Of Paradise could have produced, ere fallen
From innocence. Now therefore bend thine ear
To supplication, hear his sighs though mute;
Unskilful with what words to pray, let me
Interpret for him, me his advocate
And propitiation, all his works on me
Good or not good engraft, my merit those
Shall perfect, and for these my death shall pay.
Accept me, and in me from these receive
The smell of peace toward mankind, let him live   38
Before thee reconciled, at least his days
Numbered, though sad, till death, his doom (which I
To mitigate thus plead, not to reverse)
To better life shall yield him, where with me
All my redeemed may dwell in joy and bliss,
Made one with me as I with thee am one.
    To whom the Father, without cloud, serene.
All thy request for man, accepted Son,
Obtain, all thy request was my decree:
But longer in that Paradise to dwell,
The law I gave to nature him forbids:
Those pure immortal elements that know
No gross, no unharmonious mixture foul,
Eject him tainted now, and purge him off
As a distemper, gross to air as gross,   53
And mortal food, as may dispose him best
For dissolution wrought by sin, that first
Distempered all things, and of incorrupt
Corrupted. I at first with two fair gifts

28 **manuring**] Cultivating (lit. 'working with the hands'); see iv. 628.
38 **smell**] First suggestion; also, the prayers are 'clad with incense', ll. 17–18.
53 **gross ... gross**] i.e. from the pure air of paradise to air as impure as Adam has
become.

Created him endowed, with happiness
And immortality: that fondly lost,   59
This other served but to eternize woe;
Till I provided death; so death becomes
His final remedy, and after life
Tried in sharp tribulation, and refined
By faith and faithful works, to second life,
Waked in the renovation of the just,
Resigns him up with heaven and earth renewed.
But let us call to synod all the blessed   67
Through heaven's wide bounds; from them I will not hide
My judgments, how with mankind I proceed,
As how with peccant angels late they saw;   70
And in their state, though firm, stood more confirmed.

   He ended, and the Son gave signal high
To the bright minister that watched, he blew
His trumpet, heard in Oreb since perhaps   74
When God descended, and perhaps once more
To sound at general doom. The angelic blast   76
Filled all the regions: from their blissful bowers
Of amarantine shade, fountain or spring,   78
By the waters of life, where'er they sat
In fellowships of joy: the sons of light
Hasted, resorting to the summons high,
And took their seats; till from his throne supreme
The almighty thus pronounced his sovereign will.

   O sons, like one of us man is become
To know both good and evil, since his taste
Of that defended fruit; but let him boast   86
His knowledge of good lost, and evil got,
Happier, had it sufficed him to have known
Good by itself, and evil not at all.
He sorrows now, repents, and prays contrite,
My motions in him, longer than they move,   91

---

59 **that**] The former, happiness.   **fondly**] Foolishly.   67 **synod**] Meeting, spe-
cifically of an ecclesiastical council.   70 **peccant**] Sinning.   74 **Oreb**] Horeb,
where the trumpet signalled the descent of God to Mount Sinai to give Moses the
Ten Commandments.   76 **general doom**] The Judgment Day.   78 **amaran-
tine**] Immortal (from the amaranth, the legendary flower that never fades: see iii.
353 ff.).   86 **defended**] Forbidden.   91 **motions**] Workings, influence.

His heart I know, how variable and vain
Self-left. Lest therefore his now bolder hand   93
Reach also of the tree of life, and eat,
And live forever, dream at least to live
Forever, to remove him I decree,
And send him from the garden forth to till
The ground whence he was taken, fitter soil.

    Michael, this my behest have thou in charge,
Take to thee from among the cherubim
Thy choice of flaming warriors, lest the fiend
Or in behalf of man, or to invade
Vacant possession some new trouble raise: 103
Haste thee, and from the Paradise of God
Without remorse drive out the sinful pair,
From hallowed ground the unholy, and denounce   106
To them and to their progeny from thence
Perpetual banishment. Yet lest they faint
At the sad sentence rigorously urged,
For I behold them softened and with tears
Bewailing their excess, all terror hide.   111
If patiently thy bidding they obey,
Dismiss them not disconsolate; reveal
To Adam what shall come in future days,
As I shall thee enlighten, intermix
My covenant in the woman's seed renewed;
So send them forth, though sorrowing, yet in peace:
And on the east side of the garden place,
Where entrance up from Eden easiest climbs,
Cherubic watch, and of a sword the flame   120
Wide waving, all approach far off to fright,
And guard all passage to the tree of life:
Lest Paradise a receptacle prove
To spirits foul, and all my trees their prey,
With whose stolen fruit man once more to delude.

    He ceased; and the archangelic power prepared
For swift descent, with him the cohort bright
Of watchful cherubim; four faces each

---

  93 **Self-left**] If left to itself.   102–3 **invade . . . possession**] i.e. become a squatter on my untenanted land (in which case, under English law, the squatter would have a legal right to remain).   106 **denounce**] Announce.   111 **excess**] Transgression.

Had, like a double Janus, all their shape   129
Spangled with eyes more numerous than those
Of Argus, and more wakeful than to drowse,   131
Charmed with Arcadian pipe, the pastoral reed
Of Hermes, or his opiate rod. Meanwhile
To resalute the world with sacred light
Leucothea waked, and with fresh dews embalmed   135
The earth, when Adam and first matron Eve
Had ended now their orisons, and found
Strength added from above, new hope to spring
Out of despair, joy, but with fear yet linked;
Which thus to Eve his welcome words renewed.

  Eve, easily may faith admit, that all
The good which we enjoy, from heaven descends;
But that from us aught should ascend to heaven
So prevalent as to concern the mind   144
Of God high-blessed, or to incline his will,
Hard to belief may seem; yet this will prayer,
Or one short sigh of human breath, upborne
Even to the seat of God. For since I sought
By prayer the offended Deity to appease,
Kneeled and before him humbled all my heart,   150
Methought I saw him placable and mild,
Bending his ear; persuasion in me grew
That I was heard with favour; peace returned
Home to my breast, and to my memory
His promise, that thy seed shall bruise our foe;
Which then not minded in dismay, yet now
Assures me that the bitterness of death
Is past, and we shall live. Whence hail to thee,
Eve rightly called, mother of all mankind,
Mother of all things living, since by thee   160
Man is to live, and all things live for man.
  To whom thus Eve with sad demeanour meek.

---

129 **double Janus**] Janus, guardian of gateways, had two faces looking forward and back; the double Janus, or Janus Quadrifrons, had four faces looking towards the four compass points.   131 **Argus**] A hundred-eyed monster set by Juno to watch Io, with whom Jove was in love. He was charmed to sleep and killed by Hermes/Mercury; see *Metamorphoses*, i. 625 ff.   135 **Leucothea**] Goddess of the dawn. 144 **prevalent**] Forceful.   159–60 **rightly ... living**] Etymologically, Eve (in Hebrew *Chava*) is cognate with *chai*, life. Cf. Genesis 3: 20.

Ill worthy I such title should belong
To me transgressor, who for thee ordained
A help, became thy snare; to me reproach
Rather belongs, distrust and all dispraise:
But infinite in pardon was my judge,
That I who first brought death on all, am graced
The source of life; next favourable thou,
Who highly thus to entitle me vouchsaf'st,   170
Far other name deserving. But the field
To labour calls us now with sweat imposed,
Though after sleepless night; for see the morn,
All unconcerned with our unrest, begins
Her rosy progress smiling; let us forth,
I never from thy side henceforth to stray,
Where'er our day's work lies, though now enjoined
Laborious, till day droop; while here we dwell,
What can be toilsome in these pleasant walks?
Here let us live, though in fallen state, content.   180
    So spake, so wished much-humbled Eve, but fate
Subscribed not; nature first gave signs, impressed
On bird, beast, air, air suddenly eclipsed
After short blush of morn; nigh in her sight
The bird of Jove, stooped from his airy tower,   185
Two birds of gayest plume before him drove:
Down from a hill the beast that reigns in woods,   187
First hunter then, pursued a gentle brace,   188
Goodliest of all the forest, hart and hind;
Direct to the eastern gate was bent their flight.
Adam observed, and with his eye the chase
Pursuing, not unmoved to Eve thus spake.
    O Eve, some further change awaits us nigh,
Which heaven by these mute signs in nature shows
Forerunners of his purpose, or to warn
Us haply too secure of our discharge   196
From penalty, because from death released
Some days; how long, and what till then our life,
Who knows, or more than this, that we are dust,
And thither must return and be no more.

---

185 **bird of Jove**] Eagle.   **stooped**] Having swooped down.   **tower**] High flight.
187 **beast . . . woods**] Lion.   188 **brace**] Pair.   196 **secure**] Confident.

Why else this double object in our sight
Of flight pursued in the air and o'er the ground
One way the self-same hour? why in the east
Darkness ere day's mid-course, and morning light
More orient in yon western cloud that draws   205
O'er the blue firmament a radiant white,
And slow descends, with something heavenly fraught.

    He erred not, for by this the heavenly bands   208
Down from a sky of jasper lighted now   209
In Paradise, and on a hill made alt,   210
A glorious apparition, had not doubt
And carnal fear that day dimmed Adam's eye.   212
Not that more glorious, when the angels met
Jacob in Mahanaim, where he saw   214
The field pavilioned with his guardians bright;
Nor that which on the flaming mount appeared
In Dothan, covered with a camp of fire,   216
Against the Syrian king, who to surprise
One man, assassin-like had levied war,
War unproclaimed. The princely hierarch   220
In their bright stand, there left his powers to seize   221
Possession of the garden; he alone,
To find where Adam sheltered, took his way,
Not unperceived of Adam, who to Eve,
While the great visitant approached, thus spake.

    Eve, now expect great tidings, which perhaps
Of us will soon determine, or impose
New laws to be observed; for I descry
From yonder blazing cloud that veils the hill
One of the heavenly host, and by his gait   230
None of the meanest, some great potentate
Or of the thrones above, such majesty

---

205 **orient**] Bright.   208 **by this**] By this time.   209 **lighted**] Alighted.
210 **made alt**] Halted; a technical military expression.   212 **carnal**] Unholy,
deriving from his sinful nature.   214 **Mahanaim**] Lit. 'armies', 'encampments',
the name given by Jacob to the place where he saw the army of angels (Genesis 32: 1–2).
216 **Dothan**] Modern Tell Dotha, strategic town near Samaria.   216–20 **that . . .
unproclaimed**] When the Syrian king attempted to seize the prophet Elisha, who had
warned the Israelites against him, an angelic army 'full of horses and chariots of fire'
appeared to protect him (2 Kings 6: 13–17).   **princely hierarch**] Michael (see l. 99).
221 **stand**] Station, another technical military term.

Invests him coming; yet not terrible,
That I should fear, nor sociably mild,
As Raphael, that I should much confide,
But solemn and sublime, whom not to offend,
With reverence I must meet, and thou retire.
He ended; and the archangel soon drew nigh,
Not in his shape celestial, but as man
Clad to meet man; over his lucid arms   240
A military vest of purple flowed
Livelier than Meliboean, or the grain   242
Of Sarra, worn by kings and heroes old   243
In time of truce; Iris had dipped the woof;   244
His starry helm unbuckled showed him prime
In manhood where youth ended; by his side
As in a glistering zodiac hung the sword,   247
Satan's dire dread, and in his hand the spear.
Adam bowed low, he kingly from his state
Inclined not, but his coming thus declared.

    Adam, heaven's high behest no preface needs:
Sufficient that thy prayers are heard, and death,
Then due by sentence when thou didst transgress,
Defeated of his seizure many days
Given thee of grace, wherein thou mayst repent,
And one bad act with many deeds well done
Mayst cover: well may then thy Lord appeased
Redeem thee quite from Death's rapacious claim;
But longer in this Paradise to dwell
Permits not; to remove thee I am come,   260
And send thee from the garden forth to till
The ground whence thou wast taken, fitter soil.

    He added not, for Adam at the news
Heart-struck with chilling gripe of sorrow stood,   264
That all his senses bound; Eve, who unseen
Yet all had heard, with audible lament
Discovered soon the place of her retire.   267

---

240 **lucid**] Shining.   242 **Meliboean**] Meliboea, in Thessaly, supplied the ancient world with the finest purple dye. **grain**] Dye.   243 **Sarra**] Tyre, also famous for its dyes; Tyrian purple was the colour of Roman imperial robes. 244 **Iris ... woof**] Thereby making the cloth iridescent; Iris was goddess of the rainbow.   247 **zodiac**] The heavenly sphere containing the constellations. 264 **gripe**] Spasm, pang.   267 **Discovered**] Revealed. **retire**] Withdrawal.

O unexpected stroke, worse than of death!
Must I thus leave thee Paradise? thus leave
Thee native soil, these happy walks and shades,
Fit haunt of gods? where I had hope to spend,
Quiet though sad, the respite of that day   272
That must be mortal to us both. O flowers,
That never will in other climate grow,
My early visitation, and my last
At even, which I bred up with tender hand
From the first opening bud, and gave ye names,
Who now shall rear ye to the sun, or rank
Your tribes, and water from the ambrosial fount?
Thee lastly nuptial bower, by me adorned
With what to sight or smell was sweet; from thee
How shall I part, and whither wander down
Into a lower world, to this obscure   283
And wild, how shall we breathe in other air
Less pure, accustomed to immortal fruits?
    Whom thus the angel interrupted mild.
Lament not Eve, but patiently resign
What justly thou hast lost; nor set thy heart,
Thus over-fond, on that which is not thine;
Thy going is not lonely, with thee goes
Thy husband, him to follow thou art bound;
Where he abides, think there thy native soil.
    Adam by this from the cold sudden damp   293
Recovering, and his scattered spirits returned,
To Michael thus his humble words addressed.
    Celestial, whether among the thrones, or named
Of them the highest, for such of shape may seem
Prince above princes, gently hast thou told
Thy message, which might else in telling wound,
And in performing end us; what besides   300
Of sorrow and dejection and despair
Our frailty can sustain, thy tidings bring,
Departure from this happy place, our sweet
Recess, and only consolation left

272 respite] 'Time granted ... until the coming of' (OED), a usage apparently
peculiar to Milton; the word was normally used in the sense of reprieve, postpone-
ment, cessation of labour.   283 to] In comparison with.   293 damp] 'Dazed or
stupefied condition', 'state of dejection, depression of spirits' (OED).

Familiar to our eyes, all places else
Inhospitable appear and desolate,
Nor knowing us nor known: and if by prayer
Incessant I could hope to change the will
Of him who all things can, I would not cease
To weary him with my assiduous cries: *310*
But prayer against his absolute decree
No more avails than breath against the wind,
Blown stifling back on him that breathes it forth:
Therefore to his great bidding I submit.
This most afflicts me, that departing hence,
As from his face I shall be hid, deprived
His blessèd countenance; here I could frequent,
With worship, place by place where he vouchsafed
Presence divine, and to my sons relate;
On this mount he appeared, under this tree   *320*
Stood visible, among these pines his voice
I heard, here with him at this fountain talked:
So many grateful altars I would rear
Of grassy turf, and pile up every stone
Of lustre from the brook, in memory,
Or monument to ages, and thereon
Offer sweet smelling gums and fruits and flowers:
In yonder nether world where shall I seek
His bright appearances, or footstep trace?
For though I fled him angry, yet recalled   *330*
To life prolonged and promised race, I now
Gladly behold though but his utmost skirts
Of glory, and far off his steps adore.
    To whom thus Michael with regard benign.
Adam, thou know'st heaven his, and all the earth,
Not this rock only; his omnipresence fills
Land, sea, and air, and every kind that lives,
Fomented by his virtual power and warmed: *338*
All the earth he gave thee to possess and rule,
No despicable gift; surmise not then
His presence to these narrow bounds confined
Of Paradise or Eden: this had been
Perhaps thy capital seat, from whence had spread

338 **Fomented**] Fostered, cherished.   **virtual**] Strong, effective.

All generations, and had hither come
From all the ends of the earth, to celebrate
And reverence thee their great progenitor.
But this pre-eminence thou hast lost, brought down
To dwell on even ground now with thy sons:
Yet doubt not but in valley and in plain
God is as here, and will be found alike   *350*
Present, and of his presence many a sign
Still following thee, still compassing thee round
With goodness and paternal love, his face
Express, and of his steps the track divine.
Which that thou mayst believe, and be confirmed
Ere thou from hence depart, know I am sent
To show thee what shall come in future days
To thee and to thy offspring; good with bad
Expect to hear, supernal grace contending   359
With sinfulness of men; thereby to learn
True patience, and to temper joy with fear
And pious sorrow, equally inured
By moderation either state to bear,
Prosperous or adverse: so shalt thou lead
Safest thy life, and best prepared endure
Thy mortal passage when it comes. Ascend
This hill; let Eve (for I have drenched her eyes)
Here sleep below while thou to foresight wak'st,
As once thou slept'st, while she to life was formed.
    To whom thus Adam gratefully replied.
Ascend, I follow thee, safe guide, the path
Thou lead'st me, and to the hand of heaven submit,
However chastening, to the evil turn   '
My obvious breast, arming to overcome   374
By suffering, and earn rest from labour won,
If so I may attain. So both ascend
In the visions of God: it was a hill
Of Paradise the highest, from whose top
The hemisphere of earth in clearest ken   379
Stretched out to the amplest reach of prospect lay.
Not higher that hill nor wider looking round,
Whereon for different cause the tempter set

359 **supernal**] Heavenly.   374 **obvious**] Exposed.   379 **ken**] View.

Our second Adam in the wilderness,
To show him all earth's kingdoms and their glory.   384
His eye might there command wherever stood
City of old or modern fame, the seat
Of mightiest empire, from the destined walls
Of Cambalu, seat of Cathayan khan   388
And Samarkand by Oxus, Temir's throne,   389
To Paquin of Sinaean kings, and thence   390
To Agra and Lahore of great mogul   391
Down to the golden Chersonese, or where   392
The Persian in Ecbatan sat, or since   393
In Hispahan, or where the Russian czar   394
In Moscow, or the sultan in Bizance,   395
Turkestan-born; nor could his eye not ken
The empire of Negus to his utmost port   397
Ercoco and the less maritime kings   398
Mombasa, and Quiloa, and Melind,   399
And Sofala thought Ophir, to the realm   400
Of Congo, and Angola farthest south;
Or thence from Niger flood to Atlas mount
The kingdoms of Almansor, Fez and Sus,   403
Morocco and Algiers, and Tremisen;   404
On Europe thence, and where Rome was to sway
The world: in spirit perhaps he also saw   406

382–4 **tempter ... glory**] For Satan's temptation of Christ in the wilderness see Matthew 4: 8, Luke 4: 5.   388 **Cambalu**] Cambaluc, capital of Mongolian Cathay. 389 **Oxus**] Or Amu Darya, central Asian river.   **Temir**] Timur or Tamburlaine, the Tartar king.   390 **Paquin**] Peking, or Beijing.   **Sinaean**] Chinese (as distinct from that part of Cathay ruled by the Mongols).   391 **Agra and Lahore**] Mughal capitals in northern India.   392 **golden Chersonese**] Rich Malacca and Thailand. 393 **Ecbatan**] Ecbatana, ancient capital of the Persian kings.   393–4 **since ... Hispahan**] Isfahan became the Persian capital around 1600.   395 **Bizance**] Byzantium, or Constantinople, which fell to the Turks in 1453.   397 **Negus**] Title of the king of Abyssinia.   398 **Ercoco**] Archico, a Red Sea port in modern Ethiopia. 399 **Mombasa ... Melind**] Ports on the coast of Kenya (Melind = Malindi). **Quiloa**] The modern Kilwa, on the coast of Tanzania.   400 **Sofala**] Now Beira, in Mozambique. **thought**] Thought to be.   **Ophir**] The biblical kingdom from which Solomon's ships brought gold and jewels (1 Kings 10: 11).   403 **Almansor**] 'The victorious', a title of Mohammedan princes; specifically here the Amir Mohammed of Cordova (939–1002), king of Andalusia, who consolidated and greatly extended the Muslim control of Spain and North Africa. **Fez**] In Morocco. **Sus**] Tunis. 404 **Tremisen**] The modern Tlemcen, in Algeria.   406 **in spirit**] Not physically, because of the earth's curvature.

Rich Mexico the seat of Montezume,
And Cuzco in Peru, the richer seat
Of Atabalipa, and yet unspoiled   409
Guiana, whose great city Geryon's sons   410
Call El Dorado: but to nobler sights
Michael from Adam's eyes the film removed
Which that false fruit that promised clearer sight
Had bred; then purged with euphrasy and rue   414
The visual nerve, for he had much to see;
And from the well of life three drops instilled.
So deep the power of these ingredients pierced,
Even to the inmost seat of mental sight,
That Adam now enforced to close his eyes,
Sunk down and all his spirits became entranced:
But him the gentle angel by the hand
Soon raised, and his attention thus recalled.

    Adam, now ope thine eyes, and first behold
The effects which thy original crime hath wrought
In some to spring from thee, who never touched
The excepted tree, nor with the snake conspired,   426
Nor sinned thy sin, yet from that sin derive
Corruption to bring forth more violent deeds.

    His eyes he opened, and beheld a field,
Part arable and tilth, whereon were sheaves   430
New reaped, the other part sheep-walks and folds;
I' the midst an altar as the landmark stood
Rustic, of grassy sward; thither anon
A sweaty reaper from his tillage brought
First fruits, the green ear, and the yellow sheaf,
Unculled, as came to hand; a shepherd next   436
More meek came with the firstlings of his flock
Choicest and best; then sacrificing, laid

---

409 **Atabalipa**] Atahualpa, defeated by Pizarro in 1533.   410 **Geryon's sons**]
The Spanish. Geryon was a three-headed (or three-bodied) monster who inhabited an
island off the Spanish coast. To kill him and bring back his oxen was one of the labours
of Hercules. He is identified in Dante with Fraud, and Spenser uses him specifically
as an allegory of Spanish oppression (*Faerie Queene*, v. x. 8).   414 **euphrasy**]
Or eyebright, a herb used in poultices for the eyes.   **rue**] Also said to improve eyesight.
426 **excepted**] Forbidden.   430 **tilth**] Cultivated land.   436 **Unculled**]
Unselected, i.e. picked at random (as opposed to Abel's 'choicest and best' offering,
l. 438).

The innards and their fat, with incense strewed,
On the cleft wood, and all due rites performed.
His offering soon propitious fire from heaven
Consumed with nimble glance, and grateful steam;   442
The other's not, for his was not sincere;
Whereat he inly raged, and as they talked,
Smote him into the midriff with a stone
That beat out life; he fell, and deadly pale
Groaned out his soul with gushing blood effused.   447
Much at that sight was Adam in his heart
Dismayed, and thus in haste to the angel cried.

    O teacher, some great mischief hath befallen
To that meek man, who well had sacrificed;
Is piety thus and pure devotion paid?

    To whom Michael thus, he also moved, replied.
These two are brethren, Adam, and to come
Out of thy loins; the unjust the just hath slain,
For envy that his brother's offering found
From heaven acceptance; but the bloody fact   457
Will be avenged, and the other's faith approved
Lose no reward, though here thou see him die,
Rolling in dust and gore. To which our sire.

    Alas, both for the deed and for the cause!
But have I now seen death? Is this the way
I must return to native dust? O sight
Of terror, foul and ugly to behold,
Horrid to think, how horrible to feel!

    To whom thus Michael. Death thou hast seen
In his first shape on man; but many shapes
Of death, and many are the ways that lead
To his grim cave, all dismal; yet to sense
More terrible at the entrance than within.   470
Some, as thou saw'st, by violent stroke shall die,
By fire, flood, famine, by intemperance more
In meats and drinks, which on the earth shall bring
Diseases dire, of which a monstrous crew
Before thee shall appear; that thou mayst know

---

442 **nimble glance**] Quick flash.   **grateful**] Pleasing.   429-47 **His eyes . . . effused**] For the murder of Abel by Cain see Genesis 4.   457 **fact**] Deed; generally used in the period for a criminal act.

What misery the inabstinence of Eve
Shall bring on men. Immediately a place
Before his eyes appeared, sad, noisome, dark,
A lazar-house it seemed, wherein were laid   479
Numbers of all diseased, all maladies
Of ghastly spasm, or racking torture, qualms   481
Of heart-sick agony, all feverous kinds,
Convulsions, epilepsies, fierce catarrhs,
Intestine stone and ulcer, colic pangs,
Demoniac frenzy, moping melancholy
And moon-struck madness, pining atrophy,
Marasmus, and wide-wasting pestilence,   487
Dropsies, and asthmas, and joint-racking rheums.
Dire was the tossing, deep the groans, despair
Tended the sick busiest from couch to couch;
And over them triumphant Death his dart
Shook, but delayed to strike, though oft invoked
With vows, as their chief good, and final hope.
Sight so deform what heart of rock could long
Dry-eyed behold? Adam could not, but wept,
Though not of woman born; compassion quelled   496
His best of man, and gave him up to tears
A space, till firmer thoughts restrained excess,
And scarce recovering words his plaint renewed.

    O miserable mankind, to what fall   500
Degraded, to what wretched state reserved!
Better end here unborn. Why is life given
To be thus wrested from us? rather why
Obtruded on us thus? who if we knew
What we receive, would either not accept
Life offered, or soon beg to lay it down,
Glad to be so dismissed in peace. Can thus
The image of God in man created once
So goodly and erect, though faulty since,

---

479 **lazar-house**] Hospital, especially one for lepers, but here (as the next lines
make clear) for all diseases.   481 **qualms**] Fits.   485–7 **Demoniac ... pestilence**]
Lines added in 1674.   **moon-struck madness**] Literally translating 'lunacy'.
Marasmus] Diseases that cause the body to waste away.   496 **Though ... born**]
Echoing *Macbeth*, IV. i. 80, and elsewhere in the play, referring to Macduff; the impli-
cation here is that compassion is a female quality deriving from the mother, and is
essentially unmanly—Macduff disputes the point in IV. iii. 220 ff.

To such unsightly sufferings be debased   510
Under inhuman pains? Why should not man,
Retaining still divine similitude
In part, from such deformities be free,
And for his maker's image sake exempt?
    Their maker's image, answered Michael, then
Forsook them, when themselves they vilified
To serve ungoverned appetite, and took
His image whom they served, a brutish vice,
Inductive mainly to the sin of Eve.   519
Therefore so abject is their punishment,
Disfiguring not God's likeness, but their own,
Or if his likeness, by themselves defaced
While they pervert pure nature's healthful rules
To loathsome sickness, worthily, since they
God's image did not reverence in themselves.
    I yield it just, said Adam, and submit.
But is there yet no other way, besides
These painful passages, how we may come
To death, and mix with our connatural dust?
    There is, said Michael, if thou well observe   530
The rule of not too much, by temperance taught
In what thou eat'st and drink'st, seeking from thence
Due nourishment, not gluttonous delight,
Till many years over thy head return:
So mayst thou live, till like ripe fruit thou drop
Into thy mother's lap, or be with ease
Gathered, not harshly plucked, for death mature:
This is old age; but then thou must outlive
Thy youth, thy strength, thy beauty, which will change
To withered weak and grey; thy senses then
Obtuse, all taste of pleasure must forego,   541
To what thou hast, and for the air of youth
Hopeful and cheerful, in thy blood will reign
A melancholy damp of cold and dry   544
To weigh thy spirits down, and last consume
The balm of life. To whom our ancestor.

---

519 **Inductive . . . to**] Leading directly to (a repetition of).   541 **Obtuse**] i.e. no
longer acute.   544 **damp**] Depression.   **cold and dry**] In the old physiology, the
humours of phlegm and black bile, producing a melancholic temperament.

Henceforth I fly not death, nor would prolong
Life much, bent rather how I may be quit
Fairest and easiest of this cumbrous charge,
Which I must keep till my appointed day
Of rendering up, and patiently attend
My dissolution. Michael replied,   552
    Nor love thy life, nor hate; but what thou liv'st
Live well, how long or short permit to heaven:
And now prepare thee for another sight.

    He looked and saw a spacious plain, whereon   556
Were tents of various hue; by some were herds
Of cattle grazing: others, whence the sound
Of instruments that made melodious chime
Was heard, of harp and organ; and who moved
Their stops and chords was seen: his volant touch   561
Instinct through all proportions low and high   562
Fled and pursued transverse the resonant fugue.   563
In other part stood one who at the forge   564
Labouring, two massy clods of iron and brass
Had melted (whether found where casual fire   566
Had wasted woods on mountain or in vale,
Down to the veins of earth, thence gliding hot
To some cave's mouth, or whether washed by stream
From underground) the liquid ore he drained
Into fit moulds prepared; from which he formed
First his own tools; then, what might else be wrought
Fusile or graven in metal. After these,   573
But on the hither side a different sort   574
From the high neighbouring hills, which was their seat,
Down to the plain descended: by their guise

551–2 **Of rendering ... replied**] In 1667 the passage reads 'Of rend'ring up.
Michael to him replied'. **attend**] Await.   556 ff. The scene is based on Genesis 4:
19–22, the account of the three sons of Cain's descendant Lamech: Jabal, 'father of such
as dwell in tents and have cattle', Jubal, 'father of all such as handle the harp and organ',
and Tubal-cain ('Tubal the smith'), 'an instructor of every artificer in brass and
iron'. 561 **volant**] Flying.   562 **Instinct**] Both impelled and innate, intuitive.
proportions] Harmonies, musical relationships.   563 **fugue**] Lit. 'flight'.
564 ff. Milton's account of the discovery of metals derives from Lucretius, *De Rerum
Natura*, v. 1241–68.   566 **casual**] Accidental.   573 **fusile**] By melting. **After
these . . .**] The vision (ll. 573–627) of the 'sons of God' (see l. 622) alludes to Genesis 6:
2–4, but depends largely on patristic commentators. See also iii. 461–4.   574 **the
hither side**] The west; Cain's descendants lived east of Eden.

Just men they seemed, and all their study bent
To worship God aright, and know his works
Not hid, nor those things last which might preserve
Freedom and peace to men: they on the plain
Long had not walked, when from the tents behold
A bevy of fair women, richly gay
In gems and wanton dress; to the harp they sung
Soft amorous ditties, and in dance came on:
The men though grave, eyed them, and let their eyes
Rove without rein, till in the amorous net
Fast caught, they liked, and each his liking chose;
And now of love they treat till the evening star   588
Love's harbinger appeared; then all in heat
They light the nuptial torch, and bid invoke
Hymen, then first to marriage rites invoked;   591
With feast and music all the tents resound.
Such happy interview and fair event
Of love and youth not lost, songs, garlands, flowers,
And charming symphonies attached the heart   · 595
Of Adam, soon inclined to admit delight,
The bent of nature; which he thus expressed.

　　True opener of mine eyes, prime angel blessed,
Much better seems this vision, and more hope
Of peaceful days portends, than those two past;
Those were of hate and death, or pain much worse,
Here nature seems fulfilled in all her ends.

　　To whom thus Michael. Judge not what is best
By pleasure, though to nature seeming meet,
Created, as thou art, to nobler end
Holy and pure, conformity divine.
Those tents thou saw'st so pleasant, were the tents
Of wickedness, wherein shall dwell his race
Who slew his brother; studious they appear
Of arts that polish life, inventors rare,   610
Unmindful of their maker, though his Spirit
Taught them, but they his gifts acknowledged none.
Yet they a beauteous offspring shall beget;
For that fair female troop thou saw'st, that seemed

---

588 **evening star**] Venus.　　591 **Hymen**] God of marriage.　　595 **sym-
phonies**] Harmonies.　　**attached**] Seized.

Of goddesses, so blithe, so smooth, so gay,
Yet empty of all good wherein consists
Woman's domestic honour and chief praise;
Bred only and completed to the taste
Of lustful appetance, to sing, to dance,   619
To dress, and troll the tongue, and roll the eye.   620
To these that sober race of men, whose lives
Religious titled them the sons of God,
Shall yield up all their virtue, all their fame
Ignobly, to the trains and to the smiles   624
Of these fair atheists, and now swim in joy,
(Erelong to swim at large) and laugh; for which
The world erelong a world of tears must weep.
    To whom thus Adam of short joy bereft.
O pity and shame, that they who to live well
Entered so fair, should turn aside to tread   630
Paths indirect, or in the mid-way faint!
But still I see the tenor of man's woe
Holds on the same, from woman to begin.
    From man's effeminate slackness it begins,
Said the angel, who should better hold his place
By wisdom, and superior gifts received.
But now prepare thee for another scene.
    He looked and saw wide territory spread
Before him, towns, and rural works between,
Cities of men with lofty gates and towers,
Concourse in arms, fierce faces threatening war,   641
Giants of mighty bone, and bold emprise;   642
Part wield their arms, part curb the foaming steed,
Single or in array of battle ranged
Both horse and foot, nor idly mustering stood;
One way a band select from forage drives
A herd of beeves, fair oxen and fair kine   647
From a fat meadow ground; or fleecy flock,
Ewes and their bleating lambs over the plain,
Their booty; scarce with life the shepherds fly,
But call in aid, which makes a bloody fray;

---

619 **appetance**]   Appetite.   620 **troll**]   Wag.   624 **trains**]   Wiles.
641 **Concourse**] 'Hostile encounter' (*OED*).   642 **emprise**] Undertaking, with
chivalric overtones.   647 **beeves**] Cattle (plural of 'beef').

With cruel tournament the squadrons join;
Where cattle pastured late, now scattered lies
With carcasses and arms the ensanguined field   654
Deserted: others to a city strong
Lay siege, encamped; by battery, scale, and mine,   656
Assaulting; others from the wall defend
With dart and javelin, stones and sulphurous fire;
On each hand slaughter and gigantic deeds.
In other part the sceptred heralds call
To council in the city gates: anon
Grey-headed men and grave, with warriors mixed,
Assemble, and harangues are heard, but soon
In factious opposition, till at last
Of middle age one rising, eminent   665
In wise deport, spake much of right and wrong,
Of justice, of religion, truth and peace,
And judgment from above: him old and young
Exploded and had seized with violent hands,   669
Had not a cloud descending snatched him thence
Unseen amid the throng: so violence
Proceeded, and oppression, and sword-law
Through all the plain, and refuge none was found.   673
Adam was all in tears, and to his guide
Lamenting turned full sad; O what are these,
Death's ministers, not men, who thus deal death
Inhumanly to men, and multiply
Ten thousandfold the sin of him who slew
His brother; for of whom such massacre
Make they but of their brethren, men of men?   680
But who was that just man, whom had not heaven
Rescued, had in his righteousness been lost?
        To whom thus Michael. These are the product
Of those ill-mated marriages thou saw'st:
Where good with bad were matched, who of themselves

---

654 **ensanguined**] Bloody.   656 **scale**] Ladder.   665 **Of middle age one**]
Enoch, the father of Methusaleh, a just man who was 'translated' to heaven in 'middle
age', i.e. at the age of 365 years, half the lifespan of the patriarchs. See Genesis 5: 17–24
and the pseudepigraphical Book of Enoch, which was partly known to Milton.
669 **Exploded**] Lit. 'hissed off the stage' (opposite of applauded).   638–73 **He
looked . . . was found**] The fourth vision recalls Homer's description of the shield
made by Hephaestos for Achilles, *Iliad*, xviii. 478–616.

Abhor to join; and by imprudence mixed,
Produce prodigious births of body or mind.
Such were these giants, men of high renown;
For in those days might only shall be admired,
And valour and heroic virtue called;   *690*
To overcome in battle, and subdue
Nations, and bring home spoils with infinite
Manslaughter, shall be held the highest pitch
Of human glory, and for glory done
Of triumph, to be styled great conquerors,
Patrons of mankind, gods, and sons of gods,
Destroyers rightlier called and plagues of men.
Thus fame shall be achieved, renown on earth,
And what most merits fame in silence hid.
But he the seventh from thee, whom thou beheld'st   *700*
The only righteous in a world perverse,
And therefore hated, therefore so beset
With foes for daring single to be just,
And utter odious truth, that God would come
To judge them with his saints: him the most high
Rapt in a balmy cloud with wingèd steeds
Did, as thou saw'st, receive, to walk with God
High in salvation and the climes of bliss,
Exempt from death; to show thee what reward
Awaits the good, the rest what punishment;   *710*
Which now direct thine eyes and soon behold.
    He looked, and saw the face of things quite changed,
The brazen throat of war had ceased to roar,
All now was turned to jollity and game,
To luxury and riot, feast and dance,   *715*
Marrying or prostituting, as befell,
Rape or adultery, where passing fair   *717*
Allured them; thence from cups to civil broils.
At length a reverend sire among them came,   *719*
And of their doings great dislike declared,
And testified against their ways; he oft

---

700 **he the seventh from thee**] Enoch was seven generations removed from Adam.
715 **luxury**] Lasciviousness.   717 **passing fair**] Both surpassing beauty and pretty
passers-by.   719 ff. For the flood see Genesis 6: 9–9: 17 and the analogous account of
Deucalion's flood in *Metamorphoses*, i. 262–347.

Frequented their assemblies, whereso met,
Triumphs or festivals, and to them preached
Conversion and repentance, as to souls
In prison under judgments imminent:
But all in vain: which when he saw, he ceased
Contending, and removed his tents far off;
Then from the mountain hewing timber tall,
Began to build a vessel of huge bulk,
Measured by cubit, length, and breadth, and height,
Smeared round with pitch, and in the side a door   731
Contrived, and of provisions laid in large
For man and beast: when lo a wonder strange!
Of every beast, and bird, and insect small
Came sevens, and pairs, and entered in, as taught   735
Their order: last the sire, and his three sons
With their four wives; and God made fast the door.
Meanwhile the south wind rose, and with black wings
Wide hovering, all the clouds together drove
From under heaven; the hills to their supply
Vapour, and exhalation dusk and moist,   741
Sent up amain; and now the thickened sky   742
Like a dark ceiling stood; down rushed the rain
Impetuous, and continued till the earth
No more was seen; the floating vessel swum
Uplifted; and secure with beakèd prow
Rode tilting o'er the waves, all dwellings else
Flood overwhelmed, and them with all their pomp
Deep under water rolled; sea covered sea,
Sea without shore; and in their palaces
Where luxury late reigned, sea monsters whelped
And stabled; of mankind, so numerous late,
All left, in one small bottom swum embarked.   753
How didst thou grieve then, Adam, to behold
The end of all thy offspring, end so sad,
Depopulation; thee another flood,
Of tears and sorrow a flood thee also drowned,
And sunk thee as thy sons; till gently reared

---

731 **Smeared . . . pitch**] In order to caulk the ark.   735 **sevens, and pairs**] Noah was ordered to take seven pairs of clean beasts and two of unclean beasts (Genesis 7: 2). 741 **exhalation dusk**] Dark fog.   742 **amain**] Violently.   753 **bottom**] Boat.

By the angel, on thy feet thou stood'st at last,
Though comfortless, as when a father mourns   *760*
His children, all in view destroyed at once;
And scarce to the angel utter'dst thus thy plaint.
    O visions ill foreseen! better had I
Lived ignorant of future, so had borne
My part of evil only, each day's lot
Enough to bear; those now, that were dispensed
The burden of many ages, on me light
At once, by my foreknowledge gaining birth
Abortive, to torment me ere their being,
With thought that they must be. Let no man seek   *770*
Henceforth to be foretold what shall befall
Him or his children, evil he may be sure,
Which neither his foreknowing can prevent,
And he the future evil shall no less
In apprehension than in substance feel
Grievous to bear: but that care now is past,
Man is not whom to warn: those few escaped   *777*
Famine and anguish will at last consume
Wand'ring that wat'ry desert: I had hope
When violence was ceased, and war on earth,
All would have then gone well, peace would have crowned
With length of happy days the race of man;
But I was far deceived; for now I see
Peace to corrupt no less than war to waste.
How comes it thus? unfold, celestial guide,
And whether here the race of man will end.
To whom thus Michael. Those whom last thou saw'st
In triumph and luxurious wealth, are they
First seen in acts of prowess eminent
And great exploits, but of true virtue void;   *790*
Who having spilled much blood, and done much waste
Subduing nations, and achieved thereby
Fame in the world, high titles, and rich prey,
Shall change their course to pleasure, ease, and sloth,
Surfeit, and lust, till wantonness and pride
Raise out of friendship hostile deeds in peace.
The conquered also, and enslaved by war

777 **Man is not whom**] There is no man left

Shall with their freedom lost all virtue lose
And fear of God, from whom their piety feigned
In sharp contest of battle found no aid   *800*
Against invaders; therefore cooled in zeal
Thenceforth shall practise how to live secure,
Worldly or dissolute, on what their lords
Shall leave them to enjoy; for the earth shall bear
More than enough, that temperance may be tried: 805
So all shall turn degenerate, all depraved,
Justice and temperance, truth and faith forgot;
One man except, the only son of light
In a dark age, against example good,
Against allurement, custom, and a world
Offended; fearless of reproach and scorn,
Or violence, he of their wicked ways
Shall them admonish, and before them set
The paths of righteousness, how much more safe,
And full of peace, denouncing wrath to come   815
On their impenitence; and shall return
Of them derided, but of God observed
The one just man alive; by his command
Shall build a wondrous ark, as thou beheld'st
To save himself and household from amidst
A world devote to universal rack.   821
No sooner he with them of man and beast
Select for life shall in the ark be lodged,
And sheltered round, but all the cataracts
Of heaven set open on the earth shall pour
Rain day and night, all fountains of the deep
Broke up, shall heave the ocean to usurp
Beyond all bounds, till inundation rise
Above the highest hills: then shall this mount
Of Paradise by might of waves be moved
Out of his place, pushed by the hornèd flood,   831
With all his verdure spoiled, and trees adrift
Down the great river to the opening gulf,
And there take root an island salt and bare,

---

805 **tried**] Tested.   815 **denouncing**] Proclaiming.   821 **devote**] Doomed
rack] Ruin.   831 **hornèd**] Branching.

The haunt of seals and orcs, and seamews' clang.   835
To teach thee that God attributes to place
No sanctity, if none be thither brought
By men who there frequent, or therein dwell.
And now what further shall ensue, behold.

   He looked, and saw the ark hull on the flood,   840
Which now abated, for the clouds were fled,
Driven by a keen north wind, that blowing dry
Wrinkled the face of deluge, as decayed;
And the clear sun on his wide watery glass
Gazed hot, and of the fresh wave largely drew,
As after thirst, which made their flowing shrink
From standing lake to tripping ebb, that stole   847
With soft foot towards the deep, who now had stopped
His sluices, as the heaven his windows shut.
The ark no more now floats, but seems on ground
Fast on the top of some high mountain fixed.
And now the tops of hills as rocks appear;
With clamour thence the rapid currents drive
Towards the retreating sea their furious tide.
Forthwith from out the ark a raven flies,
And after him, the surer messenger,
A dove sent forth once and again to spy
Green tree or ground whereon his foot may light;
The second time returning, in his bill
An olive leaf he brings, pacific sign: 860
Anon dry ground appears, and from his ark
The ancient sire descends with all his train;
Then with uplifted hands, and eyes devout,
Grateful to heaven, over his head beholds
A dewy cloud, and in the cloud a bow
Conspicuous with three listed colours gay,   866
Betok'ning peace from God, and cov'nant new.
Whereat the heart of Adam erst so sad
Greatly rejoiced, and thus his joy broke forth.
   O thou who future things canst represent

---

835 **orcs**] Whales; also applied 'to more than one vaguely identified ferocious sea-monster' (*OED*). **seamew's clang**] Gull's cry.   840 **hull**] Drift.
847 **tripping**] Running.   865–6 **bow … gay**] The rainbow, striped ('*listed*') with the three primary colours, red, yellow, and blue.

As present, heavenly instructor, I revive
At this last sight, assured that man shall live
With all the creatures, and their seed preserve.
Far less I now lament for one whole world
Of wicked sons destroyed, than I rejoice
For one man found so perfect and so just,
That God vouchsafes to raise another world
From him, and all his anger to forget.
But say, what mean those coloured streaks in heaven,
Distended as the brow of God appeased,   880
Or serve they as a flowery verge to bind
The fluid skirts of that same watery cloud,
Lest it again dissolve and shower the earth?
    To whom the archangel. Dextrously thou aim'st;
So willingly doth God remit his ire,
Though late repenting him of man depraved,
Grieved at his heart, when looking down he saw   887
The whole earth filled with violence, and all flesh
Corrupting each their way; yet those removed,
Such grace shall one just man find in his sight,
That he relents, not to blot out mankind,
And makes a covenant never to destroy
The earth again by flood, nor let the sea
Surpass his bounds, nor rain to drown the world
With man therein or beast; but when he brings
Over the earth a cloud, will therein set
His triple-coloured bow, whereon to look
And call to mind his covenant: day and night,
Seed time and harvest, heat and hoary frost
Shall hold their course, till fire purge all things new,   900
Both heaven and earth, wherein the just shall dwell.

---

880 **Distended**] Spread (as God's brow is now relaxed).   886–7 **repenting . . .
heart**] Milton's syntax is much more ambiguous than his source, Genesis 6: 6: 'it
repented the Lord that he had made man on the earth, and it grieved him at his heart.'

BOOK XII

The Argument

The angel Michael continues from the flood to relate what shall
succeed; then, in the mention of Abraham, comes by degrees to
explain, who that seed of the woman shall be, which was promised
Adam and Eve in the Fall; his incarnation, death, resurrection, and
ascension; the state of the church till his second coming. Adam
greatly satisfied and recomforted by these relations and promises
descends the hill with Michael; wakens Eve, who all this while had
slept, but with gentle dreams composed to quietness of mind and
submission. Michael in either hand leads them out of Paradise,
the fiery sword waving behind them, and the cherubim taking their
stations to guard the place.

As ONE who in his journey bates at noon,   1
Though bent on speed, so here the archangel paused
Betwixt the world destroyed and world restored,
If Adam aught perhaps might interpose;
Then with transition sweet new speech resumes.   5
  Thus thou hast seen one world begin and end;
And man as from a second stock proceed.
Much thou hast yet to see, but I perceive
Thy mortal sight to fail; objects divine
Must needs impair and weary human sense:
Henceforth what is to come I will relate,
Thou therefore give due audience, and attend.
This second source of men, while yet but few,
And while the dread of judgment past remains
Fresh in their minds, fearing the Deity,
With some regard to what is just and right
Shall lead their lives, and multiply apace,
Labouring the soil, and reaping plenteous crop,
Corn wine and oil; and from the herd or flock,
Oft sacrificing bullock, lamb, or kid,   20
With large wine-offerings poured, and sacred feast,
Shall spend their days in joy unblamed, and dwell
Long time in peace by families and tribes

1 **bates**] Pauses.   1-5 Added in 1674, when Book 10 of the first edition became
Books 11 and 12 of the second.

Under paternal rule; till one shall rise   24
Of proud ambitious heart, who not content
With fair equality, fraternal state,
Will arrogate dominion undeserved
Over his brethren, and quite dispossess
Concord and law of nature from the earth,
Hunting (and men not beasts shall be his game)
With war and hostile snare such as refuse
Subjection to his empire tyrannous:
A mighty hunter thence he shall be styled
Before the Lord, as in despite of heaven,
Or from heaven claiming second sovereignty;
And from rebellion shall derive his name,   36
Though of rebellion others he accuse.
He with a crew, whom like ambition joins
With him or under him to tyrannize,
Marching from Eden towards the west, shall find
The plain, wherein a black bituminous gurge   41
Boils out from underground, the mouth of hell;
Of brick, and of that stuff they cast to build   43
A city and tower, whose top may reach to heaven;
And get themselves a name, lest far dispersed
In foreign lands their memory be lost
Regardless whether good or evil fame.
But God who oft descends to visit men
Unseen, and through their habitations walks
To mark their doings, them beholding soon,
Comes down to see their city, ere the tower
Obstruct heaven towers, and in derision sets
Upon their tongues a various spirit to rase   53
Quite out their native language, and instead
To sow a jangling noise of words unknown:
Forthwith a hideous gabble rises loud
Among the builders; each to other calls
Not understood, till hoarse, and all in rage,

24 **one**] Nimrod; the account alludes to Genesis 10: 8–10, but Nimrod's connection with the Tower of Babel derives from later commentators, beginning with Josephus, *Antiquities*, I. iv. 2.   36 **from . . . name**] Nimrod was etymologized (incorrectly) from the Hebrew verb 'to rebel'.   41 **gurge**] Whirlpool.   43 **cast**] Determine. 53 **various**] Changeable; 'calculated to cause difference or dissimilarity' (*OED* 5b, the only citation for the latter sense).   **rase**. Erase.

As mocked they storm; great laughter was in heaven
And looking down, to see the hubbub strange
And hear the din; thus was the building left
Ridiculous, and the work Confusion named.   62
    Whereto thus Adam fatherly displeased.
O execrable son so to aspire
Above his brethren, to himself assuming
Authority usurped, from God not given:
He gave us only over beast, fish, fowl
Dominion absolute; that right we hold
By his donation; but man over men
He made not lord; such title to himself   70
Reserving, human left from human free.
But this usurper his encroachment proud
Stays not on man; to God his tower intends
Siege and defiance: wretched man! what food
Will he convey up thither to sustain
Himself and his rash army, where thin air
Above the clouds will pine his entrails gross,
And famish him of breath, if not of bread?
    To whom thus Michael. Justly thou abhorr'st
That son, who on the quiet state of men
Such trouble brought, affecting to subdue   81
Rational liberty; yet know withal,
Since thy original lapse, true liberty
Is lost, which always with right reason dwells   84
Twinned, and from her hath no dividual being: 85
Reason in man obscured, or not obeyed,
Immediately inordinate desires
And upstart passions catch the government
From reason, and to servitude reduce
Man till then free. Therefore since he permits   90
Within himself unworthy powers to reign
Over free reason, God in judgment just
Subjects him from without to violent lords;
Who oft as undeservedly enthral
His outward freedom: tyranny must be,
    Though to the tyrant thereby no excuse.

---

62 **Confusion**] Incorrectly thought to be the etymological meaning of Babel.
81 **affecting**] Presuming.   84 **right reason**] The inherent ability to perceive the
good; conscience.   85 **dividual**] Separate.

Yet sometimes nations will decline so low
From virtue, which is reason, that no wrong,
But justice, and some fatal curse annexed
Deprives them of their outward liberty,
Their inward lost: witness the irreverent son,
Of him who built the ark, who for the shame
Done to his father, heard this heavy curse,
Servant of servants, on his vicious race.   104
Thus will this latter, as the former world,
Still tend from bad to worse, till God at last
Wearied with their iniquities, withdraw
His presence from among them, and avert
His holy eyes; resolving from thenceforth
To leave them to their own polluted ways;
And one peculiar nation to select   111
From all the rest, of whom to be invoked,
A nation from one faithful man to spring:
Him on this side Euphrates yet residing,   114
Bred up in idol worship; O that men
(Canst thou believe?) should be so stupid grown,
While yet the patriarch lived, who scaped the flood,   117
As to forsake the living God, and fall
To worship their own work in wood and stone
For gods! yet him God the most high vouchsafes
To call by vision from his father's house,
His kindred and false gods, into a land
Which he will show him, and from him will raise
A mighty nation, and upon him shower
His benediction so, that in his seed
All nations shall be blest; he straight obeys,
Not knowing to what land, yet firm believes:
I see him, but thou canst not, with what faith
He leaves his gods, his friends, and native soil
Ur of Chaldaea, passing now the ford   130
To Haran, after him a cumbrous train   131

101–4 **irreverent . . . race**] Ham, Noah's son, whose irreverence consisted of seeing his father drunk and naked; in punishment Noah condemned Ham's son Canaan to permanent servitude, Genesis 9: 25.   111 **peculiar**] Particular.   114 **Him**] Abraham; the biblical account is in Genesis 11: 27 ff.   117 **the patriarch . . . flood**] Noah.   130 **Ur**] On the west bank of the Euphrates.   130–1 **ford . . . Haran**] Haran is east of the Euphrates, about 400 miles north-west of Ur.

Of herds and flocks, and numerous servitude;   132
Not wand'ring poor, but trusting all his wealth
With God, who called him, in a land unknown.
Canaan he now attains, I see his tents
Pitched about Sechem, and the neighbouring plain   136
Of Moreh; there by promise he receives
Gift to his progeny of all that land;
From Hamath northward to the desert south   139
(Things by their names I call, though yet unnamed)
From Hermon east to the great western sea,   141
Mount Hermon, yonder sea, each place behold
In prospect, as I point them; on the shore
Mount Carmel; here the double-founted stream
Jordan, true limit eastward; but his sons   145
Shall dwell to Senir, that long ridge of hills.   146
This ponder, that all nations of the earth
Shall in his seed be blessèd; by that seed
Is meant thy great deliverer, who shall bruise
The serpent's head; whereof to thee anon
Plainlier shall be revealed. This patriarch blessed,
Whom faithful Abraham due time shall call,
A son, and of his son a grandchild leaves,   153
Like him in faith, in wisdom, and renown;
The grandchild with twelve sons increased, departs
From Canaan, to a land hereafter called
Egypt, divided by the river Nile;
See where it flows, disgorging at seven mouths
Into the sea: to sojourn in that land
He comes invited by a younger son   160
In time of dearth, a son whose worthy deeds
Raise him to be the second in that realm

132 **servitude**] Servants.   136 **Sechem**] Or Shechem, near Mount Gerizim and
Mount Ebal, site of Abraham's first encampment in Canaan. The account of the journey
is based on Genesis 12: 5–6.   139 **Hamath**] On the River Orontes in Syria, 120
miles north of Damascus. It marked the northern border of the Promised Land (see
Numbers 34: 8 and Joshua 13: 5–6). **desert south**] The Wilderness of Zin, the
southern border.   141 **Hermon**] The sacred mountain, the eastern boundary.
great western sea] The Mediterranean.   144–5 **double-founted ... Jordan**]
Milton relied on an incorrect tradition that the Jordan springs from two streams
called the Jor and the Dan.   146 **Senir**] A peak (not a ridge) of Mount
Hermon.   153 **son ... grandchild**] Isaac and Jacob.   160 **younger son**]
Joseph; the subsequent account follows Exodus.

Of Pharaoh: there he dies, and leaves his race
Growing into a nation, and now grown
Suspected to a sequent king, who seeks   165
To stop their overgrowth, as inmate guests
Too numerous; whence of guests he makes them slaves
Inhospitably, and kills their infant males:
Till by two brethren (those two brethren call
Moses and Aaron) sent from God to claim
His people from enthralment, they return
With glory and spoil back to their promised land.
But first the lawless tyrant, who denies   173
To know their God, or message to regard,
Must be compelled by signs and judgments dire;
To blood unshed the rivers must be turned,   176
Frogs, lice and flies must all his palace fill
With loathed intrusion, and fill all the land;
His cattle must of rot and murrain die,
Botches and blains must all his flesh emboss,   180
And all his people; thunder mixed with hail,
Hail mixed with fire must rend the Egyptian sky
And wheel on the earth, devouring where it rolls;
What it devours not, herb, or fruit, or grain,
A darksome cloud of locusts swarming down
Must eat, and on the ground leave nothing green:
Darkness must overshadow all his bounds,
Palpable darkness, and blot out three days;
Last with one midnight stroke all the first-born
Of Egypt must lie dead. Thus with ten wounds
The river dragon tamed at length submits   191
To let his sojourners depart, and oft
Humbles his stubborn heart, but still as ice
More hardened after thaw, till in his rage
Pursuing whom he late dismissed, the sea
Swallows him with his host, but them lets pass
As on dry land between two crystal walls,
Awed by the rod of Moses so to stand
Divided, till his rescued gain their shore:

---

165 **Suspected to**] Distrusted by.   173 **denies**] Refuses.   176 ff. **to blood . . .**]
The ten plagues are described in Exodus 7–12.   180 **blains**] Swollen sores.
emboss] Cover with swellings.   191 **river dragon**] The epithet is from Ezekiel 29: 3.

Such wondrous power God to his saint will lend,   200
Though present in his angel, who shall go
Before them in a cloud, and pillar of fire,
By day a cloud, by night a pillar of fire,   203
To guide them in their journey, and remove
Behind them, while the obdurate king pursues:
All night he will pursue, but his approach
Darkness defends between till morning watch;   207
Then through the fiery pillar and the cloud
God looking forth will trouble all his host
And craze their chariot wheels: when by command   210
Moses once more his potent rod extends
Over the sea; the sea his rod obeys;
On their embattled ranks the waves return,
And overwhelm their war: the race elect   214
Safe towards Canaan from the shore advance
Through the wild desert, not the readiest way,
Lest entering on the Canaanite alarmed
War terrify them inexpert, and fear
Return them back to Egypt, choosing rather   219
Inglorious life with servitude; for life
To noble and ignoble is more sweet
Untrained in arms, where rashness leads not on.
This also shall they gain by their delay
In the wide wilderness, there they shall found
Their government, and their great senate choose   225
Through the twelve tribes, to rule by laws ordained:
God from the mount of Sinai, whose grey top
Shall tremble, he descending, will himself
In thunder lightning and loud trumpets' sound
Ordain them laws; part such as appertain   230
To civil justice, part religious rites
Of sacrifice, informing them, by types
And shadows, of that destined seed to bruise
The serpent, by what means he shall achieve

---

200 **saint**] Holy man, Moses.   202–3 **Before . . . fire**] From Exodus 13: 21.
207 **defends**] Wards off attack, protects; syntactically 'between' precedes the verb.
210 **craze**] Crack; the account is in Exodus 14.   214 **war**] Army.   216–19 **not
the readiest way . . . rather**] Milton's explanation for the Israelites' thirty-eight years
in the desert is from Exodus 13: 17–18.   225 **great senate**] The Seventy Elders
(Exodus 24: 1–9 and Numbers 11: 16–30).

Mankind's deliverance. But the voice of God
To mortal ear is dreadful; they beseech
That Moses might report to them his will,
And terror cease; he grants what they besought   238
Instructed that to God is no access
Without mediator, whose high office now
Moses in figure bears, to introduce   241
One greater, of whose day he shall foretell,
And all the prophets in their age the times
Of great Messiah shall sing. Thus laws and rites
Established, such delight hath God in men
Obedient to his will, that he vouchsafes
Among them to set up his tabernacle,   247
The holy one with mortal men to dwell:
By his prescript a sanctuary is framed
Of cedar, overlaid with gold, therein
An ark, and in the ark his testimony,
The records of his covenant, over these
A mercy-seat of gold between the wings   253
Of two bright cherubim, before him burn
Seven lamps as in a zodiac representing
The heavenly fires; over the tent a cloud
Shall rest by day, a fiery gleam by night,
Save when they journey, and at length they come,
Conducted by his angel to the land
Promised to Abraham and his seed: the rest
Were long to tell, how many battles fought,
How many kings destroyed, and kingdoms won,
Or how the sun shall in mid heaven stand still
A day entire, and night's due course adjourn,   264
Man's voice commanding, sun in Gibeon stand,   265
And thou moon in the vale of Aialon,   266

237–8 **That ... cease**] 'Speak thou with us and we will hear: but let not God speak with us, lest we die' (Exodus 20: 19).   240–1 **mediator ... bears**] i.e. Moses prefigures Christ as a mediator between God and man.   247 **tabernacle**] See Exodus 25–6.   253 **mercy-seat**] The gold covering over the ark, conceived as the seat of God.   263–4 **the sun ... entire**] When Joshua defeated the Amorites (Joshua 10: 13). They had negotiated a treaty with Joshua under false pretences, and when the deception was discovered Joshua commanded the sun and moon to stand still 'until the people had avenged themselves upon their enemies'.   265 **Gibeon**] Now el-Jib, about five miles north of Jerusalem, capital of the Hivites, an Amorite tribe. 266 **Aialon**] Or Aijalon, a town and valley about fourteen miles north of Jerusalem.

Till Israel overcome; so call the third   267
From Abraham, son of Isaac, and from him
His whole descent, who thus shall Canaan win.
    Here Adam interposed. O sent from heaven,
Enlightener of my darkness, gracious things
Thou hast revealed, those chiefly which concern
Just Abraham and his seed: now first I find
Mine eyes true opening, and my heart much eased,
Erewhile perplexed with thoughts what would become
Of me and all mankind; but now I see
His day, in whom all nations shall be blessed,
Favour unmerited by me, who sought
Forbidden knowledge by forbidden means.
This yet I apprehend not, why to those
Among whom God will deign to dwell on earth   280
So many and so various laws are given;
So many laws argue so many sins
Among them; how can God with such reside?
    To whom thus Michael. Doubt not but that sin
Will reign among them, as of thee begot;
And therefore was law given them to evince   287
Their natural pravity, by stirring up   288
Sin against law to fight: that when they see
Law can discover sin, but not remove,
Save by those shadowy expiations weak,
The blood of bulls and goats, they may conclude
Some blood more precious must be paid for man,
Just for unjust, that in such righteousness
To them by faith imputed, they may find   295
Justification towards God, and peace
Of conscience, which the law by ceremonies
Cannot appease, nor man the moral part
Perform, and not performing cannot live.
So law appears imperfect, and but given

---

267 **so call the third**] Jacob was given the name Israel after his fight with the angel
(Genesis 32: 28); the name was interpreted to mean 'he wrestles with God', though
more properly it would mean 'God wrestles'; neither etymology, however, has any sound
basis.   287 **evince**] 'Make manifest' (*OED* 5); 'overcome' (*OED* 1).   288 **natural
pravity**] Original sin.   295 **imputed**] Vicariously imparted (alluding to the doctrine
of imputed righteousness, whereby Christ's virtue is transferred to Christians through
their faith: see iii. 291).

With purpose to resign them in full time   301
Up to a better covenant, disciplined
From shadowy types to truth, from flesh to spirit,   303
From imposition of strict laws, to free
Acceptance of large grace, from servile fear
To filial, works of law to works of faith.
And therefore shall not Moses, though of God
Highly beloved, being but the minister
Of law, his people into Canaan lead;
But Joshua whom the gentiles Jesus call,
His name and office bearing, who shall quell
The adversary serpent, and bring back
Through the world's wilderness long wandered man
Safe to eternal paradise of rest.   314
Meanwhile they in their earthly Canaan placed
Long time shall dwell and prosper, but when sins   316
National interrupt their public peace,
Provoking God to raise them enemies:
From whom as oft he saves them penitent
By judges first, then under kings; of whom
The second, both for piety renowned
And puissant deeds, a promise shall receive
Irrevocable, that his regal throne
Forever shall endure; the like shall sing
All prophecy, that of the royal stock
Of David (so I name this king) shall rise
A son, the woman's seed to thee foretold,   327
Foretold to Abraham, as in whom shall trust
All nations, and to kings foretold, of kings
The last, for of his reign shall be no end.
But first a long succession must ensue,
And his next son for wealth and wisdom famed,   332

301 **resign**] Consign.   303 **From . . . truth**] From the prefigurings of the Old
Testament to Christian truth. On the Christian notion of typology, see Erich Auerbach,
'Figura', in *Scenes from the Drama of European Literature* (1959); as applied to Milton,
see William Madsen, *From Shadowy Types to Truth* (1968), and Edward Tayler, *Milton's
Poetry* (1979).   310–14 **Joshua . . . rest**] Moses was not permitted to lead the
Israelites into Canaan; the charge fell to his successor Joshua. Joshua thus was taken to
prefigure Jesus, an identification confirmed by the fact that the name Jesus is the Greek
version of Joshua, meaning 'God the saviour'.   316 **but**] Except.   327 **A son**]
Jesus' human ancestry was traced back to David.   332 **his next son**] Solomon.

The clouded ark of God till then in tents
Wandering, shall in a glorious temple enshrine.
Such follow him, as shall be registered
Part good, part bad, of bad the longer scroll,
Whose foul idolatries, and other faults
Heaped to the popular sum, will so incense   338
God, as to leave them, and expose their land,
Their city, his temple, and his holy ark
With all his sacred things, a scorn and prey
To that proud city, whose high walls thou saw'st
Left in confusion, Babylon thence called.
There in captivity he lets them dwell
The space of seventy years, then brings them back,
Remembering mercy, and his covenant sworn
To David, stablished as the days of heaven.
Returned from Babylon by leave of kings
Their lords, whom God disposed, the house of God
They first re-edify, and for a while   350
In mean estate live moderate, till grown   351
In wealth and multitude, factious they grow;
But first among the priests dissension springs,
Men who attend the altar, and should most
Endeavour peace: their strife pollution brings
Upon the temple itself: at last they seize
The sceptre, and regard not David's sons,   357
Then lose it to a stranger, that the true   358
Anointed king Messiah might be born
Barred of his right; yet at his birth a star

338 **Heaped . . . sum**] On top of those of the people; Solomon's idolatry and subjection to women are described in i. 399-405.   348-50 **by leave . . . re-edify**] The Persian kings under whom the Temple was rebuilt are Cyrus, who permitted the Jews to return to Palestine in 538 BC and authorized the reconstruction, Darius Hystaspis, in whose reign the Temple was completed, and Artaxerxes, who in 458 BC allowed Ezra to lead a large group of exiles back to Jerusalem (recounted in Ezra).   351 **In mean estate**] Temperately, in moderation.   355-7 **strife . . . sceptre**] 2 Maccabees 3-4 records the conflicts over the high priesthood in the second century BC. The usurpation of ll. 356-7, by which the Jewish theocracy was changed into a kingship, is that of Aristobulus I, of the priestly Asmonean family, who succeeded to the high priesthood on his father's death in 104 BC but then proclaimed himself king.   358 **stranger**] Antipater the Idumean, governor of Jerusalem under the Romans from 61 BC and Procurator of Judaea from 47 BC. Jesus was born during the reign of his son, Herod the Great.

Unseen before in heaven proclaims him come,
And guides the eastern sages, who inquire
His place, to offer incense, myrrh, and gold;
His place of birth a solemn angel tells
To simple shepherds, keeping watch by night;
They gladly thither haste, and by a choir
Of squadroned angels hear his carol sung.
A virgin is his mother, but his sire
The power of the most high; he shall ascend
The throne hereditary, and bound his reign
With earth's wide bounds, his glory with the heavens.

    He ceased, discerning Adam with such joy
Surcharged, as had like grief been dewed in tears,   373
Without the vent of words, which these he breathed.

    O prophet of glad tidings, finisher
Of utmost hope! now clear I understand   376
What oft my steadiest thoughts have searched in vain,
Why our great expectation should be called
The seed of woman: virgin mother, hail,
High in the love of heaven, yet from my loins
Thou shalt proceed, and from thy womb the Son
Of God most high; so God with man unites.
Needs must the serpent now his capital bruise   383
Expect with mortal pain: say where and when
Their fight, what stroke shall bruise the victor's heel.

    To whom thus Michael. Dream not of their fight,
As of a duel, or the local wounds
Of head or heel: not therefore joins the Son
Manhood to Godhead, with more strength to foil
The enemy; nor so is overcome
Satan, whose fall from heaven, a deadlier bruise,
Disabled not to give thee thy death's wound:
Which he, who comes thy saviour, shall recure,   393
Not by destroying Satan, but his works
In thee and in thy seed: nor can this be,
But by fulfilling that which thou didst want,   396
Obedience to the law of God, imposed
On penalty of death, and suffering death,

---

373 **as . . . been**] Which would have been, like grief.   375–6 **finisher / Of**] i.e.
who has ended with.   383 **capital**] Both mortal, and on his head.   393 **recure**]
Cure.   396 **want**] Lack.

The penalty to thy transgression due,
And due to theirs which out of thine will grow:
So only can high justice rest apaid.   401
The law of God exact he shall fulfil
Both by obedience and by love, though love
Alone fulfil the law; thy punishment
He shall endure by coming in the flesh
To a reproachful life and cursèd death,
Proclaiming life to all who shall believe
In his redemption, and that his obedience
Imputed becomes theirs by faith, his merits   409
To save them, not their own, though legal works.   410
For this he shall live hated, be blasphemed,
Seized on by force, judged, and to death condemned
A shameful and accurst, nailed to the cross
By his own nation, slain for bringing life;
But to the cross he nails thy enemies,
The law that is against thee, and the sins
Of all mankind, with him there crucified,
Never to hurt them more who rightly trust
In this his satisfaction; so he dies,   419
But soon revives, Death over him no power
Shall long usurp; ere the third dawning light
Return, the stars of morn shall see him rise
Out of his grave, fresh as the dawning light,
Thy ransom paid, which man from death redeems,
His death for man, as many as offered life
Neglect not, and the benefit embrace
By faith not void of works: this Godlike act
Annuls thy doom, the death thou shouldst have died,
In sin forever lost from life; this act
Shall bruise the head of Satan, crush his strength
Defeating Sin and Death, his two main arms,
And fix far deeper in his head their stings
Than temporal death shall bruise the victor's heel,   433
Or theirs whom he redeems, a death like sleep,

401 **apaid**] Satisfied.   409 **Imputed**] Vicariously imparted (see 1. 295).
410 **though . . . works**] Though all that they did was in accordance with the law; the
point is that salvation comes through faith, not works.   419 **satisfaction**] i.e. of
God's justice; technical theological language.   433 **temporal**] In time, temporary,
referring not only to the death of the body, but of the soul too.

A gentle wafting to immortal life.
Nor after resurrection shall he stay
Longer on earth than certain times to appear
To his disciples, men who in his life
Still followed him; to them shall leave in charge   439
To teach all nations what of him they learned
And his salvation, them who shall believe
Baptising in the profluent stream, the sign   442
Of washing them from guilt of sin to life
Pure, and in mind prepared, if so befall,
For death, like that which the redeemer died.
All nations they shall teach; for from that day
Not only to the sons of Abraham's loins
Salvation shall be preached, but to the sons
Of Abraham's faith wherever through the world;
So in his seed all nations shall be blessed.   450
Then to the heaven of heavens he shall ascend
With victory, triumphing through the air
Over his foes and thine; there shall surprise
The serpent, prince of air, and drag in chains
Through all his realm, and there confounded leave;
Then enter into glory, and resume
His seat at God's right hand, exalted high
Above all names in heaven; and thence shall come,
When this world's dissolution shall be ripe,
With glory and power to judge both quick and dead,   460
To judge the unfaithful dead, but to reward
His faithful, and receive them into bliss,
Whether in heaven or earth, for then the earth
Shall all be paradise, far happier place
Than this of Eden, and far happier days.
   So spake the archangel Michael, then paused,
As at the world's great period; and our sire   467
Replete with joy and wonder thus replied.
   O goodness infinite, goodness immense!   469
That all this good of evil shall produce,
And evil turn to good; more wonderful
Than that which by creation first brought forth

---

439 **Still**]   Always.   442 **profluent**]   Running.   460 **quick**]   living.
467 **period**] Ending.   469 **immense**] Lit. 'without measure'.

Light out of darkness! full of doubt I stand,
Whether I should repent me now of sin
By me done and occasioned, or rejoice
Much more, that much more good thereof shall spring,
To God more glory, more good will to men
From God, and over wrath grace shall abound.
But say, if our deliverer up to heaven
Must reascend, what will betide the few   *480*
His faithful, left among the unfaithful herd,
The enemies of truth; who then shall guide
His people, who defend? will they not deal
Worse with his followers than with him they dealt?

   Be sure they will, said the angel; but from heaven
He to his own a comforter will send,   *486*
The promise of the Father, who shall dwell
His spirit within them, and the law of faith
Working through love, upon their hearts shall write,
To guide them in all truth, and also arm
With spiritual armour, able to resist
Satan's assaults, and quench his fiery darts,
What man can do against them, not afraid,
Though to the death, against such cruelties
With inward consolations recompensed,
And oft supported so as shall amaze
Their proudest persecutors: for the spirit
Poured first on his apostles, whom he sends
To evangelize the nations, then on all
Baptized, shall them with wondrous gifts endue   *500*
To speak all tongues, and do all miracles,
As did their Lord before them. Thus they win
Great numbers of each nation to receive
With joy the tidings brought from heaven: at length
Their ministry performed, and race well run,
Their doctrine and their story written left,
They die; but in their room, as they forewarn,   *507*
Wolves shall succeed for teachers, grievous wolves,   *508*
Who all the sacred mysteries of heaven

   486 **a comforter will send**] The Holy Spirit (see John 15: 26).   507 **room**]
Place.   508 **grievous wolves**] Quoting Acts 20: 29; Milton applies the prophecy to
the history of the Church in *Of Reformation*.

To their own vile advantages shall turn   510
Of lucre and ambition, and the truth
With superstitions and traditions taint,
Left only in those written records pure,
Though not but by the spirit understood.
Then shall they seek to avail themselves of names,
Places and titles, and with these to join
Secular power, though feigning still to act
By spiritual, to themselves appropriating
The spirit of God, promised alike and given
To all believers; and from that pretence,
Spiritual laws by carnal power shall force
On every conscience; laws which none shall find
Left them enrolled, or what the spirit within   523
Shall on the heart engrave. What will they then
But force the spirit of grace itself, and bind
His consort liberty; what, but unbuild
His living temples, built by faith to stand,
Their own faith not another's: for on earth
Who against faith and conscience can be heard
Infallible? yet many will presume: 530
Whence heavy persecution shall arise
On all who in the worship persevere
Of spirit and truth; the rest, far greater part,
Will deem in outward rites and specious forms
Religion satisfied; truth shall retire
Bestuck with slanderous darts, and works of faith
Rarely be found: so shall the world go on,
To good malignant, to bad men benign,
Under her own weight groaning till the day
Appear of respiration to the just,   540
And vengeance to the wicked, at return
Of him so lately promised to thy aid
The woman's seed, obscurely then foretold,
Now amplier known thy saviour and thy Lord,
Last in the clouds from heaven to be revealed
In glory of the Father, to dissolve   546

522–3 none . . . enrolled] Which will not be found recorded for them (i.e. in the
Scriptures).   540 respiration] Respite, a breathing-space.   546 dissolve]
Destroy.

Satan with his perverted world, then raise
From the conflagrant mass, purged and refined,
New heavens, new earth, ages of endless date
Founded in righteousness and peace and love   550
To bring forth fruits joy and eternal bliss.
    He ended; and thus Adam last replied.
How soon hath thy prediction, seer blessed,
Measured this transient world, the race of time,
Till time stand fixed: beyond is all abyss,
Eternity, whose end no eye can reach.
Greatly instructed I shall hence depart,
Greatly in peace of thought, and have my fill
Of knowledge, what this vessel can contain;
Beyond which was my folly to aspire.   560
Henceforth I learn, that to obey is best,
And love with fear the only God, to walk
As in presence, ever to observe
His providence, and on him sole depend,
Merciful over all his works, with good
Still overcoming evil, and by small
Accomplishing great things, by things deemed weak
Subverting worldly strong, and worldly wise
By simply meek; that suffering for truth's sake
Is fortitude to highest victory,   570
And to the faithful death the gate of life;
Taught this by his example whom I now
Acknowledge my redeemer ever blessed.
    To whom thus also the angel last replied:
This having learned, thou hast attained the sum
Of wisdom; hope no higher, though all the stars
Thou knew'st by name, and all the ethereal powers,
All secrets of the deep, all nature's works,
Or works of God in heaven, air, earth, or sea,
And all the riches of this world enjoyed'st,   580
And all the rule, one empire; only add
Deeds to thy knowledge answerable, add faith,
Add virtue, patience, temperance, add love,
By name to come called Charity, the soul
Of all the rest: then wilt thou not be loath
To leave this Paradise, but shalt possess
A paradise within thee, happier far.

Let us descend now therefore from this top
Of speculation; for the hour precise   589
Exacts our parting hence; and see the guards,
By me encamped on yonder hill, expect
Their motion, at whose front a flaming sword,   592
In signal of remove, waves fiercely round;
We may no longer stay: go, waken Eve;
Her also I with gentle dreams have calmed
Portending good, and all her spirits composed
To meek submission: thou at season fit
Let her with thee partake what thou hast heard,
Chiefly what may concern her faith to know,
The great deliverance by her seed to come   600
(For by the woman's seed) on all mankind.
That ye may live, which will be many days,
Both in one faith unanimous though sad,
With cause for evils past, yet much more cheered
With meditation on the happy end.

   He ended, and they both descend the hill;
Descended, Adam to the bower where Eve
Lay sleeping ran before, but found her waked;
And thus with words not sad she him received.

   Whence thou return'st, and whither went'st, I know;   610
For God is also in sleep, and dreams advise,
Which he hath sent propitious, some great good
Presaging, since with sorrow and heart's distress
Wearied I fell asleep: but now lead on;
In me is no delay; with thee to go,
Is to stay here; without thee here to stay,
Is to go hence unwilling; thou to me
Art all things under heaven, all places thou,
Who for my wilful crime art banished hence.
This further consolation yet secure   620
I carry hence; though all by me is lost,
Such favour I unworthy am vouchsafed,
By me the promised seed shall all restore.

   So spake our mother Eve, and Adam heard
Well pleased, but answered not; for now too nigh

588–9 **top / Of speculation**] Both mountain-top vantage point and high philo-
sophical inquiry.   591–2 **expect ... motion**] Await their orders to move.

The archangel stood, and from the other hill
To their fixed station, all in bright array
The cherubim descended; on the ground
Gliding meteorous, as evening mist   629
Risen from a river o'er the marish glides,   630
And gathers ground fast at the labourer's heel
Homeward returning. High in front advanced,
The brandished sword of God before them blazed
Fierce as a comet; which with torrid heat,
And vapour as the Lybian air adust,   635
Began to parch that temperate clime; whereat
In either hand the hastening angel caught
Our lingering parents, and to the eastern gate
Led them direct, and down the cliff as fast
To the subjected plain; then disappeared.   640
They looking back, all the eastern side beheld
Of Paradise, so late their happy seat,
Waved over by that flaming brand, the gate
With dreadful faces thronged and fiery arms:
Some natural tears they dropped, but wiped them soon;
The world was all before them, where to choose
Their place of rest, and providence their guide:
They hand in hand with wandering steps and slow,
Through Eden took their solitary way.

629 **meteorous**] Meteoric.   630 **marish**] Marsh.   635 **adust**] Scorched.
640 **subjected**] Lying below.

ROBERT LOUIS STEVENSON	**Kidnapped** and **Catriona**
	The Strange Case of Dr Jekyll and Mr Hyde and **Weir of Hermiston**
	Treasure Island
BRAM STOKER	**Dracula**
WILLIAM MAKEPEACE THACKERAY	**Vanity Fair**
OSCAR WILDE	**Complete Shorter Fiction**
	The Major Works
	The Picture of Dorian Gray
DOROTHY WORDSWORTH	**The Grasmere and Alfoxden Journals**
WILLIAM WORDSWORTH	**The Major Works**

The Oxford World's Classics Website

www.worldsclassics.co.uk

- Information about new titles
- Explore the full range of Oxford World's Classics
- Links to other literary sites and the main OUP webpage
- Imaginative competitions, with bookish prizes
- Peruse the Oxford World's Classics Magazine
- Articles by editors
- Extracts from Introductions
- A forum for discussion and feedback on the series
- Special information for teachers and lecturers

www.worldsclassics.co.uk

American Literature

British and Irish Literature

Children's Literature

Classics and Ancient Literature

Colonial Literature

Eastern Literature

European Literature

History

Medieval Literature

Oxford English Drama

Poetry

Philosophy

Politics

Religion

The Oxford Shakespeare

A complete list of Oxford Paperbacks, including Oxford World's Classics, Oxford Shakespeare, Oxford Drama, and Oxford Paperback Reference, is available in the UK from the Academic Division Publicity Department, Oxford University Press, Great Clarendon Street, Oxford OX2 6DP.

In the USA, complete lists are available from the Paperbacks Marketing Manager, Oxford University Press, 198 Madison Avenue, New York, NY 10016.

Oxford Paperbacks are available from all good bookshops. In case of difficulty, customers in the UK can order direct from Oxford University Press Bookshop, Freepost, 116 High Street, Oxford OX1 4BR, enclosing full payment. Please add 10 per cent of published price for postage and packing.